Editor's Note

This book originated with a specific purpose – to form part of an Open University third-level course. *Education: Structure and Society* is one component of a course – Education, Economy and Politics – which also includes personal tuition, a basic correspondence text, BBC radio and television programmes and other prescribed books, of which the most relevant to the reader of this volume is *Readings in the Theory of Educational Systems* edited by Earl Hopper (Hutchinson, 1971). I have deliberately avoided including pieces which already appear there. We are also able to send some offprints (for instance of journal articles) to Open University students. In editing this Reader, therefore, I have deliberately kept in mind the requirements both of students enrolled for the Education, Economy and Politics course, and also of other students and laymen who are interested in this development of the social explanation of education.

I am greatly indebted to Mr S. A. Hussein of Keele University, a consultant to the course, for cooperation on the first part of this volume.

I am also particularly indebted to Mr D. Mackinnon of the Educational Studies Faculty at the Open University for invaluable research services and coordinating editorial work on the text of the reader. I must also thank Mrs Pat O'Farrell for her conscientious secretarial work. I am also grateful to the course team[1] for general suggestions and to Mr Roger Lubbock, Co-ordinating Editor at the Open University, for his advice on and handling of the book.

Despite the invaluable services of all these people, I have chosen the pieces in this volume, and therefore am solely responsible for any mistaken choices or other errors in the pages which follow.

1. Course Team: R. E. Bell, B. R. Cosin, I. R. Dale, D. Holms, R. Hooper, K. Little, D. Mackinnon, W. Prescott, D. F. Swift (chairman), P. E. Woods; Consultants: D. S. Byrne, A. H. Halsey, E. Hopper, S. A. Hussein, C. L. Jones, D. Smith and W. Williamson.

Penguin Education

Education:
Structure and Society

Selected Readings
Edited by B. R. Cosin

Education: Structure and Society

Selected Readings

Edited for the Education, Economy and Politics course team by B. R. Cosin at The Open University

Penguin Books
in association with
The Open University Press

Penguin Books Ltd, Harmondsworth,
Middlesex, England
Penguin Books Inc, 7110 Ambassador Road,
Baltimore, Md 21207, USA
Penguin Books Australia Ltd,
Ringwood, Victoria, Australia

First published 1972
This selection copyright © The Open University, 1972
Introduction and notes copyright © The Open University, 1972

Copyright acknowledgement for items in this volume
will be found on page 292

Made and printed in Great Britain by
Cox & Wyman Ltd, London, Reading and Fakenham
Set in Monotype Times

Contents

Introduction

We may distinguish two traditional lines in the sociology of education: analysis of educational achievement in terms of stratification patterns, and the treatment of educational organizations as social systems.[1] Given the generally (though loosely) economic definition of stratification prevailing, not to mention the politically reformist orientations of many workers in the former tradition, it was natural that a long stage in the sociology of education should be marked by a reader with the title *Education, Economy and Society*[2]; in a sense this volume is a development of that tradition and even of that reader. It followed that the relationship between educational success and failure and the membership of particular social classes should constitute one of the focuses of attention, and that sociologists should look to economics in general, and to the specific discipline of the economics of education in particular, for underpinning and further development of their approach. In addition, given the absence of political criteria from the definition of stratification, there should be no systematic political element in the sociology of education (compared with the more or less systematic presence of economic definitions and assumptions at least); and also that the general assumptions associated with this approach should be congruent with the widespread demand for equality of opportunity as defined by concrete (rather than formal) access to *educational* advantages, and by access via the educational system to upward social mobility.

In order to explain class-linked differences in 'educability' (an individual's capacity to meet the demands of the educational system) such components as cognitive style, language and intrinsic motivation to 'achieve' were studied; but a necessary further development has been the study of how these qualities operated systematically in the classroom, lecture hall or study, and how they came to function as criteria of success and failure. In order to do this, recent workers have been studying the relation between social structure and 'knowledge', used in the wide sense of the sociology of knowledge to include a vast and disparate mass of cognitive and ideational elements. The study of the social structure within the school or college has necessarily been constituted very largely by the study of its (differentiated) culture and of the systematically differential distribution of knowledge (in

1. For a more general and also more detailed conspectus, see Basil Bernstein's *Sociology and the Sociology of Education*, published as the last correspondence text of Course E282 *School and Society* by the Open University.

2. A. H. Halsey, J. Floud and C. A. Anderson (eds.), Free Press, 1961.

senses of varying wideness) and ignorance. This is true for one of two reasons: either by virtue of the perspectives which see social structure composed of differentially allocated and differential 'knowledges'; or by virtue of the specific role and mode of operation of the school, operating as it does to distribute knowledge of the world, of the 'self' and so on, in a specific combination with its selective function. This distinguishes it from the economic and political systems, which characteristically operate with major sanctions different from simple expulsion, to produce different effects (power, income, wealth, etc.). We hope that this Reader will provide means for more thorough thinking about the systematic relations and disparities between these three structural elements of society.

Part One
Education and the Economy

To date, the economics of education has mainly studied two aspects of the relations between the educational system and the economy: the relations between the increase in gross educational provision general throughout the advanced industrial countries in the present century (particularly since 1945 and especially at the tertiary level) and rates of economic growth, and the relation between an increase in earning power of individuals and the amount of their educational experience or exposure. Both of these approaches have clearly raised several types of question. First, strictly economic questions of the validity of the measurement of economic performance (connected with differences in the definitions of gross national product, of economic performance itself, and so on). Second, questions of the nature of economic institutions, of what may be called in general the economic level of society. These may be termed questions of political economy – the extent to which the traditional definitions of the economics of education capture the systematic relationships between the educational system, and what may be a broader and deeper system of social relations of production, distribution, exchange and consumption than is contained within the definitions mentioned above. Third, questions of a more general sociological nature, which are none the less specifically concerned with the place of 'knowledge' (again in the very broad sense of the sociology of knowledge) in the two systems, with technical information and productive skills as part of the productive process, and with the systematic relations between the two. These relations may be of various types. They may be relations of *identity* (skills and so on are directly transmitted in the school or another formal educational institution, though this is rare and overall is decreasing in frequency). They may be of technical/technological *support*: individuals may be prepared for the receipt or development of technical skills or information for example by means of the provision of literacy (which is only one, though a crucial, example). And lastly they may be relations of *ideological support*: individuals may be systematically informed/misinformed about their likely place in the process of production, about that process in general, and about society at large. This last relationship connects economic and political aspects, for political and economic ideologies are closely linked if not interdependent. Since the first part of this book deals with the relations between the educational system and the economy, and the second with its relations with the political system, the relationship serves to support the unity of this volume.

The Readings from Bowen and Bowman are both surveys of the literature on the economics of education. Bowen concentrates in greater depth on the principal problems of the relation between education and economic growth; while Bowman's article is further ranging and includes more treatment of the organization of the educational system. Since they list and discuss the main problems with which the economics of education has been concerned, it is hoped that they will provide a background to the understanding of later Readings, and a basis for the provision of the achievement of more concrete and substantial specification of the relationships between the economy and the educational system. In this interest, Denison briefly summarizes the ways in which education can contribute to economic growth.

Landes provides a comparative account of the educational system in Britain and Germany in the eighteenth and nineteenth centuries. He shows that there was a chronological discrepancy between the development of the educational system and industrialization. He raises the important question of the reason for this discrepancy.

The next Readings specify in more detail how one might envisage an answer to this question, outlining various relations between science, technology and education. Killingsworth analyses the effect of automation, a specific type of technical change, on the pattern of the demand for labour. He goes on to discuss the correspondence between that pattern and the combination and range of learning and training provided by the educational system. Venn provides a descriptive account of the interrelationship between technical change and the nature of the work performed by labour on the one hand, and the role of educational systems in the formation of the labour force on the other. Bernal seeks to specify the nature of the relationship between sciences and technology; an historical relationship in that it varies from one epoch to another, with the educational system playing a central role in determining its nature. Ashby provides a further specification with his discussion of the provision and development of technical education in Britain. His main argument is that international differences played a determining role in the provision of technical education and in its further development in Britain.

Galbraith returns to a broader perspective, as do the two Readings from Marx. Galbraith focuses on the changes in the organization of the production of commodities and technical knowledge in industrialized economies. According to him, these changes imply an irregular rate of development of industrialized economies; and further, these changes have corresponding effects at the socio-political level.

The excerpt from Marx's *Capital* is concerned with the representation of the process of production in social terms. Notice that Marx objects to a purely technical definition of tools and machines on the grounds that it does not contribute to the knowledge of social laws. While reading the text it is important to take into account Marx's definition of production by means of machinery and the manner in which he uses this definition to analyse the social effect of this form of production, and to specify further the space in which the educational system and the economy interrelate. Lastly, the brief excerpts from his *Critique of the Gotha Programme* (the 1875 political programme of the German Social Democratic Party) outline elements of a communist criticism of its demands *vis-à-vis* education. Particularly noteworthy is his demand for a combination of (supervised and limited) productive labour (i.e. participation in the production of commodities) with education.

We have here, then, a directly political position on the educational relevance of the economy, stemming from the various perspectives on the production and location of skill, technique and knowledge in both systems. The second part of the book will provide more systematic materials relevant to the foundation and criticism of this final excerpt and in general the political interpretation of external social influences on the educational system.

1 W. G. Bowen

Assessing the Economic Contribution of Education

W. G. Bowen, 'Assessing the economic contribution of education: an appraisal of alternative approaches', *Higher Education. Report of the Committee under the Chairmanship of Lord Robbins 1961–63*, London, HMSO, 1963, Appendix IV, pp. 73–96. Cmnd 2154–4.

Of late, economists have been spending considerable time attempting to assess the economic contribution of education, and one of the hallmarks of the burgeoning literature is the variety of approaches that have been employed. The variety of tacks taken can, I suppose, be regarded as a tribute to the inventiveness of the profession, as an index of the complexity of the problem(s), or as an indicator of the fact that we simply don't know as yet how best to proceed.

The preparation of this paper has been based on the premise that at this stage it might be helpful to have a critical appraisal of the main approaches that have been tried. It is hoped that this exercise may be of some use to persons trying to interpret the results of the research that has been carried out thus far and perhaps also to persons contemplating new research.

The reader should know that I myself have not contributed to the body of literature under discussion and that I therefore write somewhat in the capacity of an outsider – a role which has some fairly obvious advantages and disadvantages. It should also be said that most of the ideas expressed in this paper are the common property of economists. I make no special claim to originality.

The following discussion is couched mainly in analytical terms, although references to data problems and to actual findings are interspersed throughout. The focus is on major approaches, not on individual studies.[1]

Four main approaches (each having a number of variants) can be distinguished: the simple correlation approach; the residual approach; the returns-to-education approach; and the forecasting-manpower-needs approach. In this paper each of these methods of analysis is discussed in turn, but considerably more space is devoted to the returns-to-education approach than to any of the others.

1. For a more broadly-gauged and comprehensive survey of work in the area of the economics of education, see Rivlin (1962); Harris (1962) includes a wealth of material and references germane to the problems of planning and financing higher education. Vaizey (1962) contains discussions of many of the topics treated below.

The simple correlation approach

In the generic sense, this approach consists of correlating some overall index of educational activity with some index of the level of economic activity.

Inter-country comparisons (cross-sectional)

Inter-country correlations at a fixed point in time constitute one well-known member of this group. Svennilson, Edding and Elvin, for example, have correlated enrolment ratios and GNP per capita, and have found that there is indeed a positive relationship, although there is also considerable dispersion, particularly among the countries falling in the middle range (1961).

Comparisons of this kind serve a number of useful purposes. For one thing, they enable countries to see their own educational efforts in the perspective of what is being done elsewhere, and thus can serve to disturb complacency. Comparisons between countries in similar economic circumstances may also provide at least a rough idea of what is possible, with 'possible' defined in terms of actual educational outlays in countries having an approximately equal GNP per capita. Comparisons between countries at different stages of economic development may provide the less-advanced countries with a rough notion of what general level of educational activity is associated with a more advanced stage of economic development – so long as one remembers that standards in this respect, as in so many others, have a habit of changing rapidly.

The construction of meaningful inter-country comparisons is, of course, beset by many practical problems. We can leave aside the problem of obtaining comparable GNP figures – provided we realize that we are leaving aside a subject to which a whole segment of professional literature has been devoted. Finding comparable indices of educational activity (or attainment) is no less difficult, given the pronounced inter-country variations in educational systems.[2] If expenditure data are used, it is essential that cognizance be taken of the opportunity costs (foregone output) involved in having students attend school rather than work.[3] It is also necessary to recognize

2. The debate in the British House of Commons on the Government's policies toward university education illustrates beautifully the way in which different measures of educational activity can lead to radically different conclusions. Mr Gaitskell, leading off for the Opposition, cited estimates of total university students as a proportion of the total population in various countries to show how far Britain was lagging behind other countries. Mr Henry Brooke, replying for the Government, cited percentages of the relevant age group *graduating* from universities to show that in fact Britain was doing better than many of the same Western European countries mentioned by Mr Gaitskell (see *Hansard*, v. 657, no. 91 (5 April 1962) pp. 719 ff., and especially pp. 726, 734–6).

3. In the case of the United States Schultz (1960) has estimated that opportunity costs were equal to about three-fifths of the total costs of high-school and college education in 1956.

that equal resource expenditures in two countries imply equal educational output only if resources are used with the same degree of efficiency in both countries – and we know astonishingly little about how efficiency is to be defined and measured, in spite of a recent upsurge of interest in the subject.

The practical problems of constructing indices can no doubt be solved to a tolerably satisfactory extent, and emphasis ought not to be placed here. It is the more basic question of what cause and effect relationship is bound up in education–GNP correlations[4] that deserves emphasis. A positive correlation can be viewed as evidence in support of the proposition that spending money on education is an important way of raising a country's GNP. But the same correlation can also be viewed as evidence in support of the proposition that education is an important consumer good on which countries elect to spend more as their GNP rises.[5]

The trouble is that these propositions are almost certainly both true *to some extent* – and, in the absence of other information, we have no way of disentangling the two relationships. The inescapable conclusion is that simple education–GNP correlations, in and of themselves, cannot tell us anything about the quantitative dimensions of the contribution that education makes to economic growth.[6]

Inter-temporal correlations

A second basic variant of the simple correlation approach consists of correlating education and GNP within a given country over time. Schultz has recently made a correlation of this type for the US over the period 1900 to 1956, and, treating education solely as a consumer good, he found that the income-elasticity of demand for education was 3·5 (1961a, p. 60).[7] But treating education solely as a consumer good begs the question of course (as Schultz is the first to admit), and one must conclude that here again the two-way causation problem makes it impossible to give a satisfactory interpretation to the figures.

4. From here on, all general references to correlations between education and GNP should be interpreted to mean correlations between *relative* measures of educational activity (e.g. proportions of the total population in school or fractions of the total GNP spent on education) and GNP per capita.

5. This assumes that the income-elasticity of demand for education is greater than unity and that any negative substitution effect, arising as a consequence of the (likely) possibility that the price of education will go up relative to other prices, will be swamped by the positive income effect. These assumptions seem reasonable.

6. There are, of course, many other considerations in addition to the two-way causation problem that make it difficult to interpret cross-sectional correlations between education and GNP. Apart from the universal problem of holding other things constant, there are time-lag and external economies problems, both of which will be discussed below in other contexts.

7. Harris (1949, pp. 160–72) has also made correlations of this kind.

Attempts at inter-temporal correlations also highlight the timing problem that plagues many approaches. Education is a long-lived asset, in that an educated man presumably contributes more on account of his education, not just one year after his graduation, but for much of the rest of his life. If a country doubled its expenditure on education in year t, the positive economic effects ought not to be looked for in year t's GNP figures (which actually will be lower because students who would have worked are now in school), but in the figures for all the years from, say, $t+4$ on.[8]

Inter-industry and inter-firm correlations

Just as countries differ in the relative emphasis placed on education, so do industries and firms within industries. While it is difficult to find an entirely satisfactory way of measuring an industry's emphasis on 'education', we can perhaps think in terms of such measures as the proportion of the work force that has had training beyond the secondary-school level or the percentage of gross receipts spent on research and development activities. Correlations can then be made between one of these indices of educational emphasis and the profitability of the industry or firm. Comparisons of this type can, of course, be made on a cross-sectional basis within a single country, over time, or on an inter-country basis. The rest of this discussion will deal only with the one-country, cross-sectional case, although many of the comments will also be applicable to inter-temporal and inter-country comparisons.

The first thing to be said is that we should certainly not expect to find all of the industries (or firms) under investigation using the same combination of inputs. Differences in the technological possibilities open to firms engaged in different lines of business, and differences in the relative scarcity of various inputs in the geographical areas where the firms happen to be located would both tend to produce differences in the relative emphasis placed on 'educationally-heavy' inputs. It is this line of reasoning that has led Jewkes to object to the argument that the industries spending comparatively little on research and development should try to raise themselves to the standards of expenditure characteristic of other industries (1960).

The usual profit-maximization model of firm behaviour does indeed

8. The best way of surmounting this problem is by measuring the total *stock* of education at different points in time, not just the current level of educational activity. (For a recent attempt at this, see Schultz, 1961a, pp. 64 ff. Note, however, that in some of his work Schultz suggests the desirability of calculating a kind of present value of the stock by weighting younger persons more heavily than older persons; this makes good sense if one wants to know what the economic worth of the stock is, but not if one just wants to relate current educational attainments to current economic output.) Stock measurements are also better than flow measurements, in the case of cross-sectional inter-country comparisons, for exactly the same reasons.

suggest the likelihood that firms in different circumstances will employ different combinations of inputs, but the model does *not* suggest that there should be any systematic difference between profit levels in industries using an exceptionally large amount of any particular input (trained manpower in this case) and industries using relatively small amounts of the input. And this is why inter-industry correlations between emphasis on educational inputs and profitability may prove to be of real interest. If a pronounced positive correlation were to be found, there would indeed be something to be explained.

This kind of inter-industry or inter-firm correlation has a real advantage over the more aggregative kinds of education–GNP correlations, in that the two-way causation problem is not so serious. We do not usually think of firms 'consuming' education simply because they 'like it' in the way that we think of individual persons partaking of education for its own sake. Even if we concede that modern-day firms have a certain element of the consumer mentality in their make-up (and thus may simply enjoy, for status or other reasons, having some high-powered scientists about), this element is surely not as pronounced as in the household sector of the economy. Consequently, a positive correlation here would at the very least suggest the possibility that differences in expenditures on educationally-heavy inputs have helped to create profit differences; that a disequilibrium situation still persists, and that a shift of resources toward the educationally-heavy inputs would be justified purely on the private profitability criterion.[9]

Mention should be made of one serious pitfall in making inter-industry correlations of this kind. It may be that industries which place a relatively heavy emphasis on educational inputs also happen to be industries which enjoy an above-average degree of market power, and that the apparent relation between relatively high profits and educational inputs is better interpreted as a reflection of the profitability of market power than as a reflection of the profitability of emphasizing educational inputs. Actually, for reasons advanced by Schumpeter and others, expenditures on trained manpower (a key ingredient in the process of innovation) and degree of market power may be inextricably bound up in many instances. This cross-relationship would certainly have to be studied carefully by anyone intent on carrying out a serious inquiry into correlations between profitability and educational inputs.[10]

9. It should be recognized that the shift of resources could take one of two forms: first, there might simply be an increase in expenditure on trained manpower by the firms and industries that had lagged behind in this respect; second, there might be a shift of resources away from industries in which the nature of activities did not justify spending more money on trained manpower, and toward those industries where the emphasis on trained manpower was already comparatively great.

10. Another type of objection that can be raised against this sort of inquiry is that,

Inter-industry correlations will most certainly not answer many of the crucial questions involved in assessing the economic contribution of education – for instance, the importance of external economies will not be reflected. Research along these general lines does appear to offer at least a modest promise of being helpful, however, and deserves to be encouraged.

The residual approach

In general terms, this approach consists of taking the total increase in economic output of a country over a given period of time, identifying as much of the total increase as possible with measurable inputs (capital and labour being the two measurable inputs usually chosen) and then saying that the residual is attributable to the unspecified inputs. It is because education and advances in knowledge are usually regarded as the most important of the unspecified inputs that this approach deserves to be discussed in the context of the contribution-of-education question.

When it comes to actually implementing the residual approach, there are a number of alternative techniques that can be adopted, only a few of which will be mentioned here. First, it is possible to proceed by calculating an input series for the labour input (based, for instance, on hours worked), a separate, constant-price input series for the capital input, and then combining these two input series into an overall arithmetic index of inputs (using the relative shares of labour and capital in the total GNP as weights). Next the rate of increase in this aggregate input series is compared with the rate of increase in an aggregate output series (also expressed in constant prices); and by simply subtracting it is possible to obtain a measure of the contribution of the 'residual' or 'third factor'.

Kendrick of the National Bureau of Economic Research has followed this general procedure, and he has found that for the US economy, over the period between 1889 and 1957, the combined input index increased at an average rate of 1·9 per cent per annum and the output index increased about 3·5 per cent per annum, leaving a 'residual' increase of about 1·6 per cent per annum (called by Kendrick the increase in 'total factor productivity') (1961, Table 6, p. 79). Thus, 46 per cent of the increase in total output is ascribed to the residual. The contribution of the residual can also be expressed as a percentage of the increase in output per unit of labour input, rather than as a percentage of the increase in total output. Following this

---

if industry would gain by devoting a larger part of its collective resources to educationally-oriented inputs, it would automatically do so. But this line of argument overlooks the very real possibility that ignorance of rewards is particularly likely to exist in this nebulous area, and that imperfections in capital markets may prevent the raising of new capital and the interchange of capital between industries both of which are necessary for an equilibrium situation to obtain.

procedure (and working with a figure of 2·0 per cent per year as the average rate of increase in output per unit of labour input)[11] it is possible to attribute roughly 80 per cent of the increased output per unit of labour input to the residual, with only about 20 per cent being attributed to increases in the stock of physical capital.

Solow and others have followed a somewhat different procedure, the basic difference being that Solow *et al.* have made explicit assumptions about the nature of the underlying production function. Dealing with a linear, homogeneous production function, and assuming that technical change is 'neutral' (i.e. in and of itself does not alter the rate of substitution between capital and labour), the residual has been found to equal roughly 90 per cent of the increase in output per man-hour in the US economy between 1915 and 1955.[12]

In some respects the recent study by Denison of the sources of US economic growth (1962) constitutes a third variant of the residual approach, in that Denison estimates the effect of *advances in knowledge* by simply subtracting the rate of growth attributable to all the other inputs he identifies from the total rate of growth. Denison ends up with a residual that is very much smaller than any of the figures given above, but this is because he has made separate estimates of the contributions of factors such as formal education and economies of scale, which have been included in the residual category by most other authors. And, in making his estimate of the contribution of formal education, Denison has employed the direct returns-to-education approach, which is discussed in considerable detail in the next section of this paper.

Before moving on to this topic, however, a few general comments concerning the residual approach are in order. Viewed from the standpoint of a desire to know something about the economic contribution of education, the residual approach has two main defects.

Taking the more technical of the two problems first, neither the National Bureau of Economic Research work nor the production function procedure takes adequate account of the interplay between capital inputs and the

11. Actually, the 2·0 per cent figure (taken from Table 1, p. 60 of Kendrick's study) is not strictly comparable with the figures given above in that it is for only the private sector of the economy, whereas the earlier figures were for the national economy as a whole. However, over long periods, the differences involved in these two types of measures are slight.

12. The 90 per cent figure has been taken from a paper by Massell (1960). Massell adopts the theoretical approach originally used by Solow (1957), but deals with somewhat different data and makes slightly different adjustments for factors such as idle capital. Actually Solow ended up with a figure of 87 per cent and so the results are really very similar. Domar presents a lucid discussion of Solow's work and of the work of others (1961).

advancing knowledge component of the residual. As Domar put it in commenting on Solow's work, capital in this context 'does not serve as the instrument for the introduction of technical change into the production process . . . (It is simply) wooden ploughs piled up on the top of existing wooden ploughs' (1961, p. 712).

Another way of making essentially the same point (or at least a very closely-related point) is by noting that available indices of capital inputs generally fail to reflect improvements in the quality, or 'productivity', of capital. Anderson (1961) has shown that the apparent historical decline in the constant-price capital output ratio is misleading for this very reason. The source of the problem is that, while the deflation of money measures of national income to a constant-price basis is done by using prices per unit of *output* (thus catching improvements in output per unit of input), money measures of capital are deflated on an elements-of-cost basis which cannot reflect improvements in the productivity of the capital equipment itself. (If a constant amount of labour and materials goes into two capital assets produced in different years, the deflated values will be equal, even though the newer capital asset may produce much more than did the older capital asset.) Consequently, the 'true' contribution of physical capital is likely to have been somewhat greater than the figures cited earlier suggest, and the 'true' size of the residual correspondingly smaller.

The more general difficulty is, of course, the 'residual' nature of the 'residual'. For reasons noted above, the residual, as usually measured, no doubt embodies the results of some secular improvement in the quality of capital assets; it also encompasses changes in output attributable to economies of scale, to improvements in the health of the labour force, to informal as well as formal education, to changes in the product mix, to reorganizations of the economic order, and to who knows what else. Moses Abramovitz has called it a 'measure of our ignorance' (1956, p. 11).[13] The heterogeneity of the elements that go to make up the residual means, of course, that a large residual cannot safely be interpreted as a mandate for more spending on any particular project, whether it be a massive research and development effort or better school lunches.

However, the size of the residual certainly does serve as a mandate to explore in detail the economic effects of activities often neglected. It seems clear that the simple accumulation of physical capital, in and of itself, has not played the dominant role in economic growth sometimes ascribed to it.

13. It is to the great credit of the authors of the estimates of the residual that without exception they have repeatedly emphasized this aspect of its character.

The direct returns-to-education approach

An obvious way of studying the economic consequences of education is by contrasting the lifetime earnings of people who have had 'more' education with the lifetime earnings of people who have had 'less' education. The difference in lifetime earnings can then be expressed as an annual percentage rate of return on the costs involved in obtaining the education.[14] Actually, as the following discussion is likely to make painfully clear, this approach, like so many others, is deceptively simple.

At the outset it is useful to distinguish two ways of looking at direct returns to education: (a) the personal profit orientation; (b) the national productivity orientation.

The 'personal profit orientation' consists of looking at differences in the net earnings of people with varying amounts of education as evidence of the amount of personal financial gain that can be associated with the attainment of a given level of education. This is, of course, the relevant orientation for the individual trying to make private calculations (in a country where students pay a substantial share of educational costs), and it can also be argued that evidence of this kind is germane to a country's decision as to what fraction of the costs of education should be borne by the students themselves.

The 'national productivity orientation' consists of looking at education-related earnings differentials as partial evidence of the effects of education on the output of the country, and is based on the premise that in a market economy differences in earnings reflect differences in productivity. This orientation is relevant to the question of whether society as a whole is investing the right share of its resources in education.

From the standpoint of procedures and problems, these two ways of looking at direct returns to education are sufficiently similar to allow us to discuss them together, although there are also differences which will require comment from time to time. Right here it is worth noting that in calculating rates of return the relevant concept of educational cost depends on the investigator's orientation (only private costs, including opportunity costs, are relevant to an assessment of the private rate of return, whereas all costs, including public subsidies, are relevant to the measurement of direct social returns) as does the relevant concept of earnings (after tax in the private-returns case, before tax in the social-returns case). Other differences will be touched on in due course.

So far we have spoken of two groups of persons: a group having 'more'

14. For references to some early studies of this kind, see Walsh (1935, p. 235). Among the more recent studies, Becker's work has received by far the most attention from professional economists, although only a preliminary report on his research has been published so far (1960).

education and a group having 'less' education. When it comes to calculating actual rates of return, however, this vague dichotomy will not do, and many of the recent studies have calculated separate rates of return for each stage of the educational process. While there is obviously much to be said for dividing education into stages, the results can be misleading if looked at in isolation from one another. Calculating the rate of return on primary education by comparing the net earnings of persons who have completed just the primary grades with the net earnings of persons who have not had even this much education is bound to produce an erroneously low result in that no account is taken of the fact that primary education is a stepping stone to secondary and college education. The value of the option to continue one's education ought to be included in the rate of return on both primary and secondary education, and the value of this option obviously depends on the rate of return to be had from the higher levels of education and on the probability that the option will be exercised. Education must be viewed as a series of related steps. Weisbrod has made this point quite clearly, and, to illustrate the order of magnitude involved, has shown that recognizing the value of the option to obtain additional education raises the expected 1939 rate of return on grade school education from a previous estimate of 35 per cent to 52 per cent (1962).

Separate rates of return can also be calculated for males and females, for persons of different races, and so on. One of Becker's most interesting (and disturbing) findings is that whereas the rate of return on the cost of college education was 9 per cent for urban white males in the United States as of 1950, the comparable rate of return for non-whites was about two percentage points lower than this – presumably because of greater job discrimination against college-educated non-whites than against other non-whites (1960, pp. 347–8).

The rate-of-return approach has many attractions, not the least of which is that educational benefits are related to educational costs in a way that holds out the hope of providing useful information concerning the adequacy of the overall level of investment in education and the extent to which economic benefits accrue directly to private individuals. But the implementation of this approach is also subject to many difficulties, which must be examined in some detail if we are to minimize the risk of misinterpreting results.

The 'holding-other-things-constant' problem

Unfortunately for purposes of analysis, groups with differing amounts of education tend to differ systematically in terms of other attributes which are also likely to influence relative earnings. An oft-quoted (and justifiable) criticism of many studies purporting to show that a person could add 'X' thousand dollars to his lifetime income by going to college is that they attribute results to education which were caused, *in part,* by differences in intelligence, ambition, family connections, and so on. At the same time, it must be emphasized that this problem has been recognized by the investigators themselves and that attempts have been made to adjust for differences in factors such as ability and family background.[15]

No one would claim that the efforts to date have been entirely satisfactory, and one of the reasons is the difficulty of obtaining satisfactory measures of such elusive variables as ability and motivation. (It is much easier to adjust for differences in mortality rates and unemployment experience.) We also need to know more than we do at present about the relationship between different *levels* of ability and differences in earnings associated with varying amounts of formal education. The results of a questionnaire study reported by Bridgman suggest that differences in earnings (between college graduates and 'comparable' high-school graduates) were greatest for those of highest ability (Harris, 1960, p. 178). The relation between levels of intellectual ability and the likelihood that one will profit economically from higher education deserves much more study, particularly in the context of discussions concerning the extension of higher education to a larger proportion of a given population.

Do earnings measure productivity?

The question of whether differences in relative earnings reflect differences in productivity does not arise so long as one looks at returns to education solely from the personal profit point of view. But, if we wish to interpret rates of return on education as indicative of over- or under-investment in education from the national productivity point of view, then this question becomes very important indeed.

In general, in an economy where relative earnings are subject to the push and pull of market forces, we should certainly expect to find relatively high earnings accruing to persons possessing special skills which enable them to make a greater economic contribution than the average person. However,

15. Becker has standardized his data for differences in ability on the basis of test score information, and for differences in unemployment and mortality as well. He reports (1960, p. 349) that adjusting for differential ability reduces the rate of return on a college education by about two percentage points (from 11 to 9 per cent). Results of detailed case-study type inquiries into the education–ability–earning relationship have been reported by Wolfle and Bridgman in the volume of papers edited by Harris (1960, pp. 178–9, pp. 180–84). Denison, in his CED study of the sources of economic growth, has reduced actual earnings differentials by one-third in order to take account of the effects of characteristics correlated with education (especially ability), but he acknowledges in a very forthright fashion that this adjustment represents nothing more than a rough guess on his part as to the quantitative importance of differences in ability and in other associated factors (1962, pp. 69–70).

there are also reasons for thinking that earnings differentials may not always be an accurate reflection of differences in marginal productivities, and the likely effects of these other considerations on rate-of-return figures must be examined carefully.

'Conspicuous production' and 'tradition-bound' wage structures

The link between relative wages and marginal productivities will be weakened to the extent that employers do not set wages so as to maximize their profits. The phrase 'conspicuous production' refers to the possibility that some employers may choose to hire college graduates (and pay them 'college graduate' salaries) for jobs which do not really require college training. Instances of this type can no doubt be found in a country such as the United States, but I suspect that we tend to exaggerate the frequency with which bosses insist on paying extra for unnecessary qualifications.[16]

The phrase 'tradition-bound wage structures' refers to what may well be a more important variant of non-profit-maximizing behaviour. Persons who have studied the so-called 'underdeveloped countries' have noted a tendency to continue paying relatively high salaries to educated persons in, for example, the Government service, when such a salary policy is no longer necessary from a recruitment standpoint (Harbison, 1961). In countries where the salary structure is rigid because of status overtones, calculations of monetary returns to education can be very misleading as a guide to educational policy.

The non-monetary attractions of jobs open to graduates

All occupations have their non-monetary pluses and minuses, and the wage structure presumably adjusts accordingly – occupations which are dirty, hard or unpleasant in any respect will be characterized by higher earnings than those which require the same kinds of qualifications but which are cleaner, easier, more interesting, have a higher status appeal, and so on. There would be no need to dwell on the existence of these non-monetary attractions if they were of roughly the same order of importance in the case

16. It may well be that as a higher proportion of the people in a country receive a college education, employers, in order to recruit people possessing a certain level of ability, will find themselves forced to recruit college graduates – even though college training may be unnecessary for the job. However, this situation ought not to be confused with the 'conspicuous production' case. To the extent that these people are paid higher salaries solely because of their basic ability, employers cannot be accused of non-profit-maximizing behaviour. Actually this kind of situation affords an excellent illustration of the need to avoid attributing higher salaries due to ability differentials to education (as discussed above), but it is quite different from a situation in which an employer pays more to a college graduate holding a particular job just because he is a college graduate.

of jobs open to highly-educated persons and jobs open to persons with less education. In actual fact, however, it seems clear that non-monetary attractions are much greater in the case of the usual jobs filled by college graduates; hence, non-monetary considerations cannot be dismissed as a neutral factor.[17]

It may also be mentioned in passing that there is likely to be an income effect at work here, and that the higher the real income of a society, the greater the weight that the society as a whole is likely to put on the non-monetary side of occupational choice. The President of an American University remarked not long ago that as real income continues to rise we may well see the day when a garbage collector is paid more than a full professor.

The important question is: how (if at all) should one adjust rates of return to take account of differences in non-monetary advantages? This is a very troublesome question at the conceptual level, as well as at the empirical level, and part of the explanation is that the answer depends on whether one is looking at returns to education from the personal profit or national productivity point of view.

From the standpoint of the individual gain from education (personal profit), it seems clear that we ought to add in a sum approximating the dollar equivalent of the non-monetary advantages. Non-monetary advantages certainly do accrue to the individuals concerned and increase their welfare. At the moment, quantitative estimates are lacking, but my guess is that taking account of this consideration would increase the calculated rate of return on higher education (and especially on graduate education) to a very marked extent.

From the national productivity standpoint, one might think at first that a similar upward adjustment is required.[18] But, to the extent that the non-monetary aspects of employment are purely a supply-side phenomenon (that is, affect only the willingness of individuals to take jobs at alternative

17. I grant that attitudes toward the non-monetary attractions of certain jobs vary significantly from one person to the next; and I also grant that my own preferences no doubt influence my judgement on this point. But it still seems safe to say that, if salaries were the same and if qualifications were not a constraint, most people would prefer the kinds of jobs that are in fact open only (or mainly) to holders of degrees. Studies that have been made of popular attitudes towards various vocations support this position. (A poll conducted for the President's Commission on Higher Education and cited by Harris, 1949, p. 7 showed that, with regard to prestige, virtually all occupations ranked in the top twenty-five by a cross-section of Americans would normally require a college education but most others would not.)

18. This seems to be Villard's position (see his criticism of Becker's work, 1960, p. 376). Many other writers have said essentially the same thing, and I should add that at one point I too shared this position. As the rest of this discussion indicates, I have now revised my views; I have Ralph Turvey to thank for forcing me to think this problem through more fully.

rates of pay and not the costs incurred by employers in hiring additional men), this is not so. The greater the non-monetary attractions of any occupation, the greater the number of people who will be willing to enter the occupation at a given wage and thus the greater the ability of the employer to hire a given number of people at a lower rate of pay. The extent of non-monetary attractions determines the position of the supply curve of labour, but this does not alter the fact that the employer will still pay that money wage which will equal the value of the marginal product produced by the last man hired. If there were suddenly a sharp increase in the non-monetary attractions of a particular occupation, the result would be a south-easterly shift of the supply schedule (more people willing to enter the occupation at each possible wage) and a movement along the demand (marginal revenue productivity) schedule to a new equilibrium characterized by a lower relative wage and a larger number of people engaged in the occupation. To put the matter another way, if we compare two occupations for which there are identical marginal revenue productivity schedules but which differ in their non-monetary attractions, we should expect to find a lower wage and a larger number of persons engaged in the more attractive of the two occupations – and the discrepancy in relative wages would measure the difference in *marginal* productivities.[19]

The above line of argument holds only to the extent that non-monetary attractions are truly 'non-monetary' and do not cost the employer anything. This is generally true of such attractions as prestige, but it may not be true of attractions such as subsidized housing, subsidized travel and long, paid vacations. Allowances for 'fringe benefits' of this type should be added to the basic wage, and it may be that fringes of this kind are more common in occupations filled by relatively well-educated people. An upward adjustment in the rate of return on education should be made to take account of any such discrepancies that can be shown to exist.

19. The reason for going through this much detail (and presenting what will appear to professional economists to be a very elementary exposition) is that there have been some misunderstandings, most of which no doubt stem from mixing together the personal profit and national productivity orientations. A major source of confusion to many persons not trained as professional economists is the fact that the 'productivity' of an occupation cannot be thought of as a mixed magnitude but must be expected to vary according to the number of persons engaged in the occupation – and it is the productivity of the last person employed (the marginal productivity) which is relevant for most purposes. The fact that in equilibrium (at the level of employment where it will not pay the employer either to add or lay off one more man) the marginal revenue product (and thus the wage) in occupation 'A' may be lower than in occupation 'B' does not mean that at other levels of employment this same relationship between the marginal productivities would necessarily hold; nor does it mean that if the same number of persons were employed in each occupation the marginal productivity in occupation 'A' would still be lower than in occupation 'B' – it might or it might not.

There is one final point – the argument presented here is based on the assumption that persons interested in rates of return on education, from what we have called the 'national productivity' standpoint, are concerned solely with the effects of education on the nation's GNP. If one wishes to work from a broader national frame of reference and look at the effects of education on the total 'welfare' of the citizenry, then once again, as in the case of the personal profit orientation, a full adjustment for non-monetary attractions is in order since such attractions most certainly do contribute to the aggregate welfare of the populace.

External economies, indirect benefits or social benefits

Anyone using direct returns to education as a guide to the proper level of spending must recognize that rates of return based on the relative earnings of groups of individuals will never reflect the external economies (or indirect benefits, or social benefits, depending on one's terminological preferences) generated by education. By definition, external economies consist of those benefits which are not confined to individual economic units – and thus do not show up in the relative earnings of identifiable groups – but which 'spill-over' to the economy as a whole, raising the level of real income and welfare generally.

While external effects are by no means confined to education, education is probably more likely to generate indirect benefits than any other single activity of comparable scope. Without pretending to present anything resembling a complete catalogue, it may be useful to mention a few of the main kinds of external effects.

As everyone knows, the educational process is intimately related to advances in knowledge, and it is equally clear that advances in knowledge can have important economic effects. Yet, because new ideas are not used up by being understood, and because the results of basic research are rapidly disseminated free of charge (over the entire world in many cases), the economic contribution of basic research will not be fully reflected in the relative earnings of the producers of this new knowledge.[20] Nor is it just research in natural science that has important economic consequences – it would be interesting to know the magnitude of the increase in real incomes that has stemmed from our improved understanding of how to prevent large-scale unemployment.

There are also, of course, important social and political benefits of education which accrue to the populace as a whole – a better informed electorate, more culturally alive neighbourhoods, a healthier and less crime-prone population, and so on. What is not always recognized is that these

20. W. Leontief presents a lucid discussion of the underlying reasons why advances in knowledge have the attributes of indirect benefits in his preface to Silk (1960).

social and political consequences may in turn have significant economic effects – the efficiency with which goods are exchanged is obviously enhanced by general literacy. To the extent that education reduces crime (even if only by keeping children off the streets during the day) the country can shift resources that would have had to be used for the police function to other ends, and so on.

While education could conceivably entail social costs as well as social benefits (for instance by producing a class of unemployed, unproductive, frustrated and socially-destructive intellectuals), there is no doubt that on balance the positive benefits are paramount. However, it is one thing to be able to say that external benefits are obviously very important and quite another to know what order of magnitude to attach to the word 'very'. I think that most people who have worked actively on the problem of estimating national returns to education are agreed that this is the biggest unsolved riddle of all. At the present time all we know is that estimates of direct returns ought to be adjusted upward to take account of external economies – we do not know how much of an adjustment to make or even how to go about finding out how much of an adjustment to make.[21]

Collective power

Finally, it is worth noting that the existence of collective power in certain sectors may influence relative earnings. It has been argued, for example, that some part of the relatively high earnings enjoyed by doctors in the United States should be attributed directly to the effectiveness of the American Medical Association in limiting entry and keeping fees high.[22]

In interpreting the implications for educational policy of an 'artificially' high rate of return of this kind, it is necessary to be very careful indeed. While the wage will be higher than under competitive conditions, so will marginal productivity (because of a smaller active labour input), and therefore an increased investment in this particular type of activity would be called for. The fact that in cases of this type relatively high rates of return have been caused in part by organized power groups (rather than solely by ignorance, underestimates of returns by policy makers, or imperfections in the capital market) makes no difference at all to the basic conclusion – that the relatively high rates of return imply under-investment and a misallocation of resources. But the cause of the relatively high rate of return

21. Some progress can be reported, however. Weisbrod (1962) has suggested ways of estimating the value of savings in terms of certain 'avoidance costs' (i.e. costs that, were it not for education, we would have had to incur for, say, added police protection). Others have attempted direct assessments of the economic value of various kinds of basic research. But all would agree that there is room for much more work on this problem.

22. The classic is by Friedman and Kuznets (1946).

has, of course, important implications for the selection of the most appropriate remedial policy measure – a relatively high rate of return attributable to the exercise of market power may be best treated by trying to eliminate the source of the market imperfection.[23]

The consumption versus *investment problem*

Critics of the direct returns-to-education approach have repeatedly emphasized that such calculations ignore the so-called 'consumption' or 'cultural' contributions of education. The point is that education presumably has purposes besides that of increasing a person's potential economic productivity – yet it is only his economic productivity (and in fact only that part of his economic productivity which passes through the market mechanism)[24] that enters into the measurement of returns to education.

Thus, no account is taken of the value of the current consumption enjoyed by the student who may say that his college years were 'the best years of his life'. (True, there may be some students who regard education as a painful process to be endured for the sake of future gain, but such students would no doubt turn out to be in the minority, especially if forced to contrast the net attractions of being a student with the net attractions of what in fact they would be doing if they were not students rather than with the attractions of what they would like to be doing.) In the case of primary education, parents no doubt derive immediate pleasure from having the children in school rather than at home, apart from that felt by the children .

It is also generally agreed that education confers long and lasting benefits of a consumption variety by extending the range of activities which a person is able to enjoy during his leisure hours. For many people, education has no doubt awakened interests which have been a source of pleasure over an entire lifetime. In this sense, education can be thought of as conferring a durable consumer good of great value.

The important question is not whether education is a source of present and future pleasure – unquestionably it is, quite apart from its effects on one's ability to obtain a satisfying and productive job – but how, if at all, estimates of the direct monetary returns to education should be adjusted to take account of such considerations.

Certainly the individual trying to decide whether or not to continue his

23. I am indebted to Thomas Ribich for helpful comments on the subject-matter of this paragraph.

24. The importance of non-market production furthered by education is illustrated by Weisbrod's estimate that the annual value of services performed by persons who fill out their own income tax returns has amounted to about sixty-six million dollars, which is almost 1 per cent of elementary school costs. Were this service provided through the market it would, of course, be priced and included in the national income (this estimate comes from Weisbrod, 1962).

education will want to add his own estimate of 'consumption' values to his estimate of job-related values in coming to a decision.

To calculate a national rate-of-return figure, Schultz has argued that the way to proceed is by first identifying the consumption component of educational costs, and then subtracting this amount from total educational costs in order to arrive at the base level of costs which can properly be used (in conjunction with earnings data) to calculate the rate of return on the investment portion of educational expenditures. If we suppose, for example, that half of all educational costs can be regarded as consumption outlays, then it would follow that the rate of return on educational investment was twice as high as the figure suggested by a simple comparison of differential earnings with total educational costs – Becker's 9 per cent rate of return would be raised to 18 per cent (1961b; pp. 12–13).

The above approach suffers from two related limitations. First of all, it is exceedingly difficult to estimate the so-called consumption component of educational costs. As Schultz himself has emphasized, to a large degree the consumption and investment components of a person's education are inextricably bound up. In our better educational systems, pure enjoyment (present and future) is in the nature of the case obtained simultaneously with the training necessary for a future career. Distinctions based on 'general' or 'liberal arts' courses *versus* 'vocational' courses fail to appreciate both that general courses can make a great contribution to one's ability to do many kinds of work well and that the so-called vocational courses can often be highly stimulating and enjoyable. In short, we must recognize that here we are dealing with a joint cost problem in which essentially the same inputs are transmuted simultaneously into two end-products (professional preparation and pleasure).

In the second place, even if we somehow succeed in isolating a pure consumption element, subtracting this portion of costs from total educational costs is a valid procedure only if we are prepared to assume that society values this 'educational consumption' as highly as it values all alternative kinds of consumption – ranging from cars to public parks. This implicit assumption must be made explicit and defended. The problem is, of course, complicated by the fact that the consumption and investment aspects noted above are complementary – society does not really have the option of ceasing to make expenditures on the consumption aspect of education (assuming for the sake of argument that a higher value was attached to public parks) without simultaneously curtailing expenditures on the investment aspect.

Given this situation, the logical way to proceed is to make an explicit evaluation of the worth of the consumption contributions of education to society (expressed in dollar terms), next add this sum to the monetary returns from education, and then compare the total benefits to the total costs in order to see if the undertaking as a whole is sufficiently worthwhile to merit devoting more resources to it. The evaluation of the consumption component depends, of course, on society's preferences and cannot be deduced in a mechanical way from any known set of figures. This is also true of parks and many other things, and the difficulties involved in making this kind of evaluation certainly do not justify the easy escape of ignoring the value of the consumption benefits altogether.[25]

The discount rate (or 'other' rate of return) problem

Since the monetary benefits of education accrue over time, it is necessary to use some discount factor to take account of the fact that a dollar earned tomorrow is less valuable than a dollar earned today, and computations of the present value of the future stream of benefits to be expected from education are, of course, very sensitive to the discount factor used. Houthakker has made some calculations (based on 1950 census data for the US) which indicate that the capital value (present value) at age fourteen of before-tax lifetime income associated with four or more years of college ranged from a figure of $280,989 if a zero discount rate is used, to $106,269 at a 3 per cent rate of discount, to $47,546 at 6 per cent and to $30,085 at 8 per cent (1959, Table 2, p. 26). Unfortunately, there is no simple answer to the question of what is the right discount factor, and this question has in fact been the subject of considerable debate.

Before going any further, it must be emphasized that this same question has, of course, to be faced by the investigator who prefers to express his results in terms of an internal rate of return rather than in terms of a present value figure. True enough, the internal rate of return figure is obtained simply by finding that rate which makes the estimated future gain in earnings equal to the present cost of obtaining the education, and no discount factor enters into this calculation. But, once one has obtained the internal rate of return on education, it is then necessary to decide which other rate of return is to be compared with the rate of return on education in order to determine whether this is relatively high or low. Thus, the 'other' rate of return used for comparative purposes serves the same function that the discount factor serves in the case of present value calculations.

Some authors have used 4 per cent as the discount factor (or the other rate of return) on the ground that this is roughly the long-term rate of interest and represents the cost that the government itself must incur in borrowing money. To the extent that one is prepared to assume that in fact

25. It may be noted in passing that the existence of a significant *personal* consumption component in the educational benefit stream also raises some nice questions germane to the issue of who should pay for education.

W. G. Bowen 33

it is going to be the government that will be providing any additional funds for education, there is much to be said for using a figure of this kind.

However, if we assume that individual students (or their families) are the ones contemplating investing in education, then a higher rate is surely appropriate, partly to take account of the greater risk involved in financing a single (typical) individual than in financing a large group. An individual would find it simply impossible to borrow educational funds on the private market at anything like 4 per cent interest.[26]

Becker (1960, pp. 348–9) has made use of a comparative rate of return in the neighbourhood of 9–10 per cent, on the ground that this is roughly the average rate of return on private investment in the United States – businesses would certainly be reluctant to undertake any project that did not promise to yield at least this high a rate of return. The argument is, of course, that if we can earn 9–10 per cent on alternative investments, a purely economic case for investing relatively more in education would have to be based on at least as high a rate of return on education.

From the standpoint of the large private investor, the logic of this argument is unassailable, provided that there are no appreciable differences in the degree of risk involved (and whether this proviso holds I do not know). But, whether this is the appropriate rate for the purposes of government policy can be questioned on the ground that, for a host of primarily political reasons (and this does not mean they are bad reasons), the actual alternative investment opportunities open to the government may not be nearly so lucrative. (In the US economy at any rate, there is a strong presumption that public funds will not be invested in such commercially profitable fields as chemicals, applied electronics, soft-drink production and the like, but rather in such activities as running the post office and supporting agricultural prices, as well as in research and development and education.)

A rather different approach to this 'other rate of return' question has been taken by Denison. His argument is that even if Becker were right in concluding that the rate of return on college education was about the same as the rate of return on private investment, 'college education for more students could fail to make a net contribution to economic growth only if it replaced investment in capital goods by an amount equal to its full cost (including the value of the work not performed by the additional college students)' (1962, p. 78). Denison goes on to argue that in fact the great bulk of expenditures on higher education comes from what would have been con-

26. It is true that individual universities, charitable groups, and some governments will make loans at lower rates of interest. The individual with access to such sources should, of course, calculate accordingly. However, since special terms of this sort do not reflect current market demands for loanable funds, they are of limited use as a guide to social policy (they in fact already reflect social policy).

sumption expenditures rather than from the savings-investment stream. Thus, he concludes that 'additional college enrolments would make a net contribution to growth even if the rate of return on a college education were only a small fraction of that on capital investment in other "things"' (1962, p. 78).

This approach (which really amounts to combining a calculation of the rate of return on private investment with a calculation of the amount of private investment that would be displaced by more spending on education) makes perfect sense if one is interested exclusively in economic growth as the objective of public policy. These days many people would no doubt agree that for political as well as economic reasons growth deserves more emphasis as a policy objective and that the US should be devoting a larger share of total resources to investments of *all* types. There is also a strong case, on welfare grounds, for recognizing that postponing present consumption entails sacrifices, and that an appropriate discount factor must be used to allow for such sacrifices.

Danger of extrapolating the past

The rates of return that I have been discussing are, of course, *average* rates of return for *past* periods, and so the question naturally arises: are there any particular cautions that must be borne in mind when using such rates of return as a guide to future actions?

The first answer to this question is that we should, of course, prefer to have a *marginal* rate of return figure rather than an average figure, since we are especially interested in the consequences of marginal changes in educational expenditures. Unfortunately, no direct way of estimating a marginal rate of return has as yet been found, and so we are forced to address ourselves to the question of whether we might expect the marginal figure to differ from the average figure in any systematic way. If we make the usual assumption that the conditions of a competitive market equilibrium obtained at the time the earnings and cost measurements were taken, then it follows that the average value can be regarded as equal to the marginal value, and this problem of the relationship between average and marginal values can be disposed of accordingly. Actually, this is taking too easy a way out in that the profit-maximization considerations which push industries to the equilibrium level of output are presumably less operative in the education field. None the less, for want of a better assumption, we must act as if the past average rate of return were equal to the marginal rate of return.

Moving now to the question of how accurate a guide to future rates of return is afforded by the average rates computed for past periods, it has been argued by Renshaw that the (marginal) rate of return applicable to additional investments is apt to be below the calculated average rates by virtue of the law of diminishing returns and because of 'the likelihood that any general increase in educational attainment will be accompanied by a decrease in the average level of ability' (1960).

Renshaw himself admits that 'dynamic factors . . . might act to maintain a *constant* marginal rate of return over time in the face of increases in the average level of educational attainment' (1960, my italics), and others, reasoning on the grounds that we are now entering a period in which knowledge and education will be of unparalleled importance, have suggested that rapid increases in the demand for skilled manpower could quite conceivably *raise* the marginal rate of return over time. Evidence of past trends in earnings differentials associated with various levels of education is of some relevance in this context. Miller has found that in the United States over the years since 1939, contrary to the expectations of some analysts, the economic advantages associated with the completion of additional years of schooling have *not* diminished, in spite of the fact that an ever-increasing proportion of the population has been educated (1960).[27]

Predicting the future rates of return that will be associated with possible expansion in education is likely to be more difficult than making similar predictions for other activities, for three main reasons: (a) so much depends on the quality of the additional students, a factor which is variable and hard to judge – when one is considering whether or not to produce more shoes, it can be safely assumed that the extra shoes produced will be much like their predecessors, but in education the extra student may turn out to be an academic failure or an Einstein; (b) the future educational requirements of a country will depend to a substantial degree on future discoveries and advancements in knowledge – which are almost impossible to foresee; (c) education is such a long process, and education once acquired is such a long-lived asset, that educational decisions must be based on an unusually long time-horizon.

In any case there is no avoiding the necessity of predictions – and past experience, modified by our understanding of trends and new developments, is likely to provide a better basis for decisions than implicit guesses predicated on unstated assumptions.

It is hoped that the above discussion has helped to clarify some of the reasons why various users of the direct-returns approach have drawn somewhat different conclusions from their work. Procedural choices and decisions have to be made at many steps in the analysis, and personal judgements and value preferences inevitably enter in.

None the less, the results obtained for the US economy offer rather

27. Becker (1960, pp. 347–8) has also reported roughly constant rates of return for the two years of 1940 and 1950.

consistent (some might say surprisingly consistent) support for the notion that education, on the average, has paid significant financial as well as non-financial rewards. The evidence is quite strong that individuals with the requisite ability have been well advised to continue their education through university level – and there is no reason to think that this pattern will not continue.

The difficulties involved in identifying earnings differentials with productivity differentials force one to be somewhat more cautious in drawing sweeping conclusions as to the effects of education on national output. However, here too the burden of proof is surely on those who would play down the economic importance of education. The likely existence of obscured relationships between ability and earnings constitutes the main reason for supposing that rate-of-return figures have an upward bias, and even after allowing (as best he could) for this cross-relation, Becker still obtained a 9 per cent per annum figure. When we then recognize that on top of this 9 per cent one surely must make some allowance for external benefits, and for the non-pecuniary contributions of education (if one wishes to think in terms of total welfare and not just in terms of GNP figures), the grounds for thinking that past investments in education have paid handsome returns to the nation as a whole are quite impressive.

It would be utter folly to pretend that the rate-of-return approach is free of troublesome difficulties or that it can be relied on to prove conclusively to a staunch unbeliever that investing resources in education makes good economic sense. But this approach does have three rather important appeals: (a) it enables us to obtain results in a form which permits comparisons of costs with benefits; (b) it permits us, in making calculations, to examine the quantitative effect on our results of alternative assumptions about such things as the proper discount rate and the effect of ability differentials on earnings differentials; and (c) as I hope the above discussion and the references to work in progress have shown, this approach is susceptible to further refinement and holds out the possibility that further research will remedy some of the present difficulties.

My own conclusion is that we have learned a great deal from the work that has already been done and that additional research along these lines – including more investigations into the external economies problem – ought certainly to be encouraged.

The forecasting-manpower-needs approach

This paper would be incomplete if it did not include at least a brief commentary on the 'forecasting-manpower-needs' approach to educational planning. No more than a brief commentary will be attempted here, however, partly because this approach falls a bit outside the scope of the present paper, in that this approach is not really directed at assessing the economic contribution of education, and partly because I am simply not sufficiently familiar with the important work in this field that has been done in France and in certain of the so-called underdeveloped countries.[28]

The objective of all 'forecasts' (or 'projections', the two terms will be used interchangeably here) of manpower needs is, of course, to provide the persons responsible for educational planning with information as to the likely future needs of the economy for persons with various kinds of training. Such forecasts can be expressed in terms of broad aggregates of people (e.g. all those completing a course of secondary or higher education), or in terms of much more specific occupational categories (e.g. botanists and teachers of mathematics).

A variety of methods has been used in arriving at manpower projections: (a) employers have been asked to specify how many persons with certain kinds of qualifications they will need, a given number of years in the future, and the responses have then been aggregated; (b) present ratios of trained manpower to total employment have been projected into the future on the basis of demographic information and, in some cases, assumptions about likely shifts in the relative importance of different industry groups; (c) the above method has been refined to take account of past *trends* in the utilization of manpower; (d) in projecting the manpower needs of the newly developing countries, recourse has been had to present ratios between skilled manpower and the total work force in countries at more advanced stages of economic development.

The great appeal of this general line of approach is that it offers definite guidelines framed in the terms in which decisions must actually be made. Whereas the returns-to-education approach hopes to tell us only whether, at a point in time, it is likely that we are spending too much or too little on education, manpower studies often culminate in recommendations that 'X' number of new student places in field 'Y' should be created by year 'Z'. This type of advice is obviously much more useful to the practical policy maker (or much more embarrassing, if he does not happen to agree with it).[29]

28. The reader interested in delving into the manpower projection literature would do well to look at the papers prepared for the Washington OECD Conference (fall of 1961), at a general summary paper by Mills (in Mushkin, 1962), at the various reports published in the United Kingdom by the Committee on Scientific Manpower (the Zuckerman Committee), at Payne's excellent summary of British experience in this field (1960), and at the commentary and references contained in Vaizey (1962). The continuing controversy in both the United States and the United Kingdom over the alleged 'shortage' of scientific manpower is also relevant – see, for example, the article by Hansen (1961), and the paper by Jewkes (1960).

29. It should be noted, however, that simply creating a given number of additional

On the negative side of the ledger, a criticism of many manpower projections made to date is that they have been disproved rather speedily by the march of events. While I know of no really ambitious study that has compared a large number of manpower projections with actual happenings, I suspect that such a study would reveal a rather systematic tendency for projections to understate the true future demand for trained manpower.

Reasons why manpower projections may be considerably off target are not hard to find. A major problem is that neither individual employers nor professional investigators are able to foresee the implications of new scientific developments. A second problem is that the manpower projections I know about have not succeeded in taking account of the elasticity of substitution between capital and labour and between highly-trained manpower and less-highly-trained manpower. There are few, if any, products that can be produced by only one specific combination of manpower, materials and machinery, and as the relative scarcity of the various factors changes one would expect adjustments in factor proportions to follow.

These projection difficulties are particularly pronounced in the case of persons whose training is general, and it is for this reason that many manpower studies have dealt only with groups such as engineers – and, of course engineers can upset supply and demand forecasts by taking managerial posts which are not 'just' engineering jobs. At the other end of the spectrum, projecting the demand for very specific occupations is also fraught with risks in that advancements in knowledge (or miscalculations of any kind) can lead to a very large proportionate error; the reason for concern about the possibility of such errors is not just that national plans may have to be modified, but that students making irrevocable career choices may have been misled. (The great potential influence of manpower projections on career choices is, for this very reason, a cause of real concern to a number of people.)

Manpower projections as a guide to policy are also subject to a still more fundamental criticism, which is implicit in my earlier comment, to the effect that this approach is not really directed at assessing the economic contribution of education. The point is that estimates of the future number of people with a given kind of training who are 'needed' or 'wanted' are rather devoid of meaning unless one also has a good idea of the relation between the benefits to be obtained by having this number of trained persons *and the costs involved in having them.* To the basic question of whether a

---

student places in a particular subject will not lead to a concomitant increase in the number of graduates unless labour-market incentives are strong enough to entice suitable candidates to accept the places. Labour-market policy and educational policy can be pursued independently of one another only at the risk of producing anomalous results.

country is well advised to devote more of its resources to training manpower, estimates of future 'needs', unless based on a balancing of costs and benefits, do not really provide much guidance.

The conclusion to draw from this is that manpower projections ought not to be viewed as an alternative method of approach, but as a way of obtaining information that can usefully be incorporated into broader-gauged analyses. Many manpower studies are already being carried out in the context of some kind of more general economic exercise, and all one can hope is that this trend will continue. At a more specific level, it would seem that future research along the manpower-projection line might fruitfully concentrate on the elasticity-of-substitution question and on the costs of inducing more people to move into various occupations.

A final comment

The reactions of persons interested in the relations between educational policy and economic policy to the kinds of analyses discussed in this paper are bound to depend on what they expected to find.

Two kinds of people, in particular, will be disappointed at the progress made to date in assessing the economic contribution of education. The first group consists of those who have already reached a firm conclusion as to what ought to be done about educational spending, and who are looking for conclusive 'proof' to support their point of view. The second group consists of those who have an entirely open mind on the subject and are looking for purely 'scientific' evidence that will settle the matter one way or another.

The work done thus far will evoke a happier response from those who want, and will use, as much help as can be obtained from careful analysis, but who are also prepared to invest their own efforts in interpreting the results in the context of the limitations of the methods employed and with reference to their own values.

It must also be said that the kinds of research described in this paper will positively displease some people – especially those who feel that educational policy discussions ought not to be 'contaminated' by references to costs and economic consequences. But surely one can feel strongly about the non-economic objectives of education and still acknowledge the importance of *also* weighing likely economic effects in arriving at policy decisions. A good case can be made (at least to economists) that this is a field in which economic issues are inevitably involved and that therefore economists must do what they can to clarify the consequences of alternative courses of action. As more and more money is spent on education, the old undocumented assertions that 'we know' or 'we believe' that 'education pays', will prove less and less satisfactory to the private and public groups who have to pay the mounting bills. Surely the issue is not whether attempts should be made to apply the techniques of economic analysis to education, but how best to do so.

Almost without exception, the persons who have actually done the kinds of research described above have been commendably modest in describing their success – and well they should be, for there is certainly much that is unknown. The mark of how far we still have to go is that economists who have strong personal opinions about the proper course of educational policy are not likely to have their opinions shaken by the results of their own research. It is becoming more and more difficult to reconcile any conclusion with the evidence, and this is the mark of progress.

References

ABRAMOVITZ, M. (1956), 'Resources and output trends in the United States since 1870', occasional paper no. 52, National Bureau of Economic Research, New York.

ANDERSON, P. S. (1961), 'The apparent decline in the capital output ratios', *Q. J. Econ.*, vol. 75, pp. 615–34.

BECKER, G. (1960), 'Is there underinvestment in college education?', *Amer. Econ. Rev.*, vol. 50, no. 2, pp. 346–54.

DENISON, E. F. (1962), 'The sources of economic growth in the United States and the alternatives before us', supplementary paper no. 13, Committee for Economic Development, New York.

DOMAR, E. (1961), 'On the measurement of technological change', *Econ. J.*, vol. 71, pp. 709–29.

FRIEDMAN, M., and KUZNETS, S. S. (1946), *Income from Independent Professional Practice*, National Bureau of Economic Research.

HANSEN, W. L. (1961), 'The "shortage" of engineers', *Rev. Econ. and Stats.*, vol. 43, pp. 251–6.

HARBISON, F. H. (1961), paper prepared for the OECD conference on education, Washington.

HARRIS, S. (1949), *The Market for College Graduates*, Harvard University Press.

HARRIS, S. (ed.) (1960), *Higher Education in the United States: The Economic Problems*, Harvard University Press.

HARRIS, S. (1962), *Higher Education: Resources and Finance*, McGraw-Hill.

HOUTHAKKER, H. S. (1959), 'Education and income', *Rev. Econ. and Stats.*, vol. 41, pp. 24–7.

JEWKES, J. (1960), 'How much science?', *Econ. J.*, vol. 70, pp. 1–16.

KENDRICK, J. W. (1961), *Productivity Trends in the United States*, Princeton University Press for National Bureau of Economic Research.

MASSELL, B. F. (1960), 'Capital formation and technological change in United States manufacturing', *Rev. Econ. and Stats.*, vol. 42, pp. 182–8.

MILLER, H. P. (1960), 'Annual and lifetime income in relation to education 1939–59', *Amer. Econ. Rev.*, vol. 50, pp. 962–86.

MILLS (1962), in S. J. Mushkin (ed.), *Economics of Higher Education*, US Department of Health, Education and Welfare, Office of Education.

PAYNE, G. L. (1960), *Britain's Scientific and Technological Manpower*, Stanford University Press.

RENSHAW, E. F. (1960), 'Estimating the returns to education', *Rev. Econ. and Stats.*, vol. 42, pp. 318–24.

RIVLIN, A. (1962), in S. J. Mushkin (ed.), *Economics of Higher Education*, US Department of Health, Education and Welfare, Office of Education.

SCHULTZ, T. W. (1960), 'Capital formation by education', *J. Polit. Econ.*, vol. 68, pp. 571–83.

SCHULTZ, T. W. (1961a), 'Education and economic growth', *Yearbook of the National Society for the Study of Education*.

SCHULTZ, T. W. (1961b), 'Investment in human capital', *Amer. Econ. Rev.*, vol. 51, pp. 1–17.

SILK, L. (1960), *The Research Revolution*, McGraw-Hill.

SOLOW, R. M. (1957), 'Technical change and the aggregate production function', *Rev. Econ. and Stats.*, vol. 39, pp. 312–20.

SVENNILSON, I., EDDING, F., and ELVIN, H. (1961), 'Targets for education in Europe 1970', paper prepared for Washington Conference of the OECD, p. 75.

VAIZEY, J. (1962), *The Economics of Education*, Faber.

VILLARD, H. H., *et al.* (1960), 'Investing in education and research: discussion', *Amer. Econ. Rev.*, vol. 50, pp. 370–78.

WALSH, J. R. (1935), 'The capital concept applied to man', *Q. J. Econ.*, vol. 49, pp. 255–85.

WEISBROD, B. (ed.) (1962), 'Education and investment in human capital', *J. Polit. Econ.*, pp. 106–23.

2 M. J. Bowman

The Human Investment Revolution in Economic Thought

M. J. Bowman, 'The human investment revolution in economic thought', *Sociology of Education*, vol. 39, 1966, pp. 111–38.

In his selective annotated bibliography of work in *The Economics of Education*, published in 1964, Mark Blaug listed 420 items (excluding other bibliographies). Education in the earlier history of economic thought was deliberately omitted, so that this is in fact a list of twentieth-century items, published in English. Although a few selections in relatively conventional educational finance are included, the bulk of the citations deal with relations between education and income distribution, effects of education on productivity, the spread of education and economic growth, schooling *versus* on-the-job training as human-resource formation, concepts and measures of human capital, social benefit–cost analysis, and educational policy – and also (less fully indexed) the literature on manpower requirements forecasting and manpower planning along with that (still very limited) on the economics of educational planning.

Of these 420 items, I found on a rough count that fourteen had appeared before 1940, six appeared in the decade of the 1940s, and nineteen in the years 1950 through 1954. The remaining 381 items, constituting 91 per cent of the total, appeared within the decade 1955–64 (or were in press in 1964); 283 of these 381 appeared in 1960 or later. The revised bibliography, to come out in 1966, will contain a thousand items, most of the added ones being post-1960 contributions. Even allowing for a selection bias against earlier work, the pace at which social scientists (and pseudo-social scientists) are adding to the printed pages on the economics of education is stunning.

This florescence of a new speciality in economics is closely allied to a shift of economic theory toward emphasis on *creative* man. The economics of information, communication, transfer of knowledge and know-how is growing on all fronts, including study of how innovations come about and their effects upon every aspect of economic life. In fact the 1965 meeting of the American Economic Association was built around the key themes of innovation, knowledge and education. Among the titles of papers directly concerned with education were: 'Education and the personal distribution of income', 'Investment in the education of the poor: a pessimistic report', 'Measurement of the quality of schooling', 'Investment in humans, technological diffusion and economic growth', 'The tax treatment of individual expenditures for research and education', 'The effect of education on labor force participation', 'Skill, earnings and the growth of wage supplements', 'A planning model for the efficient allocation of resources in education', 'A linear programming model for educational planning in an underdeveloped economy', 'Labor skills and comparative advantage', 'International flows of human capital'. The last paper of the sessions was entitled 'Trends, cycles and fads in economic writing'!

The investment orientation

A year or two ago it was still possible to give a reasonably adequate picture of what was happening in 'the economics of education' by classifying work under a few main headings,[1] ignoring odd items scattered here and there. However, this will no longer suffice. Furthermore, with the building up of empirical–analytical work close to the cores of theoretical economic systems, the economics of education itself takes off from such cores. Or restating the same point, the economics of education is genuinely economics, rather than a collection of techniques of estimation and special isolated investigations, only to the extent to which it is geared into a systematic body of economic thought.

With these considerations in mind, I have elected to focus this paper around a core concept that has come as something of a revolution in economic thought, that of investment in human beings. For as soon as such an approach is taken really seriously and followed through into its important ramifications, the economics of education begins (as it has begun) an infiltration into economics generally.

In an investment orientation to education we are concerned above all with the relations between the resources utilized to form human competencies (resource costs of education – whether in school, on the job, or elsewhere) and the increments to productivity that result. That is, an investment view of education entails cost–benefit assessments, sometimes from an individual decision-maker's point of view, sometimes from a school principal's point of view, and sometimes from the point of view of a government or of a society as a whole. But this is resource allocation; how can there be anything *new* about this? Hasn't the idea of investment in human beings been lying around for a long time? It may help to take a quick look at a few high points in the history of economic thought.

Evidently the mercantilists had some sort of appreciation of the invest-

1. The usual categorization is that used by William Bowen: (1) cross-country comparisons of income and education indices; (2) longitudinal 'aggregate input–output' studies of national income growth (most of which had no education in them, however); (3) the so-called 'rate-of-return'; and Bowen's analysis still constitutes an excellent starting point (see Bowen, 1964a; 1964b; Reading 1 in this volume).

ment in man idea, for they laid great stress on the importance of 'art and ingenuity', or skilled manpower, as a key to growth in national wealth, and William Petty even attempted to measure 'human capital'. But the mercantilists were not human investment men, for they did not follow through with their observations concerning human skills and productivity to analyse costs and returns. They had yet no system of economic thought, no analytical framework for doing this. Adam Smith reversed the mercantilist view, concerning himself with efficiency in the 'education industry', but primarily as an industry producing consumer services. In fact Smith believed that economic progress was based on division of labor and that it would reduce rather than raise supplies of human skills and demands for them. Both Smith and Malthus were concerned with education for the betterment of man, not for the creation of human resources. Malthusianism does indeed bring education back into the economics of growth, but walking backwards as it were, education would contribute to population control and hence raise or maintain national income by *reducing* the numbers in the labor force. There would seem to be nothing at all closely related to contemporary human investment concepts in all this. However, turning the pages of *The Wealth of Nations* we come to Smith's analogies between men and machines, where acquisition of skills is viewed specifically as an investment – an unambiguous anticipation of recent work. Through the middle years of the nineteenth century the neo-classicists often considered education in its relations to social stratification and social mobility and the segmentalization of labor markets, but this again was not an investment approach as such. Alfred Marshall went further, including discussion of the socio-economics of 'talent wastage'. These sections of his work probably come the closest of all, prior to the twentieth century, to many modern discussions of investment in human beings. But Marshall stopped short when he discarded the notion of 'human capital'. It was Irving Fisher, in his highly abstract capital theory, who brought the human component of capital fully into the fold. Fisher was not particularly interested in education, however. What he did was to place the emphasis in dealing with capital where it logically must be. Capital is something (a stock) that yields a flow of services over time. Whether the physical entity in which the capital stock is embodied can be bought and sold is a matter of degree (in modern terminology, degree of 'liquidity'), and is not a defining criterion. But resources put into schooling are (among other things) investments in the acquisition of potential future income streams, whether looked at from the individual or from the societal point of view. This is a kind of capital formation. It is the formation of human capital in that the stock that will yield the future income stream is embodied in human beings.

As the reader will be aware, the view of education as an investment in the creation of future income streams is a special view of education. It says nothing about education as a pleasurable (or painful) 'consumer' experience while in school. It says nothing about education for citizenship or political ends generally. What it says about education as either a private or a societal investment in the acquisition of a future income stream depends upon how we define 'income' and, in applied economics, on what elements of income get measured – directly or indirectly. In practice what is most easily measured is money income, but there is also the 'real income' potential of the capacity to 'do it yourself', whether this is home carpentry or filling out your own income-tax form. Where income in kind is an important part of total real income, as in subsistence farming, incorporation of such earnings as income estimates becomes essential; this is an important consideration in attempts to compare income positions or assess economic returns to schooling in less developed countries. Along with income in kind there is also the problem of returns to education that enter the future income stream, in a broad definition of income, as psychic satisfactions – whether as enjoyment of leisure or as non-monetary satisfactions associated with the kinds of jobs to which more education may give access. Clues as to the likely importance of the latter may sometimes be derived indirectly, from observation of large cost–benefit discrepancies working persistently against highly educated people in some occupations. However, the main concern of the investment orientation to education is with the formation of human capital that will yield flows of services that are *transferable* and could thus be measured in 'rental' or 'hire' terms (whether or not a man in fact works for himself or rents his services to others).

More difficult than the treatment of individual incomes in kind, though equally or more important, is the assessment of *indirect* economic returns to education from a societal point of view. Just adding up the observed returns to individuals may not give the right answer; in fact it would give a truly right answer only by accident. This is the pervasive problem of 'external' effects, economies of scale, and shifts in production functions, that plagues all study of economic growth. There is nothing in this that is peculiar to education, although the untutored wayfarer in the literature might easily be led to believe that education was especially 'difficult'. Exactly the same problems arise in attempts to assess societal effects of any sort of investment, whether in physical capital in the private sectors of the economy, in physical infra-structure, such as roads and dams, or in the formation of human competencies at school and on the job. In fact, there is ferment today on all of these fronts, and treatment of physical capital is being drastically overhauled as part of the modern effort to analyse factor substitutions and complementarities and the processes of economic growth and development in a dynamic world.

Finally, whether we look from an individual or a societal perspective, it should be noted that expressing income in money terms is simply a way of measuring a mix of goods and services; as such it is essential for useful analysis of the most basic questions. Money is of course a necessity for the operation of a complex economy, as the Russians discovered, whether or not overt prices are the proper weights or measures to use in assessing costs and benefits or talking about 'national income'. Where observed prices are clearly inappropriate measures, economists substitute for them what has come to be termed 'shadow prices' – estimates of more nearly 'correct' value measures. The analysis of relations between education of various levels and kinds and occupational roles is exceedingly important, and much of this work has been done without regard to earnings. However, in an investment view, occupations are intervening variables between human competencies, however acquired, and the incomes these human resources yield (their 'productivity'). Similarly, the acquisition of competencies or gains in achievement scores in school are intervening variables between inputs of teacher and student time and the future earnings of graduates.

It is convenient to distinguish four main foci of the economics of education viewed as an investment in human beings. These are:

1. Global or aggregative measurements of the magnitude of human capital formation and of its contribution to national income growth.

2. Applications of micro-decision theory to analysis of demands for schooling and supplies of educated people, career choices, factors that determine the nature and extent of on-the-job training, income and opportunity distribution, and constraints on mobility and freedom of choice.

3. Contemporary and a few historical investigations into determinants of demands for educated or trained people, changes in those demands with economic development, and dynamic interactions between human-resource demands and supplies.

4. Methodological research in the development and application of systematized procedures and criteria for educational planning. Cutting across these, sometimes merely as stated and unstated assumptions but sometimes of major direct concern, are technical parameters involved in the use of resources (including student time) to form human competencies and those involved in the combining of human skills with other resources in productive activity. Expressed in terms of substitutions and complementaries among resources in their employment for various purposes (e.g. various combinations of inputs of teacher time, student time, and library facilities to produce 'learning') these technical alternatives are called 'production functions'. Many of the most impassioned arguments among these econ-

omists who have become involved in discussions of social-decision models and planning, go back to differences in (unproven) beliefs about production functions in human learning and in human-resource use.

In the aggregate

The global or aggregative measurement of relations between human-resource development and national income is discussed in every article on contemporary work in the economics of education, even though aggregative input–output analysis has by no means a monopoly of the economics of education and its beginnings had nothing to do with education at all. The explanation is that it has probably done more to convince economists of the importance of studying education than has any other single academic endeavor. That impact tells us something about the sociology of the growth of knowledge rather than evidencing any intrinsic merits in aggregate production-function analysis. But if we judge it by the scope and importance of innovative research in all directions that it has stimulated, the naïve discovery of our ignorance – now called 'the residual' – must go down as a major event. Given the mixed scientific, econometric and polemical character of aggregate input–output history, perhaps I may be forgiven if I sum it up in a dialectical sequence. For it did more than anything else to set the stage for the 'human investment revolution' of the 1950s, so ably fostered by the innovative entrepreneurial genius of Schultz.

That revolution, like all well-behaved revolutions, can claim its historical thesis and antithesis. Thesis in this case was the labor theory of value, according to which men were most assuredly 'capital' in Fisher's definition, Marxism to the contrary notwithstanding.[2] Furthermore, the formation of physical capital in Austrian economics depended upon a 'subsistence fund' to maintain workers while they devoted their time to constructing implements of further production instead of goods for immediate consumption.[3]

Both the labor theory of value in its original sense and the Austrian 'roundaboutness' theory of capital had largely disappeared from the main stream of economics by the 1930s, even though a few modern economists like to count in 'labor efficiency units' and Marx has contributed more to modern economics than is commonly recognized. With the formalization of value theory 'factors of production' had become abstractions and Man had become a purified indifference surface, addicted to geometry and calculus. But Man and his labor were still on a par with other agents of production.

2. Note, however, that the original labor theory of value was modified in Soviet practice, where a training and crude manpower and materials planning view took hold, reminiscent more of the mercantilists than of Ricardo.

3. For a quick picture of where everyday man has stood in the history of economics see Bowman (1951).

Antithesis came with Keynes's *General Theory*. For all the variants of Keynesianism shared in a trait that is significant for the present discussion (as in many other contexts). They shifted the emphasis of a whole generation of economists from viewing labor as an active agent of production to viewing labor as a passive agent that would find employment only if there were a high enough rate of 'investment' and, most especially, of investment in the production of physical producer capital. Furthermore, out of Keynes's great but ambiguous polemic, written initially to deal with economic fluctuations and persistent unemployment, came some quite remarkable progeny – long-term 'growth' theories in which virtually everything was explained by the amount of physical capital and its rate of increase.

So it was that economists set themselves up for a series of pragmatic–political and theoretical–econometric shocks. For it was obvious after the Second World War that physical capital worked its miracles only in lands where there were many qualified men who knew how to use it (the Marshall Plan countries and Japan). And the econometricians discovered that their old aggregate capital–output ratios weren't behaving properly. Nor did un-differentiated 'labor' combined with capital inputs do any better. By conventional measures econometricians were accounting for economic growth only when there was very little growth to explain. For the period from the late 1920s to the 1950s in Western Europe and Japan they were doing very badly indeed, explaining half or less of national income growth.

Reactions to the large residuals were almost as various as the economists who looked at them, but even those who strove hardest to rehabilitate theories of investment in physical capital as the chief key to growth had to draw implicitly upon learning and creative man. This is least evident in Solow's 'vintage capital' articles (in particular, 1962). Having labeled the residual 'technical change' he argued that such change could take place only as it was embodied in new physical capital; hence even after correcting for price level changes, a dollar spent on physical capital in 1965 should count as more than a dollar so spent in 1964 or 1963. In fact Solow constructed a 'vintage' model of physical capital inputs that did the job *too* successfully. Among other things, it left all quality improvements in labor *un*embodied, a neglect that might have passed before but could hardly get by once the monolithic capital–output models had been challenged on 'quality' grounds. Furthermore, what is the process whereby technological change takes place and gets itself embodied? Another reaction to the residual has been to step up research on investments-in-research by industry, government and other agencies. This gets a little closer to investment in man. Meanwhile Lundberg, in Sweden, came up with the 'Horndal effect' – steady growth in productivity in a firm with little or no change in its physical capital. What did this have to say about human learning and productivity?

By contrast, Arrow would probably be more inclined to count his article on 'Learning by doing' (1962) in the physical capital than in the educational investment camp, though I would plant it quite firmly in both at once. He argued that (1) people learn by being challenged with new experiences, (2) gross investment in physical capital (before depreciation) is the best index of rate of exposure to learning situations, and hence (3) the best measure of capital inputs into aggregate production is gross physical-capital formation, and the use of net values has underestimated the role of physical capital in economic growth. Looked at in another way, which was not Arrow's, his thesis could be turned around to read: (1) increases in skill and knowledge are the main key to growth, (2) exposure to new situations speeds learning, and hence (3) rapid replacement of obsolescent equipment is a sound investment in man and through man in economic growth. Neither statement is more correct, or incorrect, than the other.

Two other scholars who have recently concerned themselves with aggregate input–output analysis introduced schooling of the labor force explicitly. One is Griliches, who started out with a study of social returns to investment in research on hybrid corn. Subsequently, in connection with his very interesting (and sophisticated) work on aggregate production functions and technological progress in selected sectors of the American economy, he found that rising levels of education have made a significant contribution to productivity in both agriculture and manufacturing industries (1963; 1964; 1965). Meanwhile, Denison has given us 'The sources of economic growth in the United States and the alternatives before us' (1962). This book attempts to measure every sort of input Denison could identify, including educational attainments of the labor force. Every measured input is assumed to yield constant returns per unit, so that, for example, the fourth year of secondary school embodied in a male member of the labor force will make the same additional contribution to national income in 1956 as in 1929. The education parts of Denison's study were presented in fuller form as the first (and most discussed) major paper in a 1964 conference of the OECD Study Group in the Economics of Education (1964). Given his assumptions, Denison attributed to education 23 per cent of the growth in total national income and 42 per cent of the growth in *per capita* income in the United States over the period 1929–57. In fact, though he did not say so, Denison included in his measure of education's contributions the net contributions of on-the-job training as well as of schooling embodied in the labor force. For this reason among many others, it would be quite unjustified to draw any general conclusions from his estimates, for what schooling contributes depends upon the factors with which human skills are combined in production and the opportunities for on-the-job learning and training, which are in turn functions of the pace of change.

Schultz is unique among those who have analysed empirical aggregate input–output series in that he explicitly linked his analysis with the theme of investment in human beings. This led him, among other things, to measure the value of student time as a labor input into the educational process.[4] On conservative assumptions he showed that earnings foregone (the measure of student inputs) accounted for over half of the total costs of secondary and higher education in the United States. Also, he estimated that over the period from 1900 to 1956 total investments in 'human capital formation' in schools rose from 9 to 34 per cent of total investments in physical capital formation. But the significance of his book (1963), and the numerous closely related articles that he has written on this subject is not the least dependent upon his rather vulnerable methods of estimating education's contributions, or even on his more valid empirical estimates of the magnitude of human capital formation measured in cost terms. Rather it is in the combination of detail and sweeping vision with which he argues the human investment revolution (see also Schultz, 1964).

Investments in human beings and micro-decision theory

The second major focus of work on the economics of education as an investment centers on decision theories framed as testable behavioral hypotheses, and the analysis of major institutional influences and constraints upon private investment choices with respect to schooling and on-the-job training. Decision theory in this context is micro cost–benefit analysis. I have already indicated that it has a wide range of potential uses in the study of economic structure and processes, although taken by itself it also has severe limitations and should not be casually introduced in analysis of economic growth or used without other supplementary analytical tools as a guide in making large-scale educational decisions. The decision units on which such analysis focuses are either individuals (or their parents) or business firms; the decisions concern what people invest in themselves (in school and also, indirectly, on the job) and what firms put into the training of employees. It must be stressed, however, that the economist is not concerned, as is the psychologist, with explaining individual behavior *per se*. If people behave *as if* they were economically rational, that is quite enough, provided we are dealing with multiple decision units.

In applying economic decision theory to analysis of education as self-investment, the first question is then: do individuals behave in an economically rational manner with respect to investment in the acquisition of future potential earnings streams via schooling? The first economist to pose

4. The fullest presentation of these estimates and their interpretation is in Schultz (1960).

this question explicitly, and to test it in cost–benefit terms was Walsh (1935). He asked: did doctors, lawyers, engineers get back more or less than they put into qualifying themselves, taking into account the delays in their earnings and the lifetime paths of their income streams? What about men who invested in college training instead of entering the labor market when they completed secondary school? Walsh's method of taking into account the timing of earnings was to discount income streams at an 'external rate' of 4 per cent to get their 'present values' for comparison with what the education cost. The 'present' in this context is the date at which the decision to continue in college or in post-college education is made. If Walsh had used a higher (lower) rate as the implied basis for comparison with alternative investments, his present value estimates would of course have been lower (higher). Although he did not discuss foregone earnings as a cost, his method in fact took them into account when he set up his earnings streams. The earnings of college graduates start four years later than for high-school graduates, and foregone earnings are there in the income streams of the high-school graduates with which the college streams are compared.[5] Unfortunately, Walsh's pioneer effort went virtually unnoticed until after World War II; the time was not yet ripe.

A much more elaborate study, of incomes of doctors and dentists in independent professional practice, was published by Friedman and Kuznets (1946). Again using an 'external' 4 per cent discount rate, they found doctors to do much better than dentists, and they asked a series of questions as to why this should be the case. How far might income differences be explained by differences in ability, or by differential non-monetary preferences or satisfactions unfavorable to doctors (which seemed on the face of it unlikely). Or again, what evidence was there of monopolistic constraints on entry into training for the higher paying professions? Although this work has been sharply attacked, it too was undeniably a pioneer study, and demonstrated something of what could be done with such an approach. At the same time it gave explicit attention to many of the problems that must be solved in adjusting observed education–income relationships to take account of variables such as ability and parental status. It set the stage also for a number of subsequent studies of the economics of investment in training for the professions.

The empirical study of investment in education that evoked really widespread reactions was first reported on in 1960 in a preliminary article by Becker. He asked: 'is there under-investment in college education?' (1960). There were evidently two reasons why this drew so much attention. First,

5. Walsh made the mistake of also introducing a cost of subsistence estimate into his cost figures, thereby biasing his findings downward with respect to benefit–cost ratios. Subsistence clearly is not a cost of education; it is a cost of remaining alive.

Schultz had paved the way with his writing concerning education as an investment in economic growth, even though there was no 'growth' in Becker's analysis. Second, as soon as a man talks about too much or too little he is talking societal effects and normative economics; even if measurements of social costs and benefits could be unambiguously pinpointed (which they clearly cannot) there will always be plenty of men to rise to such bait. Starting from the private side, in essence Becker's analysis was essentially like Walsh's, except for one thing. Instead of taking an arbitrary external rate of return with which to discount earning streams and estimate 'present values', Becker asked the question: what is the rate of return that the average man investing in a college education will make on that investment? If that rate, termed an 'internal rate', is higher than the returns he could get in alternative investments (and higher than his own subjective time preference), then it is evidently a good investment. In figuring private costs the public subsidy to schooling is of course ignored, and the increments to income streams are adjusted to deduct associated increments in income taxes. But Becker then asked the more nearly social question: Including public subsidies to schooling in the cost measures, and measuring returns by pre-tax increments to income streams, what is the social or 'total' internal rate of return on investment in a college education? His conclusion was that it was about in line with alternatives, that there was neither significant under- nor over-investment in college education. His internal rate of return estimates were attacked as too high because he ignored ability, too low because he ignored indirect returns, fallacious because incomes are (it was asserted) poor measures of productivity, and so on. For several years most educational and manpower planners who had heard about this and the other US rate-of-return studies that followed either ignored or attacked the work; a few complained that this was all very well in the United States, where we had census tabulations on incomes by age and educational attainment, but that it was impractical elsewhere.[6] Meanwhile Becker went on to construct a theoretical model that incorporated business decisions and on-the-job training in the same broad framework – supported by Mincer as his empirical mind and conscience (1962).[7] But before taking a look at

6. The leadership of American economists in the development and empirical testing of models for analysis of investment in education rests firmly upon the imaginative and yet unwitting contributions of sociologists, demographers, and very practical market analysts in private business. It is these people who persuaded the US Census to put earnings and educational attainments into the 1940 census, along with breaks by sex, age, race, and region. These data were improved in the 1950 and especially the 1960 census, and will be even better in 1970. They are the envy of economists in other lands concerned with human-resource problems.

7. See their articles and others in the special October 1962 supplement of the *Journal of Political Economy* on 'Investment in human beings'. Schultz's introduction is well worth reading even by those who will find some of the other papers too technical.

that tour-de-force, let us see what has been going on even without on-the-job refinements.

First, what has been happening in other countries? Using either external or internal rate of return techniques (or both) estimates of direct private and social cost–benefit relationships have been made in at least the following: Canada, England, India (two studies), Israel, Japan, Mexico, Nigeria, Venezuela, and even (a confidential report) the USSR. In two cases, Mexico and Nigeria, the authors gathered their own data, demonstrating that meaningful information could be obtained for this purpose more, not less, readily than for the heretofore more popular and common 'manpower' studies. For Nigeria and in a second small non-representative study (not yet completed) in England,[8] the analysis is differentiated by types of secondary and higher education as well as level of schooling. Findings in these studies are varied, but indicate consistent patterns in relation to other known characteristics of social-status structures and constraints associated with educational structures and selection policies Thus far there is no evidence that there actually is, in less developed countries, the relative shortage of men with secondary-level education that has been so often asserted in the literature – a fact that suggests on the one hand a need for more intensive examination of distortions in labor-market structures and processes that determine how men's skills are used, and on the other hand, a serious reconsideration of just what the evidence is with respect to the economics of the education mix in countries at lower and middle stages of development. For at least Mexico, Nigeria, and apparently (taking cruder evidence) most of East Africa, the returns to later years of primary schooling are especially high, as they are also in the United States. The limited available information with respect to technical schools in Nigeria[9] supports findings by Foster (1965, 1966), Callaway (1963, 1964), and others that in West Africa these schools are poor private and public investments, at least as they stand at the present time and in existing labor market settings.

It should be noted that only the Mexican study among those outside of the United States includes adjustments of any kind to correct for ability or for parental status. Carnoy (1964) found that among urban males in Mexico standardizing for parental occupation had little effect; it actually raised, instead of lowering, estimated returns to university education. There is some evidence to suggest that in Japan and the United States ability factors play an especially significant part in the observed income differentials as between

8. The findings of a pilot study of eight firms in electrical engineering, together with interesting background analysis and rate of return estimates, are reported in Blaug, Peston, and Ziderman (1966). See also Blaug (1965).

9. Included in a linear programming study by Samuel Bowles. I will come back to this later.

the lowest and next-lowest educational attainment groups; men with less than eight years of schooling are becoming such a small group in those countries as to be clearly selected out for defective ability and (in the United States) exceptional cultural deprivation.

In the United States, both private and 'total' rate-of-return and present-value studies have multiplied. In some cases the empirical analysis concentrates primarily upon sorting out the returns or benefits side, without explicit comparisons of returns with costs. Most of the work on relation between educational attainments and incomes in agriculture, using small area or state data, has this focus on the linkage between schooling and incomes. Welch (1966) has gone further. Using a number of sources, including state reports and the one-in-a-thousand tapes from the 1960 US census, he has attempted to identify characteristics of schools that may be associated with interstate differences in agricultural income of men with any given number of years of schooling (after controlling for other inputs into agriculture). His best predictors were teacher salaries and school size, both of which are of course correlated with degree of rural 'urbanization'.

The first study of which I am aware in which data from the 1940 or 1950 censuses were used to analyse regional and racial differences in relations between educational attainments and incomes was Anderson (1955). Though costs of schooling were not estimated, the relative gross returns to schooling were discussed in incentive terms. Zeman included schooling (along with region) in his analysis of 1939 earnings differentials between urban whites and Negroes (1958). Becker analysed rates of return to whites and to non-whites separately. Also, he attempted (1965) some adjustments of the income differentials associated with college education to allow for differences in ability. The most refined analysis of income differentials by race and region is in Hanoch's Chicago dissertation (1965). Using the one-in-a-thousand sample tapes he was able to make a number of important adjustments in the income figures and to try out a large number of control variables. Comparing Hanoch's findings with the internal rates of return computed earlier by Hansen (1963) from unadjusted income data, the most notable modification is in raising the estimated white male rate of return to investment in some college (without college completion) from around 5 to 7 per cent in the North and 9 per cent in the South, while at the same time reducing the rates of return to investment in the last two years of college from about 15 to 12 per cent in the North and 11 per cent in the South. Taking into account the fact that even with all his adjustments Hanoch did not have scores on intelligence or achievement tests,[10] this substantially

10. Concerning potentials for interdisciplinary effort that relates to rate-of-return analysis, see Bowman (1962). That article points also to the limitations and potentials of rate-of-return analysis. For a more critical view of rate-of-return work, see chapter 3

modifies the previous unfavorable investment image for junior colleges, even though it hardly points to them as a priority investment. The evident priority is in getting genetically normal people at the educational bottom effectively into the main stream. But this brings us also to the problem of market discrimination against groups, especially Negroes.

Among Hanoch's most striking findings are that the private internal rate of return to two years of college among northern non-white men was negative and that among northern non-whites the life–income patterns of those who had completed college ran close to the life incomes of those who were only high-school graduates.

On the whole Hanoch's findings are consistent with the education–income patterns delineated in Bowman (1965b), which shows median and upper and lower quartile earnings of white and of non-white males by educational attainments for two age groups, 25–34 and 45–54, in 1939, 1949 and 1959. Income gradients by schooling were consistently steeper for whites than for non-whites and steeper in the South than in the North. Furthermore, these patterns were remarkably stable over time. This study, like Anderson's earlier work, pointed especially to the Southern drag at the bottom combined with convergence into the national economy at the top, both in proportions of the adult population which had completed high school or better and in the incomes of college graduates.

Thus far no one has estimated returns to increments of schooling received in the South by men moving into the North (whether white or non-white). One of the major difficulties is evident: how far can years of schooling (at lower costs) in the South prepare a man for the jobs open to a Northerner with the same number of years of schooling?[11] Nevertheless, micro-decision theory has been applied to analysis of both intra- and inter-national migration of human capital. Sjaastad has analysed migration within the United States as a private investment (1962). Grubel and Scott (1966) are applying private decision theory to analysis of international migration in selected professions, especially between the United States and Canada,[12] and a doctoral candidate in Comparative Education at the University of Chicago (Robert Myers) is pressing further with some aspects of this problem. Both the Grubel and

---

in Vaizey (1962). He has written extensively on many aspects of the economics of education.

11. It was this problem of differences in school 'quality', defined in terms of the economic productivity potential acquired by students, to which Welch was directing his efforts in his study (1966).

12. The main study is in final stages of revision. However, a stimulating and thought-provoking paper that challenges many of the recent 'brain drain' arguments was presented at the 1965 meeting of the American Economic Association, and appears in the Proceedings (May 1966).

Scott study and that by Myers are concerned also with social benefit–cost theory in application to international migration and, in Myers's case, to study abroad. Meanwhile, of special interest in the context of American debates over Federal and local roles in financing education, Weisbrod treated a 'community' as an abstracted economic decision-unit to build up an educational investment cost–benefit analysis that takes into account migration into and out of the community. He applied this to illustrative cases (1965).

'Far out', though not necessarily unimportant on that account, are attempts to build indirect or vicarious individual satisfactions into decision models and analysis of voting behavior with respect to public investments in education. The most formalized (and hence the most likely to be ignored or unjustifiably ridiculed by economists as well as sociologists) is Stubblebine's abstract analysis of preference functions, voting behavior, and the private–public mix in educational expenditure (1965). It is my prediction that his paper will prove important to quite pragmatically oriented researchers in this field, appearances to the contrary notwithstanding.

Very different and much less formal treatments of the rationale of incorporating indirect individual satisfactions in a socio-economic analysis of public investments may be found in work by Scott on parks and fisheries (1964) and in my treatments of vicarious and related satisfactions as returns to social investments in Appalachia (Bowman and Haynes, 1963, ch. 12).[13] This brings up, incidentally, a whole range of work that I have had to neglect here, the growing research on causes of school dropouts and effects of training and retraining programs. Some of the best work on these problems is of course being done by sociologists, but the interesting thing is that some of their work fits very tidily into the economist's investment-decision framework. A striking example is Duncan's article on relations between unemployment and school dropout rates (1965).[14]

Finally, let us come back into the heat of micro-decision theory in its applications to human investment, to look at the Becker–Mincer treatment of on-the-job training (Becker, 1962; Mincer, 1962). They make no distinction between 'training' and 'learning', but tie their analysis to the opportunity–cost concept.

All costs are opportunity costs. In other words, what something 'costs' is

13. Also, a brief but more formal statement of the same idea is included in Anderson and Bowman (forthcoming).

14. There is of course an extensive literature in economics on 'structural unemployment' *versus* deficiency of aggregate demand which is highly relevant in assessing the economics of public investments in youth and adult training programs, along with empirical research on the early results of particular programs. And economists must be as interested as sociologists in Dentler and Warshauer (1965).

what must be given up to get it. Though this concept is at the heart of economics, it has all too often been either ignored or inappropriately applied (and attacked).[15] Next to his vital role as leader in the revolution of thought concerning the importance of human resources in economic growth, Schultz's most important contribution was the great stress that he placed upon one element of opportunity costs, the earnings students forego while attending school.[16]

In essence, what Becker did was to carry Schultz's student-foregone incomes the next step, to income a man may forego now in order to take a job in which he will learn more (whether through formal training or by more informal experience).[17] So long as what he learns is transferable from one firm to another and he is free to move, the difference between his current take-home pay and what he could earn measures the extent of his on-the-job investment in his own human-capital formation. This is Becker's 'general' skills case,[18] and it is the assumption upon which Mincer based estimates of the extent of on-the-job training associated with various levels of education in schools in the United States in 1939, 1949 and 1958. Mincer's findings indicated very substantial investments in on-the-job training and learning in the United States, and a substantial increase in those investments. Valued in cost terms, the aggregate of investments in human beings on the job has consistently exceeded investments in learning in schools.

All that Mincer needed to make these estimates was the data used in analyses of internal rates of return to schooling – that is, direct schooling costs and life-income streams. In fact one of the things that Becker's analysis showed up very clearly was that computed internal rates of return to investment in schooling were in fact average rates to investments in schooling and complementary on-the-job training. This is an exceedingly important fact to keep in mind, and it is not dependent for its validity upon any restrictive assumptions. Actually Mincer had to make assumptions much more restrictive than Becker's theory to get his empirical on-the-job

15. For a discussion of this concept in its multiple dimensions and applications, see Bowman (1966). The last section of this paper includes also a theoretical contrast of the Mincer model and an alternative one.

16. Notice that teacher salaries are indicators of costs from a societal point of view only to the extent to which they measure what teachers would produce in other activities – the best alternative 'opportunity'. On the other hand, to the school principal a teacher's salary is a direct measure of what he could buy for the school if he didn't hire the teacher, and hence from his point of view it is a very exact measure of 'opportunity cost'.

17. Machlup also makes effective use of opportunity cost estimations for important components of his measures (1962).

18. For a further discussion of Becker's and other categorizations of skills, as these may be pertinent to analysis of on-the-job training, see Bowman (1965a).

training estimates – the most critical was the assumption that the average rate of return to schooling and on-the-job training jointly was also the marginal rate to each successive on-the-job investment in one's self.

It is as easy to attack the Becker–Mincer work as to attack the theory of pure competition, which certainly does not dispose of it. Even when their assumptions are not satisfied, the analytical tools they provide form an extremely important point of departure for other future studies, using other assumptions and testing the validity of those assumptions in diverse institutional settings.

Human resource demands, supplies and development

None of the kinds of studies thus far discussed has focused attention upon determinants of demands for human skills and how those demands change. In their first approximations, which is where most of them have stopped, the rate-of-return studies have treated the census cross-section income–education data for a given year as though the age patterns in that year represented the income path that would be traced out through real time (or had been so traced) by any cohort of men with the indicated schooling. Projection of such patterns into the future assumes that demands for the better educated will rise with increases in their relative numbers in such a way as to maintain the same real incomes (correcting for inflation). A similar assumption underlies the aggregative approach to assessing education's contribution to growth as applied by both Denison and Schultz. Unfortunately, to go at the problem the other way and attempt to assess determinants of demand change and to measure such change is fraught with difficulties.

Most of the attempts to examine demand changes have been associated with 'manpower planning'. Since it ignores costs of human-resource development it is only at a half-way point toward an investment orientation to economic analysis of education, and I shall therefore be brief. European economists and planners have devoted the major part of their efforts in 'the economics of education' to such work, and some Americans have also been very active in these endeavors.[19] In many instances manpower planning has been no more than naïve projections of past trends, though in some cases the work has been technically intricate and very ingenious. The underlying assumptions are very different from those that have usually charac-

19. At one time or another, most of the major manpower planning endeavors have been at least summarized in OECD publications, which are the best place to start to get an international view, at least for the more developed parts of the world. Elsewhere the manpower planning work has frequently been tied in with the work of UNESCO. For a relatively sophisticated and yet eminently readable introduction to this field, and its relations to educational planning, see Parnes (1962).

terized 'aggregate production function' studies or attempts to extend rate-of-return analysis to social planning.[20] For the manpower planners assume very rigid demand structures at any given national income level, even though those structures may shift drastically through time. So far projection has not been very successful, though the attempts have constituted a valuable learning experience for those involved. Manpower planning has forced also a closer inspection of the links between schooling and job skills, including quite elaborate technical (non-economic) analyses of these relationships.[21] However, manpower planning does not incorporate in its models any analysis of interactive processes between human resource demands and supplies.

Both historical studies and those cross-national comparisons that go analytically beyond the level of searching for coefficients to plug into manpower projections must and do look at interactive development processes. There are more historical materials on these problems, and with more modern relevance, than is commonly assumed, and these are slowly being explored. I cannot summarize the historical work here, partly because what I know of it is so scattered and diverse. It must suffice to note that the investment view of human resources is beginning to make itself felt in this sort of work too. There is much to be done in painstaking historical investigation of relationships between evolving institutional characteristics of a society and the evolving loci and extent of private and public investment in human resource development.[22]

So far as I am aware, the first cross-national comparison that went beyond simple cross-tabulations of literacy rates against per capita incomes was a small essay by Bowman and Anderson (1963). Controlling for 'energy potential' and the proportion of the population engaged in agriculture, that study examined world regions separately. The most striking conclusions were

1. An apparent threshold effect of something like 40 per cent adult literacy, as a necessary but not sufficient condition of economic emergence.

2. Negligible income effects of proportions of the adult population with secondary schooling once those with primary schooling were taken into account (excepting countries with over 90 per cent literate).

20. For a sharp summing up of the extremes in the rationale of rate-of-return *v.* manpower-planning views of the economics of education and the markets for human skills, see Blaug (1966).

21. An outstanding contribution in this area is Eckaus (1964). See also Wilkinson (1964). This dissertation includes, among other things, a sample survey of employers' perceptions of training requirements (ch. 5) and a 'present value' analysis from a special run of income–age–education data in the Canadian census (ch. 6).

22. Some initial explorations are included in Anderson and Bowman (1965a).

3. That income positions in the 1930s explained enrolment rates in the 1950s better than schooling in the 1930s explained income in the 1950s.

Already some of these relationships are changing among countries in the lower and middle income ranges; the world-wide emphasis upon education both as an instrument variable in public policy oriented to growth and as a national prestige symbol is producing a situation in which schooling must almost inevitably lead economic development rather than following upon it. Partly we have of course the chicken-and-the-egg, but the relationship is not quite so closed a circle as that.

In 1964, Harbison and Myers published their book, *Education, Manpower and Economic Growth*. This book is two things. It is an enlightening and perceptive discussion of situations the authors have observed in many countries. It is also a set of cross-tabulations of and simple correlations among indexes of human resource development (school enrolments by levels and by types of curricula within higher education, expenditures on education), proportions of the population in selected occupations, and national income. They construct a composite education index by which they classify countries. In their recommendations the authors lay stress, and with good reason, on the important role of informal education and training and learning on the job. Unfortunately, however, their statistical evidence does not support the inferences they try to draw with respect to emphasis upon secondary schooling and especially vocational and technical education.

The latest and technically most sophisticated of the cross-national studies is that by Galenson and Pyatt, prepared for the International Labor Office (1964). This work might equally well have been classified with the aggregate production function studies discussed earlier. It is an investigation into determinants of growth in labor productivity over the years 1951–61 in fifty-two nations. The capital–input figures are adjusted to allow for improvements by 'vintages' but indexes of labor quality are also used. Unfortunately, the education variables, as with Harbison and Myers, were enrolment data. Evidently school enrolments *reflect* income; they cannot explain it except as they are proxies (which they may well be) for the educational attainments of the adult labor force. We must still wait for such a study using educational characteristics of the labor force itself (not available in most countries), or introducing lead education variables from enrolment rates of a previous period. It should be added that the physical–capital investment ratio taken by itself accounted for only 9 per cent of the variation in growth of labor productivity for all countries together, the percentage being highest in the wealthy nations (20 per cent) and lowest in the poor ones (5 per cent). Given rate of growth in labor productivity as the dependent variable and taking physical capital investment ratio, calories consumed per head, and enrolments in higher education as the independent variables gave an overall coefficient of determination (R^2) of 0·47.

The economics of educational planning

Even a smattering of historical awareness is enough to demonstrate that educational planning is not new. Neither is participation of economists in such planning (witness, for example, Nassau Senior in nineteenth-century England). We can go further. The tensions between centralized control of education and planning strategies that give greater scope to local and private decision-making in education is at least a hundred if not several hundred years old, both in practice and in papers in 'political economy'. And 'economic' considerations in educational planning have always been multiple; they have not been confined to the 'cost-saving' that was so often the lay image only a decade ago. It would be difficult to find a more clearcut example of a 'manpower' orientation to educational policy than that of Peter the Great. And if 'manpower' is a little less obvious in the Morrill Act which established the land-grant college system in the United States, this is only because a frontier democratic rebellion against classical education joined social–political pressures with economic pragmatism. If we are to look for the most deliberative and all-inclusive human-development planning we probably must turn to Japan, beginning from the early Meiji period; for then, as now, the Japanese have taken an integrated view of the learning process in schools and on the job, and policies have been developed accordingly.

What, then, has changed? For one thing, the last of the bastions of the sacredness of education have been shaken. Even in the holiest of ivory towers and elitist cultures it is becoming respectable to say out loud that one of the most important things schooling can do is to raise human productive capacities, capacities to do work that puts ever increasing demands upon men's mind. Economics, like sex, is becoming almost respectable parlor conversation! But this is only part of the story. The rest may be summed up by saying that educational planning has become Educational Planning, and in a world community. For the first time, it has become methodologically self-conscious, and it is generating 'experts' (with or without expertise).

Methodological self-consciousness has both its advantages and its disadvantages. So far as formalized solutions are concerned, there is an evident bias toward consideration of the more easily measured variables and criteria of evaluation – hence, typically, toward the economic. On the other hand, as the most recent efforts attest, the non-economic variables that enter as constraints can easily dominate the solutions. Under such circumstances the economic aspect of educational planning comes to be a posting of what the non-economic constraints are costing a society. But turning things around again, methodological self-consciousness without methodological sophistication holds the ever present danger of reifying invalid assumptions and by rigidifying policy making those assumptions self-fulfilling. And technical virtuosity misapplied can aggravate future adjustment problems quite as readily as more sophisticated and subtle planning may ease or prevent them. My concern in this brief final section is not with the pros and cons, the potentials and the limitations or dangers of planning, however.[23] Rather, in line with the main theme of this paper, I would ask what use planning models have made of the human-investment concept, and what have attempts at such planning contributed to our understanding of how the various components of the educational system may combine and change through time in a reasonably efficient interaction with economic development.

Up to about 1963, economists who participated actively in human-resource development planning were concerned almost exclusively with manpower planning, and this meant projections of manpower requirements geared in varying degrees into general economic planning. However, there was in fact little integration between manpower and educational plans.

The first steps toward a formal integration of manpower with educational planning was taken by Tinbergen and some of his associates (Tinbergen and Correa, 1962; Tinbergen and Bos, 1964; Tinbergen, Bos et al., 1965). They started at first with an extremely simplified model that resembled manpower planning in that it assumed fixed coefficients in the relation between growth of each type or level of manpower and growth of national income. However, the Tinbergen models defined their manpower categories by educational attainments, thus jumping the hurdle of linking skills to schooling. Furthermore, they used three manpower (educational) categories only. This had the advantage of admitting flexibility of skill combinations within the broad categories even though not between them. It had the parallel disadvantage, however, that the practical problems of deciding which types of schools and curricula to expand or contract were untouched. Moreover, except that they included importation of high-level manpower as a possibility, the Tinbergen models matched the manpower ones in ignoring costs. They were not properly speaking social decision models at all. What, then, did they contribute, and why have they received so much attention?

The second part of this question is easily answered: Tinbergen's approach was close enough to the thinking of the manpower planners to get a hearing, and his model incorporated only variables for which empirical data were readily available in most OECD countries. As I see them, his main contributions were three: First, he demonstrated the difficulties of

23. Many of these matters are discussed in Anderson and Bowman (1965b).

rapid transitions, the internal inconsistencies inherent in many manpower goals that disregarded intervening processes of educational adaptation between the planning and the target dates. This laid the groundwork for development of programming models that would take into account the intricate interdependencies involved in educational expansion. Second, his models stimulated empirical research in a series of countries that has resulted in a relatively orderly process of revision of both the models themselves and perceptions of the range of alternatives in patterns of adjustment between economic and educational development. Finally, in introducing choice between importing more qualified manpower and producing it at home, Tinbergen stepped toward cost–benefit analysis; this was a partial or limited 'optimization' problem, and as such constituted a critical departure from the conventions of prior manpower analysis.

Meanwhile there had been a running battle between the manpower planners and those who argued that internal rate-of-return analysis (or present-value–cost comparisons derived from education–age–income data) could provide useful guidelines for social investment planning. Or perhaps it would be more accurate to say that a few economists were conducting this battle on the sidelines, while most of those engaged actively in manpower planning went their way undisturbed. (So, for that matter, did most of the 'rate-of-returners'.) However, at least a partial joining of these approaches seems now to be on the way. There are three recent efforts to apply systems analysis (in these cases linear programming) to educational planning, and all use at least some elements of both cost–benefit and manpower planning methods. These are a study by Jean Benard (1965), not yet applied in practice, a study by Irma Adelman (1966) using Argentine data, and a study of Northern Nigeria by Samuel Bowles (n.d.; 1965).

The Benard and Adelman models apply to the total economy, though working out the education sector in special detail. Bowles's model is for the education sector only, taking inputs into that sector from elsewhere as exogenous variables or constraints. None treat on-the-job training explicitly, though I understand that Bowles has done the preliminary work for its inclusion. Benard and Bowles take experience into account whereas Adelman does not. All three distinguish technical or vocational from other types of schools.

Since the Benard model has not yet been applied empirically, I shall say only a word or two about it. The model is set up to solve for maximization of national income. Working in an environment in which neo-classical economics and rate-of-return analysis is automatically suspect, special care is taken in developing the argument for measuring inputs and outputs in money terms, for considering life age–income patterns, and for discounting. In some other respects he incorporates manpower-planning assumptions, however, placing his model somewhere between the Adelman model (closest to manpower) and the Bowles model (closest to the rate-of-return orientation).

The Adelman model is worked out for each of three objective functions:

1. Maximization of the discounted sum of GNP (using a 5 per cent discount rate).
2. Maximization of growth of the GNP from the base year to a designated future target year.
3. Minimization of the discounted sum of net foreign capital inflows.

As in manpower planning, this model generates its demands upon the educational system from the production (the non-education) side of the economy. It measures human resources in 'labor efficiency units' which are in principle based upon observed education–income data *within* each of three manpower categories. However, like conventional manpower studies, it allows no substitution among these categories and it assumes fixed ratios of labor-efficiency units to outputs. Also, the proportion of men with each educational attainment who enter any given manpower category is predetermined. The industry mix and hence the overall manpower category mix can vary. Thus the model allows for interaction between the demand and supply sides of human resource development.[24] It is in the cost–benefit family in that it compares the marginal social benefit of each type of education (what it adds at the margin to GNP) with its marginal social cost, or 'opportunity cost', given the cultural, political, or other constraints imposed on the model. As with the Benard, Bowles and other linear programming models, it is possible also to measure the marginal social economic cost of adhering to particular non-economic constraints.

Adelman introduces her findings with many caveats. One in particular should be noted: in the absence of education–income data for Argentina her measures of labor-efficiency units were inevitably crude. Also, she used a simple variant of her model that required that all manpower must be home produced. Bearing these facts and other cautions in mind, it is interesting nevertheless to look at some of her results. First, her solution gave top priority to university education, and to such an extent that the rest of the educational program hung upon it. However, her findings suggested that the removal of constraints (or assumptions) inhibiting expansion of junior colleges relative to universities might raise total output of the economy substantially. Unfortunately, her findings for both university education and

24. The model includes behavioral balance-of-payments constraints, constraints defining the maximum rate at which new investment can be absorbed, specification of an income-savings function, as well as its specifications more directly related to manpower and education.

the university dropout group were highly sensitive to the ratios estimated for her labor-efficiency units. The firmest of her findings, quite insensitive to any plausible changes in labor efficiency units and unaffected by constraints on the model, concerned vocational-technical schools. They simply washed out; what they contributed could not match their costs.

The Bowles model concentrates upon the education sector. Treating inputs into that sector from the rest of the economy as exogenously determined, he sets up as his objective function the maximization of the excess of total economic benefits over costs of education. The problem is one of resource allocation within education, studied in sequence over an eight-year time period. He included the choice between importation of qualified manpower and its home production in his problem, however. Furthermore, he tested for choices among alternative 'educational technologies', like team teaching. Like Tinbergen (and unlike Adelman) he classified labor directly by educational attainments, without introducing any intervening specifications of occupations or skills between his educational categories and associated incomes.[25] Like both Schultz and Denison, he assumes unchanging prices or rental values of men of given age and educational attainments (again implying either high substitutability in production or, more plausibly, changes in demands that match changes in supplies to maintain human resource prices unchanged). Boundary conditions that set limits on his solutions include, for example, socially or politically conditioned minima with respect to numbers of students in secondary school and feasibility limits on the pace of expansion of facilities. Solutions were derived for several paces of change in the quality mix of teachers in primary schools.

The first thing Bowles demonstrates, unambiguously, is that existing educational plans for Northern Nigeria were simply impossible of realization. As a matter of simple arithmetic, in the immediate future Northern Nigeria could not simultaneously upgrade teachers, maintain teacher–pupil ratios and expand primary enrolments as specified in government plans. But to arrive at this conclusion did not require a linear programming model. More interesting was the fact that in all his solutions there was an initial lag in primary education because of the teacher problem but thereafter it took over, and together with higher education dominated the secondary level. Secondary school leavers directly entering the labor force were a very low priority. Technical and vocational secondary schools were again washed out; they are too expensive. To sum up, when costs are taken into account the allocation of resources within education that have been advocated by manpower planners were virtually reversed, even when the unemployment

25. Bowles obtained these data directly, by field work. He points out that this can be done much more easily and at less expense than is entailed in getting the kinds of data used by manpower planners, at least in developing nations.

adjustments were deliberately biased against those entering the labor force from primary schools. Furthermore, test runs showed that in the Northern Nigerian context the solutions were insensitive to a wide range of variations in ratios of incomes of various educational groups as one or another increased. On the other hand, the solutions were highly sensitive to some of the constraints set up by existing regulations and institutional practice.

As Bowles himself has remarked, 'there is nothing in all this that you couldn't do on the back of an envelope – if you had enough envelopes'. But the 'if' is important; it refers to the extreme complexity of the web of interdependencies, even in a simplified programming model. On the other hand, such models cannot give out theoretical formulations of relationships that are not put into them in the first place. Their main contribution to positive science (as against public decisions) is indirect. It is in their capacity to identify which constraints are important, which are not – and so to point to problems that may be especially worthy of research, and of innovative *search*. Bowles's work is especially interesting from this point of view because he presses further into educational systems than has any other economist model-builder. This brings us to where educators and educational administrators in particular might well take over.

Although I have heard it rumored that a graduate student in California is currently attempting to apply systems analysis to intra-educational decisions at a subnational level,[26] there is only one man of whom I have any direct knowledge who has been opening up this field in anything like a balanced way. I refer to Thomas, in educational administration at the University of Chicago. He delineates (forthcoming) a framework for applying systems analysis to the educational decision process in a multi-stage input–output scheme.[27] Productivity is *value added*, whether measured by performance on tests (for example) or, ultimately, by increments to earning capacity. His methods are very similar to Bowles's, but with much more complex sets of input–output matrices. This is cost–benefit analysis of a subtle and complicated kind. In empirical application it entails among other things the identification of sets of intra-education production functions, building in part on prior empirical research in educational psychology and educational administration but requiring in the main the design of new empirical studies. Thomas is stimulating just such endeavors, especially in that ambiguous territory where economist, sociologist and educator must converge. The multiplier process is indeed at work, and none of us need pause for lack of a new challenge and a new opportunity!

26. The student in question is Dr L. P. Nordell, whose dissertation on an input–output model of the Californian educational system was submitted to the University of California, Berkeley, 1967.

27. As partial background, see James, Thomas and Dyck (1963).

References

ADELMAN, I. (1966), 'A linear programming mode of educational planning: a case study of Argentina', in I. Adelman and E. Thorbecke (eds.), *The Theory and Design of Economic Development*, Johns Hopkins Press.

ANDERSON, C. A. (1955), 'Regional and racial differences in relations between income and education', *School Rev.*, January, pp. 38–45.

ANDERSON, C. A., and BOWMAN, M. J. (eds.) (1965a), *Education and Economic Development*, Aldine.

ANDERSON, C. A., and BOWMAN, M. J. (1965b), 'Theoretical considerations in educational planning' in D. Adams (ed.), *Educational Planning*, Syracuse University Press.

ANDERSON, C. A., and BOWMAN, M. J. (forthcoming), 'Interdisciplinary aspects of the theory of regional development', in J. G. Maddox (ed.), a symposium.

ARROW, K. (1962), 'Learning by doing', *Rev. Econ. Stud.*, vol. 29, no. 2.

BECKER, G. (1960), 'Is there underinvestment in college education?' *Amer. Econ. Rev.*, vol. 50, no. 2, pp. 346–54.

BECKER, G. (1962), 'Investment in human capital: a theoretical analysis', *Investment in Human Beings*, supplement to *J. Polit. Econ.*, vol. 70, no. 5, pt 2.

BECKER, G. (1965), *Human Capital*, Princeton University Press.

BENARD, J. (1965), 'Analyse des relations entre production, travail et éducation à l'aide d'un modèle dynamique d'optimation', CEPREL, Arcueil. Reprinted as 'General optimization model for the economy and education'. *Mathematical Models in Educational Planning*, OECD, 1967.

BLAUG, M. (1964), *A Selected Annotated Bibliography in the Economics of Education*, Institute of Education, University of London; revised as *Economics of Education: A Selected Annotated Bibliography*, Pergamon Press, 1966.

BLAUG, M. (1965), 'The rate of return on investment in education in Great Britain', *Manchester School*.

BLAUG, M. (1966), 'An economic interpretation of the private demand for education', *Economica*, May, pp. 166–82.

BLAUG, M., PESTON, M. H., and ZIDERMAN, A. (1966), *The Utilization of Educated Manpower in Industry*, London School of Economics, mimeo; Oliver & Boyd, 1967.

BOWEN, W. G. (1964a), 'Assessing the contribution of education', *Economic Aspects of Higher Education*, OECD.

BOWEN, W. G. (1964b), *Economic Aspects of Education*, Industrial Relations Section, Princeton University.

BOWLES, S. (n.d.), 'A planning model for the efficient allocation of resources in education', mimeo.

BOWLES, S. (1965b), 'Efficiency in the allocations of resources is education: a planning model with application to Northern Nigeria', Harvard Ph.D. Dissertation. Reprinted in M. Blaug (ed.), *Economics of Education 2*, Penguin, 1969.

BOWMAN, M. J. (1951), 'The consumer in the history of economic doctrine', *Amer. Econ. Rev.*, vol. 41, no. 2, pp. 1–18.

BOWMAN, M. J. (1962), 'Converging concerns of economists and educators', *Comp. Educ. Rev.*, October, pp. 111–20.

BOWMAN, M. J. (1965a), 'From guild to infant-training industries', in C. A. Anderson and M. J. Bowman (eds.), *Education and Economic Development*, Aldine.

Bowman, M. J. (1965b), 'Human inequalities and southern underdevelopment' in J. W. McKie (ed.), *Education and the Southern Economy*, supplement to *Southern Econ. J.* vol. 32, no. 1, pt 2.

Bowman, M. J. (1966), 'Costing of human-resource development' and comments on the paper, *Proceedings of the 1963 Conference of the International Economics Association on The Economics of Education*, Macmillan.

Bowman, M. J., and Anderson, C. A. (1963), 'Concerning the role of education in development', in C. Geertz (ed.), *Old Societies and New States*, Free Press.

Bowman, M. J., and Haynes, W. W. (1963), *Resources and People in East Kentucky*, Johns Hopkins Press.

Callaway, A. (1963), 'Unemployment among African school leavers', *J. Mod. African Stud.*, vol. 1, no. 3, pp. 351–7. Reprinted in M. Blaug (ed.), *Economics of Education 2*, Penguin, 1969.

Callaway, A. (1964), 'Nigeria's indigenous education: the apprentice system', *J. African Stud.*, University of Ife, vol. 1, no. 1.

Carnoy, M. (1964), 'Cost and return to schooling in Mexico', Chicago Ph.D. Dissertation; published as 'Rates of return to schooling in Latin America', *J. Hum. Res.*, vol. 2, no. 1, pp. 359–74, 1967.

Denison, E. F. (1962), 'The sources of economic growth in the United States and the alternatives before us', supplementary paper no. 13, Committee for Economic Development, New York.

Dentler, R. A., and Warshauer M. E. (1965), *Big City Dropouts*, Columbia University Press.

Duncan, B. (1965), 'Dropouts and the unemployed', *J. Polit. Econ.*, vol. 73, no. 2.

Eckhaus, R. S. (1964), 'Economic criteria for education and training', *Rev. Econ. and Stats.*, vol. 46, pp. 181–90.

Foster, P. (1965), 'The vocational school fallacy' in C. A. Anderson and M. J. Bowman (eds.), *Education and Economic Development*, Aldine.

Foster, P. (1966), *Education and Social Change in Ghana*, University of Chicago Press.

Friedman, M., and Kuznets, S. S. (1946), *Income from Independent Professional Practice*, National Bureau of Economics Research.

Galenson, W., and Pyatt, G. (1964), *The Quality of Labor and Economic Development in Certain Countries*, International Labor Office.

Griliches, Z. (1963), 'The sources of measured productivity growth in U.S. Agriculture, 1940–60', *J. Polit. Econ.*, vol. 71, no. 4.

Griliches, Z. (1964), 'Research expenditures, education and the agricultural production function', *Amer. Econ. Rev.*, vol. 54, no. 6.

Griliches, Z. (1965), 'Production functions in manufacturing, some preliminary results', mimeo.

Grubel, H. G., and Scott, A. D. (1966), 'The international flow of human capital', *Amer. Econ. Rev.*, vol. 56, no. 2, pp. 268–75. Reprinted in M. Blaug (ed.), *Economics of Education 2*, Penguin, 1969.

Hanoch, G. (1965), 'Personal earnings and investment in schooling', Chicago Ph.D. Dissertation. Reprinted as 'An economic analysis of earnings and schooling', *J. Hum. Res.*, vol. 2, no. 3, pp. 310–30.

Hansen, L. (1963), 'Total and private rates of return to investment in schooling', *J. Polit. Econ.*, vol. 71, pp. 128–40.

Harbison, F., and Myers, C. A. (1964), *Education, Manpower and Economic Growth*, McGraw Hill.

JAMES, H. T., THOMAS, J. A., and DYCK, H. J. (1963), *Wealth, Expenditure and Decision Making for Education*, U S Department of Health, Education and Welfare, Cooperative Research Project No. 1241, Stanford.

MACHLUP, F. (1962), *The Production and Distribution of Knowledge in the United States*, Princeton University Press.

MINCER, J. (1962), 'On-the-job training costs, returns and some implications', *Investment in Human Beings*, supplement to *J. Polit. Econ.*, vol. 70, no. 5, pt 2.

PARNES, H. S. (1962), *Forecasting Educational Needs for Social and Economic Development*, OECD.

SCHULTZ, T. W. (1960), 'Capital formation by education', *J. Polit. Econ.*, vol. 68, pp. 571–83.

SCHULTZ, T. W. (1963), *The Economic Value of Education*, Columbia University Press.

SCHULTZ, T. W. (1964), *Transforming Traditional Agriculture*, Yale University Press.

SCOTT, A. D. (1964), 'The valuation of game resources, some theoretical aspects' in J. W. McKie (ed.), *Education and the Southern Economy*, supplement to *Southern Econ.*, vol. 32, no. 1, pt 2.

SJAASTAD, L. A. (1962), 'The costs and returns of human migration', in *Investment in Human Beings*, supplement to *J. Polit. Econ.*, vol. 70, no. 5, pt 2.

SOLOW, R. M. (1962), 'Technical progress, capital formation and economic growth', *Amer. Econ. Rev.*, vol. 52, no. 2, pp. 76–86.

STUBBLEBINE, W. C. (1965), 'Institutional elements in the financing of education', in J. W. McKie (ed.), *Education and the Southern Economy*, supplement to *Southern Econ. J.*, vol. 32, no. 1, pt 2.

Study Group in the Economics of Education (1964), 'Measuring the contribution of education to economic growth', in *The Residual Factor and Economic Growth*, OECD.

THOMAS, J. A. (forthcoming), *Productivity in Education*.

TINBERGEN, J., and BOS, H. C. (1964), 'A planning model for the educational requirements of economic development', in *The Residual Factor and Economic Growth*, OECD.

TINBERGEN, J., BOS, H. C. *et al.* (1965), *Econometric Models of Education*. Reprinted in M. Blaug (ed.), *Economics in Education 2*, Penguin, 1969.

TINBERGEN, J., and CORREA, H. (1962), 'Quantitative adaptation of education to accelerated growth', *Kyklos*, vol. 15.

VAIZEY, J. (1962), *The Economics of Education*, Faber.

WALSH, J. R. (1935), 'The capital concept applied to man', *Q. J. Econ.*, vol. 49, pp. 255–85.

WEISBROD, B. A. (1964), *External Benefits of Public Education*, Industrial Relations Section, Princeton University.

WELCH, F. (1966), 'Measurement of the quality of schooling', *Amer. Econ. Rev.*, May, pp. 379–92, a summary of 'Determinants of the return to schooling in rural farm areas, 1959', an unpublished dissertation.

WILKINSON, B. W. (1964), 'Some economic aspects of education in Canada', Massachusetts Institute of Technology Ph.D. Dissertation. Reprinted as *Studies in the Economics of Education*, occasional paper no. 4, 1966, Economics and Research Branch, Department of Labor, Canada.

ZEMAN, M. (1958), 'Quantitative analysis of white–non-white income differentials in the United States', Chicago Ph.D. Dissertation.

3 D. S. Landes

Industry, Skills and Knowledge

Excerpts from D. S. Landes, *The Unbound Prometheus*, Cambridge University Press, 1969, pp. 339–48.

Skills are learned. And the supply of skills to industry is essentially dependent on education. To observe this, however, is merely to state a truism. To do more, one must begin by breaking down this omnibus word 'education' and relating its content to the requirements of production.

By education we really mean the imparting of four kinds of knowledge, each with its own contribution to make to economic performance:

1. The ability to read, write and calculate.

2. The working skills of the craftsman and mechanic.

3. The engineer's combination of scientific principle and applied training.

4. High-level scientific knowledge, theoretical and applied.

In all four areas, Germany represented the best that Europe had to offer; in all four, with the possible exception of the second, Britain fell far behind.

The first raises special problems of evaluation. It is not easy to define and assess the relationship of primary education to industrial efficiency. The more obvious connections are probably the least important. Thus, although certain workers – supervisory and office personnel in particular – must be able to read and do the elementary arithmetical operations in order to perform their duties, a large share of the work of industry can be performed by illiterates; as indeed it was, especially in the early days of the Industrial Revolution. Probably the main economic advantages of an extensive, well-run system of compulsory elementary education, therefore, are first, the foundation it provides for more advanced work, and second, its tendency to facilitate and stimulate mobility and to promote thereby a selection of talent to fit the needs of the society. It helps optimize, in short, the allocation of human resources.

Yet it is one thing to point out the significance of this mechanism and another to measure its effectiveness. No empirical studies of the relationships between education and selection on the one hand, between selection and industrial performance on the other, exist for our period. All we have is qualitative observations, plus data on length and generality of schooling and on some of the more elementary cognitive consequences of instruction – notably percentages of literacy. The rest we are obliged to infer.

For what these data are worth – and they are subject to serious caution when used for international comparisons – they show an enormous gap between British and German achievements in this area. On the one hand, we have a nation that until the closing decades of the century preferred to leave schooling to the zeal, indifference or exploitation of private enterprise. It was not only a question of *laissez-faire*. For every idealist or visionary who saw in education the path of an enlightened citizenry, there were several 'practical' men who felt that instruction was a superfluous baggage for farm labourers and industrial workers. These people, after all, had been ploughing fields or weaving cloth since time beyond recall without knowing how to read or write; not only was there no reason to change now, but in the last analysis, all they would learn in school was discontent. As a result of this indifference and resistance, it was not until 1870 that local boards were empowered to draft by-laws of compulsory attendance; and not until 1880 was primary instruction made obligatory throughout the kingdom.

Under the circumstances, Britain did well to have roughly half of her school-age children receiving some kind of elementary instruction around 1860. At least this was the finding of the Newcastle Commission, which was exceptionally tolerant of hearsay evidence and tended to view the situation with invincible optimism (Parliamentary Papers, 1861, XXI, Cd 2794). There was good reason to believe that many if not most of these students honoured their classrooms by their absence more than their presence; and that in some of the large industrial centres, attendance was lower in the 1860s than it had been a generation before (Smith, 1931, pp. 280–81). Even granting the accuracy of the Newcastle estimates, one notes that only two-fifths of these children went to schools inspected by the state; and only one quarter of these remained long enough to enter the upper classes, the only ones that were 'reasonably efficient'.

The situation improved considerably in later years. At least attendance increased sharply from 1870 on and the content of elementary education was enriched by the simple act of assimilating the instruction of the generality of schools to the modest standards of the inspected institutions. Even so, the system remained sterilized by invidious prejudice and the constraints of pathological social conditions. Thus it was widely assumed that aptitude for instruction – or more subtly, ability to use instruction – was a function of class, and that the content and level of training should be suited to the student's station in life. 'The Education Act of 1870,' wrote H. G. Wells, 'was not an Act for common universal education, it was an Act to educate the lower classes for employment on lower-class lines, and with specially trained, inferior teachers who had no university quality' (*Experiment in Autobiography* quoted in Lowndes, 1937, p. 5). In short, it was not intended to find and advance talent. But one could go further: whatever the ostensible aims of compulsory elementary education, its essential function (what Robert Merton might call its latent function) was not even to instruct. Rather it was to discipline a growing mass of disaffected proletarians and integrate them into British society. Its object was to civilize the barbarians; as Her Majesty's Inspector for London put it, 'if it were not for her five hundred elementary schools London would be overrun by a horde of young savages' (Lowndes, 1937, p. 19).

Compulsory elementary education goes back in parts of Germany to the sixteenth century; in Prussia, Frederick the Great issued his *General Landschulreglement* in 1763. The quality of the instruction was often poor – teaching posts were long looked upon as excellent places for old soldiers – but improved with time. By the early nineteenth century, the school systems of Germany were famed throughout Europe, and travellers like Madame de Staël and observers like Victor Cousin made it a point to visit and examine this greatest achievement of a knowledge-hungry people.

The obligation of children to attend primary school was enforced – as laws usually are in Germany: in Prussia in the 1860s, the proportion of children of school age attending class was about $97\frac{1}{2}$ per cent;[1] in Saxony, it was actually over 100 per cent.[2] More important than quantitative results, however, were the character and content of the system. To begin with, it was the expression of a deep-rooted conviction that schooling was a cornerstone of the social edifice; that the state not only had an obligation to instruct its citzenry, but found its advantage therein, since an educated people is a moral and strong people. Secondly, the very antiquity of the system obviated the emphasis on debarbarization that marked the first generation of compulsory education in Britain. Observers from abroad were impressed by the neatness and decorum of German schoolchildren, from whatever class; the schools were consequently free to concentrate their efforts on instruction. Thirdly, schooling tended to last longer than in Britain, and the elementary classes were linked to so-called 'middle' and secondary grades in such a way that some selection of talent occurred. The process was only moderately effective; in large areas, particularly rural districts, it was inoperative. Yet even in the middle decades of the nineteenth century, visitors were impressed

1. It had been 43 per cent in 1816, 68 per cent in 1846 (Dieterici, 1847, p. 47).
2. The excess is to be accounted for by children under six or over fourteen years of age, and by a number of foreign students (Ministre de l'Agriculture, du Commerce et des Travaux Publics, 1865).

by the catholicity of recruitment of the continuation (as well as the elementary) schools: 'They are generally very well attended by the children of small shopkeepers,' wrote Joseph Kay, 'and contain also many children from the poorest ranks of society' (1850, pt 2, p. 227).[3]

It hardly needs saying that the above discussion does some violence to the complexity of the contrast between the two countries. One can find some striking bright spots in the British achievement – certain elementary and grammar schools, for example, which provided excellent instruction to poor scholars and children of well-to-do parents alike; just as one can find among the Junkers of East Elbia instances of a benighted hostility to education to match anything in Britain (Samuel and Thomas, 1949, pp. 6–7). Similarly, one could discuss endlessly the merits of the educational philosophies of the two countries, not only because the subject is intrinsically open to contention, but because it is almost impossible to reconcile the contradictory mass of impressionistic evidence. Was one system of elementary instruction more given to 'cramming' than another? one more practical, the other more liberal? one more devoted to facts, the other to ability to think? No categorical answer is possible.

The link between formal vocational, technical and scientific education on the one hand and industrial progress on the other is more direct and evident. Moreover, it became closer in the course of the nineteenth century, for reasons that can be deduced from our earlier discussion of technology. To begin with, the greater complexity and precision of manufacturing equipment and the closer control of quality, in conjunction with the growing cost of inefficiency and pressure of competition, conduced to higher standards of technical knowledge and proficiency, especially on the upper levels of the productive hierarchy and among the designers of industrial plant. Secondly, the high cost of equipment made on-the-job training increasingly expensive and helped break down an apprenticeship system that had long been moribund. And finally, the changed scientific content of technology compelled supervisory employees and even workers to familiarize themselves with new concepts, and enhanced enormously the value of personnel

3. Kay returns to this theme repeatedly: 'I *constantly* found the children of the highest and of the lowest ranks sitting at the same desk' (p. 209; also pp. 74–5, 80).

Compare the introduction of universal education in Japan in the 1870s, which was hastened and facilitated by similarly deep-rooted social values. According to Ronald Dore, the acceptance of the Confucian principle that virtue consists in knowledge of one's station and respect for one's superiors, implied the necessity of education for all, but especially for the lower classes, who had that much more virtue to acquire (1965, ch. 10, 'The Legacy'). The system ostensibly aimed, then, at least before the Meiji period, at reducing ambition and mobility. Yet latent functions are often more important than manifest ones, and history is full of unanticipated consequences.

trained to keep abreast of scientific novelty, appreciate its economic significance, and adapt it to the requirements of production.

It would serve no useful purpose to paint in detail the familiar chiaroscuro of the late and stunted growth of technical and scientific education in Britain as against the vigorous, precociously developed German system. Briefly, where Britain left technical training, like primary education, to private enterprise, which led in the event to a most uneven and inadequate provision of facilities, the German states generously financed a whole gamut of institutions, erecting buildings, installing laboratories, and above all maintaining competent and, at the highest level, distinguished faculties. Until the middle of the century, Britain had nothing but the young University of London, the good, bad and indifferent mechanics' institutes, occasional evening lectures or classes, and courses in the rudiments of science in a few enlightened secondary and grammar schools. After that, improvement came slowly, though the pace picked up measurably after about 1880. The first gains came around the middle of the century in scientific education (Royal College of Chemistry in 1845; Government School of Mines, 1851; Owen's College, Manchester, 1851; university degrees in science, 1850s); they came at the highest level and for many years were partially vitiated by the above-mentioned failure of the primary and secondary schools to find and prepare recruits. Technical and vocational training had to wait another generation and suffered right through the inter-war period from the same handicap. On the eve of the First World War, the British system still had a long way to go to catch up with the German – at least from the standpoint of economic productivity. (There were social and psychological aspects of the Teutonic system that gave outsiders pause.) The long chorus of anguish from otherwise sober savants, writing in the press, addressing the public, or testifying before a remarkable series of parliamentary commissions from 1867 on bears witness to the high cost of this educational backwardness.

More important than the lag itself are the reasons. Essentially they boil down to demand, for a free society generally gets the educational system it wants, and demand was once again a function in part of British industrial priority and German emulation.

As we have seen, even elementary education encountered suspicion and resistance in England; *a fortiori*, technical instruction. There were those industrialists who feared it would lead to the disclosure of or diminish the value of trade secrets. Many felt that 'book learning' was not only misleading but had the disadvantage of instilling in its beneficiaries or victims – depending on the point of view – an exaggerated sense of their own merit and intelligence. Here management was joined by foremen and master craftsmen who, products of on-the-job apprenticeship, despised or feared – in any case, resented – the skills and knowledge of the school-trained technician. Still other employers could not see spending money on anything that did not yield an immediate return, the more so as the notions imparted by these classes and institutes almost invariably called for new outlays of capital.

A few were afraid of raising up competition.[4] But most would have snorted at the very idea: they were convinced the whole thing was a fraud, that effective technical education was impossible, scientific instruction unnecessary. Their own careers were the best proof of that: most manufacturers had either begun with a minimum of formal education and come up through the ranks or had followed the traditional liberal curriculum in secondary and sometimes higher schools. Moreover, this lesson of personal experience was confirmed by the history of British industry. Here was a nation that had built its economic strength on practical tinkerers – on a barber like Arkwright, a clergyman like Cartwright, an instrument-maker like Watt, a professional 'amateur inventor' like Bessemer, and thousands of nameless mechanics who suggested and effected the kind of small improvements to machines and furnaces and tools that add up eventually to an industrial revolution. She was proud of these men – listen to Lowthian Bell citing in reply to criticism of British technical shortcomings the names of Darby and Cort (*Journal of the Iron and Steel Institute*, 1878, p. 315).

In many trades there developed a mystique of practical experience. Consider the implications of the following question at the Parliamentary Inquiry of 1885:

You know perfectly well that in every mill there is one man who can spin very much better than anyone else, and if you wanted a finer number, that was the man that was put on. Without a technical school you have always some man of that kind; do you think any technical school would turn out any number of those men in a mill? (Parliamentary Papers, 1886, XXI, 'Commission on Depression of Trade and Industry', Q. 5173).

And one manufacturer in the tinplate trade, denying the importance of trained engineers, remarked that what was needed was 'practical men who were in sympathy with their rolls and everything else. They could do a lot with their machinery if they were in sympathy with it' (Minchinton, 1954–5).

Moreover, even when employers did come to recognize the need for trained technical personnel, they yielded grudgingly. The underpaid 'scientists' were put in sheds, reclaimed workrooms and other improvised quarters that hardly permitted controlled conditions and accurate tests. Their work was one cut above the rule-of-thumb techniques of the skilled workman; it was far below that of the German laboratory researcher (see Stead, 1896; Burn,

4. In 1884 Huxley stigmatized this 'miserable sort of jealous feeling about the elevation of their workmen' (cited in Cotgrove, 1957, p. 24).

1940, p. 178; *Final Report of the Committee on Industry and Trade*, Cd 3282, 1929, p. 214).

In sum, job and promotion opportunities for graduates in science and technology were few and unattractive. The most remunerative field, in spite of what has been said, was chemistry, and even there the best positions were often reserved for men trained abroad; undoubtedly the mediocre quality of many British graduates served to reinforce the scepticism of management. There was just about nothing for physicists until the last decade of the nineteenth century. The worst situation was in the lower ranks, on the level of vocational training, where students occasionally suffered for their ambition: a witness before the Committee on Scientific Education of 1868 testified that only one in four of those who attended vocational classes of the Science and Art Department in the 1850s got back into his trade (in Cotgrove, 1957, p. 51, n. 1). In 1884 the Royal Commission on Technical Instruction reported: 'We believe that many workmen are disposed to attach too little value to the importance of acquiring knowledge of the principles of science, because they do not see their application' (in Cotgrove, 1957, p. 40). No wonder. No wonder also that the most gifted of those few young men who had the means to pursue their education beyond the intermediate level followed the traditional liberal curriculum to careers in the civil service, to pursuit of the genteel county life, or to the kind of post in industry or trade – and there were many – that called for a gentleman and not a technician.

The contrast with German attitudes is hard to exaggerate. For an ambitious nation, impatient to raise its economy to the level of the British, vexed if not humiliated by its dependence on foreign experts, an effective system of scientific and technical training was the foundation and promise of wealth and aggrandizement. A veritable cult of *Wissenschaft* and *Technik* developed. The kings and princes of central Europe vied with one another in founding schools and research institutes and collected savants (even humanistic scholars like historians!) as their predecessors of the eighteenth century had collected musicians and composers; or as the courts of the Italy of the *cinquecento*, artists and sculptors. The people came to gape at the *Hochschulen* and universities with the awe usually reserved for historical monuments. Most important, entrepreneurs prized the graduates of these institutions and often offered them respected and often powerful positions – not only the corporate giants with their laboratory staffs of up to a hundred and more, but the small firms also, who saw in the special skills of the trained technician the best defence against the competition of large-scale production.

There is keen irony in all this. We have noted how a British observer of the mid-nineteenth century was impressed by the 'social democracy' of the

German classroom; yet this is precisely what had struck continental travellers of the eighteenth century as one of the peculiar virtues of the British society of that period. To be sure, higher schooling in those days was confined to a very small fraction of the population; even the children of wealthy families often received little formal instruction; so that such equality as prevailed was as much or more one of ignorance than of knowledge. But that is the point: it did not make that much difference in the eighteenth century how much instruction a man had received. The recruitment of talent was on other grounds; wide avenues of mobility were open to the unschooled as well as the schooled; and many a man taught himself or learned by experience the knowledge and skills he required for his work.

With industrialization and the proliferation of bureaucracy in business as well as government, however, formal education took on steadily increasing importance as the key to occupational, hence social, preferment. This is not to say that the system or content of instruction was well suited to the requirements of the economy and polity; merely that schooling came more and more to govern recruitment of talent.

This is a task that a school system is in theory ideally equipped to perform. It is of its essence objective, grading and advancing students on the basis of ability and work – except where competition has been deliberately excluded from the classroom. Yet in fact, the selective efficiency of the system depends directly on its own circumstances and principles of recruitment, and these reflect in turn the values and attitudes of its creators and clientele.

Once again, timing and intent are crucially important. In Britain, where technological change came early, a new industrial society had already taken shape by the time the schools were built; so that these embodied not only the prejudices and cleavages of the established order, but the material inequalities. For members of the poorer classes, it was not only presumptuous to covet a more than minimal education; it was pecuniarily impossible – not so much because of the direct outlays required (though these were often a serious deterrent) as because of the earnings that would have to be foregone. It was the opportunity cost of instruction that made it the almost exclusive prerogative of the well-to-do. The school system, in other words, which might have been the great force for social mobility and advancement by talent, became a powerful crystallizer, defending the positions of a newly entrenched Establishment by giving it a quasi-monopoly of such knowledge and manners (including speech pattern) as the society valued.

Some of this was also true of German education, but to a much smaller degree – and differences in history are almost always a question of degree. The Germans developed their schools in advance of and in preparation for industrialization. The system was meant to strengthen the polity and economy not only by instruction, but also by finding and training talent, and while it necessarily fell short of its objectives, the elements of intent and direction were critically important. Hence one of the strangest paradoxes in modern history: that on the one hand, a liberal society standing out from all others in the eighteenth century for equality and mobility of status, should have lost something of these during the very period of its progressive political democratization; while on the other, a far more authoritarian society, characterized in its pre-industrial period by a clearly defined, fairly rigid hierarchy of rank, should have developed a more open structure, without corresponding political change (see Kay, 1850, pt 2, pp. 74–5; Trevelyan, 1922, p. 353).

References

BURN, D. L. (1940), *The Economic History of Steelmaking, 1867–1939: A Study in Competition*, Cambridge University Press.

COTGROVE, S. F. (1957), *Technical Education and Social Change*, Allen & Unwin.

DIETERICI, C. F. W. (ed.) (1847), *Mitteilungen des Statistisches Bureaus in Berlin*, Statistishches Bureau, Prussia.

DORE, R. (1965), *Education in Tokugawa Japan*, University of California Press.

KAY, J. (1850), *The Social Condition and Education of the People in England and Europe*, London.

LOWNDES, G. A. N. (1937), H. G. Wells's *Experiment in Autobiography*, quoted in *The Silent Social Revolution: An Account of the Expansion of Public Education in England and Wales, 1895–1935*.

MINCHINTON, W. E. (1954–5), 'The tinplate maker and technical change', *Explorations in Entrepreneurial History*, vol. 7.

MINISTRE DE L'AGRICULTURE DU COMMERCE ET DES TRAVAUX PUBLICS (1865), *Enquête sur l'enseignement professionnel*, Paris.

SAMUEL, R. H., and THOMAS, R. H. (1949) *Education and Society in Modern Germany*, London.

SMITH, F. (1931), *A History of English Elementary Education, 1760–1902*.

STEAD, J. E. (1896), *Journal of the Iron and Steel Institute*, vol. 49, p. 119.

TREVELYAN, G. M. (1922), *British History in the Nineteenth Century and After, 1782–1919*, Longman.

4 E. F. Denison with J. P. Poullier

Education of the Labor Force

Excerpts from E. F. Denison with J. P. Poullier, *Why Growth Rates Differ*,
The Brookings Institution, Washington, D.C., 1967, pp. 78–80, 106–8.

Education as a source of growth defined

This chapter attempts to measure the improvement in the quality of labor
in the 1950–62 period that resulted from increased education of the labor
force. Comparisons of the quality of labor, as affected by education, are
also attempted between countries, but are much less satisfactory than the
intertemporal comparisons. They are affected to a much greater extent by
limitations of information and technique and also encounter the inherent
difficulties of comparing different educational systems.

This chapter is concerned only with the quality of labor. It is not
concerned with all the direct and indirect effects of education upon
output. Thus, it is necessary to clarify at the outset the relationship
between education and the classification of growth sources adopted in this
study:

1. The value of the work an individual can perform is greatly affected by his
educational background. To count a high-school or college graduate as
only the same amount of labor, on the average, as an elementary-school
graduate of the same age and sex would be altogether unsatisfactory. The
more educated groups earn more and contribute more to the national
product. If workers with one level of education earn 50 per cent more, on the
average, than *otherwise similar* individuals with less education, they will be
counted in this chapter as 50 per cent more labor. The reason is by now
familiar: Average earnings of large groups of individuals are taken to be
proportional to the average values of their marginal products.

The upward trend in education apparent in both Europe and the United
States has meant that the skills and versatility of labor have been upgraded.
There has been a shift in occupational composition toward occupations in
which workers typically have higher levels of education and, more importantly, there has been an increase in the skills of individuals within what is
conventionally termed an occupation, often with considerable changes in
the work actually performed. This increase in the quality of labor has been a
source of increase in national income. Quality indexes are developed in this

chapter to measure the increase in the ability of workers to contribute to production as a result of additional education.

2. It is essential to distinguish between: (a) society's stock of knowledge relevant to production, which (along with other conditions) governs the output obtained with given inputs; and (b) the quantity and quality of inputs (including the education of the labor force) that govern the output obtained with a given stock of knowledge. This chapter is concerned only with the latter.

Increases in output resulting from advances in society's stock of knowledge are credited in my classification to the growth source, 'advances of knowledge'. This does not, of course, deny that the education of the labor force as a whole, and particularly the number of highly educated individuals, may be among the factors that influence the pace of inventions, new ways of organizing production, and new business practices that reduce unit costs and increase the output *that can be obtained with given inputs* (including labor of constant skills).

3. A better educated work force – from top management down – will be better able to learn about and to utilize the most efficient production practices known. The effect of education on this ability is one aspect of the quality of labor measured here, in so far as it is reflected in earning differentials. Consequently, the growth source 'changes in the lag in the application of knowledge' (discussed in chapter 20 [of the original book]), does not include changes brought about as an incidental result of changes in the amount of education of the labor force; it is confined to the effects of other changes, such as improvement in channels of information, opportunities to observe the practices of other firms or countries, and changes in the age of the capital stock. I would not pretend this distinction is precise, but it is clear enough for general understanding.

4. While education may affect the pace of advances in knowledge, it is also true that advances of knowledge change the content of education; what is taught in a physics or economics course today is not what was taught a generation ago, and this is one of the main ways in which new knowledge is disseminated. If what is taught in schools and colleges lags further behind or more closely approaches the current state of the arts, this can influence changes in the lag of actual practice behind the best known. It is not reflected in my quality indexes for the education of the labor force, which take no account of the content of courses.

5. Most individuals in school do not work and those who do usually work part time. Hence, extending schooling for young people immediately influences at least three measures of labor input that have already been examined: Employment is reduced, average hours of work may be lowered,

and (since the proportion of young people in the labor force is reduced) the age composition is improved. The net effect of these three changes is to reduce total labor input while raising the average quality of labor. Cross-sectional data suggest that the reduction in employment is later offset by a tendency for more education to raise labor force participation rates.[1] I do not trace these effects back to education, but leave them classified as effects of employment, hours or the age–sex composition of employment.[2] It should be noted that the timing of these effects bears no close relationship to changes in the education of the labor force.

6. The more years an individual spends in school the higher is the age at which he enters the labor force. This means that the more educated individuals in any age group have had less work experience than the less educated. In measuring the effect of education on the quality of labor by quality indexes, I measure the excess of the benefit from longer education over the associated loss from curtailed work experience.[3]

7. Additional education, especially general education, presumably increases versatility, mobility and awareness of employment opportunities. For this reason individuals with more education are more likely than those with less education to find employment where, given their abilities, their marginal value products are greatest. This is one of the subsidiary reasons they earn more. If they lose their positions because of shifts in the demand for labor, they are likely to be able to shift to alternative jobs with less (if any) reduction of earnings and less loss of time in unemployment. These advantages of education are reflected in the education quality indexes. [. . .]

Relationship between levels and changes in education: future trends

Education of the labor force had an unusual characteristic as an income determinant in that the gap between the United States and Europe was widening in favor of the United States from 1950 to 1962. Another unusual feature was that, based on United States weights, the educational quality of North-West European labor in 1960 was almost the same as in the United States as recently as 1950; it was much above the quality index of the United States in 1925 when real national income per person employed approximated the 1960 North-West European level. A rough estimate would

1. This effect is best known and most pronounced for women and older men but in the United States is evidently also present to a small degree among men in the prime working ages (see Bowen and Finegan, 1966).

2. Any effect of education upon the hours worked by employed persons who have completed their education *is* classified as an effect of education (see p. 85 of the original book).

3. As will be seen, this is accomplished by basing the weights for individuals with different amounts of education on earnings differentials based on age groups rather than length-of-experience groups.

Table 1 Time spent in school by recent students[a] and possible alternative adjustments to 1960 education quality indexes

| | Time per year of schooling | | | Time spent in school during school career | | | | | Possible adjustment (in percentage points) to education quality adjustment indexes, based on hours per year |
| | | | | Number | | United States equivalent years based on annual hours[c] | Indexes (United States = 100) | | |
Area	Number of scheduled days per year[b] (1)	Number of scheduled hours per day[b] (2)	Number of scheduled hours per year (3)	Years (4)	Scheduled hours (5)	(6)	Years (7)	Scheduled hours (8)	(9)
United States	180	5·69	1024	12·90	13,210	12·90	100	100	
North-West Europe	200	5·32	1069	10·26	10,968	10·71	80	83	2·7
Belgium	198	5·39[d]	1071	11·39	12,199	11·91	88	92	3·1
Denmark	212	5·08	1079	8·84	9539	9·32	69	72	2·9
France	184	5·54	1019	10·74	10,944	10·69	83	83	−0·3
Germany	229	4·83	1110	9·13	10,134	9·90	71	77	4·6
Netherlands	202	5·41	1092	10·43	11,390	11·12	81	86	4·1
Norway	193[e]	5·62	1086	9·99	10,849	10·59	77	82	3·6
United Kingdom	189	5·64[f]	1069	10·96	11,716	11·44	85	89	2·9
Italy	202	4·47	902	8·86	7992	7·80	69	60	−6·4

Source: See Appendix F, Section III, for derivation [pp. 399–401 of the original book].

a Students in school in 1957–8.
b Part days are counted as half a day.
c Calculated by multiplying the United States figure from column (4) by column (8) (before rounding).
d Assumed to be the same as in the Netherlands in each age group.
e Assumed to be the same as in Sweden in each school grade.
f Assumed to be the same as in the United States in each school grade.

put the 1925 United States index at about 80 (United States in 1960 equal to 100) which is much below the 1960 indexes of 92 to 96 for the North-West European countries and only equal to the 1960 Italian index.[4]

Available information suggests that, in the United States, the educational quality of labor will rise during the 1960s about as much as it did in the 1950s while, in the North-West European countries, the rise will be more rapid in the 1960s. Projections indicate the average rate of increase in the education quality indexes (in North-West European weights) will be higher in the 1960s than the 1950s by something like 0·15 percentage points in Belgium, France and the United Kingdom, and 0·05 points in Norway.[5] Only Belgium and Italy seem likely to match the United States increase. Education is therefore likely to remain a factor operating towards widening the gap in income levels between the United States and North-West Europe.

A final calculation gives an indication of the longer run outlook. This is

Table 2 **Mean years of education of the labor force, by sex, 1950 and 1962**

	Males			Females		
Area	1950	1962	Increase 1950–62	1950	1962	Increase 1950–62
United States	9·68	10·68	1·00	10·01	11·08	1·07
Adjusted for attendance[a]	7·59	9·25	1·66	7·87	9·62	1·75
North-West Europe						
Belgium	7·98	8·93	0·95	7·95	8·81	0·86
Denmark	7·46	7·82	0·36	7·55	7·83	0·28
France	8·09	8·65	0·56	7·89	8·51	0·62
Germany	7·93	8·24	0·31	7·95	8·19	0·24
Netherlands	8·43	9·11	0·68	8·35	9·02	0·67
Norway	7·90	8·40	0·50	7·70	8·28	0·58
United Kingdom	9·16	9·71	0·55	9·43	9·86	0·43
Adjusted for attendance[a]	8·56	9·36	0·80	8·96	9·54	0·57
Italy	4·23	5·10	0·87	3·89	4·88	0·99

Sources: See text and Appendix F, Section II, for derivation [pp. 373–403 of the original book].

[a] Years of education of labor force members reduced to equivalence with years of education of postwar students by allowing for absenteeism and, in the United States, extension of the school year outside large cities.

4. The extrapolation from 1950 to 1925 is based on my earlier study (Denison, 1962), but after sharply reducing the adjustment for days of schooling in accordance with changes introduced in the present study.

5. The statement with respect to the United States is based on previous projections by the author. (A new projection of the labor force by amount of education, made by the US Department of Labor, is contained in the *Manpower Report of the President*, March 1966, p. 218.)

the amount by which the average years of schooling being provided about the middle of the postwar period, in 1957–8 (Table 1), exceeds the average years of education of the 1962 labor force (Table 2). For the latter calculation I use a simple average of the figures for males and females. The differences are given in the first column below. The second column shows the

Differences in years of full-time schooling		
	1957–8 students minus 1962 labor force	1962 male labor force minus 1950 male labor force
Italy	3·9	0·9
United States	3·5 (2·0)	1·7 (1·0)
Belgium	2·5	1·0
France	2·2	0·6
Norway	1·6	0·5
United Kingdom	1·5 (1·2)	0·8 (0·6)
Netherlands	1·4	0·7
Denmark	1·0	0·4
Germany	0·9	0·3

However, it excludes persons who will be under twenty-five years of age and the education classes are somewhat condensed. Estimates for the European countries are all deduced from projected changes in the average number of years of education; data are described in Appendix F, Section II [pp. 373–403 of the original book].

increase that took place from 1950 to 1962 in average years of schooling of male members of the labor force (Table 2). Figures in parentheses exclude adjustments for changes in days attended per year.

The first column suggests that Italy, the United States and Belgium can anticipate the largest increases in the education of the labor force in the future; France, Norway, the United Kingdom and the Netherlands are in an intermediate position; and Denmark and Germany can expect the smallest increases. This broad grouping is the same as that observed in the second column for actual changes from 1950 to 1962. The difference between the education recently being provided the younger generation in Italy and the education of the labor force in Italy is particularly noteworthy. It is a very favorable factor for future growth. Among the large countries of North-West Europe, the future increase in education suggested for France is bigger than that for the United Kingdom, and that for Germany is especially small.[6] Indeed, one can infer directly from column 4 of Table 1 that, in the absence of a major change in education provided for young people,

6. Attention is also called to Appendix F, Section II [pp. 373–403], in which it is shown that the younger age groups in Germany have but little more education than the older age groups soon to leave the labor force.

Germany is heading toward a position in which its labor force will have the least full-time education of any of the countries covered except Italy, and eventually little, if any, more than Italy.[7] One would have to attach great weight to the part-time education provided by the part-time Berufsschule to avoid the conclusion that the future position of Germany with respect to the education of the labor force will become decidedly inferior to that of its neighbors. There appears to be substance to the comment that Germany has been 'living off the educational capital it built up before and during the war'.[8]

Use of enrolment ratios for a year later than 1957–8 in the comparisons would yield somewhat different results, of course, and educational changes still to be made will affect the more distant future. But the course of changes in the education of the labor force for a long time to come will be largely determined by changes that have already occurred and that can be observed in a classification of the adult population by amount of education. The education of most of the labor force for decades ahead has already been determined.

7. The figure in Table 1 for average years of education in Denmark in 1957–8 is below that for Germany, but allowance should be made for the higher age at which education is being received in Denmark; in addition Danish enrolment ratios are now rising.

8. Unidentified 'independent expert' quoted by Olsen in the *New York Times*, 13 January 1965.

References

BOWEN, W. G. and FINEGAN (1966), Papers and Proceedings, *Amer. Econ. Rev.*, May, pp. 567–82.

DENISON, E. F. (1962), 'The sources of economic growth in the United States and the alternatives before us', supplementary paper no. 13, Committee for Economic Development, New York.

in this table, I think, is the one showing the very large decrease in the un-employment rate of college graduates.

In a sense, these unemployment figures are only the part of the iceberg that is above the water. For a better understanding of their significance, we must consider also the changes in demand and supply that took place at the various educational levels between 1950 and 1962. Figure 1 shows (for males eighteen and over) the percentage changes in the supply of labor (labor force), in the demand for labor (employment), and in unemployment rates at various levels of educational attainment between 1950 and 1962. The left-hand bars show labor force changes, the center bars show employment changes, and the right-hand bars show unemployment rate changes. The three bars at the far right of the chart show these changes for all groups combined; these aggregates obviously conceal some differences between educational levels which are of cardinal importance.

Table 1 **Education and unemployment, April 1950 and March 1962** (males eighteen and over)

	Unemployment rates		Percentage change, 1950 to 1962
Years of school completed	1950	1962	
0 to 7	8·4	9·2	+9·5
8	6·6	7·5	+13·6
9 to 11	6·9	7·8	+13·0
12	4·6	4·8	+4·3
13 to 15	4·1	4·0	−2·4
16 or more	2·2	1·4	−36·4
All groups	6·2	6·0	−3·2

The bars for the group of zero to seven years of education show that the number of this group in the labor force declined very greatly from 1950 to 1962; but the jobs held by this group declined even more, so that its un-employment rate went up. The supply of labor with eight years of education also decreased, and the demand for this group decreased even more, and its unemployment rate increased by more than the increase in rate for the zero to seven classification. We see a different relationship between supply and demand in the nine to eleven years of education group. Supply increased; demand also increased, but by less than the increase in supply, so that a high unemployment rate resulted here too. The high-school graduates (twelve years of education) fared somewhat better. There was a substantial increase in supply in this group, and demand also kept pace, so that this group's unemployment rate went up by less than the rates of the less educated groups. The groups with college training were quite fortunate, especially those with at least four years of college. The supply of men with thirteen to fifteen years of education increased by almost 50 per cent, but the jobs for them increased by slightly more, so that their unemployment rate (which was already low) went down slightly. The experience of the group with sixteen or more years of education was particularly striking. The supply of men in this group increased by 75 per cent, but the jobs for them increased even more than that, so that their unemployment rate went down by more than a third.

It is important to note that all of the improvement in the unemployment situation in 1962, as compared with 1950, was concentrated in the elite group of our labor force – the approximately 20 per cent with college training. In all of the other categories, which have about 80 per cent of the labor force, unemployment rates were substantially higher in 1962 than in 1950. These figures, I contend, substantiate the thesis that the patterns of demand for labor have been twisted faster than the patterns of supply have changed, and that as a result we had a substantially greater degree of labor-market imbalance in 1962 than in 1950.

But these figures do not fully reveal the power of the labor-market twist. The 'labor force' enumeration includes (with minor exceptions) only those who say that they have jobs or that they have actively sought work in the week preceding the survey. Those who have been out of work so long that they have given up hope and are no longer 'actively seeking' work – but who would take a job if one were available – are simply not counted either as unemployed or as a member of the labor force. The percentage of a given category of the total population that is 'in the labor force' (under the foregoing definition) is expressed as the 'labor force participation rate'. It seems probable that worsening employment prospects for a particular group over a long period would force down the labor force participation rate – i.e. would squeeze a number of people out of the labor market altogether, in the sense that they would give up the continuing, active search for jobs. Conversely, it seems probable that improving employment prospects would tend to pull more people into the labor market and thus to raise the labor force participation rate. These two trends are indeed observable since 1950. The squeezing out of people at the lower end of the educational ladder and the pulling in of people at the upper end is another manifestation of the labor-market twist. Table 2 presents the pertinent figures for males.

This table tells us that the participation rates at the lower end of the educational scale, which were already relatively low in 1950, had gone much lower by 1962. At the other end of the scale, participation rates had gone up by 1962. (The reason why the increase for college graduates was so small is that even in 1950 their participation rates in the prime age groups – especially twenty-five to fifty-four – were already quite high, in some categories 98 or

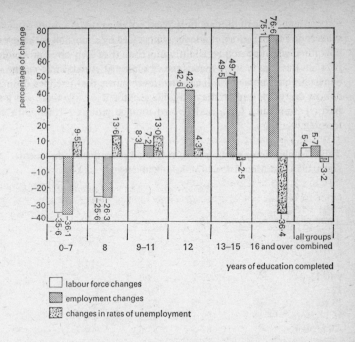

Figure 1 The changing structure of labor force, employment and unemployment, 1950–62 (males, eighteen and over)

99 per cent.) Some of the decline in participation rates at the lower end of the scale is due to higher average ages, with a larger proportion in this group (as compared with upper groups) attaining the age of sixty-five and voluntarily retiring. But that is by no means the whole story. A detailed comparison by age group as well as by educational level shows that declines occurred at almost every age level in the non-college category, while there was a rise in participation rates for a majority of the age groups of men with college training.

Table 2 **Labor force participation rates and educational attainment, April 1950 and March 1962 (males, eighteen and over)**

Years of school completed	Labor force participation rates		Percentage change in rate, 1950 to 1962
	1950	1962	
0 to 4	74·6	58·2	−22·0
5 to 7	85·0	74·6	−14·4
8	88·1	78·2	−12·7
9 to 11	92·1	88·8	−3·9
12	94·0	90·7	−3·7
13 to 15	79·6	83·0	+5·4
16 or more	92·1	92·3	+0·2
All groups	87·6	83·5	−4·7

Source: The population data are from the 1950 census. The 1962 figures are from unpublished data supplied by the US Bureau of Labor Statistics.

The important point that I want to make with these figures is that in all likelihood the official unemployment statistics substantially understate the size of the labor surplus of men with limited education. If we found jobs for most of those now officially reported as unemployed, the news of improving opportunities would undoubtedly bring back into the labor force many men who are not now counted as members of it. Unfortunately, we cannot count on the same flexibility of supply at the top of the educational scale. Even the most extreme pressures of demand cannot pull the participation rate much above 98 or 99 per cent, which (as just stated) is the current rate in some college-trained age groups.

Our overall unemployment rate has now been above 5 per cent for more than five years, and we cannot be sure what effects a substantial increase in spending by consumers, businesses and government (i.e. an increase in aggregate demand) would have on the patterns of employment, unemployment and labor-force participation just discussed. Many respected economists believe, as one of them once put it, that the hard core of unemployment is made of ice, not rock, and that it would melt away if overall demand rose high enough. As already noted, the Council of Economic Advisers has virtually guaranteed that the administration's tax-cut program – which in its current version would put about $11 billion in the hands of consumers and businesses – would reduce unemployment to an 'interim target' rate of 4 per cent by 1966. This line of reasoning assumes (either implicitly or sometimes explicitly) that no serious bottlenecks of labor supply would appear before the achievement of the overall un-employment rate of 4 per cent. I seriously question the validity of this critically important assumption under the labor-market conditions of today and the foreseeable future.

The benefits of a decline in the overall rate of unemployment appear to be quite unevenly distributed among the educational attainment groups that we have been considering. The year 1957 was the last one in which we had an unemployment rate as low as 4 per cent. It is instructive to see how the patterns of unemployment changed from 1950, when the overall rate was above 6 per cent, to 1957, and then again to 1962, which had about the same overall rate as 1950. This comparison is made in two forms in Table 3. This table shows the actual unemployment rates for the various educational attainment groups in those three years, and it also expresses the unemploy-ment rate for each group in each of the three years as a ratio of the rate for all of the other groups combined. (Thus, the zero to seven years of edu-cation group had an unemployment rate about 50 per cent higher than all other groups combined in 1950; its rate was more than double the rate for all other groups in 1957; and its rate was 70 per cent higher in 1962.)

Clearly, unemployment at the bottom of the educational scale was relatively unresponsive to general increases in the demand for labor, while

Table 3 Actual and relative unemployment rates by educational attainment, April 1950, March 1957 and March 1962 (males, eighteen and over)

| | Unemployment rates | | | | | |
| | Actual percentages | | | Relative[1] | | |
Years of school completed	1950	1957	1962	1950	1957	1962
0 to 7	8·4	6·9	9·2	154	203	170
8	6·6	4·4	7·5	108	110	132
9 to 11	6·9	4·7	7·3	115	120	142
12	4·6	3·0	4·8	70	67	75
13 to 15	4·1	2·7	4·0	64	64	65
16 or more	2·2	0·6	1·4	34	14	21
All groups	6·2	4·1	6·0	(1)	(1)	(1)

1. The relative unemployment rate is the ratio between the percentage unemploy-ment rate for a given educational attainment group and the percentage unemployment rate for all other groups at the same point in time.

C. C. Killingsworth 93

there was very strong responsiveness at the top of the educational scale. The percentage unemployment rate for college graduates in 1957 merits close attention. It was an almost incredible 0·6 per cent. I have queried the experts in the Bureau of Labor Statistics on this figure, and they assure me that they have no less confidence in it than in the other 1957 figures. Surely a figure as low as that represents what is sometimes called 'overfull' employment – i.e. demand which seriously exceeds supply.

Bear in mind that the unemployment rates for the lower educational attainment groups (those with 80 per cent of the men) are now higher than in 1950, and that the unemployment rate for college graduates is now substantially lower than in 1950. Also bear in mind that the labor force participation rate figures strongly suggest a large and growing 'reserve army' – which is not counted among the unemployed – at the lower educational levels, and that there is no evidence of any such reserve of college-trained men. Finally, bear in mind the differences between the lower end of the educational scale and the upper end in responsiveness to overall decreases in the unemployment rate.

When you put all of these considerations together, I believe that you are ineluctably led to the conclusion that long before we could get down to an overall unemployment rate as low as 4 per cent, we would have a severe shortage of workers at the top of the educational ladder. This shortage would be a bottleneck to further expansion of employment. I cannot pinpoint the level at which the bottleneck would begin to seriously impede expansion; but, on the basis of the relationships revealed by Table 3, it seems reasonable to believe that we could not get very far below a 5 per cent overall unemployment level without hitting that bottleneck.

Conclusion

The most fundamental conclusion that emerges from my analysis is that automation and the changing pattern of consumer wants have greatly increased the importance of investment in human beings as a factor in economic growth. More investment in plant and equipment, without very large increases in our investment in human beings, seems certain to enlarge the surplus of underdeveloped manpower and to create a shortage of the highly developed manpower needed to design, install, and man modern production facilities.

The Manpower Development and Training Act is aptly named, soundly conceived, and well administered. But I doubt that even the most enthusiastic supporters of the Manpower Development and Training Act program (and I count myself among them) would argue that its present or projected size is really commensurate with the size of the job to be done. We ought to be thinking in terms of helping two or three times as many people as this program is now expected to reach. I do not imply any criticism of the Congress in this comment, because it is my strong impression that dollars are not the limiting factor in the development of the Manpower Development and Training Act program. The real shortage in most areas, I believe, is trained manpower – specifically, qualified instructors and program administrators. It would be pointless to double or triple the appropriations for the program if the extra money could not be spent, and I doubt that it could be. Here we have an example of a present shortage of highly trained manpower, a shortage that limits the possibility of investment to remedy the educational deficiencies of the past.

Let us consider another, somewhat similar example. As we have all heard over and over again, the outlook for high-school dropouts is bleak indeed. Exhortations, no matter how well meant, are not going to cure this problem, and neither will the token fund set aside by President Kennedy for grants to local units for experimental programs in this area. But here again dollars alone are not the answer. We need many more highly skilled teachers, counselors and social workers. These, too, are in very short supply. Many other present shortages of highly trained manpower, in the private sector of the economy as well as in the public, could be cited. Unquestionably these shortages would be intensified and new ones would appear if we moved closer to full utilization of our economic potential.

To my mind, the greatest shortcoming of the administration's program for reducing unemployment is the failure to recognize the crucial need to break the trained manpower bottleneck. I recognize that the administration has recommended what many people regard as very ambitious measures for federal aid to higher education. But even if these measures were accepted in their entirety, it is most unlikely that they would suffice to break the present and prospective bottlenecks in the supply of highly educated manpower. I am not one who advocates even more billions of dollars in federal appropriations for higher education. Appropriations of such magnitude almost surely will not be given congressional approval in the foreseeable future. More important, even the largest appropriations within the realm of remote possibility would leave virtually untouched the most difficult aspect of the financing of higher education. That is the investment that the student, or his parents, must make in his subsistence costs during four or more years of training. For most students today, the minimum cost is $5000.

To put a complex matter briefly, we must find a fundamentally new approach to the financing of at least this important part of the cost of higher education. We must make it as easy for an individual to finance his own investment in higher education as it is for him to finance the purchase of a home. I have proposed (in an as yet unpublished essay) that we make provisions for loans to college students up to a maximum of $12,000, with a repayment period as long as forty years, at a subsidized interest rate of 2 per cent. Repayment should be on the basis of a flat percentage of income – a kind of social-security system in reverse. Others may think of better solutions; the means are less important than the end which is to make higher education readily available to all who can benefit from it.

I would give a considerably higher priority to the stimulation of investment in human beings than I would to such measures as the proposed tax cut. But I would still rate the tax cut as important. Denying that the tax cut is the 'ultimate weapon' against unemployment is not denying that it can make some contribution to the reduction of unemployment. After all, even to get below a 5 per cent unemployment rate would be a considerable achievement today. But a really effective attack on the complex problem of unemployment requires a whole arsenal of powerful weapons.

And we don't have all the time in the world. Human history has been described as a race between education and catastrophe. In the past dozen years, education has been falling behind in that race.

6 G. Venn

Man, Education and Work

G. Venn, 'Man, education and work', in G. L. Mangum (ed.), *The Manpower Revolution: Its Policy Consequences*, Doubleday, 1965, pp. 403–16.

Introduction

Rapid technological change has suddenly posed a significant, worldwide challenge to man's political, social, economic and educational institutions. The challenge is especially to education and specifically to the education of youth for a new world of work.

Change is the one great product of the new technology. It applies with particular force to occupational education and present efforts, or lack of effort, in vocational and technical education in schools and colleges. The essential educational problem posed by the new technology is one of educating all students for a changing world of work. Technology has created a new relationship which places education squarely between man and his work. While this relationship has traditionally been understood as holding true for some men and some work (on the professional level, for example), technology has brought us to the point where we can say this relationship now holds true for all men and all work. In a word, technology now dictates that all levels of education assume a new role in educating man for a changing world of work.

Man and work

Technological advance has obviously wrought great changes in the kind of work men do. One of a thousand possible examples is offered by the railroad industry, in which one machine with four men can lay as much track as a hundred strong-backed men would fifty years ago. Already the new technology has led us to a new stage of work activity: the Industrial Revolution shifted the emphasis from physical to manipulative; the technological explosion has shifted the emphasis from the manipulative to the cognitive. Work can no longer be defined in terms of physical effort. The forces of technology have completely changed the meaning of the word 'work' and man's relation to the world of work.

Technology has eliminated jobs at the lower levels of the employment spectrum. For example, agriculture and mining, which formerly employed large numbers of unskilled workers, have decreased jobs about 40 per cent in the last fifteen years. In 1900, 70 per cent of the labor force was engaged in production; today, the figure is less than 40 per cent. Work as it once was known is therefore no longer available to many people. In place of 'work' society has substituted the 'job'. A man's occupation in America today is his most significant status-conferring role. Without a job a man is lost and without educational preparation few jobs are available.

The new technology has also changed the opportunity for youth to enter the world of work. Yesterday, work was something many experienced before adulthood; today it marks initiation into adulthood. But today society denies opportunities for work during youth. To get a job youth must be prepared; there is no easy transition into the world of work. Over one million young men and women under twenty-two currently not in school and not at work attest to the change.

Young people today have little opportunity to observe work in a real work setting. Work is removed from the home and the neighborhood, a fact which makes intelligent transition into the world of work even more difficult. It makes occupational guidance and education necessary for all.

Work and education

Work activity has become more like education and a new and closer relationship between the two has become necessary and possible. Entry to work and job upgrading become more a matter of education and preparation for more occupations must be taught within the educational system. In the constantly accelerating job-upgrading process of technology there has been a constant accelerating of higher educational skills needed for job entry and retention. There is little work for those with little education.

While the relationship between work and education in the professions has long been understood, what must now be understood is that technology has advanced a host of other occupations to the point where the same relationships become necessary. Inexorably, just as apprenticeship gave way to professional education in law and medicine, on-the-job training is giving way to occupational education in the highly skilled and technical occupations.

Man and education

Several wide-ranging changes have marked man's entry into the technological age: the importance of the job to the individual and the fact that the job is more than ever a function of his education, the changes in the meaning of 'work', and the fact that as it becomes like education, more education for work becomes mandatory. From these changed relationships one conclusion emerges: Education links man and his work, and only a total acceptance of this fact by the educational community can meet urgent individual and national dislocations threatened by the new technology.

The chief dislocations facing the nation lie in the area of unemployment (over 5 per cent of American workers cannot find work), underemployment (thousands working at jobs which do not utilize their talents), and a worsening shortage of personnel in skilled, technical and professional occupations. In addition, the growing plight of older workers displaced by technology, the misfortune of the Negro workers, and the re-entry of women to the work force are problems of the here and now; they are not academic or theoretical.

To have status and a place in the new technological society every person must be able to make a contribution, to understand where he fits, to be needed, and to be useful – these have not changed. But to get the chance to have these needs met, a man's education is his opportunity; education is no longer simply nice for some; today it is a necessity for everyone.

The development of vocational and technical education

While vocational and technical education began in private institutes, land-grant colleges and universities, it soon found its way to the high schools, especially after the passage of the Smith–Hughes Act in 1917. Because of this federal legislation, vocational-technical education has developed several distinct characteristics: first, it has been separated from the educational mainstream; second, it has been conducted chiefly at the secondary-school level; third, it has developed great uniformity; fourth, it has been tied to the concept of practical work; fifth, it has tended to become terminal in nature; and lastly, it has been tied to categorical legislation which has restricted its development. Today it lacks prestige and status, and has not gained the needed attention of educators from other areas and levels of education.

In a real sense vocational and technical education has developed from concerns of people outside the educational community. Present technological change, however, should suggest to all educators, especially in higher education, the urgent need for their vigorous, imaginative involvement in vocational and technical education.

The present status of vocational and technical education

Current efforts to provide vocational and technical education can be described as conflicting, overlapping and insufficient. At present, less than 6 per cent of the high-school graduates in the country complete a program of occupational preparation. Emphasis is heavy on agricultural and home-making programs, yet there are farm jobs for only one in ten rural youth. Thirty per cent or more of the nation's youth fail to graduate from high school and only two in ten graduate from college. The need for post-secondary occupational education is also apparent from changing occupational patterns which by 1970 will find over half the new job opportunities in the highly skilled and technical occupations. Unfortunately there are too few occupational education opportunities beyond the high school; some states have free public post-secondary programs available to nearly all youth and adults and some states have none.

Displacement of workers by automation and technological advancement also requires a vast program of continuing occupational education. Yet, continuing occupational education is not a major purpose of most schools or institutions of higher education. In 1958–9 the median expenditure in school systems of the nation for all adult education was $1290; the median enrolment was eighty students. Except for some two-year colleges and a few colleges and universities the efforts in continuing vocational and technical education are equally dismal.

Business, industry and labor efforts have grown, but studies indicate that such programs are primarily aimed at the professional and technically educated employee. These programs do not touch those out of work, those with low-level technical skills, or those who have failed to gain previous high-level skills or education. Apprenticeship training has been decreasing each year; registered apprentices hit a peak of 230,823 in 1950 and numbered only 158,616 in January 1963.

Business and proprietary schools provide post-high school vocational and technical education for large numbers of youth but variations in quality and availability are great. Many youths and adults cannot afford the tuition charges. Some young men gain occupational education in the Armed Forces. It is estimated they provide about 10,000 entry workers into technical occupations annually. However, this training is not directed toward civilian jobs and is a minor source of an estimated annual need for 200,000 technicians.

The Area Redevelopment Act and the Manpower Development and Training Act provide funds to retrain and upgrade unemployed adults and youths and to provide needed skills in economically depressed areas. Congress is presently considering legislation which will increase the occupations for which federal funds are provided as well as broaden the kinds of training offered under present programs. Federal appropriations available for vocational and technical education are expected to increase both for public schools and for institutions of higher education. Continued separation of occupational education from the total education program, however, will not solve the problem of providing better education for all.

Manpower problems

Youth entering the labor market will increase by 46 per cent in the 1960s, accounting for nearly half the total labor force growth during this decade.

New jobs need to be created at the rate of 50,000 per week. Dr Norman C. Harris of the University of Michigan recently summarized these changes as follows:

Professional jobs, making up 6 per cent of the labor force in 1930, will probably constitute 12 per cent by 1970. At the other extreme, unskilled, semiskilled and service jobs which together accounted for 56 per cent of the labor force in the 1960s will by 1970 decrease to only 25 per cent of the labor force. But the really significant changes in our labor force, and in society in general, have occurred at the level of the semiprofessional and technical; the managerial, business and sales; and the highly skilled jobs. These jobs taken together, will account for over 50 per cent of the labor force by 1970 (1962, p. 111).

Shortages of professional, technical and highly skilled workers and of educational opportunities indicate that present efforts will not meet the manpower needs of the present or future.

Major issues in vocational and technical education

The forces of change and circumstance are altering long-held public attitudes toward the use and conservation of the nation's human resources. More people are beginning to understand the direct connection between education and national strength. The country has begun to perceive the permanent relationship between manpower needs and educational programs as a marriage of wisdom as well as one of necessity.

To further this objective certain issues and problems in vocational and technical education must be resolved.

Prestige and status for occupational education. Vocational and technical education simply does not now have the prestige and status necessary to enroll the number and kind of students who need it; its low public prestige is in part a reflection of its low status within the educational community itself. Educators must recognize the field of vocational-technical education as a necessary and legitimate form of education for our time.

Single purpose versus comprehensive institutions. The historical development of vocational and technical education in separate, single-purpose institutions has tended to identify it as a 'second-class' kind of education in the public mind, and has frequently led to its being bypassed in the ferment over educational goals, standards and methods – often deprived of valuable criticism and fresh ideas. The complete integration of vocational and technical education into the mainstream of post-secondary education will mean that agencies or institutions responsible for the conduct of general education no longer shrink from their total responsibilities to society.

Learning and education. The preoccupation with designated courses and credits as the only path to study beyond the high school has led vocational and technical programs to be considered, for the most part, terminal in nature, a disqualification for further study within education. This dissuades many students from enrolling in such programs. If the measure of education is learning, then learning in occupational courses must be given fair evaluation and credit toward placement in other educational programs.

Higher education and the average student. In the years immediately ahead the new technology will demand that at least half of all youth find employment in occupations for which one to three years of post-secondary education and training will be a necessary and proper preparation. Opportunities for this education and training must be provided within the framework of higher education. Many criteria, programs and goals established in another time for another society are no longer applicable in today's fast changing industrial democracy.

Guidance, placement and follow-up. Occupational guidance, placement and follow-up opportunities are too seldom found in American education today. Since a rapidly increasing number of occupations are now marked by educational requisites for entry and upgrading, a major responsibility for the allocation of persons to occupations rests within the educational community.

Teachers for vocational and technical education. One of the greatest single barriers to the expansion and improvement of vocational-technical education is the desperate shortage of qualified teachers and administrators. The preparatory and continuing education of such personnel must become the responsibility of the colleges and universities with experience in teacher education and schools or departments in the relevant disciplines.

Educational planning and leadership. With pressures building in legislative bodies to do something about the nation's pressing problems of unemployment and shortages of skilled manpower, there is a danger that schools and colleges may have an ill-advised crash program thrust upon them through financial forced feeding, or that the task may in part or in whole be taken out of the hands of educators altogether. Sound and forceful educational leadership at all levels must be evinced if this nation is to come to grips successfully with the new problems posed by the changing relationships between man, his education and his work.

Some premises and conclusions

Grave problems are emerging in the United States – a slow-down in economic growth, a rising number of unemployed, increasing racial tensions, growing juvenile delinquency, greater numbers on public welfare rolls, chronic economically depressed areas in the nation, rising job displacement by machines, an exploding ratio of youth to total population, and a growing disparity of educational opportunity. At the root of each of these problems is a lack of education to prepare the individual for a new world of work in a new technological society.

The human being, regardless of race, intelligence or place of birth, is the greatest resource this nation or any nation can possess. Maximum development of this resource must become a major national objective. The large numbers of youth in schools and colleges represent an opportunity to invest in the only resource which, in the long run, will bring the promise of a productive and useful life to everyone. Each time this resource is wasted, to whatever degree, it represents a tragic loss to the nation and the world.

Education is obviously not the only solution to the problem the nation faces; without education, however, the individual citizen, who must help his country solve its problems, can make little or no progress. The oft-quoted statement of Alfred North Whitehead made in 1917 seems doubly pertinent today:

In the conditions of modern life the rule is absolute, the race which does not value trained intelligence is doomed. Not all your heroism, not all your social charm, not all your wit, nor all your victories on land or at sea, can move back the finger of fate. Today we maintain ourselves. Tomorrow science will have moved forward one more step, and there will be no appeal from the judgement which will then be pronounced on the uneducated (1949 edn, p. 25).

This statement, concerned with one aspect of education and with one segment of the educational continuum, is presented on the assumption that the long neglect of vocational and technical education is at the root of many of the present economic and social problems facing the nation. Certain basic premises have evolved from this study which are fundamental in considering the role of education in a new technological society:

First. Every person must learn to read, write and compute. This concept is not new but it is obvious that any individual who cannot read, write or compute cannot function effectively in a technological age. If a child cannot learn these basic tool skills in the elementary grades then he must be taught in the high schools. This is the basic problem to the present trend which could mean seven-and-a-half to eight million school dropouts in the next ten years. No individual can solve his problem nor can the nation secure the manpower needed unless the schools achieve this goal. The margin for educational error or failure has disappeared.

Second. A new attitude toward work and a new relationship between education and the work world must be developed. Education for work must become a respected and proper responsibility for all levels of education and every educator. Too often the teacher or the school has given up on the student when he is not advised to follow the college preparatory route. The single goal, single route structure must give way to a multiprogram, flexible approach geared to the students enrolled. Occupational education must become an integral part of total education. Quality for all can no longer be defined in terms of every person meeting requirements of one curriculum. Quality cannot be 'mass' education.

Third. Special programs must be developed for youth with special needs. These youth can no longer be shunted aside by simply allowing them to drop out of school. Programs must be initiated which will continue to develop tool skills and offer vocational preparation at an early age so early school leavers have saleable job skills. It means a broad range of vocational offerings not now available in present vocational programs. It will require some of the best teachers working with these students.

Fourth. A vast expansion of post-secondary education opportunities is necessary. In the immediate future it appears that one-fourth of the nation's youth will need to complete a baccalaureate degree and an additional one-half of all youth will need one to three years of post-secondary education. The greatest expansion will be needed in vocational and technical education opportunities in comprehensive institutions of the two-year college type. Therefore, three-fourths of the youth in the nation will need post-high school education, a majority of which will be in programs geared to entry job preparation in broad occupational fields. The continuation of study in general education and areas of related special knowledge calls for a comprehensive-type institution.

Fifth. Continuing education must become a major purpose and function of education. This has been necessary for a long time in professional fields. No professional person can 'keep up' if he does not continue to learn. Technology has now made this necessary for everyone. There is no longer such a thing as terminal education. Education is going to have to provide continuing education opportunities to youth and adults in the skilled, technical and semiprofessional fields at all levels; high school, two-year college, and college and university. These programs must be different from programs offered for youth in school. They must be specifically planned for those in need of more general education, special knowledge, and new occupational skills. Continued learning must become an accepted normal activity in everyone's life and a major function of high schools and post-high school institutions.

Sixth. Local school systems and educational institutions must develop programs and services based on the national nature of change. Technology has so drastically changed time and distance that the nation is smaller than many counties were fifty years ago. The boy or girl in Mississippi needs the same occupational education opportunities as the youth in New York. Local school systems which do not have the funds nor the students to provide special programs and services will have to join forces. Post-high school education for 75 per cent of our youth must be available regardless of financial ability or place of residence. The movement of young people to places where jobs are available must be encouraged and assisted. New educational programs responsive to technological change may be unrelated to local occupations but they must be related to the future of the local boy or girl.

Seventh. Today the major responsibility for individual selection of proper educational programs and occupational preparation rests with education. In a technological age sound occupational choice and selection of educational programs is made in direct ratio to information and guidance available to the individual and the breadth of educational opportunities available. Society today provides few chances for youth to learn about occupations and little knowledge of the developing jobs resulting from technology. Guidance for occupational choice must begin in the intermediate grades and continue until the individual is placed in an entry job. The choice of educational preparation and occupational choice cannot be left to chance. Simple continuation in school in a single track approach is no longer adequate. Local school systems should accept guidance responsibility for those youth not in school as well.

Eighth. Education must accept the responsibility of entry job placement or educational reassignment for every student. Getting a job today or going on for more education is truly based on what one knows, not whom one knows. Transition from school to work becomes vastly more complex and difficult. At the present time, as Dr James B. Conant says, 'unemployment of youth is nobody's affair'. The responsibility must include the school leaver as well as the graduate. No agency in society is as familiar with the young as the school or college and the same kind of placement assistance available for the professional must be available to those in other occupations and lower educational levels. The establishment of a continuing relationship between the school and the individual is necessary to the continuing educational development of every person.

Ninth. Continued study of long-range manpower needs in terms of educational programs, facilities, organization and time factor is necessary to reduce educational lag. Today data are available which indicate future patterns of occupational change, economic growth, population change and manpower needs. However, there is no present national effort to translate these data into occupational education requirements and priorities. Interpretation of these data in terms of future educational programs, facilities, finances and time factor must be accomplished. Study and planning is needed to indicate the kinds of vocational and technical education necessary to meet individual requirements for the work world, as well as national and local needs for skilled manpower.

Tenth. Post-secondary vocational and technical education must be available at a cost to the individual which will allow people to enroll on the basis of interest and ability, rather than financial capability. It is well known that the greatest selective factor in determining who goes on for post-high school education is economic. The income level of the families of the 75 per cent of those who must obtain post-secondary education is such that many students are unable to continue their education. The wide disparity among the states for inexpensive post-secondary vocational and technical education prevents many people from obtaining necessary occupational preparation.

Eleventh. The development of an adequate occupational education program within the educational system is a prerequisite to a successful program of training, retraining and the development of occupational flexibility. In both the short run and the long run such a development would provide the basis for approaching problems of manpower development, unemployment and retraining for those technologically displaced in the labor force. Both retraining and occupational education are necessary but in the long run the greater the number of young people that participate in a complete educational program geared to develop entry work skills and occupational flexibility the less will be the need for remedial corrective measures. Preventive programs should prove less costly than rehabilitation.

The educational implication of technological change, then, imposes greater responsibilities on the educational community. In addition to the implications previously discussed technology indicates the necessity of equalizing educational opportunity and quality among the states and within areas of the state by upgrading those schools which cannot provide the necessary educational scope and quality. It implies continuing consolidation of smaller school districts and greater cooperative efforts among schools to provide adequate occupational education and special services. Technological changes also demand continuous and cooperative planning among the various levels of education and the development of long-range plans to meet the educational needs of the state and of the national needs for educated manpower. The necessity of experimentation, research, and flexible approaches to the education and occupational preparation of all people are demanded by technological change.

References

HARRIS, N. C. (1962), 'The community junior college – a solution to the skilled manpower problem', in G. K. Smith (ed.), *Higher Education in an Age of Revolution*, Association for Higher Education, Washington, D.C.

WHITEHEAD, A. N. (1949), *The Aims of Education and Other Essays*, New American Library.

7 E. Ashby

Technology Adopted

From E. Ashby, *Technology and the Academics*, Macmillan, 1966, ch. 3, pp. 50–66.

The Industrial Revolution was accomplished by hard heads and clever fingers. Men like Bramah and Maudslay, Arkwright and Crompton, the Darbys of Coalbrookdale and Neilson of Glasgow, had no systematic education in science or technology. Britain's industrial strength lay in its amateurs and self-made men: the craftsman-inventor, the mill-owner, the iron-master. It was no accident that the Crystal Palace, that sparkling symbol of the supremacy of British technology, was designed by an amateur. In this rise of British industry the English universities played no part whatever, and the Scottish universities only a very small part; indeed formal education of any sort was a negligible factor in its success. The schools attended by the prosperous classes followed a curriculum which had scarcely changed since the schooldays of John Milton two centuries earlier. For the working classes there was no systematic schooling. Illiteracy was widespread: even as late as 1841 a third of the men and nearly half the women who were married in England and Wales signed the register with a mark. There were a few 'cultivators of science' (as they were called) engaged in research, but their work was not regarded as having much bearing on education and still less on technology. There was practically no exchange of ideas between the scientists and the designers of industrial processes. The very stratification of English society helped to keep science isolated from its applications: it was admitted that the study of science for its useful applications might be appropriate for the labouring classes, but managers were not attracted to the study of science except as an agreeable occupation for their leisure.

So it came about that the first technological education in Britain was provided, not for the sons of managers in industry, but for that small minority of the working classes who could read and write: the craftsman, the foreman, the mechanic. The mechanics' institutes – one of the great educational movements in British history – had their origin in the 'anti-toga' lectures (open to the public) given by a professor of natural philosophy in Glasgow, the querulous and eccentric John Anderson, known to his students as 'Jolly Jack Phosphorus'. He occupied the chair from 1757 until 1796, and he records that in 1791 he had nearly 200 students at his classes. He is known

(Kelly, 1957)[1] to have given free tickets for his lectures to 'gardeners, painters, shopmen, porters, founders, bookbinders, barbers, tailors, potters, glassblowers, gunsmiths, engravers, brewers and turners'. He quarrelled persistently with his academic colleagues. One outcome of his animosity toward the University was his will, endowing (quite inadequately) a second university for the people of Glasgow, 'for the Improvement of Human Nature, of Science, and of the country where they live'. In 1799 George Birkbeck was appointed professor in this strange establishment. His principal duty was to give courses of lectures and scientific demonstrations to a middle-class clientele prepared to pay a fee of some two guineas. In addition to this duty Birkbeck imposed on himself another one, namely to hold on Saturday evenings a course of lectures, without any fee, for working men. Five years later Birkbeck migrated to London and there, on the strength of his experience in Glasgow, he founded the London Mechanics' Institution. The movement spread. In 1841 there were some 50,000 members in more than two hundred institutions, scattered the length and breadth of Britain. After the Great Exhibition the institutes in Yorkshire banded themselves together into a Union, with 20,000 members in a hundred affiliated branches. In 1853 the secretary of the Yorkshire Union, James Hole, published an essay (1853) in which he suggested that the mechanics' institutes should combine to become the constituent parts of a national industrial university. The Society of Arts, which had for many years been a pioneer in the applications of science to technology, encouraged the movement by arranging conferences on technical education, establishing examinations and awarding diplomas, and by trying to organize a nationwide union of mechanics' institutes (Cardwell, 1957).[2] It is interesting to speculate on the way technological education might have developed in Britain if a national industrial university had emerged from these proposals. In his evidence before a committee of the Society of Arts in 1853 the Secretary of the Royal Institution said:

As to the mechanics' institutes ... they might become to such schools as I have contemplated what the *école des arts et métiers* is to the schools in France. ... Each mechanics' institute, if appreciated, would be a self-governed and self-supporting academy for the particular speciality which the wants of the neighbourhood indicated, whether agricultural chemistry, manufacturing chemistry, mechanics, metallurgy, etc.

But the soil of general education was at that time too thin to carry a system of technical education. The mechanics' institutes failed to make any

1. This book is an authoritative account of the history of the mechanics' institutes.
2. This book has a useful summary of the influence of examinations on technical education in England and a collection of references to nineteenth-century writing on scientific and technological education.

impression on contemporary technology, partly because they catered for a class which was too illiterate, and too overworked, to absorb scientific education in the evenings; partly because industry offered no inducements to the few students who did survive the Society of Arts examinations and emerge with diplomas; and partly because many of the institutes, in order to retain their membership, dropped systematic instruction in the scientific principles of various trades in favour of popular science, entertainment and the amenities of a working-men's club. This is not to say that the mechanics' institutes were a negligible influence in the history of British education: on the contrary, they lie at the foundation of such great institutions as the Royal College of Science and Technology in Glasgow, the Heriot-Watt College in Edinburgh, and the Manchester College of Technology. But in their own generation they did not bring technology within the pale of the formal educational system.

To the general public the 1851 Exhibition was a reassurance of Britain's industrial supremacy. There were a hundred categories of manufacturers, and in most of these categories the international jury awarded prizes to British manufacturers. Nevertheless, discerning observers detected alarming evidence of competition from abroad, and foresaw Britain's need for technological education if her industrial supremacy was to be maintained.

Raw material, formerly our capital advantage over other nations, is gradually being equalized in price, and made available to all by improvements in locomotion, and Industry must in future be supported, not by a competition of local advantages, but by a competition of intellects (wrote Lyon Playfair, one of the organizers of the Great Exhibition, 1852).

The Society of Arts, encouraged by the Prince Consort, launched a campaign to persuade the Government to take some responsibility for technological education. The outcome was the establishment of the Department of Science and Art. The Department stimulated the teaching of science in schools – particularly in schools attended by the lower middle class – through a system of payment-by-results. Schools which conducted classes in mathematics or science received subsidies. Teachers received remuneration according to the number of their pupils who passed examinations. Pupils were encouraged through prizes and scholarships. For fourteen years this mercenary traffic in scientific education continued. It was criticized because it led to the mere cramming of examinees, to the teaching of the right things for the wrong reasons. But the examinations of the Department of Science and Art did inject science-teaching into some schools. In 1872, fourteen years after the scheme started, there were 948 schools in the country in receipt of grants for science teaching, and 36,783 pupils were receiving instruction in science (Balfour, 1903). In this same year a Royal Commission was set up under the Duke of Devonshire to inquire into scientific instruction and the advancement of science. The Commission made recommendations which would have been unthinkable ten years earlier (when the Clarendon Commission reported on schools) and which, alas, would not be acceptable to many headmasters even in the 1950s. The recommendations were (Royal Commission, 1875):

1. That in all Public and Endowed Schools a substantial portion of time allotted to study, should, throughout the School Course . . . be devoted to Natural Science; and we are of opinion that not less than Six hours a week on the average should be appropriated for the purpose.

2. That in all General School Examinations, not less than one sixth of the marks be allotted to Natural Science.

3. That in any Leaving Examination, the same proportion should be maintained.

Thus, by the 1870s, the schools of England were beginning to produce a flow of pupils who had passed examinations in science and who were accordingly both prepared and predisposed for the study of science and technology at universities.[3]

The expansion of undergraduate courses in science and technology had to await this supply of recruits from the schools. We have already discussed how British universities under the influence of German *Wissenschaft* adapted themselves to the teaching of experimental science. It now remains to discuss how higher technology found a place in British universities.

It was doubtless the propinquity of industrialization which persuaded the University of Glasgow to establish a chair of engineering in 1840. It is said to be the first chair of engineering in any British university, though the Jacksonian professor of natural philosophy in Cambridge was lecturing on the principles of engineering as long ago as 1796; however, Cambridge had no chair of engineering until 1875 (Baker, 1957, pp. 171, 991). The

3. If this eighty-year-old practice had continued, every pupil who qualified to enter a university through the GCE would have been able (if he had wished to do so) to enter faculties of science or technology. As matters stand, thousands of pupils are called upon to make a decision at the age of about fifteen which restricts their choice to arts faculties on the one hand or faculties of science and technology on the other. No other European country tolerates such premature specialization. The retreat from the recommendations of the Devonshire Commission is due to three main causes: (a) the transfer of the 'Science and Art schools' to the grammar-school system when state-aided secondary education was established in 1902; (b) the staffing of the new grammar schools with men from public schools and a consequent imitation by the new grammar schools of public-school education; and (c) the narrow scope and high specialization demanded for open scholarships by the universities of Oxford and Cambridge.

Glasgow chair was set up by royal warrant and was evidently not welcomed by the academics in the University: for the Senate refused to supply the first professor with a classroom until the Lord Advocate intervened on his behalf, and even as late as 1861 engineering was not 'considered a proper department in which a degree should be conferred', and the subject remained for years in the Faculty of Arts.[4] University College, London, too, has had a chair of engineering since 1841; and the University of Edinburgh in 1855 created a part-time chair of technology, which was occupied by George Wilson, regius director of the Industrial Museum of Scotland. Wilson's chair was not endowed. His classes were not part of the academic course and were not included in the curriculum. Such were the facilities for technological higher education provided by a nation which was at that time leading the world in commerce and industry. Before the 1870s there was neither an adequate supply of pupils trained in science from schools nor an adequate demand from industrialists for graduates. Training in technology was through apprenticeship, on the job; and any formal training in colleges was regarded with suspicion, as likely to lead to the disclosure of 'know-how' and trade secrets. There was no lack of warning against the inadequacy of this provision. Even the circumspect royal commissioners on the University of Cambridge suggested that the basic principles of engineering should be taught there (*Report of the Cambridge University Commission*, 1852, p. 102). But warnings were not enough; a much more powerful impact was needed to overcome public inertia toward technological education.

That impact was provided by the International Exhibition held in Paris in 1867. In 1851 British products had carried away most of the prizes. In 1867 British products received a bare dozen awards. No longer was there the reassurance of easy industrial supremacy. Instead there was alarming evidence that Britain had made little progress in the peaceful arts of industry since 1851 and that continental countries had become very serious competitors. For example, a building was being put up at Glasgow with iron girders from Belgium, and it was asserted by Lyon Playfair that Belgian girders were cheaper because the Belgians had introduced economies depending on chemical analysis of the ore and limestone and fuel (*Report of the Select Committee on Scientific Instruction*, 1868). Playfair had served on the international juries of both the 1851 and 1867 exhibitions. He was – as an ex-professor of chemistry, an influential member of Parliament, and a personal friend of the late Prince Consort – able to command a respectful hearing for his opinions. He summarized his anxieties in an open letter to Lord Taunton (who was at that time chairman of the Schools Inquiry Commission); it

4. *Fortuna Domus* (1952). A series of lectures delivered in the University of Glasgow in commemoration of the fifth century of its foundation.

was this letter which goaded Parliament to inquire seriously into the need for some state support for technological education. After reporting the widespread opinion that Britain had fallen behind her competitors in industrial progress Playfair went on to say:

The one cause upon which there was most unanimity of conviction [at the Exhibition] is that France, Prussia, Austria, Belgium and Switzerland possess good systems of industrial education for the masters and managers of factories and workshops, and that England possesses none (1867).[5]

The publication of Playfair's letter was followed by a broadside from the Society of Arts (1868), in the form of a report on technical education which followed a conference held in 1868. Correspondence, public comment and deputations to Whitehall followed, and finally the massive inertia of Parliament was overcome. The Government set up a Select Committee (*Report of the Select Committee on Scientific Instruction*, 1868) 'to inquire into the Provisions for giving Instruction in Theoretical and Applied Science to the Industrial Classes'. The Committee's report is a classic in educational history. It constitutes the blueprint for technological training which led ultimately to twentieth-century industrial Britain; for it was this Committee which produced overwhelming evidence that it was not the artisans who needed education in applied science, but the managers. On one hand 'there is a preponderance of evidence' (the Committee said)

that so far as the workmen, as distinguished from the managers, are concerned it [the acquisition of scientific knowledge] can be considered an essential element only in certain trades, or, generally, as enlarging the area from which the foremen and managers may be drawn.

On the other hand

all the witnesses ... are convinced that a knowledge of the principles of science on the part of those who occupy the higher industrial ranks ... would tend to promote industrial progress.

The Committee's recommendations are remarkable for their prescience and sanity: elementary instruction within reach of every child, elementary science as an ingredient of all schooling, the reorganization of some secondary schools as science schools, state support for 'superior colleges of science' to be established in centres of industry, the encouragement of education for higher science teachers 'by the granting of degrees in science at Oxford and Cambridge ... and by the opening of a greater number of fellowships to distinction in natural science'.

5. In its spirit of urgency the letter is very similar to contemporary pamphleteering on the need to expand technological education in Britain. For this reason it has been reproduced in full in an Appendix (p. 111) [of the original book].

Gradually, and with reluctant and inadequate state support, technology took its place in the curricula of the colleges and universities of Britain. As with science, so with technology: it was fear of industrial competition (reinforced in the twentieth century by fear of war) which pushed British governments into state support for higher technological education, and it was to the Continent that Britain turned for models of how technology should be taught. Also, as with science, the continental models for technological education were not simply copied: they were profoundly modified and adapted to suit British conditions. The chief adaptation is a fundamental one and it lies at the root of a major problem which faces British universities today. On the Continent higher technological education is not a primary responsibility of universities: it is conducted in institutions *sui generis*, called polytechnics or *Technische Hochschulen*. Thus in Western Germany higher technological education is concentrated in eight *Technische Hochschulen* which have the status and dignity of universities. With minor exceptions, the seventeen universities in Western Germany do not offer courses in technological subjects. In Britain higher technological education is a primary responsibility of universities. Colleges of Advanced Technology share this responsibility, but it is now evident that they are not going to replace universities as centres for research and teaching in higher technology. Eighteen out of twenty-two British universities include technology in the curriculum, and the great colleges of technology which do bear some resemblance to the continental polytechnics (for example, the Imperial College of Science and Technology in London, the College of Technology in Manchester, and the Royal College of Science and Technology in Glasgow) are either integral parts of universities or are affiliated to one or other of them.

This inclusion of technology in the curriculum of most British universities, and its exclusion from the curriculum of most continental universities, can be understood in the light of history. While the countries of continental Europe were being harassed and impoverished by wars and revolutions, England was exploiting her mineral resources and her work people and building up a supremacy in manufacture and trade. When peace finally came to the Continent, the countries of Europe were able to turn their attention to making up leeway in the industrial revolution. Naturally England did not encourage them in these endeavours. Until 1825 it was a penal offence to enlist English artisans for employment abroad. When Queen Victoria came to the throne the export of English spinning machinery (for example) was still prohibited. Foreign industrialists had no access to the 'know-how' of English industry. Accordingly the countries of the Continent had to discover the new technology for themselves. Their response to this challenge was to produce a new species of professional man: the manager-technologist.

The universities of Europe were not at that time appropriate places for this essentially empirical education. French universities had lost their initiative under the centralization imposed by Napoleon. German universities were too preoccupied with the philosophical ferment nurtured by Hegel and Schelling, and in any event the training of technologists was not consistent with ideas of *Lernfreiheit*. And so the production of manager-technologists was entrusted to polytechnics which in the course of the century acquired the rank and prestige of universities. In France there was already the famous *École Polytechnique* which became the prototype of all colleges of higher technology. In Germany some technical schools were raised to the status of *Technische Hochschule* and others were founded on the model of the *École Polytechnique*. In Switzerland one of the first activities under the new federal constitution was to found (after much acrimonious discussion) a central polytechnic in Zürich. In Holland a polytechnic school was opened in Delft in 1864, to train works managers, civil engineers, naval architects and science teachers for schools. The response spread even to the United States: the Massachusetts Institute of Technology was founded in 1865, to become a place 'intended for those who seek administrative positions in business . . . where a systematic study of political and social relations and familiarity with scientific methods and processes are alike essential'.

The prime purpose of this widespread system of technological education was not humanitarian: it was to enable continental countries to catch up and to overtake British industry. Accordingly the polytechnics laid emphasis upon a combination of science, technology and general knowledge, suitable for men who would direct policy in industry or state enterprises. Already by 1867 this new educational system was producing gratifying results. From the *Technische Hochschulen* Germany drew her manager-technologists; from the universities she drew her industrial chemists. There was both a demand for applied scientists and an adequate supply. Meanwhile in Britain Owens College (sixteen years after its foundation) had only 116 students; the Royal School of Mines in London had fewer than twenty matriculated students; there were forty students in the laboratory of the Royal College of Chemistry; no technology (except the fortuitous course at Cambridge mentioned on p. 111) was being taught in Oxford or Cambridge; and the efforts of the Prince Consort and his advisers to establish an industrial university in London had failed. It was under these circumstances that the British public reluctantly awoke to the need for manager-technologists in Britain. This awakening coincided in time with pressure from big centres of population to have their own facilities for higher education, not solely to provide vocational training but also to give the lower middle classes opportunities for a liberal education. So it happened that seven new colleges for higher education[6] were founded at the confluence of two currents of opinion: the one local and indigenous, generated by the University Extension Movement, in favour of regional centres for liberal education to compensate for the inaccessibility of Oxford and Cambridge; the other national and imported, in favour of institutions which would do for British industry what the great polytechnics were doing for industry on the Continent. The leaders of educational thought in Britain were under the spell of Newman's lectures and Pattison's essays and Jowett's teaching. It is not surprising, therefore, that they opposed the segregation of technological education into separate institutions. The manager-technologist must receive not only a vocational training: he must enjoy also the benefits of a liberal education; or at least he must rub shoulders with students who are studying the humanities. And so, through pamphlets, speeches, resolutions at conferences, and memoranda to committees, it became accepted policy that higher technology should be incorporated (as it already had been in Scotland and London) into the new university colleges. Moreover, those were the days when neither governments nor benefactors could easily be convinced that the lower middle classes needed the cultural benefits of higher education; and so the most powerful argument for the new university colleges was one based on their utilitarian value.[7] It was natural, therefore, that technology should be one of the subjects taught at the outset in the civic colleges. From Scotland, London and the industrial cities the teaching of higher technology spread to the older English universities, and ultimately became an integral part of the university curriculum.

Technology entered the British universities partly through a chance encounter of history and partly through the deep conviction among leaders of educational thought that scientific and technological education should not be separated from liberal studies. On the Continent the phase of founding new universities was over before the need for higher technological education arose; in Britain the phase of founding new universities (by way of university colleges teaching for degrees of the University of London) coincided with the need for higher technological education. On the Continent, universities were not sympathetic to the constraints of vocational education, except in the traditional professions already established in universities; in Britain

6. Birmingham (1880), Bristol (1876), Leeds (1874), Liverpool (1881), Newcastle (1871), Nottingham (1881) and Sheffield (1879). The circumstances of their origin are well described by Armytage (1953). This book contains the best account there is of the origin of modern British universities.

7. This argument was less persuasive in Wales. In Aberystwyth and Bangor it was the idea of a university as a place for liberal education which aroused public support (see Evans, 1953).

there was a strong utilitarian bias among the founders of university colleges, mellowed by a respect and attachment to the ideals for which Oxford and Cambridge stood.

It is, therefore, more than three generations since the decision was made to include technology in the university curriculum and not to create polytechnics on the continental model. But state support for higher technology in universities lagged far behind this decision. In 1865 the total parliamentary vote for science and technology 'for the Middle and Upper Classes, exclusive of the cost of the Queen's Colleges, Ireland', was £4812 8s. 8d., distributed among the four Scottish universities and the University of London (*Report of the Select Committee on Scientific Instruction*, p. 462). In 1889–90 the state accepted financial responsibility for technical education, local authorities were empowered to set up and to finance technical colleges, and the Science and Art Department was made the central authority for technical instruction. But this legislation worked mainly for the benefit of technical education at sub-university level; it did not confer much benefit on higher technological education. It has required more than sixty years of pamphleteering and propaganda, reinforced by the anxieties of two world wars and the fear of foreign economic competition, to persuade British parliaments to take full financial responsibility for teaching and research in higher technology. The first block grants to civic university colleges were made in 1889 (the total sum distributed was £15,000). Since then – within the lifetime of one man – parliamentary grants to British universities have increased two thousandfold. Although these vastly increased grants have been administered by the University Grants Committee (and its forerunners) with exemplary enlightenment, it cannot be said that Parliament has increased the grants solely from enlightenment. Often the spur to action has been fear, beginning with the alarm expressed as long ago as 1887, that educated Germans were penetrating Britain's oriental markets, and still continuing at the time of the 'Sputnik-hysteria' of 1957. Some German educationists (Paulsen, for example, 1906) have regretted that the *Technische Hochschulen* were not integrated with the universities of Germany, and perhaps in the long run it will be to the advantage of British higher education that the patterns of Zürich and Charlottenburg and Delft were not followed in London and Glasgow and Manchester. But the British pattern sets its problems too. It was difficult enough for British universities to adapt themselves to scientific thought; it is proving much more difficult for them to adapt themselves to technological thought. For pure scientific research is akin to other kinds of scholarship: it is disinterested, pursued for its own sake, undeterred by practical considerations or popular opinion. There is no great divergence between the attitude of the physicist toward the concept of entropy and the attitude of the philosopher toward the concept of virtue. But teaching and research in technology are unashamedly tendentious, and their tendentiousness has not been mellowed (as it has for medicine and law) by centuries of tradition. Technology is of the earth, earthy; it is susceptible to pressure from industry and government departments; it is under an obligation to deliver the goods. And so the crude engineer, the mere technologist (the very adjectives are symptoms of the attitude) are tolerated in universities because the state and industry are willing to finance them. Tolerated, but not assimilated; for the traditional don is not yet willing to admit that technologists may have anything intrinsic to contribute to academic life. It is not yet taken for granted that a faculty of technology enriches a university intellectually as well as materially. The attitude of universities toward technology is still ambiguous; until the ambiguity is resolved the universities will not have adapted themselves to one of the major consequences of the scientific revolution.

References

ARMYTAGE, W. H. G. (1935), *Civic Universities*, Benn.

BAKER J. F. (1957), 'Engineering education at Cambridge' *Proceedings of the Institute of Mechanics and Engineers*.

BALFOUR, G. (1903), *The Educational Systems of Great Britain and Ireland*, 2nd edn, Clarendon Press.

CARDWELL, D. S. L. (1957), *The Organization of Science in England*, Heinemann.

EVANS, B. E. (1953), *The University of Wales: A Historical Sketch*, Cardiff.

HOLE, J. (1853), *An Essay on the History and Management of Literary, Scientific and Mechanics' Institution*, Society of Arts.

KELLY, T. (1957), *George Birkbeck: Pioneer of Adult Education*, Liverpool University Press.

PAULSEN, F. (1906), *The German Universities and University Study*, trans. F. Thilly, Longman.

PLAYFAIR, L. (1852), *Lectures on the Results of the Great Exhibition of 1851*, London.

PLAYFAIR, L. (1867), Letter to Lord Taunton, *J. Royal Society of Arts*, vol. 15, p. 477.

ROYAL COMMISSION ON SCIENTIFIC INSTRUCTION AND THE ADVANCEMENT OF SCIENCE (1875), Sixth Report, p. 10.

SOCIETY OF ARTS (1868), Report on Technical Education, *J. Royal Society of Arts*, vol. 16.

8 J. D. Bernal

Science and Industry in the Nineteenth Century

Excerpts from J. D. Bernal, *Science and Industry in the Nineteenth Century*,
Routledge & Kegan Paul, 1953, ch. 1, pp. 3–37.

We who live in an age where science is recognized as a means of life or death, cannot fail to see all around us the consequences and even the instruments of science. That very fact, however, makes it extremely difficult to disentangle science from the social and economic factors with which it is entwined. Scientists themselves are at a loss to know how far their responsibility extends into the consequences for good or evil of discoveries and applications often made more collectively than individually. There is no recognized means of assessing the amount of a community's resources that should go to science, how it should be apportioned or indeed whether the whole matter should not be left to chance, as it has been so largely in the past.

These are not academic questions – we need the solutions to deal with our day-to-day problems and for planning the most immediate future. Yet they can be solved only by a study which takes account of how the present grew out of the past, for science and technology are pre-eminently traditional social institutions, depending for their very existence on an accumulated stock of facts and methods to a far larger degree and far more consciously than do the arts. That is why it may be of some value to examine the relations of science and technology, or, more widely, of science and industry, in an era like the nineteenth century when those relations were simpler than they are now, but yet one not so distant that we cannot appreciate from our own experiences the significance of its main movements.

Short as has been the gap in years we are now getting far enough away from the nineteenth century to be able to see its achievements in science and technology in the wide perspective of history. Nevertheless, the task of finding the relations between them is by no means an easy one. Science is still a somewhat unfamiliar part of social life and those outside its disciplines find it hard to realize the changes that have taken place in them. Consequently, many intelligent non-scientific people still think of science as it appeared to be in the nineteenth century, as the product of individual efforts of men of genius, instead of, as it now is, a highly organized new profession closely linked with industry and government. On the other hand many scientists of today, outside the older centres of learning where the ways of the past still linger, find it difficult to grasp the uncoordinated and amateur character of nineteenth-century science with little formal teaching and without research laboratories or research funds. It is almost as difficult in an age of vast engineering and chemical factories, each furnished with its own research department, to recall the intimate traditional and practical character of the old workshops and forges from which the modern giants are descended.

In fact the nineteenth century was as different from the twentieth as it was from the eighteenth. It was above all a period of expansion – expansion of population, of manufacture, of trade and of knowledge. In their time these increases seemed unlimited, they were taken to herald the achievement of a universal Progress that was reflected in the world of nature itself by the great generalization of Evolution. All this also seemed to be a most natural, as well as desirable, state of affairs. With the advent of free-trade capitalism in the mid-century, economics was deemed to have found its true laws which the ignorance and superstitition of earlier ages had hidden from sight. By abandoning all restrictions a *laissez-faire* Liberalism would achieve the best distribution of wealth by the automatic operation of the laws of the market.

What actually happened, as we know, was very different. Far from producing peaceful progress, the nineteenth century ushered in the transitional period of upheaval and violence of the twentieth century. We can see it now as a period of material and social *preparation* for a far more radical revolution of production, distribution and government. This revolution was an implicit consequence of the great new productive forces released by the scientific and technical advances achieved in principle in the eighteenth century but first realized on a large scale in practice only in the nineteenth.

Then, for the first time, it becomes possible to deal with the relations of science and technology in such a relatively short space as a hundred years. The pace of application of scientific discovery was speeding up sufficiently for the effect of discoveries made early in the century to be appreciable by its end. The use of the electric current, discovered just before the beginning of the century, was appreciable in the telegraph in the 1850s though it was only beginning to be used as electric light and power in the 1890s. In general the industry of the nineteenth century depended on the twin scientific and technical achievement of the late eighteenth century: the development of the steam engine and the establishment of a rational, quantitative chemistry. The greatest achievements of the physical sciences of the nineteenth century – the doctrine of the conservation of energy and the interchangeability of its various forms: the sciences of thermodynamics and electrodynamics – drew their inspiration from the study of practical sources of power and arose from the needs of transport and communication. Their full utilization as the basis of a rational chemical and electrical industry had to wait till the twentieth century.

For the historian a century is necessarily a most arbitrary and often inconvenient division of time; it is doubly so when the histories of two different human activities have to be considered together. A longer or shorter period, say from 1760 to 1914 or 1820 to 1870, would have advantages in considering the history of technology, the former bridging the whole of the Industrial Revolution before the period of mass production, the latter concentrating on the characteristic nineteenth-century achievements of the railway, steamship and telegraph. In the history of science, the limits are more difficult to define at the beginning and easier at the end. The era might start with Hales and Black and the beginning of the pneumatic revolution in the mid-eighteenth century or, alternatively, considering that revolution as already complete, with 1831, the year of the foundation of the British Association and the discovery of electromagnetic induction by Faraday. The end of the era is definite enough, at least for physical science, because it is marked by a breakthrough to a new and unsuspected realm of experience. This was the discovery of X-rays by Röntgen in 1895, followed almost immediately by that of the electron and radioactivity and leading to the theory of atomic structure, the central feature of twentieth-century science. The choice taken here is to limit the century in the beginning by a social fact, the outbreak of the French Revolution in 1789, and to end it by 1895, a date fixed for scientific reasons which roughly coincides with a turning-point in the development of capitalism when the division of the world into empires was completed and preparation for a new era of wars was consciously beginning. These limitations of time will not preclude a certain casting backward for origins or looking forward for consequences.

The aim of this essay is to bring out by the study of actual examples the close and necessary connections between technical developments and the advance of scientific knowledge. These connections are not limited to any period of history but have a critical importance in the nineteenth century.[1]

1. This was evident enough to far-sighted men of the time, especially to those who could see below the surface of the chaos of apparently unrelated discoveries and inventions. In 1844, almost at the outset of their career, Marx and Engels, attacking Feuerbach's idealist picture of mental progress, were writing: '... the celebrated "unity of man with nature" has always existed in industry and has existed in varying forms in every epoch according to the lesser or greater development of industry, just like the "struggle" of man with nature, right up to the development of his productive powers in a corresponding basis. Industry and commerce, production and the exchange of the necessities of life, themselves determine distribution, the structure of the different social classes and are, in turn, determined by these as to the mode in which they are carried on; and so it happens that in Manchester, for instance, Feuerbach sees only factories and machines where a hundred years ago only spinning-wheels and weaving-looms were to be seen, or in the Campagna of Rome he finds only pasture lands and swamps, where in the time of Augustus he would have found nothing but the vineyards and villas of Roman capitalists. Feuerbach speaks in particular of the

Before the Industrial Revolution, science had been an affair of courts, gentlemen and scholars, and except for the arts of navigation and war it hardly affected ordinary life. The idea that it could do so was a vision enthusiastically acclaimed but as often derided. By the twentieth century, on the other hand, the interrelations of science and technique were consciously recognized. Whether constructive or destructive ends were in view there could be no doubt that the means employed for the advancement of techniques must be scientific. The transition between the dream and the reality was effected in the nineteenth century and it is therefore specially important to inquire how and why it occurred.

Before attempting to analyse in some detail the connections between the scientific and technical developments of the nineteenth century it is useful to give a general summary of the main trends which revealed themselves in science and technology separately.

Each field, the technical as much as the scientific, has its own inner coherence, not only in the logical unfolding of new discoveries on the basis of older researches and in the making of new inventions drawing on older technical advances, but also in their being in the hands of two largely distinct sets of men, the scientists and the engineers. At the beginning of the century the personal interaction was greatest, the engineers and scientists were the same men or were close friends, but the state of the sciences themselves provided only certain limited bridges between theory and practice. On the other hand towards its end the scientists and engineers, incorporated in their distinct societies and institutions, had drawn further apart, but by then the advance of science had made its intervention into techniques possible and indeed necessary over a large part of the field, while conversely the problems, the equipment and, not least, the funds of science were provided by industry.

The main lines of scientific advance

In science, the nineteenth century was the great period of specialization, as witness the formation of the separate scientific societies to supplement the older general academies such as the Royal Society. Each discipline followed

---

perception of natural science, he mentions secrets which are disclosed only to the eye of the physicist and chemist: but where would natural science be without industry and commerce? Even this "pure" natural science is provided with an aim, as with its material, only through trade and industry, through the sensuous activity of men. So much is this activity, this unceasing sensuous labour and creation, this production, the basis of the whole sensuous world as it now exists, that, were it interrupted only for a year, Feuerbach would not only find an enormous change in the natural world, but would very soon find that the whole world of men and his own perceptive faculty, nay his own existence, were missing' (Marx and Engels, 1938, p. 36).

its own line of development, they were not yet ready for the general unification of the sciences which is the major task of the twentieth century. Such unification as occurred lay inside each science; in physics with the great generalization of the electromagnetic theory of light; in chemistry with the union of organic and inorganic through the theory of valency. Both were achieved only towards the end of the century and both seemed to indicate a finality that was soon to prove illusory. [. . .]

The main lines of technological advance

The technical developments of the nineteenth century brought about a complete transformation of the manner of life of hundreds of millions of people in countries dominated by industrial production and mechanized agriculture, and notably affected the conditions of all the remaining population of the world.[2] Nevertheless, it is principally in *quantity* that the technical transformation of the nineteenth century was remarkable; in *quality* it was much less so. The basic invention of the Industrial Revolution – the use of power-driven machinery to take the place of handicraft – had already been achieved in the eighteenth century. What happened in the nineteenth was its enormous extension, together with a steady increase in its cheapness and efficiency.

At the outset the new technical developments were highly localized. The Industrial Revolution itself had been largely limited to Britain and even to a very small part of Britain, to the half-dozen areas where coal had been available as a cheap fuel. Though its products were spread throughout the world with unprecedented speed, the methods of production, the pattern of the factory system, established itself but slowly in other areas. By the end of the century the only centres that rivalled Britain were those based on the coalfields of Pennsylvania and the Ruhr. Consequently, the pace of technical development in most traditional fields of industry was set by Britain. This remains broadly true even for the new chemical and electrical industries which later flourished in America and Germany because, at least in the nineteenth century, they still operated in a field dominated by the older industries.

To understand the pattern of technical advance it is therefore necessary, in the first place, to consider the conditions which determined it in Britain. In a bourgeois society – and Britain was the bourgeois society *par excellence* throughout the whole century – not only the day-to-day existence of technology, but its year-to-year change was determined by what profits it could

2. Out of the total estimated world population in 1901 of 1608 million, some 290 million were to be found in the countries of Britain, France, Germany, Austro-Hungary, Italy, Holland and Belgium, all of which were markedly affected by industrialization, while 600 million lived under their direct colonial control and the remaining countries, including Russia and China, were commercially dominated by them.

show which in turn depended on the state of the market. Now the great feature of nineteenth-century Britain was the rapid growth of the market, however uneven that growth was. The very cheapness of even the earlier crude machine-made goods ensured a general increase in profitable production. Exports, first of consumption goods, largely textiles, and later of production goods, largely steel and machinery, went on increasing and brought with them a corresponding increase in imports of luxuries, of raw materials and finally of food for the ever-increasing industrial population.

The pattern of production was already set – it lay in exploiting the greatest early success of the Industrial Revolution – the new machine-made textiles. There seemed even little need to make radical improvements in spinning and weaving methods – merely to increase their scale was sufficient. The production of cotton cloth had increased from forty million yards in 1785 to 6500 million yards in 1887.[3] Such a phenomenal growth would by itself imply a proportionate increase in machinery, raw materials and ancillary processes such as bleaching and dyeing. Accompanied as it was by other developments in all fields of manufacturing industry it meant a scale of demand for raw materials and products that traditional methods of production could not supply and so still further forced the pace of mechanization. In themselves, the mechanical requirements of manufacture made little demand on science, though, as will be shown, the steam engine and the machine-building industry did so. It was rather the problem of providing the necessary, though relatively small-scale, ancillaries, particularly the chemical ones, such as dyes and soaps, to replace natural products, which had become too scarce and too dear, that provoked scientific solutions.[4] The chemical industry grew up largely under the shadow of the textile industry, while the gas industry found its earliest customers in the new mills and was later in return to provide the materials for the new coal-tar dyes. Machine production needed power; power meant steam, and steam called for coal and iron. The expansion of manufactures also placed a premium on rapid and cheap transportation and assured the success of the railways and the steamers.

The railway age

Cheap coal, the new universal fuel, and cheap iron, the new universal material, now both finally replacing wood in its cruder uses, are charac-

3. From then on the rate of increase of British – though not of world – production slackened, roughly comparable figures being 8000 in 1912, the peak year, and then production itself actually fell to 3600 in 1937 and 2100 in 1950.

4. An admirable and detailed account of how this occurred in Britain, and particularly in North Britain, in the eighteenth and early nineteenth century has recently been produced by Clow and Clow (1952).

teristic of nineteenth-century industry. The production of coal went up by fifteen times – from about 10 to 150 million tons – in the century between 1780 and 1880, a great advance though only a tenth as great as the increase in output of cloth. The increased output of iron, 110 times from 68,000 to 7,750,000 tons, however, almost kept pace with that of cloth in the same period. Both coal and iron were bulky goods needed in enormous quantities and the cost of moving them tied industry largely down to the coalfields. All through the century the steam engine and the factory chimney remained the symbols of the grimy, formless, gas-lit cities of the first industrial age. Nevertheless, it was this urgent need for heavy transport that gave rise to the greatest and most characteristic innovation of the nineteenth century – the railway.

The railway came straight out of the coalmines themselves, where rails had been used at least as far back as the fifteenth century. It was the convenience of running the trucks carrying the sea coal of Newcastle down to the staithes for loading on ships that led stage by stage to radical inprovements. It was these improvements – first iron rails, then stationary engines, and finally locomotive engines – that emancipated the railway from the mine and sent it, carrying goods and passengers, first over Britain and then over the world.

What the locomotive did for land transport, the steam-boat had already been doing for some years for the cheaper water transport, and with a far wider range, especially when, with the advent of steel, the ocean-going steamer was able to supplant the sailing ship. By these means the products of the new factories were enabled to undersell and ruin native industries all over the world, and to turn undeveloped countries into virtual or actual plantations supplying raw materials for industry. Towards the end of the century this type of trade was increasing, supplemented by an export of capital goods, largely rails and mining machinery, which facilitated the collection of agricultural products and ores over a still larger area, and was balanced by an increasing import of food.

The great transport revolution of the nineteenth century owed relatively little directly to science.[5] The first railway engineers were largely self-taught men, though few had as hard a struggle as George Stephenson. It did,

5. Charles Babbage seems to have been one of the few who interested themselves scientifically in its working. In 1838 he fitted up – at his own cost, £300 – a second-class carriage where he installed a self-recording apparatus measuring both the tractive force and the components of vibration of the carriage. With this he made extensive measurements – not without danger – for five months on the new Great Western line of whose broad gauge he was an enthusiastic supporter. In this example of operational research, as in his computing machine, he was a hundred years ahead of his time (1864). Samuel Smiles and, curiously enough, Herbert Spencer were also connected with the early railways but they made no notable scientific contribution to them.

however, serve to stimulate and facilitate science in a number of different ways, particularly in geology and surveying at home and geography and biology abroad. Indeed, the great generalization of evolution was given its impetus largely as the result of the voyages of Darwin, Wallace and Huxley.

With transport went communication. The telegraph – the first practical application of the new electrical knowledge – followed the spread of the railways and was, within a few decades, to link the continents by submarine cables. Through these inventions the whole world could become one great market, in which the powers of business and finance could operate without the old limitations of space or time. Here, certainly, was a direct case of science leading industry – a small industry to be sure, but almost from the start a necessary one. And the electrical industry grew, rather more slowly than it might have done technically, as will be shown, but steadily. Towards the end of the century, the telegraph was to lead directly to the telephone, and at its very end to the wireless telegraph, the first opening of a new age of communication. The development of the telegraph provided a nursery for the young science of electromagnetism, supplying problems, part-time occupation, equipment and funds for the academic scientists and ensuring them plenty of students.

The telegraph and cable industries were also to be the source of the new electric light, traction and power industries of the 1880s and 1890s. This development, however, took the best part of half a century to realize and the reasons for the lag is one of the main questions that will be examined in the latter part of this book.

The metal industry

The great manufacturing and commercial effort of the nineteenth century could never have come into being or grown as it did, without a parallel and intense development of the old metal industries and the new industry of engineering. The needs of the new industry could not be satisfied in quantity or performance by the old universal material, wood. Wood was in fact used more than ever before, but it did not go far enough and it had not the strength for the new needs of machinery or structures. By the middle of the century cast and wrought iron had replaced wood for most machinery and was beginning to replace wood for ships and stone for bridges.

The basic inventions of the coal-fired blast furnace and of puddling and rolling had been made in the eighteenth century. They were not radically improved throughout most of the nineteenth century with the exception of the introduction of hot blast by the gas engineer J. B. Neilson in 1828.[6]

6. This development was a striking early example of the direct influence of science on an industry normally resistant to it. J. B. Neilson was not an ironmaster himself but his father had been a works engineer at one of Dr Roebuck's collieries. He became

They were, however, enormously extended, increased in scale of operation and improved in hundreds of minor ways. These changes, moreover, were largely technical, the fruits of the experience of observant iron-workers and ironmasters. The subject was largely a closed book to science. It was very different with the great revolution in metal production that occurred in the second half of the century and ushered in the age of steel. This was largely due to the entry of science – amateur in the case of Bessemer, more professional with Siemens and Gilchrist – into a traditional industry. For that reason, I have chosen it as the theme for a later chapter. The cheap steel that science thus brought in, a far stronger and more adaptable material than iron, provided and still provides the main material basis for a mechanical civilization.

Engineering

Throughout the nineteenth century the metal industry grew up with and fed an ever-expanding and diversifying machine-building and engineering industry. The nucleus of that industry had been formed in the eighteenth century through a blend of the traditions of heavy, and usually rough, construction of the smith and millwright with those of the fine workmanship of the clockmaker and instrument maker, itself an offshoot of the age-old goldsmiths' craft and allied with science since its inception in the Renaissance. Watt, trained as an instrument maker and turning himself into the first professional engine maker, may stand as the prototype of the new mathematical technical profession, while his partnership with the practical manufacturer Boulton in 1775 marked the foundation of the first engineering firm. The new industry had to find its own technicians and workers, who trained themselves as they produced the new machines. It was only by the 1820s that the next generation of men like George Stephenson, born and bred with engines, began to make themselves felt.

The aim of the industry was the production and multifarious use of power – the new power of the steam engine. The means to realize it were the development of strength in materials, and design and precision in workmanship. In its pursuit of power the new engineering industry did not so much depend on science as create it. The successive developments of the

first foreman and then manager of the new Glasgow Gas Works and picked up the necessary chemistry at the Andersonian Institution, Glasgow. This first working-class technical institute was founded in 1793 through a legacy from Dr John Anderson, the republican Professor of Natural Philosophy at the University. Its first principal was Dr Birkbeck who was later to light the lamp of higher education in London. In 1824 James Ewing, the ironmaster of Muirkirk, asked Neilson whether the variations in the yield of his furnaces could be suppressed by purifying the air used to blow them. Neilson had the ingenious idea of using the newly established principles of expansion of gases to increase the volume, and hence the speed, of the blast by heating.

steam engine – separate condenser, expansive working, compound cylinders – right down to the steam turbine at the end of the century were essentially successive essays in thermodynamics solved in practice before they were solved in theory. In Chapter 2 of the original book will be found a discussion of how the great generalizations of nineteenth-century physics, the conservation of energy and the limits of its utilization – the first and second laws of thermodynamics – arose out of attempts to understand and improve the performance of prime movers, predominantly of the steam engine.

On the side of metal working and of mechanisms, progress owed even less to science. The creators of modern machine tools – the great succession of Bramah, Maudslay, Whitworth, Roberts, Muir, Clements – all started as manual workers. They achieved, through an application of simple geometry and a deep experience of the behaviour of materials under stress, a steady improvement in accuracy and reproducibility of work. Not only did they learn how to work metal on a scale even larger than wood, but also they achieved a precision that wood could never have given.

The new accuracy was not merely pride in good craftsmanship. Left to itself that leads to beauty of form and ornament as is evident in the products of the seventeenth and eighteenth century. The working requirements of the new machines were for screws that would not work loose, for plane slides, for well-fitting pistons in accurately bored cylinders, and for wheels that must spin true. This imposed a new kind of craftsmanship, one where work was done from drawings, implying a deep understanding of three-dimensional geometry. The new engineer had in one way or another to acquire the rudiments of a scientific education. In his production fancy must be subservient to work and a new kind of beauty was created, one that appealed visually only to the initiated.

The new ability to machine metal accurately in turn made possible the series production of identical parts that could later be assembled. The impetus for this came first from America, where there was a shortage of skilled labour, with the elder Brunel, Eli Whitney and Colt. This method of manufacture started with small arms but was later to make possible the great labour-saving mechanisms of the sewing-machine, the typewriter, and the reaper and binder. But the full, logical development towards mass production by the adding of the mobile assembly line had, despite pioneer efforts in the pig slaughterhouses and in the box-car assembly in America, to wait till the twentieth century with the relatively enormous market offered by the motor car.

The multiple machines of the nineteenth century, outside the pioneer industry of textiles, notably those in the printing trade, were the fruit of much ingenuity but relied little on science and gave little back to it. The typical inventor was usually a workman or amateur who contrived to find the most convenient arrangement of wheels, rollers, cogs and levers designed to imitate the movement of the craftsman at higher speed and using steam power. The more flexible arrangements using electricity were scarcely available until well into the twentieth century.

Where the practical mechanics broke radically new ground was in the devising of machinery using forces greater than man could wield. Bramah's hydraulic press and Nasmyth's[7] steamhammer made heavy engineering possible, as the need for engines for steamers and later of guns and armour plate for battleships made it profitable. It was this development, which came in with cheap steel towards the last quarter of the century, that gave over-whelming advantages to the handful of big firms in Britain, Germany, France and America which alone could undertake this work and were the progenitors of the trusts and cartels of our time. They were even sufficiently wealthy to finance some research of their own, notably that of the steam turbine. Nevertheless, as will be shown in later chapters, the general tendency in engineering industry was to separate itself as an independent profession from the general trends of academic science. The eighteenth- and early nineteenth-century engineers, men like Smeaton, Watt and Rankine, were in the forefront of the science of their day; their successors, however eminent and successful as engineers, did not, with few exceptions like Sir Charles Parsons, contribute notably to the advance of science.

The chemical industry

It was not until the second half of the century, and only markedly so at its close, that a new and important industry – the heavy chemical industry – began to take its place beside the traditional industries. It was not based to the same extent as the electrical industry on academic science, but it tended to draw on it more and more as the century advanced, not only for improve-ments in technique but also for large-scale processes derived from laboratory experiments.

The chemical industry started and remained for most of the century largely ancillary to the textile industry. It started from the need to supply acid, alkali and soap on a scale with which the old semi-domestic chemical industry could not cope. In 1785 the first great purely scientific addition was

7. James Nasmyth is an apparent exception to the rule that early nineteenth-century engineers started as mechanics. He was the son of a respected portrait painter of Edinburgh, himself descended through a long line of master builders from the eponymous Naesmyth who won his lands in the fight against the Douglas in the thir-teenth century. His father, however, was familiar with many of the engineers of the day and young James showed an early passion for practical design and construction that won him instant employment as an assistant and not apprentice in Maudslay's shop.

made with the introduction of bleaching by chlorine and bleaching powder. By the middle of the century it was adding dyes and the beginnings of plastics with mercerization and celluloid. The first big independent development came with the discovery of the explosive properties of nitrated cotton and glycerine. This was to lead to the creation of a new explosive industry, with dynamite and cordite appropriate to the new era of mining exploitation and for the wars that were soon to come.

Because of the close and evident links between the chemical industry and the advance of chemical science from the time of the great chemical revolution there is no need here to demonstrate their interdependence. The problem is rather to unravel the closely intertwined strands of practical and theoretical considerations that led to the advance of both. The chemical factory could indeed never be far away from the laboratory where its processes had been first elaborated and in which they could be modified or superseded. In a later chapter an account will be given of examples of that interaction. It will suffice here to stress the fact that in this industry, no less than in electricity, there still remained, despite multiple links, a long lag between the laboratory and the works, and that, however scientific the principles used, the actual handling of materials in chemical factories often owed more to tradition and skill than to scientific design and operation.

Traditional methods could not cope with the enormous demands of the new industrial populations. Larger scale methods had to be found for brewing, distilling and preserving, and this opened a loophole for science, especially where new methods, such as canning and refrigeration, became technically possible. Some of the problems which affected the older science of physics and chemistry as well as the newly created science of bacteriology, are discussed in a later chapter.

Agriculture and medicine

It is not within the scope of this essay to discuss, except incidentally, the influence of the more purely biological industry – agriculture – on the progress of science as a whole. Its effects were naturally most profound on the development of biology itself, particularly in its contribution, through Darwin, to the great generalization of evolution. Nor is it within my province to discuss fully the mutual stimulation of the great art and profession of medicine and the sciences of human and animal biology, though the chemical controversy between Liebig and Pasteur discussed in Chapter 3 of the original book inevitably touches on this. I mention them here only to complete the picture of practical human activities, so as to avoid the impression that the external impetus to science in the nineteenth century came only from the predominantly physical and chemical industries.

Economic features of nineteenth-century industry

Taken in all, the enormous technical developments of the nineteenth century were aimed at achieving old-established ends by new means. To some extent this was a necessary transitional stage before the new forces, which the Industrial Revolution had liberated, could be sufficiently understood and mastered to enable new ends to be envisaged and achieved. To an even greater extent, however, it was due to the dominance throughout the whole century of a market economy concerned essentially with producing the goods that were in known demand but producing them in far larger quantities and making a far larger profit than the old handicraft industries could manage. The advantages of enormously more efficient methods of production did not accrue to the great bulk of the population of the industrial countries and still less to those in their colonial dependencies. It was largely divested from them by the operation of an unjust, unstable and wasteful economic system. The new goods involved the use of far less labour per unit of manufacture but the ingenuity that had been devoted to production had concentrated on cheapness rather than quality or serviceability. Still less was there, or could there be, an attempt to meet the real need of people by designing these objects or devices for this purpose – they were produced for profit rather than use.

Production for profit was the great motive force that had stimulated the Industrial Revolution into being. The force that continually modified production was the need to use part of that profit as further capital investment. The pressure of competition did lead to more efficient and therefore more profitable techniques – though in a very irregular way, as will be shown in later chapters – and it was here the services of science were mostly in demand. It would be more true to say that it was here that science could insinuate itself, for one leading characteristic of the chase for profit was its blindness – a blindness not concealed but even praised by the dominant advocates of *laissez-faire*.

Though free competition was still the watchword, in the latter part of the century it tended to give way to price rings, cartels and monopolies. The early successes of the new industries were making capital harder and harder to invest profitably at home. Alternative investments were found in the opening up of colonial territories and in the war preparations due to the resulting rivalries between the great powers. These could only be negotiated in larger units than the old individual entrepreneur or family firm could command. Large-scale monopoly industries did not achieve their full development till the twentieth century, but already before the end of the nineteenth the most rapidly advancing fields of technique, and consequently of science, were those in the purview of the great telegraph companies, chemical companies, steel companies and armament firms. The era of the industrial and government research laboratories, where science was organized and directed to particular ends, was just about to begin.

Relations between science and industry

The broad outlines of the development of science and of industry throughout the nineteenth century already show something of the character of the most general connections between them. Two main complementary trends are evident. On the one hand we have the scientific study of already established industrial processes, such as the use of steam engines or the making of iron, which lead to new scientific generalizations, such as the conservation of energy or radiation physics; on the other we have scientific discoveries, particularly in electricity and chemistry, that give rise to new industries such as the telegraph and synthetic dyes. These relations, now easy to recognize, were not so easily grasped at the time. Despite much lip service to the mutual dependence of science and industry the anarchic development of industry made it virtually impossible for the links between science and industry to have any rational or planned basis. Indeed, as will be shown, they were of an even more casual and individual character than those between the various branches of industry. While it was generally admitted that the age of science had arrived, little or no provision was made until the very end of the century for the development of science itself, let alone its application to practical purposes. Nevertheless it was possible for individual scientists, alone or in conjunction with far-sighted businessmen, to study some of the problems of industry and to propose solutions, some of which, though usually after a considerable lapse of time, became embodied in practice.

References

BABBAGE, C. (1864), *Passages from the Life of a Philosopher*, Longman.
CLOW, A., and CLOW, N. (1952), *The Chemical Revolution*, Batchworth.
MARX, K., and ENGELS, F. (1938), *The German Ideology*, Lawrence & Wishart.

9 J. K. Galbraith

(a) The Imperatives of Technology

J. K. Galbraith, *The New Industrial State*, Hamish Hamilton, 1971, ch. 2, pp. 11–21, 2nd edn.

On 16 June 1903, after some months of preparation which included negotiation of contracts for various components, the Ford Motor Company was formed for the manufacture of automobiles. Production was to be whatever number could be sold. The first car reached the market that October. The firm had an authorized capital of $150,000. However, only $100,000 worth of stock was issued, and only $28,500 of this was for cash. Although it does not bear on the present discussion, the company made a handsome profit that year and did not fail to do so for many years thereafter. Employment in 1903 averaged 125 men (Nevins, 1954, p. 220 and appendix).

In the spring of 1964, the Ford Motor Company introduced what is now called a new automobile. In accordance with current fashion in automobile nomenclature, it was called, one trusts inappropriately, a Mustang. The public was well prepared for the new vehicle. Plans carefully specified prospective output and sales; they erred, as plans do, and in this case by being too modest. These preparations required three and a half years. From late in the autumn of 1962, when the design was settled, until the spring of 1964, there was a fairly firm commitment to the particular car that eventually emerged. Engineering and 'styling' costs were nine million dollars; the cost of tooling up for the production of the Mustang was fifty million dollars.[1] In 1964 employment in the Ford Motor Company averaged 317,000. Assets were approximately six billion dollars (*Fortune*, 1964).

Virtually all of the effects of increased use of technology are revealed by these comparisons. We may pass them in preliminary review.

Technology means the systematic application of scientific or other organized knowledge to practical tasks. Its most important consequence, at least

1. I am grateful to Mr Walter T. Murphy of the Ford Motor Company for providing these details. In this and subsequent chapters, I have also drawn on earlier help of Robert McNamara which he gave when he was still an executive of Ford. I wish here, at the outset, not only to concede but to emphasize that one may have planning without precision of result and that there will also be occasional failures. Accordingly, to cite a failure – another Ford creation, the Edsel, comes automatically to the mind of the more impulsive critics – is not to disprove this argument.

for purposes of economics, is in forcing the division and subdivision of any such task into its component parts. Thus, and only thus, can organized knowledge be brought to bear on performance.

Specifically, there is no way that organized knowledge can be brought to bear on the production of an automobile as a whole or even on the manufacture of a body or chassis. It can only be applied if the task is so subdivided that it begins to be coterminous with some established area of scientific or engineering knowledge. Though metallurigical knowledge cannot be applied to the manufacture of the whole vehicle, it can be used in the design of the cooling system or the engine block. While knowledge of mechanical engineering cannot be brought to bear on the manufacture of the vehicle, it can be applied to the machining of the crankshaft. While chemistry cannot be applied to the composition of the car as a whole, it can be used to decide on the composition of the finish or trim.

Nor do matters stop here. Metallurgical knowledge is brought to bear not on steel but on the characteristics of special steels for particular functions, and chemistry not on paints or plastics but on particular molecular structures and their rearrangement as required.[2]

Nearly all of the consequences of technology, and much of the shape of modern industry, derive from this need to divide and subdivide tasks and from the further need to bring knowledge to bear on these fractions and from the final need to combine the finished elements of the task into the finished product as a whole. Six consequences are of immediate importance.

First. An increasing span of time separates the beginning from the completion of any task. Knowledge is brought to bear on the ultimate microfraction of the task; then on that in combination with some other fraction; then on some further combination and thus on to final completion. The process stretches back in time as the root system of a plant goes down into the ground. The longest of the filaments determines the total time required in production. The more thoroughgoing the application of technology – in common or at least frequent language, the more sophisticated the pro-

2. The notion of division of labor, an old one in economics, is a rudimentary and partial application of the ideas here outlined. As one breaks down a mechanical operation, such as the manufacture of Adam Smith's immortal pins, it resolves itself into simpler and simpler movements as in putting the head or the point on the pin. This is the same as saying that the problem is susceptible to increasingly homogeneous mechanical knowledge.

However, the subdivision of tasks to accord with area of organized knowledge is not confined to, nor has it any special relevance to, mechanical processes. It occurs in medicine, business management, building design, child and dog rearing and every other problem that involves an agglomerate of scientific knowledge.

duction process – the farther back the application of knowledge will be carried. The longer, accordingly, will be the time between the initiation and completion of the task.

The manufacture of the first Ford was not an exacting process. Metallurgy was an academic concept. Ordinary steels were used that could be obtained from the warehouse in the morning and shaped that afternoon. In consequence, the span of time between initiation and completion of a car was very slight.

The provision of steel for the modern vehicle, in contrast, reaches back to specifications prepared by the designers or the laboratory, and proceeds through orders to the steel mill, parallel provision for the appropriate metal-working machinery, delivery, testing and use.

Second. There is an increase in the capital that is committed to production aside from that occasioned by increased output. The increased time, and therewith the increased investment in goods in process, costs money. So does the knowledge which is applied to the various elements of the task. The application of knowledge to an element of a manufacturing problem will also typically involve the development of a machine for performing the function. (The word technology brings to mind machines; this is not surprising for machinery is one of its most visible manifestations.) This too involves investment as does equipment for integrating the various elements of the task into the final product.

The investment in making the original Ford was larger than the $28,500 paid in, for some of it was in the plant, inventory and machinery of those who, like the Dodge Brothers, supplied the components. But investment in the factory itself was infinitesimal. Materials and parts were there only briefly; no expensive specialists gave them attention; only elementary machinery was used to assemble them into the car. It helped that the frame of the car could be lifted by two men.

Third. With increasing technology the commitment of time and money tends to be made ever more inflexibly to the performance of a particular task. That task must be precisely defined before it is divided and subdivided into its component parts. Knowledge and equipment are then brought to bear on these fractions and they are useful only for the task as it was initially defined. If that task is changed, new knowledge and new equipment will have to be brought to bear.

Little thought needed to be given to the Dodge Brothers' machine shop, which made the engine and chassis of the original Ford, as an instrument for automobile manufacture. It was unspecialized as to task. It could have worked as well on bicycles, steam engines or carriage gear and, indeed, had been so employed. Had Ford and his associates decided, at any point, to shift from gasoline to steam power, the machine shop could have accommodated itself to the change in a few hours.

By contrast all parts of the Mustang, the tools and equipment that worked on these parts, and the steel and other materials going into these parts were designed to serve efficiently their ultimate function. They could serve only that function. Were the car appreciably altered, were it instead of a Mustang a Barracuda or possibly a Serpent, Scorpion or Roach, as one day with decent imagination there will be, much of this work would have had to be redone. Thus the firm commitment to this particular vehicle for some eighteen months prior to its appearance.

Fourth. Technology requires specialized manpower. This will be evident. Organized knowledge can be brought to bear, not surprisingly, only by those who possess it. However, technology does not make the only claim on manpower; planning, to be mentioned in a moment, also requires a comparatively high level of specialized talent. To foresee the future in all its dimensions and to design the appropriate action does not necessarily require high scientific qualification. It does require ability to organize and employ information, or capacity to react intuitively to relevant experience.

These requirements do not necessarily reflect, on some absolute scale, a higher order of talent than was required in a less technically advanced era. The makers of the original Ford were men of talent. The Dodge Brothers had previously invented a bicycle and a steam launch. Their machine shop made a wide variety of products, and Detroit legend also celebrated their imaginative exuberance when drunk. Alexander Malcolmson, who was Ford's immediate partner in getting the business under way, was a successful coal merchant. James Couzens, who may well have had more to do with the success of the enterprise than Henry Ford,[3] had a background in railroading and the coal business and went on from Ford to be Police Commissioner and Mayor of Detroit, Republican Senator from Michigan and an undeviating supporter of Franklin D. Roosevelt. Not all of the present Ford organization would claim as much reach. But its members do have a considerably deeper knowledge of the more specialized matters for which they are severally responsible.

Fifth. The inevitable counterpart of specialization is organization. This is what brings the work of specialists to a coherent result. If there are many specialists, this coordination will be a major task. So complex, indeed, will be the job of organizing specialists that there will be specialists on organ-

3. A case I have argued elsewhere (Galbraith, 1960, p. 141).

ization. More even than machinery, massive and complex business organizations are the tangible manifestations of advanced technology.

Sixth. From the time and capital that must be committed, the inflexibility of this commitment, the needs of large organization and the problems of market performance under conditions of advanced technology, comes the necessity for planning. Tasks must be performed so that they are right not for the present but for that time in the future when, companion and related work having also been done, the whole job is completed. And the amount of capital that, meanwhile, will have been committed adds urgency to this need to be right. So conditions at the time of completion of the whole task must be foreseen as must developments along the way. And steps must be taken to prevent, offset or otherwise neutralize the effect of adverse developments, and to ensure that what is ultimately foreseen eventuates in fact.

In the early days of Ford, the future was very near at hand. Only days elapsed between the commitment of machinery and materials to production and their appearance as a car. If the future is near at hand, it can be assumed that it will be very much like the present. If the car did not meet the approval of the customers, it could quickly be changed. The briefness of the time in process allowed this; so did the unspecialized character of manpower, materials and machinery.

Changes were needed. The earliest cars, as they came on the market, did not meet with complete customer approval: there were complaints that the cooling system did not cool, the brakes did not brake, the carburettor did not feed fuel to the engine, and a Los Angeles dealer reported the disconcerting discovery that, when steered, 'Front wheels turn wrong' (Nevins, 1954, p. 248). These defects were promptly remedied. They did the reputation of the car no lasting harm.

Such shortcomings in the Mustang would have been unpleasant. And they would have been subject to no such quick, simple and inexpensive remedy. The machinery, materials, manpower and components of the original Ford, being all unspecialized, could be quickly procured on the open market. Accordingly, there was no need to anticipate possible shortage of these requirements and take steps to prevent them. For the more highly specialized requirements of the Mustang, foresight and associated action were indispensable. In Detroit, when the first Ford was projected, anything on wheels that was connected with a motor was assured of acceptance. Acceptance of the Mustang could not be so assumed. The prospect had to be carefully appraised. And customers had to be carefully conditioned to want this blessing. Thus the need for planning.

The more sophisticated the technology, the greater, in general, will be all of the foregoing requirements. This will be true of simple products as they come to be produced by more refined processes or as they develop imaginative containers or unopenable packaging. With very intricate technology such as that associated with modern weapons and weaponry, there will be a quantum change in these requirements. This will be especially so if, as under modern peacetime conditions, cost and time are not decisive considerations.

Thus when Philip II settled on the redemption of England at the end of March 1587, he was not unduly troubled by the seemingly serious circumstance that Spain had no navy. Some men-of-war were available from newly conquered Portugal but, in the main, merchant ships would suffice.[4] A navy, in other words, could then be bought in the market. Nor was the destruction of a large number of the available ships by Drake at Cadiz three weeks later a fatal blow. Despite what historians have usually described as unconscionable inefficiency, the Armada sailed in a strength of 130 ships a little over a year later on 18 May 1588. The cost, though considerable, was well within the resources of the Empire. Matters did not change greatly in the next three hundred years. The *Victory*, from which Nelson called Englishmen to their duty at Trafalgar, though an excellent fighting ship, was a full forty years old at the time. The exiguous flying machines of the First World War, built only to carry a man or two and a weapon, were designed and put in combat in a matter of months.

To create a modern fleet of the numerical size of the Armada, with aircraft carriers, and appropriate complement of aircraft, nuclear submarines and missiles, auxiliary and supporting craft and bases and communications, would take a first-rate industrial power a minimum of twenty years. Though modern Spain is rich beyond the dreams of its monarchs in its most expansive age, it could not for a moment contemplate such an enterprise. In the Second World War, no combat plane that had not been substantially designed before the outbreak of hostilities saw major service. Since then the lead time for comparable *matériel* has become yet greater. In general, individuals in late middle age stand in little danger of weapons now being designed; they are a menace only to the unborn and the uncontemplated.

It is a commonplace of modern technology that there is a high measure of certainty that problems have solutions before there is knowledge of how they are to be solved. It was known in the early 1960s with reasonable certainty that men could land on the moon by the end of the decade. But many, perhaps most of the details for accomplishing this journey remained to be worked out.

4. Instructions issued from the Escorial on 31 March (see Mattingly, 1959, p. 80). Philip had, of course, been contemplating the enterprise for some years.

If methods of performing the specified task are uncertain the need for bringing organized intelligence to bear will be much greater than if the methods are still known. This uncertainty will also lead to increased time and cost and the increase can be very great. Uncertainty as to the properties of the metal to be used for the skin of supersonic transport; uncertainty therefore as to the proper way of handling and working the metal; uncertainty therefore as to the character and design of the equipment required to work it can add extravagantly to the time and cost of obtaining such a vehicle. This problem-solving, with its high costs in time and money, is a recognized feature of modern technology. It graces all modern economic discussion under the cachet of *Research and Development*.

The need for planning, it has been said, arises from the long period of time that elapses during the production process, the high investment that is involved and the inflexible commitment of that investment to the particular task. In the case of advanced military equipment, time, cost and inflexibility of commitment are all very great. Time and outlay will be even greater where, a common characteristic of weaponry, design is uncertain and where, accordingly, there must be added expenditure for research and development. In these circumstances, planning is both essential and difficult. It is essential because of the time that is involved, the money that is at risk, the number of things that can go wrong and the magnitude of the possible ensuing disaster. It is difficult because of the number and size of the eventualities that must be controlled.

One answer is to have the state absorb the major risks. It can provide or guarantee a market for the product. And it can underwrite the costs of development so that if they increase beyond expectation the firm will not have to carry them. Or it can pay for and make available the necessary technical knowledge. The drift of this argument will be evident. Technology, under all circumstances, leads to planning; in its higher manifestations it may put the problems of planning beyond the reach of the industrial firm. Technological compulsions, and not ideology or political wile, will require the firm to seek the help and protection of the state. This is a consequence of advanced technology of no small interest, and to which we shall return.

In examining the intricate complex of economic change, technology, having an initiative of its own, is the logical point at which to break in. But technology not only causes change, it is a response to change. Though it forces specialization it is also the result of specialization. Though it requires extensive organization it is also the result of organization. The changes stimulated by technology, slightly reordered for purposes of exposition, are none the less the themes of the ensuing chapters [of the original book]. First we shall look more closely at the effect of requirements of time and capital on industrial planning. Thereafter we shall look at the source and role of the capital which it employs in such large amounts. And then we shall examine the role of specialized manpower and its organization. Nor will this be the end. These themes, planning, specialization and organization, like the military symbolism of marching and combat in Protestant hymns and college sports, will recur throughout the book.

References

Fortune (1964), 'The 500 largest US industrial corporations', *Fortune Directory*, August.

GALBRAITH, J. K. (1960), 'Was Ford a fraud?', in *The Liberal Hour*, Houghton Mifflin.

MATTINGLY, G. (1959), *The Defeat of the Spanish Armada*, Houghton Mifflin.

NEVINS, A. (1954), *Ford, The Times, The Man, The Company*, Scribner.

(b) The Nature of Employment and Unemployment

J. K. Galbraith, *The New Industrial State*, Hamish Hamilton, 1971, ch. 21, pp. 33–46, 2nd edn.

There is no rate of pay at which a United States pick-and-shovel laborer can live which is low enough to compete with the work of a steam shovel as an excavator. Norbert Wiener, *Control and Communication in the Animal and the Machine*, 1948.

On few matters is the image of industrial civilization so sharp as on that of its labour force. This is a great mass – the word itself is ubiquitous – which streams in at the beginning of the shift and out at the end. It consists of comparatively unskilled operatives who guide or attend the machines and a smaller aristocracy who have skills beyond the scope of the machine. When the system is functioning well, all or nearly all are at work. When it is not, the notices appear on the board, the men remain at home and the rising percentage of unemployed in the labour force as a whole measures the extent of failure of the economic system. Similarly, when labour relations are tranquil, men pass peacefully through the gates. When they are not, a picket line appears and the plant either shuts down or functions in face of the threats of the milling crowd outside. There are others in the enterprise – managers, engineers, designers, clerks, auditors and salesmen – but they are part of a shadowed background. The labour force, that which counts, is the great homogeneous blue-collared proletariat.

The image is not yet at odds with the reality of the industrial system. But it is strongly at odds with its trend. Within the system the blue-collared proletarian is sharply in decline, both in relative numbers and in influence. And the notion of unemployment, as traditionally held, is coming year by year to have less meaning. More and more, the figures on unemployment enumerate those who are currently unemployable by the industrial system. This incapacity coexists with acute shortages of more highly qualified talent. The view of the system in the preceding chapters makes these tendencies predictable; and the statistics, which in this case are good, affirm the expectation or are consistent with it.

The industrial system, we have seen, has a strong technological orientation; indeed one of the subordinate goals of the technostructure is a showing of technical virtuosity. And the technostructure itself, among other things, is an apparatus that brings into conjunction the various branches of specialized scientific and engineering knowledge which bear on the solution of particular problems.

We have seen, also, that advanced technology in combination with high capital requirements makes planning imperative. All planning seeks, so far as may be possible, to ensure that what it assumes as regards the future will be what the future brings. This accords, too, with the concern of the technostructure for its own security, for such control minimizes the likelihood of developments which might jeopardize its earnings and thus its tenure.

These considerations tell with considerable precision the manpower requirements and labour policies of the industrial system and forecast virtually all of its principal tendencies.

That it will have a large and growing requirement for qualified talent is evident. Technology, planning and the coordination of the resulting organization all require such talent. This requirement, it is perhaps unnecessary to notice, is for *educationally* qualified, as distinct from skilled, manpower. Engineers, salesmen and sales managers, managers and management engineers, and the near infinity of other such specialists, though they are trained in their particular task, can only be so trained if they have prior preparatory education. This is not necessarily the case of the tool-and-die maker, carpenter, plasterer or other skilled craftsman. The engineer, sales manager or personnel director applies specialized mental qualifications to a particular task. He must have, before learning his particular speciality, the requisite intellectual or mental preparation. The skilled journeyman brings manual dexterity and experience to bear. For this there is no minimum educational level.

At the same time the industrial system reduces relatively, and, it seems probable, absolutely, its requirement for blue-collared workers, both skilled and unskilled.

This situation arises partly from the nature of technology. Machines do easily and well what is done by repetitive physical effort unguided by significant intelligence. Accordingly they compete most effectively with physical labour, including that of no slight dexterity and skill.[1]

But to see mechanization and automation purely as a problem in comparative cost is greatly to minimize their role – and to pay further for the error of confining economic goals, and economic calculation, to profit maximization.[2] The technostructure, as noted, seeks technical progressiveness for its own sake when this is not in conflict with other goals. More important, it seeks certainty in the supply and price of all the prime requisites of production. Labour is a prime requisite. And a large blue-collar labour force, especially if subject to the external authority of a union, introduces a major element of uncertainty and danger. Its cost is not under the control of the technostructure. Who can assess the likelihood, the costs and consequences of a strike?

In contrast mechanization adds to certainty. Machines do not go on strike. Their prices are subject to the stability which, we have seen, is inherent in the contractual relationships between large firms. The capital by which the machinery is provided comes in large proportion from the internal savings of the firm. Both its supply and cost are thus fully under the control of the firm. More white-collar workers and more members of the technostructure will be required with mechanization. But white-collar workers with rare exceptions do not join unions; they tend to identify themselves with the goals of the technostructure with which they are fused.[3] To add to the technostructure is to increase its power in the enterprise. Such is the result of replacing twenty blue-collar workers with two men who are knowledgeable on computers.

1. This is a generalization. There are numerous operations – the sensory-manipulative operations that are involved in handling a power shovel for example – which have no appreciable educational requirements but which do not lend themselves to automatic processes.

2. For such an argument see Silberman (1965). For an opposing and, I believe, more persuasive case see Seligman (1965). The word automation, narrowly construed, refers to an industrial process which provides data from its own operations and feeds this back usually through a computer to controls which fully govern the process. It thus dispenses with all direct manpower. But automatic machinery dispensing with much but not all human guidance is, of course, very important. And this too is called automation. Because of this ambiguity I have used the phrase automation sparingly and mostly where paraphrasing popular argument.

3. I return to these matters in more detail in chapters 23 and 24 [of the original book].

Thus the technostructure has strong incentives, going far beyond considerations of cost (which may themselves be important) to replace blue-collar workers.

In the eleven years from 1958 to 1969, the labour force grew by about fifteen million – from sixty-three million to just under seventy-eight million. From 1958 to 1963, however, the blue-collar labour force remained constant. Thereafter it increased by about five million. In consequence, while white-collar employment increased from 42·6 per cent of the labour force in 1958 to 47·3 per cent in 1969, the proportion of blue-collar workers dropped from 37 per cent to 36·2 per cent.[4]

The foregoing figures are for the economy as a whole, excluding only agriculture and the service industries. Thus they include blue-collar workers outside the industrial system and where, it can be assumed, the decline in relative numbers was much less. Thus from 1964 to 1969, the years when the blue-collar force was increasing by five million, it was constant or declining in steel, petroleum and tobacco production – all characteristic industries of the industrial system. In food processing and automobile production there was a modest increase[5] but from 1951 to 1969, although the total output of the automobile industry about doubled, the total number of production workers remained the same.[6]

A recent study of manpower requirements concludes that between 1966 and 1975 there will be an increase in white-collar employment of some 28 per cent. The increase in blue-collar employment is put at only 10 per cent. Much of this increase, it should be repeated, will be outside the industrial system.[7]

As the relative demand for blue-collar workers declines, the requirement for those with higher educational qualification increases. These are needed by the technostructure. And, though with more modest educational qualification, they are required for the white-collar tasks.

It follows, further, that if the educational system does not keep abreast of these requirements there will be a shortage of those with a higher educational qualification and a surplus of those with less. This is the present situation.

It is the vanity of educators that they shape the educational system to their preferred image. They may not be without influence but the decisive force is

4. *Manpower Report of the President* and *A Report on Manpower Requirements, Resources, Utilization and Training,* United States Department of Labor, March 1970, pp. 225–6.

5. pp. 267–9.

6. *Economic Report of the President,* 1970, p. 218.

7. *Tomorrow's Manpower Needs,* vol. III, *National Trends and Outlook: Occupational Employment,* Bureau of Labor Statistics, bulletin no. 1606. February 1969, p. 4.

the economic system. What the educator believes is latitude is usually latitude to respond to economic need.

In the early stages of industrialization, the educational requirement for industrial manpower was in the shape of a very squat pyramid. A few men of varying qualifications – managers, engineers, bookkeepers, timekeepers and clerks – were needed in or by the office. The wide base reflected the large requirement for repetitive labour power for which even literacy was something of a luxury. To this pyramid the educational system conformed. Elementary education was provided for the masses at minimum cost. Those who wanted more had to pay for it or to forego income while getting it. This ensured that it would be sought only by a minority. To this day the school systems of the older industrial communities in West Virginia, central and western Pennsylvania, northern New Jersey and upstate New York still manifest their ancient inferiority. It is assumed that an old mill town will have bad schools.[8]

By contrast, the manpower requirements of the industrial system are in the shape of a tall urn. It widens out below the top to reflect the need of the technostructure for administrative, coordinating and planning talent, for scientists and engineers, for sales executives, salesmen, those learned in the other arts of persuasion and for those who programme and command the computers. It widens further to reflect the need for white-collar talent. And it curves in sharply towards the base to reflect the more limited demand for those who are qualified only for muscular and repetitive tasks and who are readily replaced by machines.

This revision of educational requirements is progressive. The top of the urn continues to expand while the bottom remains the same or contracts. To this change the educational system responds. It does so with a lag which is partly in the nature of any social response. But also the newly demanded education has required a sharp break with the social attitudes of the entrepreneurs. These, as noted, held the state to be an incubus; they sought to confine it to the provision of law and order, the protection of property and the common defence. Now the technostucture of the mature corporation must acknowledge dependence on the state for a factor of production more critical for its success than capital. Such a revision of attitudes takes time and so accordingly does the public response to it.

The effect of this delayed response is that when employment is comparatively high there will be numerous vacancies for those of higher qualification and

8. Outside the industrial system, the same is true of the rural areas of the South. Here, too, the need was for crude, illiterate labour power and provision, accordingly, was made for nothing more. Northern agriculture was more demanding and the rural schools better. However, differences in income were a cause as well as a result of the difference.

most of the unemployed will be without educational qualification or without compensating work experience or seniority. There are many openings for individuals with advanced educational qualification. The ardent recruitment efforts of the industrial system in universities and colleges and, even more, its newspaper advertising, attest the fact.[9] At the same time, since these vacancies are not yet fully recognized as the normal counterpart of unemployment, statistics thereon are meagre.

The figures on the educational qualifications of the unemployed are better. In the spring of 1968, when the official unemployment rate was 3·4 per cent of the labour force it was 5·2 per cent for those with one to four years of schooling and 4·3 per cent for those with five to seven years of schooling. For those with four or more years of college, it was 1·0 per cent.[10] In March 1962, when unemployment in general was 6·0 per cent, it was 10·4 per cent for those with one to four years of schooling and 8·5 per cent for those with five to seven. Those who are unemployable eventually become discouraged (as other workers do not) and withdraw from the labour market. Estimates are available for 1962 of those not actively looking for work. When these were added to the labour force, the national unemployment rate was estimated at 7·8 per cent. For those with four years of schooling or less it was 17·2 per cent. For those with five to seven years of schooling, it was 12·2 per cent. Among those with sixteen years of schooling or more, unemployment was only 1·4 per cent. Of all those officially counted as unemployed at the time, 40 per cent had eight years of schooling or (in most cases) much less (Killingsworth, 1963).[11] Unemployment of teenagers, reflecting the combined handicap of limited work experience and, in many cases, limited schooling, was 11·8 per cent. Adding those not in the labour force it was 25·6 per cent (Bowen, 1965). Additionally, the individual with a limited number of years of schooling will, ordinarily, have had poorer schooling than the person who has had more. Two principal reasons why he discontinues school are because the schools are bad and because he is doing badly. These suggest that his few years have been less good than the average. There can be no doubt, accordingly, that the unemployed include the predicted concentration of the uneducated.[12]

9. A Boston newspaper editor noted a few years ago that his revenues from advertising of job opportunities had come to exceed that from department stores, with much less interference with editorial policy.

10. United States Bureau of Labor Statistics, Special Labor Force Report No. 103, *Educational Attainment of Workers, March 1968* (1969).

11. By way of comparison, national unemployment was estimated at 25 per cent of the civilian labour force in 1933, the worst year of the Great Depression.

12. It must be kept in mind that the educational requirements and disqualifications discussed here are those of the industrial system while the educational characteristics of the unemployed are those of the labour force as a whole. And without doubt, the opportunities for employment of those with minimal educational qualifications are better

Lack of education is not the only disability of those who are rejected by the industrial system. A large proportion are Negroes or members of other racial minorities and it has anciently been observed that the Negro worker is the last to be hired when employment is expanding and the first to be fired when it is contracting. Negroes do suffer a special handicap. But a great deal must be attributed to the low level of educational qualification among Negroes, reflecting not discrimination, *per se*, by the industrial system but prior disadvantage in schools and environment. A well-educated Negro is not so necessarily the first fired or the last hired.[13]

Some employment is also associated with industrial change – with the decline of anthracite coal-mining in central Pennsylvania, the mechanization and consolidation of mining in the bituminous region, the loss of industry by mill towns in New York, New England or elsewhere. Here again, however, much must be attributed to the exiguous educational system which served the industries of these regions where, characteristically, a boy went into the mine or mill at the earliest age at which he was capable of manual labour. A well-educated population would not have remained stranded or it would have drawn industry to itself. An aeronautical engineer, with the decline in demand for manned military aircraft, may have trouble finding employment in his speciality. But with a little training and some slight loss of dignity he becomes an excellent appliance salesman.

The point is of much importance. Unemployment in the industrial system includes those who cannot find work in their particular craft or skill. It also includes qualified workers who are in the wrong place and who are reluctant to move. The number who fall in these categories will increase as demand presses less strongly on the capacity of the labour force and unemployment rises in consequence. But the increasing educational requirements of the industrial system add to the mobility of the working force both as between occupations and regions. The skilled craftsman of modest education does not easily learn a new skill. And the risks of movement are his own. So if he establishes himself as a tool-and-die maker in Detroit there is a fair chance

---

outside the industrial system. The service industries, construction and agriculture all have a substantial continuing requirement for common labour. In the case of migrant agricultural labour, one sees again how responsive the educational system is to context. No education is required for harvesting crops. And by more or less effectively denying education to the children of those who participate, further generations of such labour are assured.

13. Although earnings of educated Negroes remain well below those of white citizens of comparable qualification. In 1968 the median earnings of Negroes with one year or more of college was 74 per cent of the earnings of Whites with the same formal qualification ('The social and economic status of Negroes in the United States, 1969', United States Bureau of the Census, *Current Population Report*, series P–23, no. 29, p. 21).

that he will remain there. The engineer or sales executive, though he is strongly specialized as to task, can acquire another perhaps less demanding qualification if he must. He is but little tied to his surroundings. If there is greater need for his speciality on the other side of the country he moves in response to a promise of employment, or is moved by his new employer as a matter of routine.

In the early 1960s economists have debated whether unemployment in the modern economy is primarily structural, which is to say the result of a poor adaptation of the worker's qualification and skills to need, or whether it is the result of a general shortage of demand. Some professional blood was spilled, for the argument had an important bearing on remedy. If unemployment was structural, the remedy was to retrain those who are out of work. But if the problem was merely a shortage of demand, then general action to increase spending or reduce taxes would suffice. The use of tax reduction as a remedy for insufficient demand has added a point to the debate. For advocates of structural causes and remedies feared that this would limit the spending on education, training and retraining which was the remedy for unemployment.

We now see the answer. Unemployment can be both structural and the result of inadequate demand but also something more. It will appear with slackening of aggregate demand and it will be among those who are most inflexibly tied to particular occupations and locations. At the same time there will be vacancies in positions requiring high and specialized qualification. Employment would be higher both with stronger demand and with a better accommodation of qualification to need.

But unemployment also reflects the cultural development of the system. It will be smaller, at any given level of demand, the better the *cultural* accommodation to the needs of the industrial system. If this accommodation is good, there will be a smaller core of functional illiterates who cannot be used at all. And there will be a larger number of people not only to fill the vacancies calling for higher qualification but also with the added mobility between occupations and regions that goes with education.[14] Modern unemployment reflects not only a shortage in aggregate demand and a poor adjustment of skills to need but a lag in cultural development.

14. In recent years, in much of Western Europe unemployment has been consistently a smaller proportion of the labour force than in the United States. Something is to be attributed to a more persistent pressure of demand and to relatively larger employment opportunities outside the industrial system. But national educational standards and, in consequence, a more homogeneously qualified labour force have certainly been contributing factors. Foreign workers of lesser educational qualifications have been added to the domestic labour force, but it has been possible for countries such as Germany, France and Switzerland to take these in the numbers needed and leave the unemployment associated with such lower qualification behind in Spain, Turkey or southern Italy.

In consequence of the foregoing, unemployment, as a simple statistical concept, now has little relevance in the industrial system. This system requires a progressive accommodation of educated manpower to its needs. If this accommodation is imperfect, there will be a shortage of workers for specialized tasks. And there will, at the same time, be unemployment. Both measure the failure in the accommodation. Depending on the qualitative nature of the failure, the unemployed will consist of those who are unemployable because of insufficient education, or those who are occupationally or geographically immobile because of the absence of education, or those who have a skill or speciality for which there is no demand and which, for reasons unrelated to education, they cannot exchange for one that is wanted. Or unemployment may have a quite different cause. It may be the result of an insufficiency of aggregate demand which reflects yet another accommodation of society to the needs of the industrial system. Simple statistics of unemployment reveal, it will be evident, almost nothing about the nature of the failure of accommodation at any given time. The crude-steel capacity of a country was once a rather good indication of its ability to build railroads and meet its other needs for steel, and the statistics on the finishing capacity told where, with expansion, idle capacity would persist or bottlenecks would occur. Technology has made such figures far less meaningful. One must now know the nature of the accommodation to the more refined, more specialized and constantly changing requirements for the metal. A surplus of steel could be combined with a severe shortage. So it is with labour. Here too one must look beyond the totals to the accommodation to educationally more refined, more specialized and constantly changing requirements. Here also totals have slight meaning. And here, as with steel, technology is one of the things that has made them so.

Much may be learned of the character of any society from its social conflicts and passions. When capital was the key to economic success, social conflict was between the rich and the poor. Money made the difference; possession or non-possession justified contempt for, or resentment of, those oppositely situated. Sociology, economics, political science and fiction celebrated the war between the two sides of the tracks and the relation of the mansion on the hill to the tenement below.

In recent times education has become the difference that divides. All who have educational advantage, as with the moneyed of an earlier day, are reminded of their *noblesse oblige* and also of the advantages of reticence. They should help those who are less fortunate; they must avoid reflecting aloud on their advantage in knowledge. But this doesn't serve to paper over the conflict. It is visible in almost every community.

Thus the city with a high rate of accommodation to the requirements of the industrial system, i.e. a good educational system and a well-qualified working force, will attract industry and have a strong aspect of well-being. It will be the natural Canaan of the more energetic among those who were born in less favoured communities. This explains the modern migration from the South, South-West and border states to California, the upper Middle West and the eastern seaboard. Many of these migrants will be unqualified for employment in the industrial system. They thus contribute heavily to welfare and unemployment rolls in the communities to which they have moved. The nature of the opprobrium to which they are subject is indicated by the appellations that are applied to them – they are hillbillies, Okies or jungle-bunnies. It is not that they are poorer but that they are culturally inferior. It is such groups, not the working proletariat, that now react in resentment and violence to their subordination.

Politics also reflects the new division. In the United States suspicion or resentment is no longer directed to the capitalists or the merely rich. It is the intellectuals – the effete snobs – who are eyed with misgiving and alarm. This should surprise no one. Nor should it be a matter for surprise when semi-literate millionaires turn up leading or financing the ignorant in struggle against the intellectually privileged and content. This reflects the relevant class distinction in our time.

A further consequence of the new pattern of employment and unemployment is that full employment, though it remains an important test of successful performance of the economic system, can be approached only against increasing resistance. For, as noted, while the unemployed are reduced in number, they come to consist more and more of those, primarily the uneducated, who are unemployable in the industrial system. The counterpart of this resistant core is a growing number of vacancies for highly qualified workers and a strong bargaining position for those who are employed. This leads to the final source of instability in the industrial system and to yet a further resort to the state.

References

BOWEN, W. G. (1965), 'Unemployment in the United States: quantitative dimensions', in W. G. Bowen and F. Harbison (eds.), *Unemployment in a Prosperous Economy*, Princeton University Press.
KILLINGSWORTH, C. C. (1963), 'Unemployment and the tax cut', Conference on Economic Security, Michigan State University, mimeo.
National Commission on Technology, Automation and Economic Progress (1966), *The Outlook for Technological Change and Employment*, Washington, D.C.
SELIGMAN, B. B. (1965), 'Automation and the unions', *Dissent*, Winter.
SILBERMAN, C. E. (1965), 'The real news about automation', *Fortune*, January.

10 Karl Marx

(a) Machinery and Modern Industry

Excerpts from Karl Marx, *Capital*, Allen & Unwin, 1946, pp. 365-82, 420-24, 491-8.* First published in English, 1889.

The development of machinery

John Stuart Mill says in his *Principles of Political Economy*: 'It is questionable if all the mechanical inventions yet made have lightened the day's toil of any human being.' That is, however, by no means the aim of the capitalistic application of machinery. Like every other increase in the productiveness of labour, machinery is intended to cheapen commodities, and, by shortening that portion of the working day, in which the labourer works for himself, to lengthen the other portion that he gives, without an equivalent, to the capitalist. In short, it is a means for producing surplus value.

In manufacture, the revolution in the mode of production begins with the labour power, in modern industry it begins with the instruments of labour. Our first inquiry then is, how the instruments of labour are converted from tools into machines, or what is the difference between a machine and the implements of a handicraft? We are only concerned here with striking and general characteristics; for epochs in the history of society are no more separated from each other by hard and fast lines of demarcation, than are geological epochs.

Mathematicians and mechanicians, and in this they are followed by a few English economists, call a tool a simple machine, and a machine a complex tool. They see no essential difference between them, and even give the name of machine to the simple mechanical powers, the lever, the inclined plane, the screw, the wedge, etc. As a matter of fact, every machine is a combination of those simple powers, no matter how they may be disguised. From the economical standpoint this explanation is worth nothing, because the historical element is wanting. Another explanation of the difference between tool and machine is that in the case of a tool, man is the motive power, while the motive power of a machine is something different from man, is, for instance, an animal, water, wind, and so on.[1] According to this, a

---

* Many footnotes are omitted. [Ed.]

1. 'From this point of view we may draw a sharp line of distinction between a tool and a machine: spades, hammers, chisels, etc., combinations of levers and of screws, in all of which, no matter how complicated they may be in other respects, man is the motive power ... all this falls under the idea of a tool; but the plough, which is drawn

plough drawn by oxen, which is a contrivance common to the most different epochs, would be a machine, while Claussen's circular loom, which, worked by a single labourer, weaves 96,000 picks per minute, would be a mere tool. Nay, this very loom, though a tool when worked by hand, would, if worked by steam, be a machine. And since the application of animal power is one of man's earliest inventions, production by machinery would have preceded production by handicrafts. When, in 1735, John Wyalt brought out his spinning machine, and began the industrial revolution of the eighteenth century, not a word did he say about an ass driving it instead of a man, and yet this part fell to the ass. He described it as a machine 'to spin without fingers'.[2]

All fully developed machinery consists of three essentially different parts, the motor mechanism, the transmitting mechanism, and finally the tool or working machine. The motor mechanism is that which puts the whole in motion. It either generates its own motive power, like the steam engine, the caloric engine, the electro-magnetic machine, etc., or it receives its impulse from some already existing natural force, like the water wheel from a head of water, the windmill from wind, etc. The transmitting mechanism, composed of fly wheels, shafting, toothed wheels, pulleys, straps, ropes, bands, pinions and gearing of the most varied kinds, regulates the motion, changes its form where necessary, as for instance, from linear to circular, and divides and distributes it among the working machines. These two first parts of the

---

by animal power, and windmills, etc., must be classed among machines' (Schulz, 1843, p. 38).

2. Before his time, spinning machines, although very imperfect ones, had already been used, and Italy was probably the country of their first appearance. A critical history of technology would show how little any of the inventions of the eighteenth century are of a single individual. Hitherto there is no such book. Darwin has interested us in the history of Nature's Technology, i.e., in the formation of the organs of plants and animals, which organs serve as instruments of production for sustaining life. Does not the history of the productive organs of man, of organs that are the material basis of all social organization, deserve equal attention? And would not such a history be easier to compile, since, as Vico says, human history differs from natural history in this, that we have made the former, but not the latter? Technology discloses man's mode of dealing with Nature, the process of production by which he sustains his life, and thereby also lays bare the mode of formation of his social relations, and of the mental conceptions that flow from them. Every history of religion, even, that fails to take account of this material basis, is uncritical. It is, in reality, much easier to discover by analysis the earthly core of the misty creations of religion, than, conversely, it is, to develop from the actual relations of life the corresponding celestialized forms of those relations. The latter method is the only materialistic, and therefore the only scientific, one. The weak points in the abstract materialism of natural science, a materialism that excludes history and its process, are at once evident from the abstract and ideological conceptions of its spokesmen, whenever they venture beyond the bounds of their own speciality.

whole mechanism are there, solely for putting the working machines in motion, by means of which motion the subject of labour is seized upon and modified as desired. The tool or working machine is that part of the machinery with which the Industrial Revolution of the eighteenth century started. And to this day it constantly serves as such a starting point, whenever a handicraft, or a manufacture, is turned into an industry carried on by machinery.

On a closer examination of the working machine proper, we find in it, as a general rule, though often, no doubt, under very altered forms, the apparatus and tools used by the handicraftsman or manufacturing workman; with this difference, that instead of being human implements, they are the implements of a mechanism, or mechanical implements. Either the entire machine is only a more or less altered mechanical edition of the old handicraft tool, as, for instance, the power-loom;[3] or the working parts fitted in the frame of the machine are old acquaintances, as spindles are in a mule, needles in a stocking-loom, saws in a sawing machine, and knives in a chopping machine. The distinction between these tools and the body proper of the machine, exists from their very birth; for they continue for the most part to be produced by handicraft, or by manufacture, and are afterwards fitted into the body of the machine, which is the product of machinery.[4] The machine proper is therefore a mechanism that, after being set in motion, performs with its tools the same operations that were formerly done by the workman with similar tools. Whether the motive power is derived from man, or from some other machine, makes no difference in this respect. From the moment that the tool proper is taken from man, and fitted into a mechanism, a machine takes the place of a mere implement. The difference strikes one at once, even in those cases where man himself continues to be the prime mover. The number of implements that he himself can use simultaneously, is limited by the number of his own natural instruments of production, by the number of his bodily organs. In Germany, they tried at first to make one spinner work two spinning wheels, that is, to work simultaneously with both hands and both feet. This was too difficult. Later, a treadle spinning wheel with two spindles was invented, but adepts in spinning who could spin two threads at once, were almost as scarce as two-headed men. The Jenny, on the

3. Especially in the original form of the power-loom, we recognize, at the first glance, the ancient loom. In its modern form, the power-loom has undergone essential alterations.

4. It is only during the last fifteen years (i.e. since about 1850), that a constantly increasing portion of these machine tools have been made in England by machinery, and that not by the same manufacturers who make the machines. Instances of machines for the fabrication of these mechanical tools are, the automatic bobbin-making engine, the card-setting engine, shuttle-making machines and machines for forging mule and throstle spindles.

other hand, even at its very birth, spun with twelve to eighteen spindles, and the stocking-loom knits with many thousand needles at once. The number of tools that a machine can bring into play simultaneously, is from the very first emancipated from the organic limits that hedge in the tools of a handicraftsman.

In many manual implements the distinction between man as mere motive power, and man as the workman or operator properly so-called, is brought into striking contrast. For instance, the foot is merely the prime mover of the spinning wheel, while the hand, worked with the spindle and drawing and twisting, performs the real operation of spinning. It is this last part of the handicraftsman's implement that is first seized upon by the Industrial Revolution, leaving to the workman, in addition to his new labour of watching the machine with his eyes and correcting its mistakes with his hands, the merely mechanical part of being the moving power. On the other hand, implements, in regard to which man has always acted as a simple motive power, as, for instance, by turning the crank of a mill, by pumping, by moving up and down the arm of a bellows, by pounding with a mortar, etc., such implements soon call for the application of animals, water and wind as motive powers. Here and there, long before the period of manufacture, and also, to some extent, during that period, these implements pass over into machines, but without creating any revolution in the mode of production. It becomes evident, in the period of Modern Industry, that these implements, even under their form of manual tools, are already machines. For instance, the pumps with which the Dutch, in 1836–7, emptied the Lake of Harlem, were constructed on the principle of ordinary pumps; the only difference being, that their pistons were driven by cyclopean steam engines, instead of by men. The common and very imperfect bellows of the blacksmith is, in England, occasionally converted to a blowing engine by connecting its arm with a steam engine. The steam engine itself, such as it was at its invention, during the manufacturing period at the close of the seventeenth century, and such as it continued to be down to 1780, did not give rise to any industrial revolution. It was, on the contrary, the invention of machines that made a revolution in the form of steam engines necessary. As soon as man, instead of working with an implement on the subject of his labour, becomes merely the motive power of an implement-machine, it is a mere accident that motive power takes the disguise of human muscle; and it may equally well take the form of wind, water or steam. Of course, this does not prevent such a change of form from producing great technical alterations in the mechanism that was originally constructed to be driven by man alone. Nowadays, all machines that have their way to make, such as sewing machines, bread-making machines, etc., are, unless from their very nature their use on a small scale is excluded, constructed to be driven both by human and by purely mechanical motive power.

The machine, which is the starting point of the industrial revolution, supersedes the workman, who handles a single tool, by a mechanism operating with a number of similar tools, and set in motion by a single motive power, whatever the form of that power may be.[5] Here we have the machine, but only as an elementary factor of production by machinery.

Increase in the size of the machine, and in the number of its working tools, calls for a more massive mechanism to drive it; and this mechanism requires, in order to overcome its resistance, a mightier moving power than that of man, apart from the fact that man is a very imperfect instrument for producing uniform continued motion. But assuming that he is acting simply as a motor, that a machine has taken the place of his tool, it is evident that he can be replaced by natural forces. Of all the great motors handed down from the manufacturing period, horse-power is the worst, partly because a horse has a head of his own, partly because he is costly, and the extent to which he is applicable in factories is very restricted. Nevertheless the horse was extensively used during the infancy of Modern Industry. This is proved, as well by the complaints of contemporary agriculturists, as by the term 'horse-power', which has survived to this day as an expression for mechanical force.

Wind was too inconstant and uncontrollable, and besides, in England, the birthplace of Modern Industry, the use of water-power preponderated even during the manufacturing period. In the seventeenth century attempts had already been made to turn two pairs of millstones with a single water wheel. But the increased size of the gearing was too much for the water power, which had now become insufficient, and this was one of the circumstances that led to a more accurate investigation of the laws of friction. In the same way the irregularity caused by the motive power in mills that were put in motion by pushing and pulling a lever, led to the theory, and the application, of the fly wheel, which afterwards plays so important a part in Modern Industry. In this way, during the manufacturing period, were developed the first scientific and technical elements of Modern Mechanical Industry. Arkwright's throstle spinning mill was from the very first turned by water. But for all that, the use of water, as the predominant motive power, was beset with difficulties. It could not be increased at will, it failed at certain seasons of the year, and, above all, it was essentially local. Not till the invention of Watt's second and so called double-acting steam engine, was a prime mover found, that begot its own force by the consumption of coal and water, whose power was entirely under man's control, that was mobile and a means of locomotion, that was urban and not, like the water

5. 'The union of all these simple instruments, set in motion by a single motor, constitutes a machine' (Babbage, 1832).

wheel, rural, that permitted production to be concentrated in towns instead of, like the water wheels, being scattered up and down the country, that was of universal technical application, and, relatively speaking, little affected in its choice of residence by local circumstances. The greatness of Watt's genius showed itself in the specification of the patent that he took out in April 1784. In that specification his steam engine is described, not as an invention for a specific purpose, but as an agent universally applicable in Mechanical Industry. In it he points out applications, many of which, as for instance, the steam hammer, were not introduced till half a century later. Nevertheless he doubted the use of steam engines in navigation. His successors, Boulton and Watt, sent to the exhibition of 1851 steam engines of colossal size for ocean steamers.

As soon as tools had been converted from being manual implements of man into implements of a mechanical apparatus, of a machine, the motive mechanism also acquired an independent form, entirely emancipated from the restraints of human strength. Thereupon the individual machine, that we have hitherto been considering, sinks into a mere factor in production by machinery. One motive mechanism was now able to drive many machines at once. The motive mechanism grows with the number of the machines that are turned simultaneously, and the transmitting mechanism becomes a widespread apparatus.

We now proceed to distinguish the cooperation of a number of machines of one kind from a complex system of machinery.

In the one case, the product is entirely made by a single machine, which performs all the various operations previously done by one handicraftsman with his tool; as, for instance, by a weaver with his loom; or by several handicraftsmen successively, either separately or as members of a system of Manufacture.[6] For example, in the manufacture of envelopes, one man folded the paper with his folder, another laid on the gum, a third turned the flap over, on which the device is impressed, a fourth embossed the device, and so on; and for each of these operations the envelope had to change hands. One single envelope machine now performs all these operations at once, and makes more than 3000 envelopes in an hour. In the London exhibition of 1862, there was an American machine for making paper cornets. It cut

6. From the standpoint of division of labour in Manufacture, weaving was not simple, but, on the contrary, complicated manual work and consequently the power-loom is a machine that does very complicated work. It is altogether erroneous to suppose that modern machinery originally appropriated those operations alone, which division of labour had simplified. Spinning and weaving were, during the manufacturing period, split up into new species, and the implements were modified and improved; but the labour itself was in no way divided, and it retained its handicraft character. It is not the labour, but the instrument of labour, that serves as the starting-point of the machine.

the paper, pasted, folded, and finished 300 in a minute. Here, the whole process, which, when carried on as Manufacture, was split up into, and carried out by, a series of operations, is completed by a single machine, working a combination of various tools. Now, whether such a machine be merely a reproduction of a complicated manual implement, or a combination of various simple implements specialized by Manufacture, in either case, in the factory, i.e. in the workshop in which machinery alone is used, we meet again with simple cooperation; and, leaving the workman out of consideration for a moment, this cooperation presents itself to us, in the first instance, as the conglomeration in one place of similar and simultaneously acting machines. Thus, a weaving factory is constituted of a number of power-looms, working side by side, and a sewing factory of a number of sewing machines all in the same building. But there is here a technical oneness in the whole system, owing to all the machines receiving their impulse simultaneously, and in an equal degree, from the pulsations of the common prime mover, by the intermediary of the transmitting mechanism; and this mechanism, to a certain extent, is also common to them all, since only particular ramifications of it branch off to each machine. Just as a number of tools, then, form the organs of a machine, so a number of machines of one kind constitute the organs of the motive mechanism.

A real machinery system, however, does not take the place of these independent machines, until the subject of labour goes through a connected series of detail processes, that are carried out by a chain of machines of various kinds, one supplementing the other. Here we have again the cooperation by division of labour that characterizes Manufacture; only now, it is a combination of detail machines. The special tools of the various detail workmen, such as those of the beaters, combers, spinners, etc., in the woollen manufacture, are now transformed into the tools of specialized machines, each machine constituting a special organ, with a special function, in the system. In those branches of industry in which the machinery system is first introduced, Manufacture itself furnishes, in a general way, the natural basis for the division, and consequent organization of the process of production.[7] Nevertheless an essential difference at once manifests itself. In

7. Before the epoch of Mechanical Industry, the wool manufacture was the predominating manufacture in England. Hence it was in this industry that, in the first half of the eighteenth century, the most experiments were made. Cotton, which required less careful preparation for its treatment by machinery, derived the benefit of the experience gained on wool, just as afterwards the manipulation of wool by machinery was developed on the lines of cotton-spinning and weaving by machinery. It was only during the ten years immediately preceding 1866, that isolated details of the wool manufacture, such as wool-combing, were incorporated in the factory system. 'The application of power to the process of combing wool ... extensively in operation since the introduction of the combing machine, especially Lister's ... undoubtedly had the

Manufacture it is the workmen who, with their manual implements, must, either singly or in groups, carry on each particular detail process. If, on the one hand, the workman becomes adapted to the process, on the other, the process was previously made suitable to the workman. This subjective principle of the division of labour no longer exists in production by machinery. Here, the process as a whole is examined objectively, in itself, that is to say, without regard to the question of its execution by human hands, it is analysed into its constituent phases; and the problem, how to execute each detail process, and bind them all into a whole, is solved by the aid of machines, chemistry, etc.[8] But, of course, in this case also, theory must be perfected by accumulated experience on a large scale. Each detail machine supplies raw material to the machine next in order; and since they are all working at the same time, the product is always going through the various stages of its fabrication, and is also constantly in a state of transition, from one phase to another. Just as in Manufacture, the direct cooperation of the detail labourers establishes a numerical proportion between the special groups, so in an organized system of machinery, where one detail machine is constantly kept employed by another, a fixed relation is established between their numbers, their size and their speed. The collective machine, now an organized system of various kinds of single machines, and of groups of single machines, becomes more and more perfect, the more the process as a whole becomes a continuous one, i.e. the less the raw material is interrupted in its passage from its first phase to its last; in other words, the more its passage from one phase to another is effected, not by the hand of man, but by the machinery itself. In Manufacture the isolation of each detail process is a condition imposed by the nature of division of labour, but in the fully developed factory the continuity of these processes is, on the contrary, imperative.

A system of machinery, whether it reposes on the mere cooperation of similar machines, as in weaving, or on a combination of different machines, as in spinning, constitutes in itself a huge automaton, whenever it is driven by a self-acting prime mover. But although the factory as a whole be driven by its steam engine, yet either some of the individual machines may require

---

effect of throwing a very large number of men out of work. Wool was formerly combed by hand, most frequently in the cottage of the comber. It is now very generally combed in the factory, and hand-labour is superseded, except in some particular kinds of work, in which hand-combed wool is still preferred. Many of the hand-combers found employment in the factories, but the produce of the hand-combers bears so small a proportion to that of the machine, that the employment of a very large number of combers has passed away' (Report of the Inspector of Factories, 31 October 1865, p. 16).

8. 'The principle of the factory system, then, is to substitute ... the partition of a process into its essential constituents, for the division or gradation of labour among artisans' (Ure, 1835, p. 20).

the aid of the workman for some of their movements (such aid was necessary for the running in of the mule carriage, before the invention of the self-acting mule, and is still necessary in fine-spinning mills); or, to enable a machine to do its work, certain parts of it may require to be handled by the workman like a manual tool; this was the case in machine-makers' workshops, before the conversion of the slide rest into a self-actor. As soon as a machine executes, without man's help, all the movements requisite to elaborate the raw material, needing only attendance from him, we have an automatic system of machinery, and one that is susceptible of constant improvement in its details. Such improvements as the apparatus that stops a drawing frame, whenever a sliver breaks, and the self-acting stop, that stops the power-loom so soon as the shuttle bobbin is emptied of weft, are quite modern inventions. As an example, both of continuity of production, and of the carrying out of the automatic principle, we may take a modern paper mill. In the paper industry generally, we may advantageously study in detail not only the distinctions between modes of production based on different means of production, but also the connection of the social conditions of production with those modes: for the old German paper-making furnishes us with a sample of handicraft production; that of Holland in the seventeenth and of France in the eighteenth century with a sample of manufacturing in the strict sense; and that of modern England with a sample of automatic fabrication of this article. Besides these, there still exist, in India and China, two distinct antique Asiatic forms of the same industry.

An organized system of machines, to which motion is communicated by the transmitting mechanism from a central automaton, is the most developed form of production by machinery. Here we have, in the place of the isolated machine, a mechanical monster whose body fills whole factories, and whose demon power, at first veiled under the slow and measured motions of his giant limbs, at length breaks out into the fast and furious whirl of his countless working organs.

There were mules and steam engines before there were any labourers, whose exclusive occupation it was to make mules and steam engines; just as men wore clothes before there were such people as tailors. The inventions of Vaucanson, Arkwright, Watt and others, were, however, practicable, only because those inventors found, ready to hand, a considerable number of skilled mechanical workmen, placed at their disposal by the manufacturing period. Some of these workmen were independent handicraftsmen of various trades, others were grouped together in manufactures, in which, as before-mentioned, division of labour was strictly carried out. As inventions increased in number, and the demand for the newly discovered machines grew larger, the machine-making industry split up, more and more, into numerous independent branches, and division of labour in these manufactures was more and more developed. Here, then, we see in Manufacture the immediate technical foundation of Modern Industry. Manufacture produced the machinery, by means of which Modern Industry abolished the handicraft and manufacturing systems in those spheres of production that it first seized upon. The factory system was therefore raised, in the natural course of things, on an inadequate foundation. When the system attained to a certain degree of development, it had to root up this ready-made foundation, which in the meantime had been elaborated on the old lines, and to build up for itself a basis that should correspond to its methods of production. Just as the individual machine retains a dwarfish character, so long as it is worked by the power of man alone, and just as no system of machinery could be properly developed before the steam engine took the place of the earlier motive powers, animals, wind, and even water; so, too, Modern Industry was crippled in its complete development, so long as its characteristic instrument of production, the machine, owed its existence to personal strength and personal skill, and depended on the muscular development, the keenness of sight, and the cunning of hand, with which the detail workmen in manufactures, and the manual labourers in handicrafts, wielded their dwarfish implements. Thus, apart from the dearness of the machines made in this way, a circumstance that is ever present to the mind of the capitalist, the expansion of industries carried on by means of machinery, and the invasion by machinery of fresh branches of production, were dependent on the growth of a class of workmen, who, owing to the almost artistic nature of their employment, could increase their numbers only gradually, and not by leaps and bounds. But besides this, at a certain stage of its development, Modern Industry became technologically incompatible with the basis furnished for it by handicraft and Manufacture. The increasing size of the prime movers, of the transmitting mechanism, and the machines proper, the greater complication, multiformity and regularity of the details of these machines, as they more and more departed from the model of those originally made by manual labour, and acquired a form, untrammelled except by the conditions under which they worked,[9] the

9. The power-loom was at first made chiefly of wood; in its improved modern form it is made of iron. To what an extent the old forms of the instruments of production influenced their new forms at first starting, is shown by, amongst other things, the most superficial comparison of the present power-loom with the old one, of the modern blowing apparatus of a blast-furnace with the first inefficient mechanical reproduction of the ordinary bellows, and perhaps more strikingly than in any other way, by the attempts before the invention of the present locomotive, to construct a locomotive that actually had two feet, which after the fashion of a horse, it raised alternately from the ground. It is only after considerable development of the science of mechanics, and accumulated practical experience, that the form of a machine becomes settled entirely in accordance with mechanical principles, and emancipated from the traditional form of the tool that gave rise to it.

perfecting of the automatic system, and the use, every day more unavoidable, of a more refractory material, such as iron instead of wood – the solution of all these problems which sprang up by the force of circumstances, everywhere met with a stumbling-block in the personal restrictions, which even the collective labourer of Manufacture could not break through, except to a limited extent. Such machines as the modern hydraulic press, the modern power-loom, and the modern carding engine, could never have been furnished by Manufacture.

A radical change in the mode of production in one sphere of industry involves a similar change in other spheres. This happens at first in such branches of industry as are connected together by being separate phases of a process, and yet are isolated by the social division of labour, in such a way, that each of them produces an independent commodity. Thus spinning by machinery made weaving by machinery a necessity, and both together made the mechanical and chemical revolution that took place in bleaching, printing and dyeing, imperative. So too, on the other hand, the revolution in cotton-spinning called forth the invention of the gin, for separating the seeds from the cotton fibre; it was only by means of this invention, that the production of cotton became possible on the enormous scale at present required. But more especially, the revolution in the modes of production of industry and agriculture made necessary a revolution in the general conditions of the social process of production, i.e. in the means of communication and of transport. In a society whose pivot, to use an expression of Fourier, was agriculture on a small scale, with its subsidiary domestic industries, and the urban handicrafts, the means of communication and transport were so utterly inadequate to the productive requirements of the manufacturing period, with its extended division of social labour, its concentration of the instruments of labour, and of the workmen, and its colonial markets, that they became in fact revolutionized. In the same way the means of communication and transport handed down from the manufacturing period soon became unbearable trammels on Modern Industry, with its feverish haste of production, its enormous extent, its constant flinging of capital and labour from one sphere of production into another, and its newly-created connections with the markets of the whole world. Hence, apart from the radical changes introduced in the construction of sailing vessels, the means of communication and transport became gradually adapted to the modes of production of mechanical industry, by the creation of a system of river steamers, railways, ocean steamers and telegraphs. But the huge masses of iron that had now to be forged, to be welded, to be cut, to be bored and to be shaped, demanded, on their part, cyclopean machines, for the construction of which the methods of the manufacturing period were utterly inadequate.

Modern Industry had therefore itself to take in hand the machine, its characteristic instrument of production, and to construct machines by machines. It was not till it did this, that it built up for itself a fitting technical foundation, and stood on its own feet. Machinery, simultaneously with the increasing use of it, in the first decades of this century, appropriated, by degrees, the fabrication of machines proper. But it was only during the decade preceding 1866, that the construction of railways and ocean steamers on a stupendous scale called into existence the cyclopean machines now employed in the construction of prime movers.

The most essential condition to the production of machines by machines was a prime mover capable of exerting any amount of force, and yet under perfect control. Such a condition was already supplied by the steam engine. But at the same time it was necessary to produce the geometrically accurate straight lines, planes, circles, cylinders, cones and spheres, required in the detail parts of the machines. This problem Henry Maudslay solved in the first decade of this century by the invention of the slide rest, a tool that was soon made automatic, and in a modified form was applied to other constructive machines besides the lathe, for which it was originally intended. This mechanical appliance replaces, not some particular tool, but the hand itself, which produces a given form by holding and guiding the cutting tool along the iron or other material operated upon. Thus it became possible to produce the forms of the individual parts of machinery 'with a degree of ease, accuracy and speed, that no accumulated experience of the hand of the most skilled workman could give'.

If we now fix our attention on that portion of the machinery employed in the construction of machines, which constitutes the operating tool, we find the manual implements reappearing, but on a cyclopean scale. The operating part of the boring machine is an immense drill driven by a steam engine; without this machine, on the other hand, the cylinders of large steam engines and of hydraulic presses could not be made. The mechanical lathe is only a cyclopean reproduction of the ordinary foot-lathe; the planing machine, an iron carpenter, that works on iron with the same tools that the human carpenter employs on wood; the instrument that, on the London wharves, cuts the veneers, is a gigantic razor; the tool of the shearing machine, which shears iron as easily as a tailor's scissors cut cloth, is a monster pair of scissors; and the steam hammer works with an ordinary hammer head, but of such a weight that not Thor himself could wield it. These steam hammers are an invention of Nasmyth, and there is one that weighs over six tons and strikes with a vertical fall of seven feet, on an anvil weighing thirty-six tons. It is mere child's play for it to crush a block of granite into powder, yet it is no less capable of driving, with a succession of light taps, a nail into a piece of soft wood.

The implements of labour, in the form of machinery, necessitate the substitution of natural forces for human force, and the conscious application of science, instead of rule of thumb. In Manufacture, the organization of the social labour-process is purely subjective; it is a combination of detail labourers; in its machinery system, Modern Industry has a productive organism that is purely objective, in which the labourer becomes a mere appendage to an already existing material condition of production. In simple cooperation, and even in that founded on division of labour, the suppression of the isolated, by the collective, workman still appears to be more or less accidental. Machinery, with a few exceptions to be mentioned later, operates only by means of associated labour, or labour in common. Hence the cooperative character of the labour process is, in the latter case, a technical necessity dictated by the instrument of labour itself. [. . .]

To work at a machine, the workman should be taught from childhood, in order that he may learn to adapt his own movements to the uniform and unceasing motion of an automaton. When the machinery, as a whole, forms a system of manifold machines, working simultaneously and in concert, the cooperation based upon it, requires the distribution of various groups of workmen among the different kinds of machines. But the employment of machinery does away with the necessity of crystallizing this distribution after the manner of Manufacture, by the constant annexation of a particular man to a particular function. Since the motion of the whole system does not proceed from the workman, but from the machinery, a change of persons can take place at any time without an interruption of the work. The most striking proof of this is afforded by the *relays system*, put into operation by the manufacturers during their revolt from 1848–50. Lastly, the quickness with which machine work is learnt by young people, does away with the necessity of bringing up for exclusive employment by machinery, a special class of operatives.[10] With regard to the work of the mere attendants, it can, to some extent, be replaced in the mill by machines,[11] and owing to its

10. When distress is very great, as, for instance, during the American Civil War, the factory operative is now and then set by the Bourgeois to do the roughest of work, such as road-making, etc. The English *ateliers nationaux* of 1862 and the following years, established for the benefit of the destitute cotton operatives, differ from the French of 1848 in this, that in the latter the workmen had to do unproductive work at the expense of the state, in the former they had to do productive municipal work to the advantage of the bourgeois, and that, too, cheaper than the regular workmen, with whom they were thus thrown into competition. 'The physical appearance of the cotton operatives is unquestionably improved. This I attribute . . . as to the men, to outdoor labour on public works' (Report of the Inspector of Factories, 31 October 1865, p.59). The writer here alludes to the Preston factory operatives, who were employed on Preston Moor.

11. An example: The various mechanical apparatus introduced since the Act of 1844

extreme simplicity, it allows of a rapid and constant change of the individuals burdened with this drudgery.

Although then, technically speaking, the old system of division of labour is thrown overboard by machinery, it hands on in the factory, as a traditional habit handed down from Manufacture, and is afterwards systematically remoulded and established in a more hideous form by capital, as a means of exploiting labour power. The life-long speciality of handling one and the same tool, now becomes the life-long speciality of serving one and the same machine. Machinery is put to a wrong use, with the object of transforming the workman, from his very childhood, into a part of a detail machine.[12] In this way, not only are the expenses of his reproduction considerably lessened, but at the same time his helpless dependence upon the factory as a whole, and therefore upon the capitalist, is rendered complete. Here as everywhere else, we must distinguish between the increased productiveness due to the development of the social process of production, and that due to the capitalist exploitation of that process. In handicrafts and manufacture, the workman makes use of a tool, in the factory, the machine makes use of him. There the movements of the instrument of labour proceed from him, here it is the movements of the machine that he must follow. In manufacture the workmen are parts of a living mechanism. In the factory we have a lifeless mechanism independent of the workman, who becomes its mere living appendage. 'The miserable routine of endless drudgery and toil in which the same mechanical process is gone through over and over again, is like the labour of Sisyphus. The burden of labour, like the rock, keeps ever falling back on the worn-out labourer' (Engels, 1845, p. 217). At the same time that factory work exhausts the nervous system to the uttermost, it does away with the many-sided play of the muscles, and confiscates every atom of freedom, both in bodily and intellectual activity. The lightening of the labour, even, becomes a sort of torture, since the machine does not free the labourer from work, but deprives the work of all interest. Every kind of

into woollen mills, for replacing the labour of children. So soon as it shall happen that the children of the manufacturers themselves have to go through a course of schooling as helpers in the mill, this almost unexplored territory of mechanics will soon make remarkable progress. 'Of machinery, perhaps self-acting mules are as dangerous as any other kind. Most of the accidents from them happen to little children, from their creeping under the mules to sweep the floor whilst the mules are in motion. Several "minders" have been fined for this offence, but without much general benefit. If machine makers would only invent a self-sweeper, by whose use the necessity for these little children to creep under the machinery might be prevented, it would be a happy addition to our protective measures' (Report of the Inspector of Factories, 31 October 1866, p. 63).

12. So much then for Proudhon's wonderful idea: he 'construes' machinery not as a synthesis of instruments of labour, but as a synthesis of detail operations for the benefit of the labourer himself.

capitalist production, in so far as it is not only a labour process, but also a process of creating surplus value, has this in common, that it is not the workman that employs the instruments of labour, but the instruments of labour that employ the workman. But it is only in the factory system that this inversion for the first time acquires technical and palpable reality. By means of its conversion into an automaton, the instrument of labour confronts the labourer, during the labour process, in the shape of capital, of dead labour, that dominates, and pumps dry, living labour power. The separation of the intellectual powers of production from the manual labour, and the conversion of those powers into the might of capital over labour, is, as we have already shown, finally completed by modern industry erected on the foundation of machinery. The special skill of each individual insignificant factory operative vanishes as an infinitesimal quantity before the science, the gigantic physical forces, and the mass of labour that are embodied in the factory mechanism and, together with that mechanism, constitute the power of the 'master'. This 'master', therefore, in whose brain the machinery and his monopoly of it are inseparably united, whenever he falls out with his 'hands', contemptuously tells them:

The factory operatives should keep in wholesome remembrance the fact that theirs is really a low species of skilled labour; and that there is none which is more easily acquired, or of its quality more amply remunerated, or which by a short training of the least expert can be more quickly, as well as abundantly, acquired. ... The master's machinery really plays a far more important part in the business of production than the labour and the skill of the operative, which six months' education can teach, and a common labourer can learn (The Master Spinners' and Manufacturers' Defence Fund, Report of the Committee, 1854, p. 17).[13]

The technical subordination of the workman to the uniform motion of the instruments of labour, and the peculiar composition of the body of work people, consisting as it does of individuals of both sexes and of all ages, give rise to a barrack discipline, which is elaborated into a complete system in the factory, and which fully develops the before mentioned labour of overlooking, thereby dividing the work people into operatives and overlookers, into private soldiers and sergeants of an industrial army.

The main difficulty [in the automatic factory] ... lay ... above all in training human beings to renounce their desultory habits of work, and to identify themselves with the unvarying regularity of the complex automaton. To devise and administer a successful code of factory discipline, suited to the necessities of factory diligence, was the Herculean enterprise, the noble achievement of Arkwright! Even at the present day, when the system is perfectly organized and its labour lightened to the utmost, it is found nearly impossible to convert persons past the age of puberty, into useful factory hands (Ure, 1835, p. 15).

13. We shall see hereafter, that the 'master' can sing quite another song, when he is threatened with the loss of his 'living' automaton.

The factory code in which capital formulates, like a private legislator, and at his own good will, his autocracy over his work people, unaccompanied by that division of responsibility, in other matters so much approved of by the bourgeoisie, and unaccompanied by the still more approved representative system, this code is but the capitalistic caricature of that social regulation of the labour process which becomes requisite in cooperation on a great scale, and in the employment in common, of instruments of labour and especially of machinery. The place of the slave driver's lash is taken by the over-looker's book of penalties. All punishments naturally resolve themselves into fines and deductions from wages, and the law-giving talent of the factory Lycurgus so arranges matters, that a violation of his laws is, if possible, more profitable to him than the keeping of them. [. . .]

As with the division of labour in the interior of the manufacturing work-shops, so it is with the division of labour in the interior of society. So long as handicraft and manufacture form the general groundwork of social pro-duction, the subjection of the producer to one branch exclusively, the break-ing up of the multifariousness of his employment,[14] is a necessary step in the development. On that groundwork each separate branch of production acquires empirically the form that is technically suited to it, slowly perfects it, and, so soon as a given degree of maturity has been reached, rapidly crystallizes that form. The only thing, that here and there causes a change, besides new raw material supplied by commerce, is the gradual alteration of instruments of labour. But their form, too, once definitely settled by ex-perience, petrifies, as is proved by their being in many cases handed down in the same form by one generation to another during thousands of years. A characteristic feature is, that, even down into the eighteenth century, the different trades were called 'mysteries' (*mystères*),[15] into their secrets none but those duly initiated could penetrate. Modern Industry rent the veil that concealed from men their own social process of production, and that turned the various, spontaneously divided branches of production into so many

14. 'In some parts of the Highlands of Scotland, not many years ago, every peasant, according to the Statistical Account, made his own shoes of leather tanned by himself. Many a shepherd and cottar too, with his wife and children, appeared at Church in clothes which had been touched by no hands but their own, since they were shorn from the sheep and sown in the flaxfield. In the preparation of these, it is added, scarcely a single article had been purchased, except the awl, needle, thimble, and a very few parts of the iron-work employed in the weaving. The dyes, too, were chiefly extracted by the women from trees, shrubs and herbs' (Stewart, 1869, vol. 8, pp. 327–8).

15. In the celebrated *Livre des métiers* of Etienne Boileau, we find it prescribed that a journeyman on being admitted among the masters had to swear 'to love his brethren with brotherly love, to support them in their respective trades, not wilfully to betray the secrets of the trade, and besides, in the interests of all, not to recommend his own wares by calling the attention of the buyers to the defects in the articles made by others'.

riddles, not only to outsiders, but even to the initiated. The principle which it pursued, of resolving each process into its constituent movements, without any regard to their possible execution by the hand of man, created the new modern science of technology. The varied, apparently unconnected, and petrified forms of the industrial processes now resolved themselves into so many conscious and systematic applications of natural science to the attainment of given useful effects. Technology also discovered the few main fundamental forms of motion, which, despite the diversity of the instruments used, are necessarily taken by every productive action of the human body; just as the science of mechanics sees in the most complicated machinery nothing but the continual repetition of the simple mechanical powers.

Modern Industry never looks upon and treats the existing form of a process as final. The technical basis of that industry is therefore revolutionary, while all earlier modes of production were essentially conservative.[16] By means of machinery, chemical processes and other methods, it is continually causing changes not only in the technical basis of production, but also in the functions of the labourer, and in the social combinations of the labour process. At the same time, it thereby also revolutionizes the division of labour within the society, and incessantly launches masses of capital and of work people from one branch of production to another. But if Modern Industry, by its very nature, therefore necessitates variation of labour, fluency of function, universal mobility of the labourer, on the other hand, in its capitalistic form, it reproduces the old division of labour with its ossified particularizations. We have seen how this absolute contradiction between the technical necessities of Modern Industry, and the social character inherent in its capitalistic form, dispels all fixity and security in the situation of the labourer; how it constantly threatens, by taking away the instruments of labour, to snatch from his hands his means of subsistence,[17] and, by suppressing his detail-function, to make him superfluous. We have seen, too, how this antagonism vents its rage in the creation of that mon-

16. 'The bourgeoisie cannot exist without continally revolutionizing the instruments of production, and thereby the relations of production and all the social relations. Conservation, in an unaltered form, of the old modes of production was on the contrary the first condition of existence for all earlier industrial classes. Constant revolution in production, uninterrupted disturbance of all social conditions, everlasting uncertainty and agitation, distinguish the bourgeois epoch from all earlier ones. All fixed, fast-frozen relations, with their train of ancient and venerable prejudices and opinions, are swept away, all new formed ones become antiquated before they can ossify. All that is solid melts into air, all that is holy is profaned, and man is at last compelled to face with sober senses his real conditions of life, and his relations with his kind' (Engels and Marx, 1848, p. 5).

17.   You take my life
    When you do take the means whereby I live. Shakespeare, *Merchant of Venice*, IV, 1.

strosity, an industrial reserve army, kept in misery in order to be always at the disposal of capital; in the incessant human sacrifices from among the working class, in the most reckless squandering of labour power, and in the devastation caused by a social anarchy which turns every economical progress into a social calamity. This is the negative side. But if, on the one hand, variation of work at present imposes itself after the manner of an over-powering natural law, and with the blindly destructive action of a natural law that meets with resistance at all points, Modern Industry, on the other hand, through its catastrophes imposes the necessity of recognizing, as a fundamental law of production, variation of work, consequently fitness of the labourer for varied work, consequently the greatest possible develop-ment of his varied aptitudes. It becomes a question of life and death for society to adapt the mode of production to the normal functioning of this law. Modern Industry, indeed, compels society, under penalty of death, to replace the detail-worker of today, crippled by life-long repetition of one and the same trivial operation, and thus reduced to the mere fragment of a man, by the fully developed individual, fit for a variety of labours, ready to face any change of production, and to whom the different social functions he performs, are but so many modes of giving free scope to his own natural and acquired powers.

One step already spontaneously taken towards effecting this revolution is the establishment of technical and agricultural schools, and of 'écoles d'enseignement professionnel', in which the children of the working men receive some little instruction in technology and in the practical handling of the various implements of labour. Though the Factory Act, that first and meagre concession wrung from capital, is limited to combining elementary education with work in the factory, there can be no doubt that when the working class comes into power, as inevitably it must, technical instruction, both theoretical and practical, will take its proper place in the working-class schools. There is also no doubt that such revolutionary ferments, the final result of which is the abolition of the old division of labour, are diametrically opposed to the capitalistic form of production, and to the economic status of the labourer corresponding to that form. But the historical development of the antagonisms, immanent in a given form of production, is the only way in which that form of production can be dissolved and a new form estab-lished. 'Ne sutor ultra crepidam' – this nec plus ultra of handicraft wisdom became sheer nonsense, from the moment the watchmaker Watt invented the steam engine, the barber Arkwright, the throstle, and the working-jeweller, Fulton, the steamship.[18]

18. John Bellers, a very phenomenon in the history of political economy, saw most clearly at the end of the seventeenth century, the necessity for abolishing the present system of education and division of labour, which beget hypertrophy and atrophy at the

So long as Factory legislation is confined to regulating the labour in factories, manufactories, etc., it is regarded as a mere interference with the exploiting rights of capital. But when it comes to regulating the so-called 'home-labour', it is immediately viewed as a direct attack on the patria potestas, on parental authority. The tender-hearted English Parliament long affected to shrink from taking this step. The force of facts, however, compelled it at last to acknowledge that Modern Industry, in overturning the economical foundation on which was based the traditional family, and the family labour corresponding to it, had also unloosened all traditional family ties. The rights of the children had to be proclaimed. The final report of the Children's Employment Commission of 1866, states: 'It is unhappily, to a painful degree, apparent throughout the whole of the evidence, that against no persons do the children of both sexes so much require protection as against their parents.' The system of unlimited exploitation of childrens' labour in general and the so-called home-labour in particular is 'maintained only because the parents are able, without check or control, to exercise this arbitrary and mischievous power over their young and tender offspring. . . . Parents must not possess the absolute power of making their children mere "machines to earn so much weekly wage". . . . The children and young persons, therefore, in all such cases may justifiably claim from the legislature, as a natural right, that an exemption should be secured to them, from what destroys prematurely their physical strength, and lowers them in the scale of intellectual and moral beings.' It was not, however, the misuse of parental authority that created the capitalistic exploitation, whether direct or indirect, of children's labour; but, on the contrary, it was the capitalistic mode of exploitation which, by sweeping away the economical basis of parental authority, made its exercise degenerate into a mischievous misuse of power. However terrible and disgusting the dissolution, under the capitalist system, of the old family ties may appear, nevertheless, Modern Industry, by assigning as it does an important part in the process of production, outside the domestic sphere, to women, to young persons, and to children of both sexes, creates a new economical foundation for a higher form of the family and of the relations between the sexes. It is, of course, just as absurd to hold the Teutonic-Christian form of the family to be absolute and final as it would be to apply that character to the ancient Roman, the ancient Greek, or the

---

two opposite extremities of society. Amongst other things he says this: 'An idle learning being little better than the learning of idleness. . . . Bodily labour, it's a primitive institution of God. . . . Labour being as proper for the bodies' health as eating is for its living; for what pains a man saves by ease, he will find in disease. . . . Labour adds oyl to the lamp of life, when thinking inflames it. . . . A childish silly employ leaves the children's minds silly' (Proposals for raising a colledge of industry of all useful trades and husbandry, 1696).

Eastern forms, which moreover, taken together form a series in historic development. Moreover, it is obvious that the fact of the collective working group being composed of individuals of both sexes and all ages, must necessarily, under suitable conditions, become a source of humane development; although in its spontaneously developed, brutal, capitalistic form, where the labourer exists for the process of production, and not the process of production for the labourer, that fact is a pestiferous source of corruption and slavery.[19]

The necessity for a generalization of the Factory Acts, for transforming them from an exceptional law relating to mechanical spinning and weaving – those first creations of machinery – into a law affecting social production as a whole, arose, as we have seen, from the mode in which Modern Industry was historically developed. In the years of that industry, the traditional form of manufacture, of handicraft, and of domestic industry, is entirely revolutionized; manufactures are constantly passing into the factory system, and handicrafts into manufactures; and lastly, the spheres of handicraft and of the domestic industries become, in a, comparatively speaking, wonderfully short time, dens of misery in which capitalistic exploitation obtains free play for the wildest excesses. There are two circumstances that finally turn the scale: first, the constantly recurring experience that capital, so soon as it finds itself subject to legal control at one point, compensates itself all the more recklessly at other points; secondly, the cry of the capitalists for equality in the conditions of competitition, i.e. for equal restraint on all exploitation of labour. On this point let us listen to two heart-broken cries. Messrs Cooksley of Bristol, nail and chain, etc., manufacturers, spontaneously introduced the regulations of the Factory Act into their business. 'As the old irregular system prevails in neighbouring works, the Messrs Cooksley are subject to the disadvantage of having their boys enticed to continue their labour elsewhere after 6 p.m. "This", they naturally say, "is an injustice and loss to us, as it exhausts a portion of the boys' strength, of which we ought to have the full benefit."' Mr J. Simpson (paper box and bagmaker, London) states before the commissioners of the Children's Employment Commission: 'He would sign any petition for it' (legislative interference) ... 'As it was, he always felt restless at night, when he had closed his place, lest others should be working later than him, and getting away his orders.' Summarizing, the Children's Employment Commission says:

It would be unjust to the larger employers that their factories should be placed under regulation, while the hours of labour in the smaller places in their own branch of business were under no legislative restriction. And to the injustice

19. 'Factory labour may be as pure and as excellent as domestic labour, and perhaps more so' (Report of the Inspector of Factories, 31 October 1865).

arising from the unfair conditions of competition, in regard to hours, that would be created if the smaller places of work were exempt, would be added the disadvantage to the larger manufacturers, of finding their supply of juvenile and female labour drawn off to the places of work exempt from legislation. Further, a stimulus would be given to the multiplication of the smaller places of work, which are almost invariably the least favourable to the health, comfort, education and general improvement of the people.

In its final report the Commission proposes to subject to the Factory Act more than 1,400,000 children, young persons and women, of which number about one half are exploited in small industries and by the so-called homework. It says,

But if it should seem fit to Parliament to place the whole of that large number of children, young persons and females under the protective legislation above adverted to ... it cannot be doubted that such legislation would have a most beneficent effect, not only upon the young and the feeble, who are its more immediate objects, but upon the still larger body of adult workers, who would in all these employments, both directly and indirectly, come immediately under its influence. It would enforce upon them regular and moderate hours; it would lead to their places of work being kept in a healthy and cleanly state; it would therefore husband and improve that store of physical strength on which their own well-being and that of the country so much depends; it would save the rising generation from that overexertion at an early age which undermines their constitutions and leads to premature decay; finally, it would ensure them – at least up to the age of thirteen – the opportunity of receiving the elements of education, and would put an end to that utter ignorance ... so faithfully exhibited in the Reports of our Assistant Commissioners, and which cannot be regarded without the deepest pain, and a profound sense of national degradation.

References

BABBAGE, C. (1832), *On the Economy of Machinery and Manufactures*, Charles Knight, London.
ENGELS, F. (1845), *Condition of the Working Class in England, 1844*, Leipzig.
ENGELS, F., and MARX, K. (1848), *Manifesto of the Communist Party*, London.
SCHULZ, W. (1843), *Die Bewegung der Produktion*, Zurich.
STEWART, D. (1869), *Works*, ed. W. Hamilton, Kelley.
URE, A. (1835), *The Philosophy of Manufactures*, London.

(b) Politics and Education

Excerpts from Karl Marx, *Critique of the Gotha Programme*, 1875; Foreign Languages Publishing House, Moscow, 1959, pp. 33–6.

'The German workers' party demands as the intellectual and ethical basis of the state:
1. Universal and *equal public education* by the state. Universal compulsory school attendance. Free instruction.'

Equal public education? What idea lies behind these words? Is it believed that in present-day society (and it is only with this one has to deal) education can be *equal* for all classes? Or is it demanded that the upper classes also shall be compulsorily reduced to the modicum of education – the elementary school – that alone is compatible with the economic conditions not only of the wage workers but of the peasants as well?

'Universal compulsory school attendance. Free instruction.' The former exists even in Germany, the second in Switzerland and in the United States in the case of elementary schools. If in some states of the latter country higher educational institutions are also 'free' that only means in fact defraying the cost of education of the upper classes from the general tax receipts. [. . .]

The paragraph on the schools should at least have demanded technical schools (theoretical and practical) in combination with the elementary school.

'*Public education by the state*' is altogether objectionable. Defining by a general law the expenditures on elementary schools, the qualifications of the teaching staff, the branches of instruction, etc., and, as is done in the United States, supervising the fulfilment of these legal specifications by state inspectors, is a very different thing from appointing the state as the educator of the people! Government and church should rather be equally excluded from any influence on the school. Particularly, indeed, in the Prusso-German Empire (and one should not take refuge in the rotten subterfuge that one is speaking of a 'state of the future'; we have seen how matters stand in this respect) the state has need, on the contrary, of a very stern education by the people. [. . .]

'*Prohibition of child labour*.' Here it was absolutely essential to state the age limit.

A *general prohibition* of child labour is incompatible with the existence of large-scale industry and hence an empty, pious wish. Its realization – if it were possible – would be reactionary, since, with a strict regulation of the working time according to the different age groups and other safety measures for the protection of children, an early combination of productive labour with education is one of the most potent means for the transformation of present-day society.

Part Two
Education and Politics

It must be admitted that the academic treatment of politics is subject to far more profound disagreements than economics. Economics had developed in the early nineteenth century a far more rigorous conceptual system, mostly agreed on by all workers in the field, than the study of politics possesses, even today. Common understanding of the disagreements within the discipline is therefore not found in political theory or science as it is in economics.

What I am attempting, therefore, in this part of the Reader, is less to set out even a basic introduction to one conceptual scheme than to outline elements of *three* such schemes, which may be displayed as more or less common to both sociology and the study of politics.[1] This is a fortunate overlap, since the socio-political study of education is overwhelmingly sociological rather than political.

The first Reading by Collins contrasts two approaches, derived from classical perspectives in sociology, to the explanation of the increased educational provision in advanced industrial countries over the last century. It attempts to deduce more or less testable hypotheses from these approaches. The first of them is functionalism. It may roughly be described as the explanation of social phenomena in terms of their contribution to the stability of the social structure. It is specified as this to yield explanations by means of a range of technical functions, interpreted as necessary to that stability. The second may be summarized equally crudely as attempting to take more account of social conflict, and refers the increase to competition for scarce resources between variously defined social groups.

Durkheim plays an important part in the history of the functionalist tradition. Another important aspect of this tradition is its stress on 'value consensus' or ideological agreement on basic issues between members of a society; in it, such consensus is regarded as a vital support of the stability of the society, and society in a sense as depending on a moral foundation in such consensus. Durkheim clearly articulates the

1. In the correspondence material which relates to this Reader, an attempt is made to suggest modes of identifying compatibilities and incompatibilities between such schemes.

thesis that education is vitally important in contributing to such consensus; further, and interestingly, he does so in a way similar to his treatment of religion in his classic *Elementary Forms of the Religious Life* – it is not values only that are instilled, but a system of ideas also, which is itself a representation of the society, and reflects its structure. There is thus, at a very high level of generality, an attempt to provide a social or societal explanation of the curricular content of education. This attempt is also made, in a very different way, in the piece by Althusser.

In the pieces by Weber, on the other hand, as in the rest of his work, we find little systematic general treatment of education. What we do find is an emphasis on the multifarious groups in societies and on the variety of the dimensions by which they may significantly be characterized. The competition between these groups for differential advantage is seen as a basic social process; but with only very general principles, such as 'rationality' or 'prestige' to unite them, it is hard to retain any *concept* of educational or social *system*. Weber stresses rather some of the possible uses to which such groups may put education. A further development of this perspective requires specification of the systematic differences within education pertaining to the differential involvement of such different groups, and a treatment of the curricular content of education in this light.

Althusser's treatment on the other hand emphasizes the unity of society – though this unity is seen as far from tranquil. All other social relations are seen as connected in the last instance to relations of economic production; and it is in all these social relations that classes exist and struggle, not only at the economic but also at the political and ideological level. Althusser is therefore committed to seeing the educational system as a site of the class struggle; for it operates within ideology in his inclusive and complex sense of the term, which is explained at length in his essay.

A more empirical discussion of the political dimensions of education is found in Morris's paper. He tries to relocate the position of the educational system within, at least nineteenth-century English, society. His article exemplifies the place of political ideology in educational provision, and also provides empirical material to be worked on in the light of the three more theoretical pieces in this section, and also of the Second Reading by Marx (10b).

We have, then, a number of different approaches to the sociological study of education and politics, which partly overlap in respect of the aspects with which they deal; and it is hoped that these Readings will contribute not only to this sociological study, but also provide concepts for the explanation of the context of directly educational policies.

11 R. Collins

Functional and Conflict Theories of Educational Stratification*

R. Collins, 'Functional and conflict theories of educational stratification',
American Sociological Review, vol. 36, 1971, pp. 1002–19.

Education has become highly important in occupational attainment in modern America, and thus occupies a central place in the analysis of stratification and of social mobility. This paper attempts to assess the adequacy of two theories in accounting for available evidence on the link between education and stratification: a functional theory concerning trends in technical skill requirements in industrial societies; and a conflict theory derived from the approach of Max Weber, stating the determinants of various outcomes in the struggles among status groups. It will be argued that the evidence best supports the conflict theory, although technical requirements have important effects in particular contexts. It will be further argued that the construction of a general theory of the determinants of stratification in its varying forms is best advanced by incorporating elements of the functional analysis of technical requirements of specific jobs at appropriate points within the conflict model. The conclusion offers an interpretation of historical change in education and stratification in industrial America, and suggests where further evidence is required for more precise tests and for further development of a comprehensive explanatory theory.

The importance of education

A number of studies have shown that the number of years of education is a strong determinant of occupational achievement in America with social origins constant. They also show that social origins affect educational attainment, and also occupational attainment after the completion of education (Blau and Duncan, 1967, pp. 163–205; Eckland, 1965; Sewell, Haller and Portes, 1969; Duncan and Hodge, 1963; Lipset and Bendix, 1959, pp. 189–92). There are differences in occupational attainment independent of social origins between the graduates of more prominent and less prominent secondary schools, colleges, graduate schools and law schools (Smigel, 1964, pp. 39, 73–7, 117; Havemann and West, 1952, pp. 179–81; Ladinsky, 1967; Hargens and Hagstrom, 1967).

* I am indebted to Joseph Ben-David, Reinhard Bendix, Bennett Berger, Margaret S. Gordon, Joseph R. Gusfield, Stanford M. Lyman, Martin A. Trow and Harold L.

Educational requirements for employment have become increasingly widespread, not only in elite occupations but also at the bottom of the occupational hierarchy (see Table 1). In a 1967 survey of the San Francisco, Oakland, and San Jose areas (Collins, 1969), 17 per cent of the employers surveyed required at least a high-school diploma for employment in even

Table 1 **Percentage of employers requiring various minimum educational levels of employees, by occupational level**

National survey, 1937–8

	Un-skilled	Semi-skilled	Skilled	Clerical	Mana-gerial	Pro-fessional
Less than high school	99	97	89	33	32	9
High-school diploma	1	3	11	63	54	16
Some college				1	2	23
College degree				3	12	52
	100	100	100	100	100	100

San Francisco Bay area, 1967

	Un-skilled	Semi-skilled	Skilled	Clerical	Mana-gerial	Pro-fessional
Less than high school	83	76	62	29	27	10
High-school diploma	16	24	28	68	14	4
Vocational training beyond high school	1	1	10	2	2	4
Some college				2	12	7
College degree					41	70
Graduate degree					3	5
	100	100	100	101	99	100
	(244)	(237)	(245)	(306)	(288)	(240)

Sources: Bell (1940, p. 264), as analysed in Thomas (1956, p. 346); and Collins (1969, Table III–1). Bell does not report the number of employers in the sample, but it was apparently large.

unskilled positions;[1] a national survey (Bell, 1940) in 1937–8 found a comparable figure of 1 per cent. At the same time, educational requirements appear to have become more specialized, with 38 per cent of the organizations in the 1967 survey which required college degrees of managers preferring business administration training, and an additional 15 per cent preferring engineering training; such requirements appear to have been

Wilensky for advice and comment; and to Margaret S. Gordon for making available data collected by the Institute of Industrial Relations of the University of California at Berkeley, under grants from the US Office of Education and US Department of Labor. Their endorsement of the views expressed here is not implied.

1. This survey covered 309 establishments with 100 or more employees, representing all major industry groups.

virtually unknown in the 1920s (Pierson, 1959, pp. 34–54). At the same time, the proportions of the American population attending schools through the advanced levels have risen sharply during the last century (Table 2). Careers are thus increasingly shaped within the educational system.

The technical-function theory of education

A common explanation of the importance of education in modern society may be termed the technical-function theory. Its basic propositions, found in a number of sources (see, for example, B. Clark, 1962; Kerr *et al.*, 1960), may be stated as follows:

1. The skill requirements of jobs in industrial society constantly increase because of technological change. Two processes are involved: (a) the proportion of jobs requiring low skill decreases and the proportion requiring high skill increases; and (b) the same jobs are upgraded in skill requirements.

2. Formal education provides the training, either in specific skills or in general capacities, necessary for the more highly skilled jobs.

3. Therefore, educational requirements for employment constantly rise, and increasingly larger proportions of the population are required to spend longer and longer periods in school.

The technical-function theory of education may be seen as a particular

Table 2 **Percentage educational attainment in the United States, 1869–1965**

Period	High-school graduates/ pop. 17 yrs. old	Resident college students/ pop. 18–21	B.A.s or 1st prof. degrees/ 1/10 of pop. 15–24	M.A.s or 2nd prof. degrees/ 1/10 of pop. 25–34	Ph.D.s/ 1/10 of pop. 25–34
1869–1870	2·0	1·7			
1879–1880	2·5	2·7			
1889–1890	3·5	3·0			
1899–1900	6·4	4·0	1·66	0·12	0·03
1909–1910	8·8	5·1	1·85	0·13	0·02
1919–1920	16·8	8·9	2·33	0·24	0·03
1929–1930	29·0	12·4	4·90	0·78	0·12
1939–1940	50·8	15·6	7·05	1·24	0·15
1949–1950	59·0	29·6	17·66	2·43	0·27
1959–1960	65·1	34·9	17·72	3·25	0·42
1963	76·3	38·0			
1965			19·71	5·02	0·73

Sources: *Historical Statistics of the United States*, Series A 28–29, H 327–338; *Statistical Abstract of the United States*, 1966, Tables 3 and 194; *Digest of Educational Statistics* (US Office of Education, 1967), Tables 66 and 88.

application of a more general functional approach. The functional theory of stratification (Davis and Moore, 1945) rests on the premises (a) that occupational positions require particular kinds of skilled performance; and (b) that positions must be filled with persons who have either the native ability, or who have acquired the training, necessary for the performance of the given occupational role.[2] The technical-function theory of education may be viewed as a subtype of this form of analysis, since it shares the premises that the occupational structure creates demands for particular kinds of performance, and that training is one way of filling these demands. In addition, it includes the more restrictive premises (1 and 2 above) concerning the way in which skill requirements of jobs change with industrialization, and concerning the content of school experiences.

The technical-function theory of education may be tested by reviewing the evidence for each of its propositions (1a, 1b and 2).[3] As will be seen, these propositions do not adequately account for the evidence. In order to generate a more complete explanation, it will be necessary to examine the evidence for the underlying functional propositions, (a) and (b). This analysis leads to a focus on the processes of stratification – notably group conflict – not expressed in the functional theory, and to the formalization of a conflict theory to account for the evidence.

Proposition (1a): *Educational requirements of jobs in industrial society increase because the proportion of jobs requiring low skill decreases and the proportion requiring high skill increases.* Available evidence suggests that this process accounts for only a minor part of educational upgrading, at least in a society that has passed the point of initial industrialization. Fifteen per cent of the increase in education of the US labor force during the twentieth century may be attributed to shifts in the occupational structure – a decrease in the proportion of jobs with low skill requirements and an increase in proportion of jobs with high skill requirements (Folger and Nam, 1964). The bulk of educational upgrading (85 per cent) has occurred *within* job categories.

2. The concern here is with these basic premises rather than with the theory elaborated by Davis and Moore to account for the universality of stratification. This theory involves a few further propositions: (c) in any particular form of society certain occupational positions are functionally most central to the operation of the social system; (d) the ability to fill these positions, and/or the motivation to acquire the necessary training, is unequally distributed in the population; (e) inequalities of rewards in wealth and prestige evolve to ensure that the supply of persons with the necessary ability or training meshes with the structure of demands for skilled performance. The problems of stating functional centrality in empirical terms have been subjects of much debate.

3. Proposition 3 is supported by Tables 1 and 2. The issue here is whether this can be explained by the previous propositions and premises.

Proposition (1b): *Educational requirements of jobs in industrial society rise because the same jobs are upgraded in skill requirements.* The only available evidence on this point consists of data collected by the US Department of Labor in 1950 and 1960, which indicate the amount of change in skill requirements of specific jobs. Under the most plausible assumptions as to the skills provided by various levels of education, it appears that the educational level of the US labor force has changed in excess of that which is necessary to keep up with skill requirements of jobs (Berg, 1970, pp. 38–60). Over-education for available jobs is found particularly among males who have graduated from college and females with high-school degrees or some college, and appears to have increased between 1950 and 1960.

Proposition (2): *Formal education provides required job skills.* This proposition may be tested in two ways: (a) Are better educated employees more productive than less educated employees? (b) Are vocational skills learned in schools, or elsewhere?

(a) *Are better educated employees more productive?* The evidence most often cited for the productive effects of education is indirect, consisting of relationships between *aggregate* levels of education in a society and its overall economic productivity. These are of three types:

(i) The national growth approach involves calculating the proportion of growth in the US Gross National Product attributable to conventional inputs of capital and labor; these leave a large residual, which is attributed to improvements in skill of the labor force based on increased education (Schultz, 1961; Denison, 1965). This approach suffers from difficulty in clearly distinguishing among technological change affecting productive arrangements, changes in the abilities of workers acquired by experience at work with new technologies, and changes in skills due to formal education and motivational factors associated with a competitive or achievement-oriented society. The assignment of a large proportion of the residual category to education is arbitrary. Denison (1965) makes this attribution on the basis of the increased income to persons with higher levels of education interpreted as rewards for their contributions to productivity. Although it is a common assumption in economic argument that wage returns reflect output value, wage returns cannot be used to prove the productive contribution of education without circular reasoning.

(ii) Correlations of education and level of economic development for nations show that the higher the level of economic development of a country, the higher the proportion of its population in elementary, secondary and higher education (Harbison and Myers, 1964). Such correlations beg the question of causality. There are considerable variations in school enrollments among countries at the same economic level, and many of these variations are explicable in terms of political demands for access to education (Ben-David, 1963–4). Also, the overproduction of educated personnel in countries whose level of economic development cannot absorb them suggests the demand for education need not come directly from the economy, and may run counter to economic needs (Hoselitz, 1965).

(iii) Time-lag correlations of education and economic development show that increases in the proportion of population in elementary school precede increases in economic development after a takeoff point at approximately 30 to 50 per cent of the seven to fourteen years old age-group in school. Similar anticipations of economic development are suggested for increases in secondary and higher education enrollment, although the data do not clearly support this conclusion (Peaslee, 1969). A pattern of advances in secondary-school enrollments preceding advances in economic development is found only in a small number of cases (twelve of thirty-seven examined in Peaslee, 1969). A pattern of growth of university enrollments and subsequent economic development is found in twenty-one of thirty-seven cases, but the exceptions (including the United States, France, Sweden, Russia and Japan) are of such importance as to throw serious doubt on any *necessary* contribution of higher education to economic development. The main contribution of education to economic productivity, then, appears to occur at the level of the transition to mass literacy, and not significantly beyond this level.

Direct evidence of the contribution of education to *individual* productivity is summarized by Berg (1970, pp. 85–104, 143–76). It indicates that the better educated employees are not generally more productive, and in some cases are less productive, among samples of factory workers, maintenance men, department-store clerks, technicians, secretaries, bank tellers, engineers, industrial research scientists, military personnel and federal civil service employers.

(b) *Are vocational skills learned in school, or elsewhere?* Specifically vocational education in the schools for manual positions is virtually independent of job fate, as graduates of vocational programs are not more likely to be employed than high school dropouts (Plunkett, 1960; Duncan, 1964). Most skilled manual workers acquire their skills on the job or casually (Clark and Sloan, 1966, p. 73). Retraining for important technological changes in industry has been carried out largely informally on-the-job; in only a very small proportion of jobs affected by technological change is formal retraining in educational institutions used (Collins, 1969, pp. 147–58; Bright, 1958).

The relevance of education for non-manual occupational skills is more difficult to evaluate. Training in specific professions, such as medicine, engineering, scientific or scholarly research, teaching and law can plausibly be considered vocationally relevant, and possibly essential. Evidences comparing particular degrees of educational success with particular kinds of occupational performance or success are not available, except for a few occupations. For engineers, high college grades and degree levels generally predict high levels of technical responsibility and high participation in professional activities, but not necessarily high salary or supervisory responsibility (Perrucci and Perrucci, 1970). At the same time, a number of practising engineers lack college degrees (about 40 per cent of engineers in the early 1950s; see Soderberg, 1963, p. 213), suggesting that even such highly technical skills may be acquired on the job. For academic research scientists, educational quality has little effect on subsequent productivity (Hagstrom and Hargens, 1968). For other professions, evidence is not available on the degree to which actual skills are learned in school rather than in practice. In professions such as medicine and law, where education is a legal requirement for admission to practice, a comparison group of non-educated practitioners is not available, at least in the modern era.

Outside of the traditional learned professions, the plausibility of the vocational importance of education is more questionable. Comparisons of the efforts of different occupations to achieve 'professionalization' suggest that setting educational requirements and bolstering them through licensing laws is a common tactic in raising an occupation's prestige and autonomy (Wilensky, 1964). The result has been the proliferation of numerous pseudo-professions in modern society; nevertheless these fail to achieve strong professional organization through lack of a monopolizable (and hence teachable) skill base. Business administration schools represent such an effort. (See Pierson, 1959, pp. 9, 55–95, 140; Gordon and Howell, 1959, pp. 1–18, 40, 324–37.) Descriptions of general, non-vocational education do not support the image of schools as places where skills are widely learned. Scattered studies suggest that the knowledge imparted in particular courses is retained only in small part through the next few years (Learned and Wood, 1938, p. 28), and indicate a dominant student culture concerned with non-academic interests or with achieving grades with a minimum of learning (Coleman, 1961; Becker, Geer and Hughes, 1968).

The technical-function theory of education, then, does not give an adequate account of the evidence. Economic evidence indicates no clear contributions of education to economic development, beyond the provisions of mass literacy. Shifts in the proportions of more skilled and less skilled jobs do not account for the observed increase in education of the American labor force. Education is often irrelevant to on-the-job productivity and is sometimes counter-productive; specifically vocational training seems to be derived more from work experience than from formal school training. The quality of schools themselves, and the nature of dominant student cultures suggest that schooling is very inefficient as a means of training for work skills.

Functional and conflict perspectives

It may be suggested that the inadequacies of the technical-function theory of education derive from a more basic source: the functional approach to stratification. A fundamental assumption is that there is a generally fixed set of positions, whose various requirements the labor force must satisfy. The fixed demand for skills of various types, at any given time, is the basic determinant of who will be selected for what positions. Social change may then be explained by specifying how these functional demands change with the process of modernization. In keeping with the functional perspective in general, the needs of society are seen as determining the behavior and the rewards of the individuals within it.

However, this premise may be questioned as an adequate picture of the fundamental processes of social organization. It may be suggested that the 'demands' of any occupational position are not fixed, but represent whatever behavior is settled upon in bargaining between the persons who fill the positions and those who attempt to control them. Individuals want jobs primarily for the rewards to themselves in material goods, power and prestige. The amount of productive skill they must demonstrate to hold their positions depends on how much clients, customers or employers can successfully demand of them, and this in turn depends on the balance of power between workers and their employers.

Employers tend to have quite imprecise conceptions of the skill requirements of most jobs, and operate on a strategy of 'satisfying' rather than optimizing – that is, setting average levels of performance as satisfactory, and making changes in procedures or personnel only when performance falls noticeably below minimum standards (Dill, Hilton and Reitman, 1962; March and Simon, 1958, pp. 140–41). Efforts to predict work performance by objective tests have foundered due to difficulties in measuring performance (except on specific mechanical tasks) and the lack of control groups to validate the tests (Anastasi, 1967). Organizations do not force their employees to work at maximum efficiency; there is considerable insulation of workers at all levels from demands for full use of their skills and efforts. Informal controls over output are found not only among production workers in manufacturing but also among sales and clerical personnel (Roy, 1952; Blau, 1955; Lombard, 1955). The existence of informal organization at the managerial level, the widespread existence of bureaucratic pathologies such as evasion of responsibility, empire-building and displacement of ends by means ('red tape'), and the fact that administrative work is only indirectly related to the output of the organization, suggest that managers, too, are insulated from strong technological pressures for use of technical skills. On all levels, wherever informal organization exists, it appears that standards of performance reflect the power of the groups involved.

In this light, it is possible to reinterpret the body of evidence that ascriptive factors continue to be important in occupational success even in advanced industrial society. The social mobility data summarized at the onset of this paper show that social origins have a direct effect on occupational success, even after the completion of education. Both case studies and cross-sectional samples amply document widespread discrimination against Negroes. Case studies show the operation of ethnic and class standards in employment based not merely on skin color but on name, accent, style of dress, manners and conversational abilities (Noland and Bakke, 1949; Turner, 1952; Taeuber, Taeuber and Cain, 1966; Nosow, 1956). Cross-sectional studies, based on both biographical and survey data, show that approximately 60 to 70 per cent of the American business elite come from upper-class and upper-middle-class families, and fewer than 15 per cent from working-class families (Taussig and Joselyn, 1932, p. 97; Warner and Abegglen, 1955, pp. 37–68; Newcomer, 1955, p. 53; Bendix, 1956, pp. 198–253; Mills, 1963, pp. 110–39). These proportions are fairly constant from the early 1800s through the 1950s. The business elite is overwhelmingly Protestant, male and completely white, although there are some indications of a mild trend toward declining social origins and an increase of Catholics and Jews. Ethnic and class background have been found crucial for career advancement in the professions as well (Ladinsky, 1963; Hall, 1946). Sexual stereotyping of jobs is extremely widespread (Collins, 1969, pp. 234–8).

In the traditional functionalist approach, these forms of ascription are treated as residual categories: carry-overs from a less advanced period, or marks of the imperfections of the functional mechanism of placement. Yet available trend data suggest that the link between social-class origins and occupational attainment has remained constant during the twentieth century in America (Blau and Duncan, 1967, pp. 81–113); the proportion of women in higher occupational levels has changed little since the late nineteenth century (Epstein, 1970, p. 7); and the few available comparisons between elite groups in traditional and modern societies suggest comparable levels of mobility (Marsh, 1963). Declines in racial and ethnic discrimination that appear to have occurred at periods in twentieth-century America may be plausibly explained as results of political mobilization of particular minority groups rather than by an increased economic need to select by achievement criteria.

Goode (1967) has offered a modified functional model to account for these disparities: that work groups always organize to protect their inept members from being judged by outsiders' standards of productivity, and that this self-protection is functional to the organizations, preventing a Hobbesian competitiveness and distrust of all against all. This argument re-establishes a functional explanation, but only at the cost of undermining the technological view of functional requirements. Further, Goode's conclusions can be put in other terms: it is to the advantage of groups of employees to organize so that they will not be judged by strict performance standards; and it is at least minimally to the advantage of the employer to let them do so, for if he presses them harder he creates dissension and alienation. Just how hard an employer *can* press his employees is not given in Goode's functional model. That is, his model has the disadvantage, common to functional analysis in its most general form, of covering too many alternative possibilities to provide testable explanations of specific outcomes. Functional analysis too easily operates as a justification for whatever particular pattern exists, asserting in effect that there is a proper reason for it to be so, but failing to state the conditions under which a particular pattern will hold rather than another. The technical version of job requirements has the advantage of specifying patterns, but it is this specific form of functional explanation that is jettisoned by a return to a more abstract functional analysis.

A second hypothesis may be suggested: the power of 'ascribed' groups may be the *prime* basis of selection in all organizations, and technical skills are secondary considerations depending on the balance of power. Education may thus be regarded as a mark of membership in a particular group (possibly at times its defining characteristic), not a mark of technical skills or achievement. Educational requirements may thus reflect the interests of whichever groups have power to set them. Weber (1968, p. 1000) interpreted educational requirements in bureaucracies, drawing especially on the history of public administration in Prussia, as the result of efforts by university graduates to monopolize positions, raise their corporate status, and thereby increase their own security and power *vis-à-vis* both higher authorities and clients. Gusfield (1958) has shown that educational requirements in the British civil service were set as the result of a power struggle between a victorious educated upper-middle-class and the traditional aristocracy.

To summarize the argument to this point: available evidence suggests that the technical-functional view of educational requirements for jobs leaves a large number of facts unexplained. Functional analysis on the more abstract level does not provide a testable explanation of which ascribed groups will be able to dominate which positions. To answer this question, one must leave the functional frame of reference and examine the conditions of relative power of each group.

A conflict theory of stratification

The conditions under which educational requirements will be set and changed may be stated more generally, on the basis of a conflict theory of stratification derived from Weber (1968, pp. 926–39; see also Collins, 1968), and from advances in modern organization theory fitting the spirit of this approach.

(a) *Status groups*. The basic units of society are associational groups sharing common cultures (or 'subcultures'). The core of such groups is families and friends, but they may be extended to religious, educational or ethnic communities. In general, they comprise all persons who share a sense of status equality based on participation in a common culture: styles of language, tastes in clothing and decor, manners and other ritual observances, conversational topics and styles, opinions and values, and preferences in sports, arts and media. Participation in such cultural groups gives individuals their fundamental sense of identity, especially in contrast with members of other associational groups in whose everyday culture they cannot participate comfortably. Subjectively, status groups distinguish themselves from others in terms of categories of *moral evaluation* such as 'honor', 'taste', 'breeding', 'respectability', 'propriety', 'cultivation', 'good fellows', 'plain folks', etc. Thus the exclusion of persons who lack the ingroup culture is felt to be normatively legitimated.

There is no *a priori* determination of the number of status groups in a particular society, nor can the degree to which there is a consensus on a rank order among them be stated in advance. These are not matters of definition, but empirical variations, the causes of which are subjects of other developments of the conflict theory of stratification. Status groups should be regarded as ideal types, without implication of *necessarily distinct* boundaries; the concepts remain useful even in the case where associational groupings and their status cultures are fluid and overlapping, as hypotheses about the conflicts among status groups may remain fruitful even under these circumstances.

Status groups may be derived from a number of sources. Weber outlines three: (a) differences in life style based on economic situation (i.e. class); (b) differences in life situation based on power position; (c) differences in life situation deriving directly from cultural conditions or institutions, such as geographical origin, ethnicity, religion, education, or intellectual or aesthetic cultures.

(b) *Struggle for advantage*. There is a continual struggle in society for various 'goods' – wealth, power or prestige. We need make no assumption that every individual is motivated to maximize his rewards; however, since power and prestige are inherently scarce commodities, and wealth is often contingent upon them, the ambition of even a small proportion of persons for more than equal shares of these goods sets up an implicit counter-struggle on the part of others to avoid subjection and disesteem. Individuals may struggle with each other, but since individual identity is derived primarily from membership in a status group, and because the cohesion of status groups is a key resource in the struggle against others, the primary focus of struggle is between status groups rather than within them.

The struggle for wealth, power and prestige is carried out primarily through organizations. There have been struggles throughout history among organizations controlled by different status groups, for military conquest, business advantage or cultural (e.g. religious) hegemony, and intricate sorts of interorganizational alliances are possible. In the more complex societies, struggle between status groups is carried on in large part *within* organizations, as the status groups controlling an organization coerce, hire or culturally manipulate others to carry out their wishes (as in, respectively, a conscript army, a business or a church). Organizational research shows that the success of organizational elites in controlling their subordinates is quite variable. Under particular conditions, lower or middle members have considerable *de facto* power to avoid compliance, and even to change the course of the organizations (see Etzioni, 1961).

This opposing power from below is strengthened when subordinate members constitute a cohesive status group of their own; it is weakened when subordinates acquiesce in the values of the organization elite. Coincidence of ethnic and class boundaries produces the sharpest cultural distinctions. Thus, Catholics of immigrant origins have been the bulwarks of informal norms restricting work output in American firms run by WASPs, whereas Protestants of native rural backgrounds are the main 'rate-busters' (Collins, Dalton and Roy, 1946). Selection and manipulation of members in terms of status groups is thus a key weapon in intraorganizational struggles. In general, the organization elite selects its new members and key assistants from its own status group and makes an effort to secure lower-level employees who are at least indoctrinated to respect the cultural superiority of their status culture.[4]

4. It might be argued that the ethnic cultures may differ in their functionality: that middle-class Protestant culture provides the self-discipline and other attributes

Once groups of employees of different status groups are formed at various positions (middle, lower or laterally differentiated) in the organization, each of these groups may be expected to launch efforts to recruit more members of their own status group. This process is illustrated by conflicts among whites and blacks, Protestants and Catholics and Jews, Yankee, Irish and Italian, etc. found in American occupational life (Hughes, 1949; Dalton, 1951). These conflicts are based on ethnically or religiously founded status cultures; their intensity rises and falls with processes increasing or decreasing the cultural distinctiveness of these groups, and with the succession of advantages and disadvantages set by previous outcomes of these struggles which determine the organizational resources available for further struggle. Parallel processes of cultural conflict may be based on distinctive class as well as ethnic cultures.

(c) *Education as status culture*. The main activity of schools is to teach particular status cultures, both in and outside the classroom. In this light, any failure of schools to impart technical knowledge (although it may also be successful in this) is not important; schools primarily teach vocabulary and inflection, styles of dress, aesthetic tastes, values and manners. The emphasis on sociability and athletics found in many schools is not extraneous but may be at the core of the status culture propagated by the schools. Where schools have a more academic or vocational emphasis, this emphasis may itself be the content of a particular status culture, providing sets of values, materials for conversation, and shared activities for an associational group making claims to a particular basis for status.

In so far as a particular status group controls education, it may use it to foster control within work organizations. Educational requirements for

---

necessary for higher organizational positions in modern society. This version of functional theory is specific enough to be subject to empirical test: are middle-class WASPs in fact better businessmen or government administrators than Italians, Irishmen or Jews of patrimonial or working-class cultural backgrounds? Weber suggested that they were in the initial construction of the capitalist economy within the confines of traditional society; he also argued that once the new economic system was established, the original ethic was no longer necessary to run it (Weber, 1930, pp. 180–83). Moreover, the functional explanation also requires some feedback mechanism whereby organizations with more efficient managers are selected for survival. The oligopolistic situation in large-scale American business since the late nineteenth century does not seem to provide such a mechanism; nor does government employment. Schumpeter, the leading expositor of the importance of managerial talent in business, confined his emphasis to the formative period of business expansion, and regarded the large, oligopolistic corporation as an arena where advancement came to be based on skills in organizational politics (1951, pp. 122–4); these personalistic skills are arguably more characteristic of the patrimonial cultures than of WASP culture.

employment can serve both to select new members for elite positions who share the elite culture and, at a lower level of education, to hire lower and middle employees who have acquired a general respect for these elite values and styles.

Tests of the conflict theory of educational stratification

The conflict theory in its general form is supported by evidence (1) that there are distinctions among status group cultures – based both on class and on ethnicity – in modern societies (Kahl, 1957, pp. 127–56, 184–220); (2) that status groups tend to occupy different occupational positions within organizations (see data on ascription cited above); and (3) that occupants of different organizational positions struggle over power (Dalton, 1959; Crozier, 1964). The more specific tests called for here, however, are of the adequacy of conflict theory to explain the link between education and occupational stratification. Such tests may focus either on the proposed mechanism of occupational placement, or on the conditions for strong or weak links between education and occupation.

Education as a mechanism of occupational placement. The mechanism proposed is that employers use education to select persons who have been socialized into the dominant status culture: for entrants to their own managerial ranks, into elite culture; for lower-level employees, into an attitude of respect for the dominant culture and the elite which carries it. This requires evidence that: (a) schools provide either training for the elite culture, or respect for it; and (b) employers use education as a means of selection for cultural attributes.

(a) Historical and descriptive studies of schools support the generalization that they are places where particular status cultures are acquired, either from the teachers, from other students, or both. Schools are usually founded by powerful or autonomous status groups, either to provide an exclusive education for their own children, or to propagate respect for their cultural values. Until recently most schools were founded by religions, often in opposition to those founded by rival religions; throughout the nineteenth century, this rivalry was an important basis for the founding of large numbers of colleges in the US, and of the Catholic and Lutheran school systems. The public-school system in the US was founded mainly under the impetus of WASP elites with the purpose of teaching respect for Protestant and middle-class standards of cultural and religious propriety, especially in the face of Catholic, working-class immigration from Europe (Crémin, 1961; Curti, 1935). The content of public-school education has consisted especially of middle-class, WASP culture (Waller, 1932, pp. 15–131; Becker, 1961; Hess and Torney, 1967).

At the elite level, private secondary schools for children of the WASP upper class were founded from the 1880s, when the mass indoctrination function of the growing public schools made them unsuitable as means of maintaining cohesion of the elite culture itself (Baltzell, 1958, pp. 327–72). These elite schools produce a distinctive personality type, characterized by adherence to a distinctive set of upper-class values and manners (McArthur, 1955). The cultural role of schools has been more closely studied in Britain (Bernstein, 1961; Weinberg, 1967), and in France (Bourdieu and Passeron, 1964), although Riesman and his colleagues (Riesman, 1958; Jencks and Riesman, 1968) have shown some of the cultural differences among prestige levels of colleges and universities in the United States.

(b) Evidence that education has been used as a means of cultural selection may be found in several sources. Hollingshead's (1949, pp. 360–88) study of Elmtown school children, school dropouts, and community attitudes toward them suggests that employers use education as a means of selecting employees with middle-class attributes. A 1945–6 survey of 240 employers in New Haven and Charlotte, NC, indicated that they regarded education as a screening device for employees with desirable (middle-class) character and demeanor; white-collar positions particularly emphasized educational selection because these employees were considered most visible to outsiders (Noland and Bakke, 1949, pp. 20–63).

A survey of employers in nationally prominent corporations indicated that they regarded college degrees as important in hiring potential managers, not because they were thought to ensure technical skills, but rather to indicate 'motivation' and 'social experience' (Gordon and Howell, 1959, p. 121). Business-school training is similarly regarded, less as evidence of necessary training (as employers have been widely sceptical of the utility of this curriculum for most positions) than as an indication that the college graduate is committed to business attitudes. Thus, employers are more likely to refuse to hire liberal-arts graduates if they come from a college which has a business school than if their college is without a business school (Gordon and Howell, 1959, pp. 84–7; see also Pierson, 1959, pp. 90–99). In the latter case, the students could be said not to have had a choice; but when both business and liberal-arts courses are offered and the student chooses liberal arts, employers appear to take this as a rejection of business values.

Finally, a 1967 survey of 309 California organizations (Collins, 1971) found that educational requirements for white-collar workers were highest in organizations which placed the strongest emphasis on normative control over their employees.[5] Normative control emphasis was indicated by (i)

5. Sample consisted of approximately one-third of all organizations with 100 or more employees in the San Francisco, Oakland and San Jose metropolitan areas. See Gordon and Thal-Larsen (1969) for a description of procedures and other findings.

relative emphasis on the absence of police record for job applicants; (ii) relative emphasis on a record of job loyalty; (iii) Etzioni's (1961) classification of organizations into those with high normative control emphasis (financial, professional services, government and other public services organizations) and those with remunerative control emphasis (manufacturing, construction and trade). These three indicators are highly interrelated, thus mutually validating their conceptualization as indicators of normative control emphasis. The relationship between normative control emphasis and educational requirements holds for managerial requirements and white-collar requirements generally, both including and excluding professional and technical positions. Normative control emphasis does not affect blue-collar education requirements.

Variations in linkage between education and occupation

The conflict model may also be tested by examining the case in which it predicts education will be relatively important or unimportant in occupational attainment. Education should be most important where two conditions hold simultaneously: (1) the type of education most closely reflects membership in a particular status group, and (2) that group controls employment in particular organizational contexts. Thus, education will be most important where the fit is greatest between the culture of the status groups emerging from schools, and the status group doing the hiring; it will be least important where there is the greatest disparity between the culture of the school and of the employers.

This fit between school-group culture and employer culture may be conceptualized as a continuum. The importance of elite education is highest where it is involved in selection of new members of organizational elites, and should fade off where jobs are less elite (either lower level jobs in these organizations, or jobs in other organizations not controlled by the cultural elite). Similarly, schools which produce the most elite graduates will be most closely linked to elite occupations; schools whose products are less well socialized into elite culture are selected for jobs correspondingly less close to elite organizational levels.

In the United States, the schools which produce culturally elite groups, either by virtue of explicit training or by selection of students from elite backgrounds, or both, are the private prep schools at the secondary level; at the higher level, the elite colleges (the Ivy League, and to a lesser degree the major state universities); at the professional training level, those professional schools attached to the elite colleges and universities. At the secondary level, schools which produce respectably socialized, non-elite persons are the public high schools (especially those in middle-class residential areas); from the point of view of the culture of WASP employers, Catholic schools (and all-black schools) are less acceptable. At the level of higher education, Catholic and black colleges and professional schools are less elite, and commercial training schools are the least elite form of education.

In the United States, the organizations most clearly dominated by the WASP upper class are large, nationally organized business corporations, and the largest law firms (Domhoff, 1967, pp. 38–62). Those organizations more likely to be dominated by members of minority ethnic cultures are the smaller and local businesses in manufacturing, construction and retail trade; in legal practice, solo rather than firm employment. In government employment, local governments appear to be more heavily dominated by ethnic groups, whereas particular branches of the national government (notably the State Department and the Treasury) are dominated by WASP elites (Domhoff, 1967, pp. 84–114, 132–7).

Evidence on the fit between education and employment is available for only some of these organizations. In a broad sample of organizational types (Collins, 1971) educational requirements were higher in the bigger organizations, which also tended to be organized on a national scale, than in smaller and more localistic organizations.[6] The finding of Perrucci and Perrucci (1970) that upper-class social origins were important in career success precisely within the group of engineers who graduated from the most prestigious engineering schools with the highest grades may also bear on this question; since the big national corporations are most likely to hire this academically elite group, the importance of social origins within this group tends to corroborate the interpretation of education as part of a process of elite cultural selection in those organizations.

Among lawyers, the predicted differences are clear: graduates of the law schools attached to elite colleges and universities are more likely to be employed in firms, whereas graduates of Catholic or commercial law schools are more likely to be found in solo practice (Ladinsky, 1967). The elite Wall Street law firms are most educationally selective in this regard, choosing not only from Ivy League law schools but from a group whose background includes attendance at elite prep schools and colleges (Smigel, 1964, pp. 39, 73–4, 117). There are also indications that graduates of ethnically-dominated professional schools are most likely to practise within the ethnic community; this is clearly the case among black professionals. In general, the evidence that graduates of black colleges (Sharp, 1970, pp. 64–7) and of Catholic colleges (Jencks and Riesman, 1968, pp. 357–66) have attained

6. Again these relationships hold for managerial requirements and white-collar requirements generally, both including and excluding professional and technical positions, but not for blue-collar requirements. Noland and Bakke (1949, p. 78) also report that larger organizations have higher educational requirements for administrative positions than smaller organizations.

lower occupational positions in business than graduates of white Protestant schools (at least until recent years) also bolsters this interpretation.[7]

It is possible to interpret this evidence according to the technical-function theory of education, arguing that the elite schools provide the best technical training, and that the major national organizations require the greatest degree of technical talent. What is necessary is to test simultaneously for technical and status-conflict conditions. The most direct evidence on this point is the California employer study (Collins, 1971), which examined the effects of normative control emphasis and of organizational prominence, while holding constant the organization's technological modernity, as measured by the number of technological and organizational changes in the previous six years. Technological change was found to affect educational requirements at managerial and white-collar (but not blue-collar) levels, thus giving some support to the technical-function theory of education. The three variables – normative control emphasis, organizational prominence and technological change – each independently affected educational require-ments, in particular contexts. Technological change produced significantly higher educational requirements only in smaller, localistic organizations, and in organizational sectors not emphasizing normative control. Organ-izational prominence produced significantly higher educational require-ments in organizations with low technological change, and in sectors de-emphasizing normative control. Normative control emphasis produced significantly higher educational requirements in organizations with low technological change, and in less prominent organizations. Thus, technical and normative status conditions all affect educational requirements; measures of association indicated that the latter conditions were stronger in this sample.

Other evidence bearing on this point concerns business executives only. A study of the top executives in nationally prominent businesses indicated that the most highly educated managers were not found in the most rapidly developing companies, but rather in the least economically vigorous ones, with highest education found in the traditionalistic financial and utility firms (Warner and Abegglen, 1955, pp. 141–3, 148). The business elite has

7. Similar processes may be found in other societies, where the kinds of organizations linked to particular types of schools may differ. In England, the elite 'public schools' are linked especially to the higher levels of the national civil service (Weinberg, 1967, pp. 139–43). In France, the elite Ecole Polytechnique is linked to both government and industrial administrative positions (Crozier, 1964, pp. 238–44). In Germany, universities have been linked principally with government administration, and business executives are drawn from elsewhere (Ben-David and Zloczower, 1962). Comparative analysis of the kinds of education of government officials, business executives, and other groups in contexts where the status group links of schools differ is a promising area for further tests of conflict and technical-function explanations.

always been highly educated in relation to the American populace, but education seems to be a correlate of their social origins rather than the determinant of their success (Mills, 1963, p. 128; Taussig and Joselyn, 1932, p. 200; Newcomer, 1955, p. 76). Those members of the business elite who entered its ranks from lower social origins had less education than the businessmen of upper and upper-middle-class origins, and those business-men who inherited their companies were much more likely to be college educated than those who achieved their positions by entrepreneurship (Bendix, 1956, p. 230; Newcomer, 1955, p. 80).

In general, the evidence indicates that educational requirements for em-ployment reflect employers' concerns for acquiring respectable and well-socialized employees; their concern for the provision of technical skills through education enters to a lesser degree. The higher the normative control concerns of the employer, and the more elite the organization's status, the higher his educational requirements.

Historical change

The rise in educational requirements for employment throughout the last century may be explained using the conflict theory, and incorporating elements of the technical-function theory into it at appropriate points. The principal dynamic has centered on changes in the supply of educated persons caused by the expansion of the school system, which was in turn shaped by three conditions:

1. Education has been associated with high economic and status position from the colonial period on through the twentieth century. The result was a popular demand for education as mobility opportunity. This demand has not been for vocational education at a terminal or commercial level, short of full university certification; the demand has rather focused on education giving entry into the elite status culture, and usually only those technically-oriented schools have prospered which have most closely associated them-selves with the sequence of education leading to (or from) the classical Bachelor's degree (Collins, 1969, pp. 68–70, 86–7, 89, 96–101).

2. Political decentralization, separation of church and state, and com-petition among religious denominations have made founding schools and colleges in America relatively easy, and provided initial motivations of competition among communities and religious groups that moved them to do so. As a result, education at all levels expanded faster in America than anywhere else in the world. At the time of the Revolution, there were nine colleges in the colonies; in all of Europe, with a population forty times that of America, there were approximately sixty colleges. By 1880 there were 811 American colleges and universities; by 1966, there were 2337. The United

States not only began with the highest ratio of institutions of higher education to population in the world, but increased this lead steadily, for the number of European universities was not much greater by the twentieth century than in the eighteenth (Ben-David and Zloczower, 1962).

3. Technical changes also entered into the expansion of American education. As the evidence summarized above indicates: (a) mass literacy is crucial for the beginnings of full-scale industrialization, although demand for literacy could not have been important in the expansion of education beyond elementary levels. More importantly, (b) there is a mild trend toward the reduction in the proportion of unskilled jobs and an increase in the proportion of highly skilled (professional and technical) jobs as industrialism proceeds, accounting for 15 per cent of the shift in educational levels in the twentieth century (Folger and Nam, 1964). (c) Technological change also brings about some upgrading in skill requirements of some continuing job positions, although the available evidence (Berg, 1970, pp. 38–60) refers only to the decade 1950–60. Nevertheless, as Wilensky (1964) points out, there is no 'professionalization of everyone', as most jobs do not require considerable technical knowledge of the order of that required of the engineer or the research scientist.

The existence of a relatively small group of experts in high-status positions, however, can have important effects on the structure of competition for mobility chances. In the United States, where democratic decentralization favors the use of schools (as well as government employment) as a kind of patronage for voter interests, the existence of even a small number of elite jobs fosters a demand for *large-scale* opportunities to acquire these positions. We thus have a 'contest mobility' school system (Turner, 1960); it produced a widely educated populace because of the many dropouts who never achieve the elite level of schooling at which expert skills and/or high cultural status are acquired. In the process, the status value of American education has become diluted. Standards of respectability are always relative to the existing range of cultural differences. Once higher levels of education become recognized as an objective mark of elite status, and a moderate level of education as a mark of respectable middle-level status, increases in the supply of educated persons at given levels result in yet higher levels becoming recognized as superior, and previously superior levels become only average.

Thus, before the end of the nineteenth century, an elementary-school or home education was no longer satisfactory for a middle-class gentleman; by the 1930s, a college degree was displacing the high-school degree as the minimal standard of respectability; in the late 1960s, graduate-school or specialized professional degrees were becoming necessary for initial entry to many middle-class positions, and high-school graduation was becoming a standard for entry to manual laboring positions. Education has thus gradually become part of the status culture of classes far below the level of the original business and professional elites.

The increasing supply of educated persons (Table 2) has made education a rising requirement of jobs (Table 1). Led by the biggest and most prestigious organizations, employers have raised their educational requirements to maintain both the relative prestige of their own managerial ranks and the relative respectability of middle ranks.[8] Education has become a legitimate standard in terms of which employers select employees, and employees compete with each other for promotion opportunities or for raised prestige in their continuing positions. With the attainment of a mass (now approaching universal) higher education system in modern America, the ideal or image of technical skills becomes the legitimating culture in terms of which the struggle for position goes on.

Higher educational requirements, and the higher level of educational credentials offered by individuals competing for position in organizations, have in turn increased the demand for education by the populace. The interaction between formal job requirements and informal status cultures has resulted in a spiral in which educational requirements and educational attainments become ever higher. As the struggle for mass educational opportunities enters new phases in the universities of today and perhaps in the graduate schools of the future, we may expect a further upgrading of educational requirements for employment. The mobilization of demands by minority groups for mobility opportunities through schooling can only contribute an extension of the prevailing pattern.

Conclusion

It has been argued that conflict theory provides an explanation of the principal dynamics of rising educational requirements for employment in America. Changes in the technical requirements of jobs have caused more

8. It appears that employers may have raised their wage costs in the process. Their behavior is nevertheless plausible, in view of these considerations: (a) the thrust of organizational research since Mayo and Barnard has indicated that questions of internal organizational power and control, of which cultural dominance is a main feature, take precedence over purely economic considerations; (b) the large American corporations, which have led in educational requirements, have held positions of oligopolistic advantage since the late nineteenth century, and thus could afford a large internal 'welfare' cost of maintaining a well-socialized work force; (c) there are interorganizational wage differentials in local labor markets, corresponding to relative organizational prestige, and a 'wage-escalator' process by which the wages of the leading organizations are gradually emulated by others according to their rank (Reynolds, 1951); a parallel structure of 'educational status escalators' could plausibly be expected to operate.

limited changes in particular jobs. The conditions of the interaction of these two determinants may be more closely studied.

Precise measures of changes in the actual technical skill requirements of jobs are as yet available only in rudimentary form. Few systematic studies show how much of particular job skills may be learned in practice, and how much must be acquired through school background. Close studies of what is actually learned in school, and how long it is retained, are rare. Organizational studies of how employers rate performance and decide upon promotions give a picture of relatively loose controls over the technical quality of employee performance, but this no doubt varies in particular types of jobs.

The most central line of analysis for assessing the joint effects of status group conflict and technical requirements are those which compare the relative importance of education in different contexts. One such approach may take organization as the unit of analysis, comparing the educational requirements of organizations both to organizational technologies and to the status (including educational) background of organizational elites. Such analysis may also be applied to surveys of individual mobility, comparing the effects of education on mobility in different employment contexts, where the status group (and educational) background of employers varies in its fit with the educational culture of prospective employees. Such analysis of 'old school tie' networks may also simultaneously test for the independent effect of the technical requirements of different sorts of jobs on the importance of education. Inter-nation comparison provides variations here in the fit between types of education and particular kinds of jobs which may not be available within any particular country.

The full elaboration of such analysis would give a more precise answer to the historical question of assigning weight to various factors in the changing place of education in the stratification of modern societies. At the same time, to state the conditions under which status groups vary in organizational power, including the power to emphasize or limit the importance of technical skills, would be to state the basic elements of a comprehensive explanatory theory of the forms of stratification.

References

ANASTASI, A. (1967), 'Psychology, psychologists, and psychological testing', *American Psychologist*, vol. 22, April, pp. 297–306.

BALTZELL, E. D. (1958), *An American Business Aristocracy*, Macmillan.

BECKER, H. S. (1961), 'Schools and systems of stratification', in A. H. Halsey, J. Floud and C. A. Anderson (eds.), *Education, Economy and Society*, Free Press, pp. 91–104.

BECKER, H. S., GEER, B., and HUGHES, E. C. (1968), *Making the Grade: The Academic Side of College Life*, Wiley.

BELL, H. M. (1940), *Matching Youth and Jobs*, American Council on Education.

BEN-DAVID, J. (1963–4), 'Professions in the class systems of present-day societies', *Current Sociology*, vol. 5, no. 12, pp. 247–330.

BEN-DAVID, J., and ZLOCZOWER, A. (1962), 'Universities and academic systems in modern societies', *Eur. J. Sociol.*, vol. 31, pp. 45–85.

BENDIX, R. (1956), *Work and Authority in Industry*, Wiley.

BERG, I. (1970), *Education and Jobs*, Praeger.

BERNSTEIN, B. (1961), 'Social class and linguistic development', in A. H. Halsey, J. Floud and C. A. Anderson (eds.), *Education, Economy and Society*, Free Press.

BLAU, P. M. (1955), *The Dynamics of Bureaucracy*, University of Chicago Press.

BLAU, P. M., and DUNCAN, O. D. (1967), *The American Occupational Structure*, Wiley.

BOURDIEU, P., and PASSERON, J. C. (1964), *Les Héritiers: Les Etudiants et la Culture*, Les Editions de Minuit.

BRIGHT, J. R. (1958), 'Does automation raise skill requirements?', *Harvard Business Review*, vol. 16, July–August, pp. 85–97.

CLARK, B. R. (1962), *Educating the Expert Society*, Chandler.

CLARK, H. F., and SLOAN, H. S. (1966), *Classrooms on Main Street*, Teachers College Press.

COLEMAN, J. S. (1961), *The Adolescent Society*, Free Press.

COLLINS, O., DALTON, M., and ROY, D. (1946), 'Restriction of output and social cleavage in industry', *Applied Anthropol.*, vol. 5, Summer, pp. 1–14.

COLLINS, R. (1968), 'A comparative approach to political sociology', in R. Bendix *et al.* (eds.), *State and Society*, Little, Brown.

COLLINS, R. (1969), 'Education and employment', unpublished Ph.D. Dissertation, University of California at Berkeley.

COLLINS, R. (1971), 'Educational requirements for employment: a comparative organizational study', unpublished manuscript.

CRÉMIN, L. A. (1961), *The Transformation of the School*, Knopf.

CROZIER, M. (1964), *The Bureaucratic Phenomenon*, Tavistock.

CURTI, M. (1935), *The Social Ideas of American Educators*, Scribners.

DALTON, M. (1951), 'Informal factors in career achievement', *Amer. J. Sociol.*, vol. 56, March, pp. 407–15.

DALTON, M. (1959), *Men Who Manage*, Wiley.

DAVIS, K., and MOORE, W. (1945), 'Some principles of stratification', *Amer. Sociol. Rev.*, vol. 10, pp. 242–9.

DENISON, E. F. (1965), 'Education and economic productivity', in S. Harris (ed.), *Education and Public Policy*, McCutchen, pp. 328–40.

DILL, W. R., HILTON, T. L., and REITMAN, W. R. (1962), *The New Managers*, Prentice-Hall.

DOMHOFF, G. W. (1967), *Who Rules America?*, Prentice-Hall.

DUNCAN, B. (1964), 'Dropouts and the unemployed', *J. Polit. Econ.*, vol. 73, April, pp. 121–34.

DUNCAN, O. D., and HODGE, R. W. (1963), 'Education and occupational mobility: a regression analysis', *Amer. J. Sociol.*, vol. 68, pp. 629–44.

ECKLAND, B. K. (1965), 'Academic ability, higher education and occupational mobility', *Amer. Sociol. Rev.*, vol. 30, pp. 735–46.

EPSTEIN, C. F. (1970), *Woman's Place: Options and Limits in Professional Careers*, University of California Press.

ETZIONI, A. (1961), *A Comparative Analysis of Complex Organizations*, Free Press.

FOLGER, J. K., and NAM, C. B. (1964), 'Trends in education in relation to the occupational structure', *Sociol. Educ.*, vol. 38, pp. 19–33.

GOODE, W. J. (1967), 'The protection of the inept', *Amer. Sociol. Rev.*, vol. 32, pp. 5–19.

GORDON, M. S., and THAL-LARSEN, M. (1969), *Employer Policies in a Changing Labour Market*, Institute of Industrial Relations, University of California.

GORDON, R. A., and HOWELL, J. E. (1959), *Higher Education for Business*, Columbia University Press.

GUSFIELD, J. R. (1958), 'Equalitarianism and bureaucratic recruitment', *Admin. Sci. Q.*, vol. 2, pp. 521–41.

HAGSTROM, W. O., and HARGENS, L. L. (1968), 'Mobility theory in the sociology of science', Paper delivered at Cornell Conference on Human Mobility, Ithaca.

HALL, O. (1946), 'The informal organization of the medical profession', *Canadian J. Econ. Polit. Sci.*, vol. 12, February, pp. 30–44.

HARBISON, F., and MYERS, C. A. (1964), *Education, Manpower and Economic Growth*, McGraw-Hill.

HARGENS, L., and HAGSTROM, W. O. (1967), 'Sponsored and contest mobility of American academic scientists', *Sociol. Educ.*, vol. 40, pp. 24–38.

HAVEMANN, E., and WEST, P. S. (1952), *They Went to College*, Harcourt, Brace & World.

HESS, R. D., and TORNEY, J. V. (1967), *The Development of Political Attitudes in Children*, Aldine.

HOLLINGSHEAD, A. B. (1949), *Elmtown's Youth*, Wiley.

HOSELITZ, B. F. (1965), 'Investment in education and its political impact', in J. S. Coleman (ed.), *Education and Political Development*, Princeton University Press, pp. 541–65.

HUGHES, E. C. (1949), 'Queries concerning industry and society growing out of the study of ethnic relations in industry', *Amer. Sociol. Rev.*, vol. 14, pp. 211–20.

JENCKS, C., and RIESMAN, D. (1968), *The Academic Revolution*, Doubleday.

KAHL, J. A. (1957), *The American Class Structure*, Holt, Rinehart & Winston.

KERR, C., DUNLOP, J. T., HARBISON, F. H., and MYERS, C. A. (1960), *Industrialism and Industrial Man*, Harvard University Press.

LADINSKY, J. (1963), 'Careers of lawyers, law practice and legal institutions', *Amer. Sociol. Rev.*, vol. 28, February, pp. 47–54.

LADINSKY, J. (1967), 'Higher education and work achievement among lawyers', *Sociol. Q.*, vol. 8, Spring, pp. 222–32.

LEARNED, W. S., and WOOD, B. D. (1938), *The Student and His Knowledge*, Carnegie Foundation for the Advancement of Teaching.

LIPSET, S. M., and BENDIX, R. (1959), *Social Mobility in Industrial Society*, University of California Press.

LOMBARD, G. F. (1955), *Behavior in a Selling Group*, Harvard University Press.

MCARTHUR, C. (1955), 'Personality differences between middle and upper classes', *J. of Abnorm. and Soc. Psychol.*, vol. 50, pp. 247–54.

MARCH, J. G., and SIMON, H. A. (1958), *Organizations*, Wiley.

MARSH, R. M. (1963), 'Values, demand, and social mobility', *Amer. Sociol. Rev.*, vol. 28, August, pp. 567–75.

MILLS, C. W. (1963), *Power Politics and People*, Oxford University Press.

NEWCOMER, M. (1955), *The Big Business Executive*, Columbia University Press.

NOLAND, E. W., and BAKKE, E. W. (1949), *Workers Wanted*, Harper.

NOSOW, S. (1956), 'Labor distribution and the normative system', *Social Forces*, vol. 30, pp. 25–33.

PEASLEE, A. L. (1969), 'Education's role in development', *Economic Development and Cultural Change*, vol. 17, April, pp. 293–318.

PERRUCCI, C. C., and PERRUCCI, R. (1970), 'Social origins, educational contexts, and career mobility', *Amer. Sociol. Rev.*, vol. 35, June, pp. 451–63.

PIERSON, F. C. (1959), *The Education of American Businessmen*, McGraw-Hill.

PLUNKETT, M. (1960), 'School and early work experience of youth', *Occupational Outlook Quarterly*, vol. 4, pp. 22–7.

REYNOLDS, L. (1951), *The Structure of Labor Markets*, Harper.

RIESMAN, D. (1958), *Constraint and Variety in American Education*, Doubleday.

ROY, D. (1952), 'Quota restriction and goldbricking in a machine shop', *Amer. J. of Sociol.*, vol. 57, March, pp. 427–42.

SCHULTZ, T. W. (1961), 'Investment in human capital', *Amer. Econ. Rev.*, vol. 51, March, pp. 1–17.

SCHUMPETER, J. (1951), *Imperialism and Social Classes*, Augustus M. Kelly.

SEWELL, W. H., HALLER, A. O., and PORTES, A. (1969), 'The educational and early occupational attainment process', *Amer. Sociol. Rev.*, vol. 34, February, pp. 82–92.

SHARP, L. M. (1970), *Education and Employment: the Early Careers of College Graduates*, Johns Hopkins Press.

SMIGEL, E. O. (1964), *The Wall Street Lawyer*, Free Press.

SODERBERG, C. R. (1963), 'The American engineer', in K. S. Lynn, *The Professions in America*, Beacon Press, pp. 203–30.

TAEUBER, A. F., TAEUBER, K. E., and CAIN, G. G. (1966), 'Occupational assimilation and the competitive process: a reanalysis', *Amer. J. of Sociol.*, vol. 72, pp. 276–85.

TAUSSIG, F W., and JOSELYN, C. S. (1932), *American Business Leaders*, Macmillan.

THOMAS, L. (1956), *The Occupational Structure and Education*, Prentice-Hall.

TURNER, R. H. (1952), 'Foci of discrimination in the employment of nonwhites', *Amer. J. Sociol.*, vol. 58, pp. 247–56.

TURNER, R. H. (1960), 'Sponsored and contest mobility and the school system', *Amer. Sociol. Rev.*, vol. 25, October, pp. 855–67.

WALLER, W. (1932), *The Sociology of Teaching*, Russell and Russell.

WARNER, W. L., and ABEGGLEN, J. C. (1955), *Occupational Mobility in American Business and Industry, 1928–1952*, University of Minnesota Press.

WEBER, M. (1930), *The Protestant Ethic and the Spirit of Capitalism*, Scribners.

WEBER, M. (1968), *Economy and Society*, Westminster Press.

WEINBERG, I. (1967), *The English Public Schools: The Sociology of Elite Education*, Atherton Press.

WILENSKY, H. L. (1964), 'The professionalization of everyone?', *Amer. J. Sociol.*, vol. 70, September, pp. 137–58.

12 Emile Durkheim

Moral Education

Excerpts from Emile Durkheim, *Moral Education*, Free Press, 1961, pp. 148–52, 228–36, 275–8. Published in French, 1925.

Such an apprenticeship,[1] which can only be quite incomplete in the family, must devolve upon the school. In fact, there is a whole system of rules in the school that predetermine the child's conduct. He must come to class regularly, he must arrive at a specified time and with an appropriate bearing and attitude. He must not disrupt things in class. He must have learned his lessons, done his homework, and have done so reasonably well, etc. There are, therefore, a host of obligations that the child is required to shoulder. Together they constitute the discipline of the school. It is through the practice of school discipline that we can inculcate the spirit of discipline in the child.

Too often, it is true, people conceive of school discipline so as to preclude endowing it with such an important moral function. Some see in it a simple way of guaranteeing superficial peace and order in the class. Under such conditions, one can quite reasonably come to view these imperative requirements as barbarous – as a tyranny of complicated rules. We protest against this kind of regulation, which is apparently imposed on the child for the sole purpose of easing the teacher's task in inducing uniformity. Does not such a system evoke feelings of hostility in the student toward the teacher, rather than the affectionate confidence that should characterize their relationship?

In reality, however, the nature and function of school discipline is something altogether different. It is not a simple device for securing superficial peace in the classroom – a device allowing the work to roll on tranquilly. It is the morality of the classroom, just as the discipline of the social body is morality properly speaking. Each social group, each type of society, has and could not fail to have its own morality, which expresses its own make-up.

Now, the class is a small society. It is therefore both natural and necessary that it have its own morality corresponding to its size, the character of its elements, and its function. Discipline is this morality. The obligations we shall presently enumerate are the student's duties, just as the civic or professional obligations imposed by state or corporation are the duties of the adult. On the other hand, the schoolroom society is much closer to the society of

1. ['Learning to do his duty because it is his duty.' Ed.]

adults than it is to that of the family. For aside from the fact that it is larger, the individuals – teachers and students – who make it up are not brought together by personal feelings or preferences but for altogether general and abstract reasons, that is to say, because of the social function to be performed by the teacher, and the immature mental condition of the students. For all these reasons, the rule of the classroom cannot bend or give with the same flexibility as that of the family in all kinds and combinations of circumstances. It cannot accommodate itself to given temperaments. There is already something colder and more impersonal about the obligations imposed by the school: they are now concerned with reason and less with feelings; they require more effort and greater application. And although – as we have previously said – we must guard against overdoing it, it is nevertheless indispensable in order that school discipline be everything that it should be and fulfil its function completely. For only on this condition will it be able to serve as intermediary between the affective morality of the family and the more rigorous morality of civil life. It is by respecting the school rules that the child learns to respect rules in general, that he develops the habit of self-control and restraint simply because he should control and restrain himself. It is a first initiation into the austerity of duty. Serious life has now begun.

This, then, is the true function of discipline. It is not a simple procedure aimed at making the child work, stimulating his desire for instruction, or husbanding the energies of the teacher. It is essentially an instrument – difficult to duplicate – of moral education. The teacher to whom it is entrusted cannot guard it too conscientiously. It is not only a matter of his own interest and peace of mind; one can say without exaggeration that the morality of the classroom rests upon his resolution. Indeed, it is certain that an undisciplined class lacks morality. When children no longer feel restrained, they are in a state of ferment that makes them impatient of all curbs, and their behavior shows it – even outside the classroom. One can see analogous situations in the family when domestic education is overly relaxed. In school, this unwholesome ferment of excitement, the result of a failure of discipline, constitutes a more serious moral danger because the agitation is collective. We must never lose sight of the fact that the class is a small society. Thus, no member of this small group acts as though he were alone; each is subject to the influence of the group, and this we must consider most carefully.

Collective action, according to the way its influence is used, may enhance the good or increase the evil. Should its influence be abnormal, then, precisely because it excites and intensifies individual energies, it drives them on the road to catastrophe with all the greater energy. This accounts for immorality developing so readily in mobs and quite often reaching an exceptional degree of violence. The mob, we know, kills easily. A mob or crowd is a society, but one that is inchoate, unstable, without regularly organized discipline. Because it is a society the strong emotional forces generated in the crowd are especially intense. Therefore, they move quickly to excesses. A forceful and complex system of regulation is required to enclose them within normal limits, to prevent them from bursting all bounds. By definition, however, a mob lacks constituted rules, regulatory organs of any sort. The forces thus set loose are left entirely to themselves; consequently, it is inevitable that they allow themselves to go beyond all limits, that they know no moderation and spill out into tumultuous, destructive, and, as a result, almost necessarily immoral disorders.

A class without discipline is like a mob. Because a given number of children are brought together in the same class, there is a kind of general stimulation deriving from the common life and imparted to all the individual activities – a stimulation that, when everything goes along normally and is well directed, emerges as more enthusiasm, more concern about doing things well than if each student were working individually. But if the teacher has not developed the necessary authority then this hyperactivity degenerates into an unwholesome ferment, and a genuine demoralization sets in, the more serious as the class is larger. This demoralization becomes obvious in that those elements of least moral value in the class come to have a preponderant place in the common life; just as in political societies during periods of great flux, one sees hosts of harmful elements come to the surface of public life, while in normal times they would be hidden in the shadows.

It is important, therefore, to react against the discredit into which, for a number of years, discipline has tended to fall. Doubtless when one examines the rules of conduct that the teacher must enforce, in themselves and in detail, one is inclined to judge them as useless vexations; and the benevolent feelings, which childhood quite naturally inspires in us, prompt us to feel that they are excessively demanding. Is it not possible for a child to be good and yet fail to be punctual, to be unprepared at the specified time for his lesson or other responsibilities, etc.? If, however, instead of examining these school rules in detail, we consider them as a whole, as the student's code of duty, the matter takes on a different aspect. Then conscientiousness in fulfilling all these petty obligations appears as a virtue. It is the virtue of childhood, the only one in accord with the kind of life the child leads at that age, and consequently the only one that can be asked of him. This is why one cannot cultivate it too conscientiously. If, in a given class, the challenge to discipline results in a kind of partial demoralization, at least one may hope that it will be only a passing thing; but if the disturbance is general, if the whole system is discredited in public opinion and in the view of teachers themselves, then public morality is touched at one of its vital sources. [. . .]

Above all we must give the child the clearest possible idea of the social groups to which he belongs. It is here that the role of the educator is most important. If the child were left to himself he would conceive of the groups in which he is implicated only imperfectly and very late. They are too vast and complex for him to see with his eyes – except, of course, the family, since it is so small he can have face-to-face contact with it. Now, in order to attach the child to these groups, which is the final goal of moral education, it is not enough to give him an image of them. Beyond this, the image must be repeated with such persistence that it becomes, through the sole fact of repetition, an integrating element in himself, such that he can no longer do without it. Once again, we can only become attached to things through the impressions or images we have of them. To say that the idea we acquire of these social groups is a part of our consciousness is really to say that it cannot disappear without creating a painful void. Not only must we repeat this representation, but in repeating it, give the idea enough colour, form and life to stimulate action. It must warm the heart and set the will in motion. The point here is not to enrich the mind with some theoretical notion, a speculative conception; but to give it a principle of action, which we must make as effective as necessary and possible. In other words, the representation must have something emotional; it must have the characteristic of a sentiment more than of a conception. Since, in the long run, one only learns to do by doing, we must multiply the opportunities in which the sentiments thus communicated to the child can manifest themselves in actions. To learn the love of collective life we must live it, not only in our minds and imaginations, but in reality. It is not enough to form in a child the potential for attaching himself to the group. We must stimulate this power by effective exercise; for only thus can it take shape and become strengthened.

In sum, by broadening gradually the consciousness of the child so as to infuse it with the idea of the social groups to which he belongs and will belong; by linking, through repetition, these ideas intimately with the greatest possible number of other ideas and feelings, so that the former are constantly called to mind and come to occupy such an important place in the child's mind that he will resist any diminution or weakening of them; by communicating them with such warmth and sincerity that their emotive power becomes an active force; by developing that power of action through exercise – such is the general method we must follow to commit the child to the collective goals that he must pursue. There is nothing in this method beyond the power of the educator since it is simply a matter of giving the child an impression, as vivid and as forceful as possible, of things as they actually exist. The problem, then, at this stage, is to find out how this method is applicable in the school. There are two vehicles at our disposal: first, the school environment itself; secondly, that which is taught. Let us examine how these instruments of action should be used to achieve the desired end.

General influence of the school environment

To understand clearly the important role that the school environment can and should play in moral education we must first realize what the child faces when he comes to school. Up to that point he has only been acquainted with two kinds of groups. In the family the sentiment of solidarity is derived from blood relationships; and the moral bonds that result from such relationships are further re-enforced by intimate and constant contact of all the associated minds and by a mutual interpenetration of their lives. Then there are little groups of friends and companions – groups that have taken shape outside the family through free selection. Now, political society presents neither of these two characteristics. The bonds uniting the citizens of a given country have nothing to do with relationships or personal inclinations. There is therefore a great distance between the moral state in which the child finds himself as he leaves the family and the one towards which he must strive. This road cannot be travelled in a single stage. Intermediaries are necessary. The school environment is the most desirable. It is a more extensive association than the family or the little societies of friends. It results neither from blood relationships nor from free choice, but from a fortuitous and inevitable meeting among subjects brought together on the basis of similar age and social conditions. In that respect it resembles political society. On the other hand, it is limited enough so that personal relations can crystallize. The horizon is not too vast; the consciousness of the child can easily embrace it. The habit of common life in the class and attachment to the class and even to the school constitute an altogether natural preparation for the more elevated sentiments that we wish to develop in the child. We have here a precious instrument, which is used all too little and which can be of the greatest service.

It is the more natural to use the school to this end since it is precisely groups of young persons, more or less like those constituting the social system of the school, which have enabled the formation of societies larger than the family. With respect to animals, Espinas has already demonstrated that groupings of birds and mammals could not have taken shape if, at a certain moment in their lives, the young had not been induced to separate from their parents and formed societies of a new type, which no longer have domestic characteristics. Indeed, wherever the family keeps its members to itself it is easily self-sufficient; each particular family tends to live its own life, an autonomous life – tends to isolate itself from other families so as to provide more easily for itself; under these conditions, it is clearly impossible for another society to be formed. The small group appears only where the new generation, once it has been brought up, is induced to free itself from the family setting to lead a collective life of a new sort. Similarly, if, from the very beginning, inferior human societies are not limited to one household, if they comprise even in their humblest form a number of families, it is largely because the moral education of children is not undertaken by their parents, but by the elders of the clan. The elders would assemble the young, after they had reached a given age, to initiate them collectively into the religious beliefs, rites, traditions – in a word, to everything constituting the intellectual and moral patrimony of the group. Because of this gathering of the young into special groups, determined by age and not by blood, extra-familial societies have been able to come into being and perpetuate them-selves. The school is precisely a group of this kind; it is recruited according to the same principle. The gatherings of young neophytes, directed and taught by the elders, which we can observe in primitive societies, are already actual school societies and may be considered as the first form of the school. In asking the school to prepare children for a higher social life than that of the family, we are only asking something that is quite in accord with its character.

Furthermore, if there is a country in which the role of the school is par-ticularly important and necessary, it is ours. In this respect, we are living under quite special conditions. Indeed, with the exception of the school, there is no longer in this country any society intermediate between the family and the state – that is to say, a society that is not merely artificial or superficial. All the groups of this kind, which at one time ranged between domestic and political society – provinces, communes, guilds – have been totally abolished or at least survive only in very attenuated form. The province and the guild are only memories; communal life is very impover-ished and now holds a very secondary place in our consciousness.

The causes of this situation are well known. In order to achieve political and moral unity, the monarchy fought all forms of local particularism; it strove to reduce the autonomy of towns and provinces, to weaken their moral individuality so as to fuse the more easily and completely into the great collective personality of France. In this regard, the Revolution con-tinued and completed the work of the monarchy. All groupings that were opposed to this great movement of national consolidation – which was the essence of the revolutionary movement – anything that was an obstacle to the unity and the indivisibility of the Republic, was broken. Moreover, the spirit that animated the men of the Revolution became quite hostile toward intermediate groupings. This is the reason why until very recently our laws were frankly hostile to societies of this kind.

Now, this state of affairs constitutes a serious crisis. For morality to have a sound basis, the citizen must have an inclination toward collective life. It is only on this condition that he can become attached, as he should, to collective aims that are moral aims *par excellence*. This does not happen automatically; above all, this inclination toward collective life can only become strong enough to shape behavior by the most continuous practice. To appreciate social life to the point where one cannot do without it, one must have developed the habit of acting and thinking in common. We must learn to cherish these social bonds that for the unsocial being are heavy chains. We must learn through experience how cold and pale the pleasures of solitary life are in comparison. The development of such a temperament, such a mental outlook, can only be formed through repeated practice, through perpetual conditioning. If, on the contrary, we are invited only infrequently to act like social beings, it is impossible to be very interested in an existence to which we can only adapt ourselves imperfectly.

The nature of political life is such that we take part in it only intermittently. The state is far away. We are not directly involved in its activity. Among events at the national level, only the most considerable have repercussions that reach us. We do not constantly encounter those great political causes that can excite us, to which we can give ourselves entirely.

If then, with the exception of the family, there is no collective life in which we participate, if in all the forms of human activity – scientific, artistic, professional, and so on – in other words, in all that constitutes the core of our existence, we are in the habit of acting like lone wolves, our social temperament has only rare opportunities to strengthen and develop itself. Consequently, we are inevitably inclined to a more or less suspicious isolation, at least in regard to everything concerning life outside the family. Indeed, the weakness of the spirit of association is one of the characteristics of our national temperament. We have a marked inclination toward a fierce individualism, which makes the obligations of social life appear intolerable to us and which prevents us from experiencing its joys.

We seem to think that we cannot participate in a society without losing our freedom and reducing our stature. Therefore, we join associations only reluctantly, and as seldom as possible. There is nothing more instructive in this respect than a comparison of the life of the German and the French student. In Germany, everything is done in a group. People sing together. They take walks together. They play together. They philosophize together, or talk about science and literature. All kinds of associations, corresponding to every kind of human activity, function in parallel ways; thus, the young man is constantly involved in group life. He engages in serious occupations in a group, and he relaxes in a group. In France, on the other hand, until very recently, the principle was that of isolation; and if the appreciation of life in common is beginning to revive, it is far from being very deep. This is true of the adult as well as the young man. The only social relations for which we show any inclination are those sufficiently external so that we commit only the most superficial part of ourselves. That is why *salon* life has taken on such importance and attained such a great development in this country. It is because it is a way of satisfying to some extent – or rather a way of pretending to satisfy – that need of sociability, which, in spite of everything, still survives in us. Need we demonstrate how illusory that satisfaction is, since that form of life in common is only a game without any connection with the serious aspects of life?

No matter how necessary it is to remedy the situation, there can be no question of reviving the groupings of the past or of allotting them their erstwhile functions; if they disappeared, it is because they were no longer consonant with the new conditions of collective existence. What we must do is to try to bring to life new groupings, which are in harmony with the present-day social order and with the principles on which it reposes. But the only way of succeeding in this is to breathe life into the spirit of association. These groups cannot be created by force. If they are to have any real life they must be created by public opinion. Men must feel the need for them and be inclined to form groups of their own accord. Thus, we seem to be caught in a vicious circle. For these associations can only be reborn if the spirit of association and the sense of the group are aroused. On the other hand, we have seen that this sense can only be acquired through practice in the context of already existing associations. We can only reanimate collective life, revive it from this torpor, if we love it; we cannot learn to love it unless we live it, and in order to do so it must exist.

It is precisely at this point that the role of the school can be considerable. It is the means, perhaps the only one, by which we can leave this vicious circle. The school is a real group, of which the child is naturally and necessarily a part. It is a group other than the family. Its principal function is not, as in the case of the family, that of emotional release and the sharing of affections. Every form of intellectual activity finds scope in it, in embryonic form. Consequently, we have through the school the means of training the child in a collective life different from home life. We can give him habits that, once developed, will survive beyond school years and demand the satisfaction that is their due. We have here a unique and irreplaceable opportunity to take hold of the child at a time when the gaps in our social organization have not yet been able to alter his nature profoundly, or to arouse in him feelings that make him partially rebellious to common life. This is virgin territory in which we can sow seeds that, once taken root, will grow by themselves. Of course, I do not mean that education alone can remedy the evil – that institutions are not necessary demanding legislative action. But that action can only be fruitful if it is rooted in a state of opinion, if it is an answer to needs that are really felt. Thus, although we could not at any time do without the school to instil in the child a social sense, although we have here a natural function from which the school should never withdraw, today, because of the critical situation in which we find ourselves, the services that the school can render are of incomparable importance. [. . .]

To become attached to society, the child must feel in it something that is real, alive and powerful, which dominates the person and to which he also owes the best of himself. To be sure, if we fall into the trap of obsolete historical teachings and tell the child that modern law was created by Napoleon, that the literature of the seventeenth century was caused by the personal influence of Louis XIV, and that Luther made Protestantism, we will simply maintain that old prejudice we were discussing a while back. This doctrine strengthens old prejudices by attributing history to the making of a few *individuals* instead of recognizing in society a definite nature of its own which imposes itself on men. Worse than that, this prejudice may lead people to identify their country with one man. Today, we no longer need dwell on this naïvely oversimplified theory of history. For a century now, historians have emphasized the action of the collective and anonymous forces, which move nations because they are the work of nations, because they emanate not from such and such an individual, but from society as a whole. The history of France alone furnishes a thousand examples which give the child an idea of the reality of this impersonal life – feudalism, the crusades, the Renaissance.

There is one thing that may have an even more forceful impact on the student's mind. It is when he is shown, not only how at every moment each of us is affected by the collective action of our contemporaries, but also how each generation depends upon previous generations, how each century continues the work of its predecessors and advances in that path that they have traced for it – even when it thinks it is proceeding in an exactly opposite direction. What more instructive spectacle than to see social life inexorably moving in its own direction despite the endlessly changing composition of its personnel. Now then, there is no need at all to engage students in abstract philosophical considerations concerning the necessity of social evolution. Nothing would be more out of place. The point is simply to give them a strong impression of what historical development is. The point is, above all, to prevent false ideas, still only too current, from taking hold; and the history of this country lends itself admirably to the type of teaching we are proposing. That history, at bottom, has a remarkable unity. Few things are easier to demonstrate than the marvellous continuity with which it develops, from the moment monarchy consolidates itself and subordinates feudalism to it, when the towns appeared, to the French Revolution. The most diverse and contrasting regimes were the unwitting instruments of this achievement, so compelling were the convergent circumstances pushing them in that direction. Absolute monarchy and revolutionary democracy are mutually exclusive; yet the former cleared the way for the latter. I have previously shown how the moral unity of this country, wrought by men of the Revolution, was prepared by the Ancien Régime. The connection between the struggle of the communes, the towns, to assert themselves on the one hand, and the French Revolution on the other is recognized today by everybody. It is also well known that the emancipation of the communes was favoured by the kings. We must nevertheless be wary of facile notions about continuity. The teaching of history would be false to its goal if it did not leave the impression that, as a well-known aphorism puts it, history neither begins nor ends anywhere. In order to secure loyalty to the ideas that found their expression at the end of the last century, we need not present them as a sort of unintelligible improvisation. Are they not, on the contrary, clothed with more authority if we show that they were actually the natural product of everything that went on before? Indeed, the glory of the men of the Revolution would not be diminished in this way; true merit is to have drawn out of the historic situation the consequences that it logically implied. Thus, the child and later the adult will understand that rights accorded him today, the liberties he enjoys, the moral dignity he feels – all this is the work not of such and such an individual or of such and such a generation but of that being, personal and impersonal at the same time, we call France. In other words, it is all of society, going back to its most remote reaches, that prepared his emancipation.

To bind the child to the social group of which he is a part, it is not enough to make him feel the reality of it. He must be attached to it with his whole being. There is only one effective way of doing this, and that is by making his society an integral part of him, so that he can no more separate himself from it than from himself. Society is not the work of the individuals that compose it at a given stage of history, nor is it a given place. It is a complex of ideas and sentiments, of ways of seeing and of feeling, a certain intellectual and moral framework distinctive of the entire group. Society is above all a consciousness of the whole. It is, therefore, this collective consciousness that we must instil in the child.

Of course, this penetration of the child's consciousness is effected in part by the mere fact of living, by the autonomous play of human relations. These ideas and sentiments are all around the child, and he is immersed in them by living. But there is another operation much too important to leave to chance. It is the business of the school to organize it methodically. An enlightened mind must select from among the welter of confused and often contradictory states of mind that constitute the social consciousness; it must set off what is essential and vital; and play down the trivial and the secondary. The teacher must bring this about and here again history will furnish him the means to this end.

The point is that to imbue children with the collective spirit it is useless to analyse it abstractly. On the contrary, they must be put in direct contact with this collective spirit. Now, what is the history of a people if not the genius of that people developing through time? By making the history of their country come alive for the children, we can at the same time make them live in close intimacy with the collective consciousness. Is it not through intimate and prolonged contact with a man that we finally get to know him? In this respect, a history lesson is the lesson of experience. But since our national character is immanent in historical events, the child would neither see nor feel them if the teacher did not try to set them off in bold relief, especially highlighting those events that merit it. Once again, the point is not to give a course on the French character. All that is needed is a knowledge of what it is and how to disentangle it from the welter of facts.

13 Max Weber

(a) Class, Status, Party

Excerpt from Max Weber, *Wirtschaft und Gesellschaft*, 1922, reprinted in Hans Gerth and C. Wright Mills (eds. and trans.), *From Max Weber: Essays in Sociology*, Routledge & Kegan Paul, 1948, pp. 180–95.

Economically determined power and the social order

Law exists when there is a probability that an order will be upheld by a specific staff of men who will use physical or psychical compulsion with the intention of obtaining conformity with the order, or of inflicting sanctions for infringement of it.[1] The structure of every legal order directly influences the distribution of power, economic or otherwise, within its respective community. This is true of all legal orders and not only that of the state. In general, we understand by 'power' the chance of a man or of a number of men to realize their own will in a communal action even against the resistance of others who are participating in the action.

'Economically conditioned' power is not, of course, identical with 'power' as such. On the contrary, the emergence of economic power may be the consequence of power existing on other grounds. Man does not strive for power only in order to enrich himself economically. Power, including economic power, may be valued 'for its own sake'. Very frequently the striving for power is also conditioned by the social 'honour' it entails. Not all power, however, entails social honour: the typical American Boss, as well as the typical big speculator, deliberately relinquishes social honour. Quite generally, 'mere economic' power, and especially 'naked' money power, is by no means a recognized basis of social honour. Nor is power the only basis of social honour. Indeed, social honour, or prestige, may even be the basis of political or economic power, and very frequently has been. Power, as well as honour, may be guaranteed by the legal order, but, at least normally, it is not their primary source. The legal order is rather an additional factor that enhances the chance to hold power or honour; but it cannot always secure them.

The way in which social honour is distributed in a community between typical groups participating in this distribution we may call the 'social

1. *Wirtschaft und Gesellschaft*, part III, ch. 4, pp. 631–40. The first sentence in paragraph one and the several definitions in this chapter which are in brackets do not appear in the original text. They have been taken from other contexts of *Wirtschaft und Gesellschaft*.

order'. The social order and the economic order are, of course, similarly related to the 'legal order'. However, the social and the economic order are not identical. The economic order is for us merely the way in which economic goods and services are distributed and used. The social order is of course conditioned by the economic order to a high degree, and in its turn reacts upon it.

Now: 'classes', 'status groups' and 'parties' are phenomena of the distribution of power within a community.

Determination of class-situation by market-situation

In our terminology, 'classes' are not communities; they merely represent possible, and frequent, bases for communal action. We may speak of a 'class' when (1) a number of people have in common a specific causal component of their life chances, in so far as (2) this component is represented exclusively by economic interests in the possession of goods and opportunities for income, and (3) is represented under the conditions of the commodity or labour markets. [These points refer to 'class situation', which we may express more briefly as the typical chance for a supply of goods, external living conditions, and personal life experiences, in so far as this chance is determined by the amount and kind of power, or lack of such, to dispose of goods or skills for the sake of income in a given economic order. The term 'class' refers to any group of people that is found in the same class situation.]

It is the most elemental economic fact that the way in which the disposition over material property is distributed among a plurality of people, meeting competitively in the market for the purpose of exchange, in itself creates specific life chances. According to the law of marginal utility this mode of distribution excludes the non-owners from competing for highly valued goods; it favours the owners and, in fact, gives to them a monopoly to acquire such goods. Other things being equal, this mode of distribution monopolizes the opportunities for profitable deals for all those who, provided with goods, do not necessarily have to exchange them. It increases, at least generally, their power in price wars with those who, being property-less, have nothing to offer but their services in native form or goods in a form constituted through their own labour, and who above all are compelled to get rid of these products in order barely to subsist. This mode of distribution gives to the propertied a monopoly on the possibility of transferring property from the sphere of use as a 'fortune', to the sphere of 'capital goods'; that is, it gives them the entrepreneurial function and all chances to share directly or indirectly in returns on capital. All this holds true within the area in which pure market conditions prevail. 'Property' and 'lack of property' are, therefore, the basic categories of all class situations. It does not matter whether these two categories become effective in price wars or in competitive struggles.

Within these categories, however, class situations are further differentiated: on the one hand, according to the kind of property that is usable for returns; and, on the other hand, according to the kind of services that can be offered in the market. Ownership of domestic buildings; productive establishments; warehouses; stores; agriculturally usable land, large and small holdings – quantitative differences with possibly qualitative consequences; ownership of mines; cattle; men (slaves); disposition over mobile instruments of production, or capital goods of all sorts, especially money or objects that can be exchanged for money easily and at any time; disposition over products of one's own labour or of others' labour differing according to their various distances from consumability; disposition over transferable monopolies of any kind – all these distinctions differentiate the class situations of the propertied just as does the 'meaning' which they can and do give to the utilization of property, especially to property which has money equivalence. Accordingly, the propertied, for instance, may belong to the class of rentiers or to the class of entrepreneurs.

Those who have no property but who offer services are differentiated just as much according to their kinds of services as according to the way in which they make use of these services, in a continuous or discontinuous relation to a recipient. But always this is the generic connotation of the concept of class: that the kind of chance in the *market* is the decisive moment which presents a common condition for the individual's fate. 'Class situation' is, in this sense, ultimately 'market situation'. The effect of naked possession *per se*, which among cattle breeders gives the non-owning slave or serf into the power of the cattle owner, is only a forerunner of real 'class' formation. However, in the cattle loan and in the naked severity of the law of debts in such communities, for the first time mere 'possession' as such emerges as decisive for the fate of the individual. This is very much in contrast to the agricultural communities based on labour. The creditor–debtor relation becomes the basis of 'class situations' only in those cities where a 'credit market', however primitive, with rates of interest increasing according to the extent of dearth and a factual monopolization of credits, is developed by a plutocracy. Therewith 'class struggles' begin.

Those men whose fate is not determined by the chance of using goods or services for themselves on the market, e.g. slaves, are not, however, a 'class' in the technical sense of the term. They are, rather, a 'status group'.

Communal action flowing from class interest

According to our terminology, the factor that creates 'class' is unambiguously economic interest, and indeed, only those interests involved in the existence of the 'market'. Nevertheless, the concept of 'class interest' is an ambiguous one: even as an empirical concept it is ambiguous as soon as one understands by it something other than the factual direction of interests following with a certain probability from the class situation for a certain 'average' of those people subjected to the class situation. The class situation and other circumstances remaining the same, the direction in which the individual worker, for instance, is likely to pursue his interests may vary widely, according to whether he is constitutionally qualified for the task at hand to a high, to an average or to a low degree. In the same way, the direction of interests may vary according to whether or not a *communal* action of a larger or smaller portion of those commonly affected by the 'class situation', or even an association among them, e.g. a 'trade union', has grown out of the class situation from which the individual may or may not expect promising results. [Communal action refers to that action which is oriented to the feeling of the actors that they belong together. Societal action, on the other hand, is oriented to a rationally motivated adjustment of interests.] The rise of societal or even of communal action from a common class situation is by no means a universal phenomenon.

The class situation may be restricted in its effects to the generation of essentially *similar* reactions, that is to say, within our terminology, of 'mass actions'. However, it may not have even this result. Furthermore, often merely an amorphous communal action emerges. For example, the 'murmuring' of the workers known in ancient oriental ethics: the moral disapproval of the work-master's conduct, which in its practical significance was probably equivalent to an increasingly typical phenomenon of precisely the latest industrial development, namely, the 'slow down' (the deliberate limiting of work effort) of labourers by virtue of tacit agreement. The degree in which 'communal action' and possibly 'societal action', emerges from the 'mass actions' of the members of a class is linked to general cultural conditions, especially to those of an intellectual sort. It is also linked to the extent of the contrasts that have already evolved, and is especially linked to the *transparency* of the connections between the causes and the consequences of the 'class situation'. For however different life chances may be, this fact in itself, according to all experience, by no means gives birth to 'class action' (communal action by the members of a class). The fact of being conditioned and the results of the class situation must be distinctly recognizable. For only then the contrast of life chances can be felt not as an absolutely given fact to be accepted, but as a resultant from either (1) the given distribution of property, or (2) the structure of the concrete economic order. It is only then that people may react against the class structure not only through acts of an intermittent and irrational protest, but in the form of rational association. There have been 'class situations' of the first category (1), of a specifically naked and transparent sort, in the urban centres of antiquity and during the Middle Ages; especially then, when great fortunes were accumulated by factually monopolized trading in industrial products of these localities or in foodstuffs. Furthermore, under certain circumstances in the rural economy of the most diverse periods, when agriculture was increasingly exploited in a profit-making manner. The most important historical example of the second category (2) is the class situation of the modern 'proletariat'.

Types of 'class struggle'

Thus every class may be the carrier of any one of the possibly innumerable forms of 'class action', but this is not necessarily so. In any case, a class does not in itself constitute a community. To treat 'class' conceptually as having the same value as 'community' leads to distortion. That men in the same class situation regularly react in mass actions to such tangible situations as economic ones in the direction of those interests that are most adequate to their average number is an important and after all simple fact for the understanding of historical events. Above all, this fact must not lead to that kind of pseudo-scientific operation with the concepts of 'class' and 'class interests' so frequently found these days, and which has found its most classic expression in the statement of a talented author, that the individual may be in error concerning his interests but that the 'class' is 'infallible' about its interests. Yet, if classes as such are not communities, nevertheless class situations emerge only on the basis of communalization. The communal action that brings forth class situations, however, is not basically action between members of the identical class; it is an action between members of different classes. Communal actions that directly determine the class situation of the worker and the entrepreneur are: the labour market, the commodities market and the capitalistic enterprise. But, in its turn, the existence of a capitalistic enterprise presupposes that a very specific communal action exists and that it is specifically structured to protect the possession of goods *per se*, and especially the power of individuals to dispose, in principle freely, over the means of production. The existence of a capitalistic enterprise is preconditioned by a specific kind of 'legal order'. Each kind of class situation, and above all when it rests upon the power of property *per se*, will become most clearly efficacious when all other determinants of reciprocal relations are, as far as possible, eliminated in their significance. It is in this way that the utilization of the power of property in the market obtains its most sovereign importance.

Now 'status groups' hinder the strict carrying through of the sheer market principle. In the present context they are of interest to us only from this one point of view. Before we briefly consider them, note that not much of a general nature can be said about the more specific kinds of antagonism between 'classes' (in our meaning of the term). The great shift, which has been going on continuously in the past, and up to our times, may be summarized although at the cost of some precision: the struggle in which class situations are effective has progressively shifted from consumption credit towards, first, competitive struggles in the commodity market and, then, towards price wars on the labour market. The 'class struggles' of antiquity – to the extent that they were genuine class struggles and not struggles between status groups – were initially carried on by indebted peasants, and perhaps also by artisans threatened by debt bondage and struggling against urban creditors. For debt bondage is the normal result of the differentiation of wealth in commercial cities, especially in seaport cities. A similar situation has existed among cattle breeders. Debt relationships as such produced class action up to the time of Cataline. Along with this, and with an increase in provision of grain for the city by transporting it from the outside, the struggle over the means of sustenance emerged. It centred in the first place around the provision of bread and the determination of the price of bread. It lasted throughout antiquity and the entire Middle Ages. The propertyless as such flocked together against those who actually and supposedly were interested in the dearth of bread. This fight spread until it involved all those commodities essential to the way of life and to handicraft production. There were only incipient discussions of wage disputes in antiquity and in the Middle Ages. But they have been slowly increasing up into modern times. In the earlier periods they were completely secondary to slave rebellions as well as to fights in the commodity market.

The propertyless of antiquity and of the Middle Ages protested against monopolies, pre-emption, forestalling and the withholding of goods from the market in order to raise prices. Today the central issue is the determination of the price of labour.

This transition is represented by the fight for access to the market and for the determination of the price of products. Such fights went on between merchants and workers in the putting-out system of domestic handicraft during the transition to modern times. Since it is quite a general phenomenon we must mention here that the class antagonisms that are conditioned through the market situation are usually most bitter between those who actually and directly participate as opponents in price wars. It is not the rentier, the shareholder and the banker who suffer the ill will of the worker, but almost exclusively the manufacturer and the business executives who are the direct opponents of workers in price wars. This is so in spite of the fact that it is precisely the cash boxes of the rentier, the shareholder and the banker into which the more or less 'unearned' gains flow, rather than into the pockets of the manufacturers or of the business executives. This simple state of affairs has very frequently been decisive for the role the class situation has played in the formation of political parties. For example, it has made possible the varieties of patriarchal socialism and the frequent attempts – formerly, at least – of threatened status groups to form alliances with the proletariat against the 'bourgeoisie'.

Status honour

In contrast to classes, *status groups* are normally communities. They are, however, often of an amorphous kind. In contrast to the purely economically determined 'class situation' we wish to designate as 'status situation' every typical component of the life fate of men that is determined by a specific, positive or negative, social estimation of *honour*. This honour may be connected with any quality shared by a plurality, and, of course, it can be knit to a class situation: class distinctions are linked in the most varied ways with status distinctions. Property as such is not always recognized as a status qualification, but in the long run it is, and with extraordinary regularity. In the subsistence economy of the organized neighbourhood, very often the richest man is simply the chieftain. However, this often means only an honorific preference. For example, in the so-called pure modern 'democracy', that is, one devoid of any expressly ordered status privileges for individuals, it may be that only the families coming under approximately the same class dance with one another. This example is reported of certain smaller Swiss cities. But status honour need not necessarily be linked with a 'class situation'. On the contrary, it normally stands in sharp opposition to the pretensions of sheer property.

Both propertied and propertyless people can belong to the same status group, and frequently they do with very tangible consequences. This 'equality' of social esteem may, however, in the long run become quite precarious. The 'equality' of status among the American 'gentlemen', for instance, is expressed by the fact that outside the subordination determined by the different functions of 'business', it would be considered strictly repugnant – wherever the old tradition still prevails – if even the richest 'chief', while playing billiards or cards in his club in the evening, would not treat his 'clerk' as in every sense fully his equal in birthright. It would be repugnant if the American 'chief' would bestow upon his 'clerk' the condescending 'benevolence' marking a distinction of 'position', which the German chief can never dissever from his attitude. This is one of the most important reasons why in America the German 'clubby-ness' has never been able to attain the attraction that the American clubs have.

Guarantees of status stratification

In content, status honour is normally expressed by the fact that above all else a specific *style of life* can be expected from all those who wish to belong to the circle. Linked with this expectation are restrictions on 'social' intercourse (that is, intercourse which is not subservient to economic or any other of business's 'functional' purposes). These restrictions may confine normal marriages to within the status circle and may lead to complete endogamous closure. As soon as there is not a mere individual and socially irrelevant imitation of another style of life, but an agreed-upon communal action of this closing character, the 'status' development is under way.

In its characteristic form, stratification by 'status groups' on the basis of conventional styles of life evolves at the present time in the United States out of the traditional democracy. For example, only the resident of a certain street ('the street') is considered as belonging to 'society', is qualified for social intercourse, and is visited and invited. Above all, this differentiation evolves in such a way as to make for strict submission to the fashion that is dominant at a given time in society. This submission to fashion also exists among men in America to a degree unknown in Germany. Such submission is considered to be an indication of the fact that a given man *pretends* to qualify as a gentleman. This submission decides, at least *prima facie*, that he will be treated as such. And this recognition becomes just as important for his employment chances in 'swank' establishments, and above all, for social intercourse and marriage with 'esteemed' families, as the qualification for duelling among Germans in the Kaiser's day. As for the rest: certain families resident for a long time, and, of course, correspondingly wealthy, e.g. 'F.F.V., i.e. First Families of Virginia', or the actual or alleged descendants of the 'Indian Princess' Pocahontas, of the Pilgrim fathers, or of the Knickerbockers, the members of almost inaccessible sects and all sorts of circles setting themselves apart by means of any other characteristics and badges . . . all these elements usurp 'status' honour. The development of status is essentially a question of stratification resting upon usurpation. Such usurpation is the normal origin of almost all status honour. But the road from this purely conventional situation to legal privilege, positive or negative, is easily travelled as soon as a certain stratification of the social order has in fact been 'lived in' and has achieved stability by virtue of a stable distribution of economic power.

'Ethnic' segregation and 'caste'

Where the consequences have been realized to their full extent, the status group evolves into a closed 'caste'. Status distinctions are then guaranteed not merely by conventions and laws, but also by *rituals*. This occurs in such a way that every physical contact with a member of any caste that is considered to be 'lower' by the members of a 'higher' caste is considered as making for a ritualistic impurity and to be a stigma which must be expiated by a religious act. Individual castes develop quite distinct cults and gods.

In general, however, the status structure reaches such extreme consequences only where there are underlying differences which are held to be 'ethnic'. The 'caste' is, indeed, the normal form in which ethnic communities usually live side by side in a 'societalized' manner. These ethnic communities believe in blood relationship and exclude exogamous marriage and social intercourse. Such a caste situation is part of the phenomenon of 'pariah' peoples and is found all over the world. These people form communities, acquire specific occupational traditions of handicrafts or of other arts, and cultivate a belief in their ethnic community. They live in a 'diaspora' strictly segregated from all personal intercourse, except that of an unavoidable sort, and their situation is legally precarious. Yet, by virtue of their economic indispensability, they are tolerated, indeed, frequently privileged, and they live in interspersed political communities. The Jews are the most impressive historical example.

A 'status' segregation grown into a 'caste' differs in its structure from a mere 'ethnic' segregation: the caste structure transforms the horizontal and unconnected coexistences of ethnically segregated groups into a vertical social system of super- and sub-ordination. Correctly formulated: a comprehensive societalization integrates the ethnically divided communities into specific political and communal action. In their consequences they differ precisely in this way: ethnic coexistences condition a mutual repulsion and disdain but allow each ethnic community to consider its own honour as the highest one; the caste structure brings about a social subordination and an acknowledgement of 'more honour' in favour of the privileged caste and status groups. This is due to the fact that in the caste structure ethnic distinctions as such have become 'functional' distinctions within the political societalization (warriors, priests, artisans that are politically important for war and for building, and so on). But even pariah people who are most despised are usually apt to continue cultivating in some manner that which is equally peculiar to ethnic and to status communities: the belief in their own specific 'honour'. This is the case with the Jews.

Only with the negatively privileged status groups does the 'sense of dignity' take a specific deviation. A sense of dignity is the precipitation in individuals of social honour and of conventional demands which a positively privileged status group raises for the deportment of its members. The sense of dignity that characterizes positively privileged status groups is naturally related to their 'being' which does not transcend itself, that is, it is to their 'beauty and excellence' ($\kappa\alpha\lambda o$-$\kappa\dot\alpha\gamma\alpha\vartheta\iota\alpha$). Their kingdom is 'of this world'. They live for the present and by exploiting their great past. The sense of dignity of the negatively privileged strata naturally refers to a future lying beyond the present, whether it is of this life or of another. In other words, it must be nurtured by the belief in a providential 'mission' and by a belief in a specific honour before God. The 'chosen people's' dignity is nurtured by a belief either that in the beyond 'the last will be the first', or that in this life a Messiah will appear to bring forth into the light of the world which has cast them out the hidden honour of the pariah people. This simple state of affairs, and not the 'resentment' which is so strongly emphasized in Nietzsche's much admired construction in the *Genealogy of Morals*, is the source of the religiosity cultivated by pariah status groups. In passing, we may note that resentment may be accurately applied only to a limited extent; for one of Nietzsche's main examples, Buddhism, it is not at all applicable.

Incidentally, the development of status groups from ethnic segregations is by no means the normal phenomenon. On the contrary, since objective 'racial differences' are by no means basic to every subjective sentiment of an ethnic community, the ultimately racial foundation of status structure is rightly and absolutely a question of the concrete individual case. Very frequently a status group is instrumental in the production of a thorough-bred anthropological type. Certainly a status group is to a high degree effective in producing extreme types, for they select personally qualified individuals (e.g. the Knighthood selects those who are fit for warfare, physically and psychically). But selection is far from being the only, or the predominant, way in which status groups are formed: political membership or class situation has at all times been at least as frequently decisive. And today the class situation is by far the predominant factor, for of course the possibility of a style of life expected for members of a status group is usually conditioned economically.

Status privileges

For all practical purposes, stratification by status goes hand in hand with a monopolization of ideal and material goods or opportunities, in a manner we have come to know as typical. Besides the specific status honour, which always rests upon distance and exclusiveness, we find all sorts of material monopolies. Such honorific preferences may consist of the privilege of wearing special costumes, of eating special dishes taboo to others, of carrying arms – which is most obvious in its consequences – the right to pursue certain non-professional dilettante artistic practices, e.g. to play certain musical instruments. Of course, material monopolies provide the most effective motives for the exclusiveness of a status group; although, in themselves, they are rarely sufficient, almost always they come into play to some extent. Within a status circle there is the question of intermarriage: the interest of the families in the monopolization of potential bridegrooms is at least of equal importance and is parallel to the interest in the monopolization of daughters. The daughters of the circle must be provided for. With an increased enclosure of the status group, the conventional preferential opportunities for special employment grow into a legal monopoly of special offices for the members. Certain goods become objects for monopolization by status groups. In the typical fashion these include 'entailed estates' and frequently also the possession of serfs or bondsmen and, finally, special trades. This monopolization occurs positively when the status group is exclusively entitled to own and to manage them; and negatively when, in order to maintain its specific way of life, the status group must *not* own and manage them.

The decisive role of a 'style of life' in status 'honour' means that status groups are the specific bearers of all 'conventions'. In whatever way it may be manifest, all 'stylization' of life either originates in status groups or is at least conserved by them. Even if the principles of status conventions differ greatly, they reveal certain typical traits, especially among those strata which are most privileged. Quite generally, among privileged status groups there is a status disqualification that operates against the performance of common physical labour. This disqualification is now 'setting in' in America against the old tradition of esteem for labour. Very frequently every rational economic pursuit, and especially 'entrepreneurial activity', is looked upon as a disqualification of status. Artistic and literary activity is also considered as degrading work as soon as it is exploited for income, or at least when it is connected with hard physical exertion. An example is the sculptor working like a mason in his dusty smock as over against the painter in his salon-like 'studio' and those forms of musical practice that are acceptable to the status group.

Economic conditions and effects of status stratification

The frequent disqualification of the gainfully employed as such is a direct result of the principle of status stratification peculiar to the social order, and of course, of this principle's opposition to a distribution of power which is regulated exclusively through the market. These two factors operate along with various individual ones, which will be touched upon below.

We have seen above that the market and its processes 'knows no personal distinctions': 'functional' interests dominate it. It knows nothing of 'honour'. The status order means precisely the reverse, viz.: stratification in terms of 'honour' and of styles of life peculiar to status groups as such. If mere economic acquisition and naked economic power still bearing the stigma of its extra-status origin could bestow upon anyone who has won it the same honour as those who are interested in status by virtue of style of life claim for themselves, the status order would be threatened at its very root. This is the more so as, given equality of status honour, property *per se* represents an addition even if it is not overtly acknowledged to be such. Yet if such economic acquisition and power gave the agent any honour at all, his wealth would result in his attaining more honour than those who successfully claim honour by virtue of style of life. Therefore all groups having interests in the status order react with special sharpness precisely against the pretensions of purely economic acquisition. In most cases they react the more vigorously the more they feel themselves threatened. Calderón's respectful treatment of the peasant, for instance, as opposed to Shakespeare's simultaneous and ostensible disdain of the *canaille* illustrates the different way in which a firmly structured status order reacts as compared with a status order that has become economically precarious. This is an example of a state of affairs that recurs everywhere. Precisely because of the rigorous reactions against the claims of property *per se*, the 'parvenu' is never accepted, personally and without reservation, by the privileged status groups, no matter how completely his style of life has been adjusted to theirs. They will only accept his descendants who have been educated in the conventions of their status group and who have never besmirched its honour by their own economic labour.

As to the general *effect* of the status order, only one consequence can be stated, but it is a very important one: the hindrance of the free development of the market occurs first for those goods which status groups directly withhold from free exchange by monopolization. This monopolization may be effected either legally or conventionally. For example, in many Hellenic cities during the epoch of status groups, and also originally in Rome, the inherited estate (as is shown by the old formula for indiction against spendthrifts) was monopolized just as were the estates of knights, peasants, priests, and especially the clientele of the craft and merchant guilds. The market is restricted, and the power of naked property *per se*, which gives its stamp to 'class formation', is pushed into the background. The results of this process can be most varied. Of course, they do not necessarily weaken the contrasts in the economic situation. Frequently they strengthen these contrasts, and in any case, where stratification by status permeates a community as strongly as was the case in all political communities of antiquity and of the Middle Ages, one can never speak of a genuinely free market competition as we understand it today. There are wider effects than this direct exclusion of special goods from the market. From the contrariety between the status order and the purely economic order mentioned above, it follows that in most instances the notion of honour peculiar to status absolutely abhors that which is essential to the market: higgling. Honour abhors higgling among peers and occasionally it taboos higgling for the members of a status group in general. Therefore, everywhere some status groups, and usually the most influential, consider almost any kind of overt participation in economic acquisition as absolutely stigmatizing.

With some over-simplification, one might thus say that 'classes' are stratified according to their relations to the production and acquisition of goods; whereas 'status groups' are stratified according to the principles of their *consumption* of goods as represented by special 'styles of life'.

An 'occupational group' is also a status group. For normally, it successfully claims social honour only by virtue of the special style of life which may be determined by it. The differences between classes and status groups frequently overlap. It is precisely those status communities most strictly segregated in terms of honour (viz. the Indian castes) who today show, although within very rigid limits, a relatively high degree of indifference to pecuniary income. However, the Brahmans seek such income in many different ways.

As to the general economic conditions making for the predominance of stratification by 'status', only very little can be said. When the bases of the acquisition and distribution of goods are relatively stable, stratification by status is favoured. Every technological repercussion and economic transformation threatens stratification by status and pushes the class situation into the foreground. Epochs and countries in which the naked class situation is of predominant significance are regularly the periods of technical and economic transformations. And every slowing down of the shifting of economic stratification leads, in due course, to the growth of status structures and makes for a resuscitation of the important role of social honour.

Parties

Whereas the genuine place of 'classes' is within the economic order, the place of 'status groups' is within the social order, that is, within the sphere of the distribution of 'honour'. From within these spheres, classes and status groups influence one another and they influence the legal order and are in turn influenced by it. But 'parties' live in a house of 'power'.

Their action is oriented towards the acquisition of social 'power', that is to say, towards influencing a communal action no matter what its content may be. In principle, parties may exist in a social 'club' as well as in a 'state'. As over against the actions of classes and status groups, for which this is not necessarily the case, the communal actions of 'parties' always mean a societalization. For party actions are always directed towards a goal which is striven for in planned manner. This goal may be a 'cause' (the party may aim at realizing a programme for ideal or material purposes), or the goal may be 'personal' (sinecures, power, and from these, honour for the leader and the followers of the party). Usually the party action aims at all these simultaneously. Parties are, therefore, only possible within communities that are societalized, that is, which have some rational order and a staff of persons available who are ready to enforce it. For parties aim precisely at influencing this staff, and if possible, to recruit it from party followers.

In any individual case, parties may represent interests determined through 'class situation' or 'status situation', and they may recruit their following respectively from one or the other. But they need be neither purely 'class' nor purely 'status' parties. In most cases they are partly class parties and partly status parties, but sometimes they are neither. They may represent ephemeral or enduring structures. Their means of attaining power may be quite varied, ranging from naked violence of any sort to canvassing for votes with coarse or subtle means: money, social influence, the force of speech, suggestion, clumsy hoax, and so on to the rougher or more artful tactics of obstruction in parliamentary bodies.

The sociological structure of parties differs in a basic way according to the kind of communal action which they struggle to influence. Parties also differ according to whether or not the community is stratified by status or by classes. Above all else, they vary according to the structure of domination within the community. For their leaders normally deal with the conquest of a community. They are, in the general concept which is maintained here, not only products of specially modern forms of domination. We shall also designate as parties the ancient and medieval 'parties', despite the fact that their structure differs basically from the structure of modern parties. By virtue of these structural differences of domination it is impossible to say anything about the structure of parties without discussing the structural forms of social domination *per se*. Parties, which are always structures struggling for domination, are very frequently organized in a very strict 'authoritarian' fashion.

Concerning 'classes', 'status groups' and 'parties', it must be said in general that they necessarily presuppose a comprehensive societalization, and especially a political framework of communal action, within which they operate. This does not mean that parties would be confined by the frontiers of any individual political community. On the contrary, at all times it has been the order of the day that the societalization (even when it aims at the use of military force in common) reaches beyond the frontiers of politics. This has been the case in the solidarity of interests among the Oligarchs and among the democrats in Hellas, among the Guelfs and among Ghibellines in the Middle Ages, and within the Calvinist party during the period of religious struggles. It has been the case up to the solidarity of the landlords (international congress of agrarian landlords), and has continued among princes (holy alliance, Karlsbad decrees), socialist workers, conservatives (the longing of Prussian conservatives for Russian intervention in 1850). But their aim is not necessarily the establishment of new international political, i.e. *territorial*, dominion. In the main they aim to influence the existing dominion.[1]

1. The posthumously published text breaks off here.

(b) The 'Rationalization' of Education and Training

Excerpt from Max Weber, *Wirtschaft und Gesellschaft*, 1922, reprinted in Hans Gerth and C. Wright Mills (eds. and trans.), *From Max Weber: Essays in Sociology*, Routledge & Kegan Paul, 1948, pp. 240–44.

We cannot here analyse the far-reaching and general cultural effects that the advance of the rational bureaucratic structure of domination, as such, develops quite independently of the areas in which it takes hold. Naturally, bureaucracy promotes a 'rationalist' way of life, but the concept of rationalism allows for widely differing contents. Quite generally, one can only say that the bureaucratization of all domination very strongly furthers the development of 'rational matter-of-factness' and the personality type of the professional expert. This has far-reaching ramifications, but only one important element of the process can be briefly indicated here: its effect upon the nature of training and education.

Educational institutions of the European continent, especially the institutions of higher learning – the universities, as well as technical academies, business colleges, gymnasiums and other middle schools – are dominated and influenced by the need for the kind of 'education' that produces a system of special examinations and the trained expertness that is increasingly indispensable for modern bureaucracy.

The 'special examination', in the present sense, was and is found also outside of bureaucratic structures proper; thus, today it is found in the 'free' professions of medicine and law and in the guild-organized trades. Expert examinations are neither indispensable to nor concomitant phenomena of bureaucratization. The French, English and American bureaucracies have for a long time foregone such examinations entirely or to a large extent, for training and service in party organizations have made up for them.

'Democracy' also takes an ambivalent stand in the face of specialized examinations, as it does in the face of all the phenomena of bureaucracy – although democracy itself promotes these developments. Special examinations, on the one hand, mean or appear to mean a 'selection' of those who qualify from all social strata rather than a rule by notables. On the other hand, democracy fears that a merit system and educational certificates will result in a privileged 'caste'. Hence, democracy fights against the special-examination system.

The special examination is found even in pre-bureaucratic or semi-bureaucratic epochs. Indeed, the regular and earliest locus of special examinations is among prebendally organized dominions. Expectancies of prebends, first of church prebends – as in the Islamite Orient and in the

Occidental Middle Ages – then, as was especially the case in China, secular prebends, are the typical prizes for which people study and are examined. These examinations, however, have in truth only a partially specialized and expert character.

The modern development of full bureaucratization brings the system of rational, specialized and expert examinations irresistibly to the fore. The civil-service reform gradually imports expert training and specialized examinations into the United States. In all other countries this system also advances, stemming from its main breeding place, Germany. The increasing bureaucratization of administration enhances the importance of the specialized examination in England. In China, the attempt to replace the semi-patrimonial and ancient bureaucracy by a modern bureaucracy brought the expert examination; it took the place of a former and quite differently structured system of examinations. The bureaucratization of capitalism, with its demand for expertly trained technicians, clerks, etc., carries such examinations all over the world. Above all, the development is greatly furthered by the social prestige of the educational certificates acquired through such specialized examinations. This is all the more the case as the educational patent is turned to economic advantage. Today, the certificate of education becomes what the test for ancestors has been in the past, at least where the nobility has remained powerful: a prerequisite for equality of birth, a qualification for a canonship, and for state office.

The development of the diploma from universities, and business and engineering colleges, and the universal clamour for the creation of educational certificates in all fields make for the formation of a privileged stratum in bureaus and in offices. Such certificates support their holders' claims for intermarriages with notable families (in business offices people naturally hope for preferment with regard to the chief's daughter), claims to be admitted into the circles that adhere to 'codes of honour', claims for a 'respectable' remuneration rather than remuneration for work done, claims for assured advancement and old-age insurance, and, above all, claims to monopolize socially and economically advantageous positions. When we hear from all sides the demand for an introduction of regular curricula and special examinations, the reason behind it is, of course, not a suddenly awakened 'thirst for education' but the desire for restricting the supply for these positions and their monopolization by the owners of educational certificates. Today, the 'examination' is the universal means of this monopolization, and therefore examinations irresistibly advance. As the education prerequisite to the acquisition of the educational certificate requires considerable expense and a period of waiting for full remuneration, this striving means a setback for talent (charisma) in favour of property. For the 'intellectual' costs of educational certificates are always low, and with the increasing volume of such certificates, their intellectual costs do not increase, but rather decrease.

The requirement of a chivalrous style of life in the old qualification for fiefs in Germany is replaced by the necessity of participating in its present rudimental form as represented by the duelling corps of the universities which also distribute the educational certificates. In Anglo-Saxon countries, athletic and social clubs fulfil the same function. The bureaucracy, on the other hand, strives everywhere for a 'right to the office' by the establishment of a regular disciplinary procedure and by removal of the completely arbitrary disposition of the 'chief' over the subordinate official. The bureaucracy seeks to secure the official position, the orderly advancement, and the provision for old age. In this, the bureaucracy is supported by the 'democratic' sentiment of the governed, which demands that domination be minimized. Those who hold this attitude believe themselves able to discern a weakening of the master's prerogatives in every weakening of the arbitrary disposition of the master over the officials. To this extent, bureaucracy, both in business offices and in public service, is a carrier of a specific 'status' development, as have been the quite differently structured officeholders of the past. We have already pointed out that these status characteristics are usually also exploited, and that by their nature they contribute to the technical usefulness of the bureaucracy in fulfilling its specific tasks.

'Democracy' reacts precisely against the unavoidable 'status' character of bureaucracy. Democracy seeks to put the election of officials for short terms in the place of appointed officials; it seeks to substitute the removal of officials by election for a regulated procedure of discipline. Thus, democracy seeks to replace the arbitrary disposition of the hierarchically superordinate 'master' by the equally arbitrary disposition of the governed and the party chiefs dominating them.

Social prestige based upon the advantage of special education and training as such is by no means specific to bureaucracy. On the contrary! But educational prestige in other structures of domination rests upon substantially different foundations.

Expressed in slogan-like fashion, the 'cultivated man', rather than the 'specialist', has been the end sought by education and has formed the basis of social esteem in such various systems as the feudal, theocratic, and patrimonial structures of dominion: in the English notable administration, in the old Chinese patrimonial bureaucracy, as well as under the rule of demagogues in the so-called Hellenic democracy.

The term 'cultivated man' is used here in a completely value-neutral sense; it is understood to mean solely that the goal of education consists in the quality of a man's bearing in life which was *considered* 'cultivated', rather than in a specialized training for expertness. The 'cultivated' personality formed the educational ideal, which was stamped by the structure of domination and by the social condition for membership in the ruling stratum. Such education aimed at a chivalrous or an ascetic type; or, at a literary type, as in China; a gymnastic-humanist type, as in Hellas; or it aimed at a conventional type, as in the case of the Anglo-Saxon gentleman. The qualification of the ruling stratum as such rested upon the possession of 'more' cultural quality (in the absolutely changeable, value-neutral sense in which we use the term here), rather than upon 'more' expert knowledge. Special military, theological and juridical ability was of course intensely practised; but the point of gravity in Hellenic, in medieval, as well as in Chinese education, has rested upon educational elements that were entirely different from what was 'useful' in one's speciality.

Behind all the present discussions of the foundations of the educational system, the struggle of the 'specialist type of man' against the older type of 'cultivated man' is hidden at some decisive point. This fight is determined by the irresistibly expanding bureaucratization of all public and private relations of authority and by the ever-increasing importance of expert and specialized knowledge. This fight intrudes into all intimate cultural questions.

During its advance, bureaucratic organization has had to overcome those essentially negative obstacles that have stood in the way of the levelling process necessary for bureaucracy. In addition, administrative structures based on different principles intersect with bureaucratic organizations. Since these have been touched upon above, only some especially important structural *principles* will be briefly discussed here in a very simplified schema. We would be led too far afield were we to discuss all the actually existing types. We shall proceed by asking the following questions:

1. How far are administrative structures subject to economic determination? Or, how far are opportunities for development created by other circumstances, for instance, the purely political? Or, finally, how far are developments created by an 'autonomous' logic that is solely of the technical structure as such?

2. We shall ask whether or not these structural principles, in turn, release specific economic effects, and if so, what effects. In doing this, one of course from the beginning has to keep his eye on the fluidity and the overlapping transitions of all these organizational principles. Their 'pure' types, after all, are to be considered merely as border cases which are especially valuable and indispensable for analysis. Historical realities, which almost always appear in mixed forms, have moved and still move between such pure types.

The bureaucratic structure is everywhere a late product of development. The further back we trace our steps, the more typical is the absence of bureaucracy and officialdom in the structure of domination. Bureaucracy has a 'rational' character: rules, means, ends and matter-of-factness dominate its bearing. Everywhere its origin and its diffusion have therefore had 'revolutionary' results, in a special sense, which has still to be discussed. This is the same influence which the advance of *rationalism* in general has had. The march of bureaucracy has destroyed structures of domination which had no rational character, in the special sense of the term. Hence, we may ask: What were these structures?

(c) Status Groups

Excerpt from Max Weber, *Wirtschaft und Gesellschaft*, 1922, reprinted in Hans Gerth and C. Wright Mills (eds. and trans.), *From Max Weber: Essays in Sociology*, Routledge & Kegan Paul, 1948, p. 405.

What is a 'status group'? 'Classes' are groups of people who, from the standpoint of specific interests, have the same economic position. Ownership or non-ownership of material goods or of definite skills constitute the 'class-situation'. 'Status' is a quality of social honour or a lack of it, and is in the main conditioned as well as expressed through a specific style of life. Social honour can stick directly to a class-situation, and it is also, indeed most of the time, determined by the average class-situation of the status-group members. This, however, is not necessarily the case. Status membership, in turn, influences the class-situation in that the style of life required by status groups makes them prefer special kinds of property or gainful pursuits and reject others. A status group can be closed ('status by descent') or it can be open.[1]

1. It is incorrect to think of the 'occupational status group' as an alternative. The 'style of life', not the 'occupation', is always decisive. This style may require a certain profession (for instance, military service), but the nature of the occupational service resulting from the claims of a style of life always remains decisive (for instance, military service as a knight rather than as a mercenary).

(d) The Chinese Literati

Excerpt from Max Weber, *Wirtschaft und Gesellschaft*, 1922, reprinted in Hans Gerth and C. Wright Mills (eds. and trans.), *From Max Weber: Essays in Sociology*, Routledge & Kegan Paul, 1948, pp. 422–33.

The development of the examination system

During the period of the central monarchy, the mandarins became a status group of certified claimants to office prebends. All categories of Chinese civil servants were recruited from their midst, and their qualification for office and rank depended upon the number of examinations they had successfully passed.

These examinations consisted of three major degrees,[1] which were considerably augmented by intermediary, repetitive and preliminary examinations as well as by numerous special conditions. For the first degree alone there were ten types of examinations. The question usually put to a stranger of unknown rank was how many examinations he had passed. Thus, in spite of the ancestor cult, how many ancestors one had was not decisive for social rank. The very reverse held: it depended upon one's official rank whether one was allowed to have an ancestral temple (or a mere table of ancestors, which was the case with illiterates). How many ancestors one was permitted to mention was determined by official rank.[2] Even the rank of a city god in the Pantheon depended upon the rank of the city's mandarin.

In the Confucian period (sixth to fifth century B.C.), the possibility of ascent into official positions as well as the system of examinations was still unknown. It appears that as a rule, at least in the feudal states, the 'great families' were in the possession of power. It was not until the Han dynasty – which was established by a parvenu – that the bestowal of offices according to merit was raised to the level of a principle. And not until the Tang dynasty, in A.D. 690, were regulations set up for the highest degree. As we have already mentioned, it is highly probable that literary education, perhaps with a few

1. The French authors for the most part designate *seng yuen, siu tsai* by 'baccalaureate' [bachelor's degree], *kiu jin* by 'licentiate' [master's degree], *tien se* by 'doctorate'. The lowest degree gave a claim to a stipend only to the top graduates. The bachelors who had received a stipend were called *lin cheng* (magazine prebendaries), bachelors selected by the director and sent to Peking were called *pao kong*, those among them who were admitted to the college *yu kong*, and those who had acquired the bachelor degree by purchase were called *kien cheng*.

2. The charismatic qualities of the descendant simply were proof for those of his sib, hence of the forebears. At the time, Chi Hwang-Ti had abolished this custom, as the son was not to judge the father. But since then almost every founder of a new dynasty has bestowed ranks to his ancestors.

exceptions, was at first actually, and perhaps also legally, monopolized by the 'great families', just as the Vedic education in India was monopolized. Vestiges of this continued to the end. Members of the imperial sib, although not freed from all examinations, were freed from the examination for the first degree. And the trustees, whom every candidate for examinations, until recently, had to name, had to testify to the candidate's 'good family background'. During modern times this testimony has only meant the exclusion of descendants of barbers, bailiffs, musicians, janitors, carriers and others. Yet alongside this exclusion there was the institution of 'candidates for the mandarinate', that is, the descendants of mandarins enjoyed a special and preferred position in fixing the maximum quota of examination candidates from each province. The promotion lists used the official formula 'from a mandarin family and from the people'. The sons of well-deserved officials held the lowest degree as a title of honour. All of which represent residues of ancient conditions.

The examination system has been fully carried through since the end of the seventh century. This system was one of the means the patrimonial ruler used in preventing the formation of a closed estate, which, in the manner of feudal vassals and office nobles, would have monopolized the rights to the office prebends. The first traces of the examination system *seem* to emerge about the time of Confucius (and Huang K'an) in the substate of Chin, a locality which later became autocratic. The selection of candidates was determined essentially by military merit. Yet, even the *Li Chi* and the *Chou Li*[3] demand, in a quite rationalist way, that the district chiefs examine their lower officials periodically with regard to their morals, and then propose to the emperor which of them should be promoted. In the unified state of the Han emperors, pacifism began to direct the selection of officials. The power of the literati was tremendously consolidated after they had succeeded in elevating the correct Kuang Wu to the throne in A.D. 21 and in maintaining him against the popular 'usurper' Wang Mang. During the struggle for prebends, which raged during the following period and which we shall deal with later, the literati developed into a unified *status group*.

Even today the Tang dynasty irradiates the glory of having been the actual creator of China's greatness and culture. The Tang dynasty, for the first time, regulated the literati's position and established colleges for their education (in the seventh century). It also created the *Han lin yuan*, the so-called 'academy', which first edited the *Annals* in order to gain precedents, and then controlled the emperor's correct deportment. Finally, after the Mongol storms, the national Ming dynasty in the fourteenth century decreed statutes which, in essence, were definitive.[4] Schools were to be set up in every

3. By the way, this is a rather certain symptom of its *recent origin*!
4. Cf. for this: Biot (1847). It is still useful.

village, one for every twenty-five families. As the schools were not subsidized, the decree remained a dead letter – or rather we have already seen which powers gained control over the schools. Officials selected the best pupils and enrolled a certain number in the colleges. In the main, these colleges have decayed, although in part they have been newly founded. In 1382, prebends in the form of rice rents were set aside for the 'students'. In 1393, the number of students was fixed. After 1370, only examined men had claims to offices.

At once a fight set in between the various regions, especially between the North and the South. The South even then supplied candidates for examinations who were more cultured, having experienced a more comprehensive environment. But the North was the military foundation stone of the empire. Hence, the emperor intervened and *punished* (!) the examiners who had given the 'first place' to a Southerner. Separate lists for the North and the South were set up, and moreover, a struggle for the patronage of offices began immediately. Even in 1387 special examinations were given to officers' sons. The officers and officials, however, went further, and demanded the right to designate their successors, which meant a demand for re-feudalization. In 1393 this was conceded, but in the end only in a modified form. The candidates presented were preferentially enrolled in the colleges, and prebends were to be reserved for them: in 1465 for three sons, in 1482 for one son. In 1453 we meet with the purchase of college places, and in 1454 with the purchase of offices. During the fifteenth century, as is always the case, these developments arose from the need for military funds. In 1492 these measures were abolished, but in 1529 they were reintroduced.

The *departments* also fought against one another. The Board of Rites was in charge of the examinations after 736, but the Board of Civil Office appointed the officials. The examined candidates were not infrequently boycotted by the latter department, the former answering by going on strike during the examinations. Formally, the minister of rites, actually, the minister of offices (the major-domo) were in the end the most powerful men in China. Then merchants, who were expected to be less 'stingy', came into office.[5] Of course, this hope was quite unjustified. The Manchus favoured the old traditions and thus the literati and, as far as possible, 'purity' in the distribution of offices. But now, as before, three routes to office existed side by side: (1) imperial favours for the sons of the 'princely' families (examination privileges); (2) easy examinations (officially every three to six years) for the lower officials by the higher officials who controlled patronage; this inevitably led each time to advancement also to higher positions; (3) the only legal way: to qualify effectively and purely by examination.

In the main, the system of examinations has actually fulfilled the functions

5. Complaints at Ma Tuan Lin, translated in Biot (1847, p. 481).

as conceived by the emperor. Occasionally (in 1372), it was suggested to the emperor – one can imagine by whom – that he draw the conclusion from the orthodox charisma of virtues by abolishing the examinations, since virtue *alone* legitimizes and qualifies. This conclusion was soon dropped, which is quite understandable. For after all, both parties, emperor and graduates, had a stake in the examination system, or at least they thought they had. From the emperor's standpoint, the examination system corresponded entirely to the role which the *mjestnitshestvo*, a technically heterogeneous means, of Russian despotism played for the Russian nobility. The system facilitated a competitive struggle for prebends and offices among the candidates, which stopped them from joining together into a feudal office nobility. Admittance to the ranks of aspirants was open to everybody who was proved to be educationally qualified. The examination system thus fulfilled its purpose.

The typological position of Confucian education

We shall now discuss the position of this educational system among the great types of education. To be sure, we cannot here, in passing, give a sociological typology of pedagogical ends and means, but perhaps some comments may be in place.

Historically, the two polar opposites in the field of educational ends are: to awaken charisma, that is, heroic qualities or magical gifts; and, to impart specialized expert training. The first type corresponds to the charismatic structure of domination; the latter type corresponds to the *rational* and bureaucratic (modern) structure of domination. The two types do not stand opposed, with no connections or transitions between them. The warrior hero or the magician also needs special training, and the expert official is generally not trained exclusively for knowledge. However, they are polar opposites of types of education and they form the most radical contrasts. Between them are found all those types which aim at cultivating the pupil for a *conduct of life*, whether it is of a mundane or of a religious character. In either case, the life conduct is the conduct of a status group.

The charismatic procedure of ancient magical asceticism and the hero trials, which sorcerers and warrior heroes have applied to boys, tried to aid the novice to acquire a 'new soul', in the animist sense, and hence, to be reborn. Expressed in our language, this means that they merely wished to *awaken* and to test a capacity which was considered a purely personal gift of grace. For one can neither teach nor train for charisma. Either it exists *in nuce*, or it is infiltrated through a miracle of magical rebirth – otherwise it cannot be attained.

Specialized and expert schooling attempts to *train* the pupil for practical usefulness for administrative purposes – in the organization of public authorities, business offices, workshops, scientific or industrial laboratories, disciplined armies. In principle, this can be accomplished with anybody, though to varying extent.

The pedagogy of cultivation, finally, attempts to *educate* a cultivated type of man, whose nature depends on the decisive stratum's respective ideal of cultivation. And this means to educate a man for a certain internal and external deportment in life. In principle this can be done with everybody, only the goal differs. If a separate stratum of warriors form the decisive status group – as in Japan – education will aim at making the pupil a stylized knight and courtier, who despises the pen-pushers as the Japanese Samurai have despised them. In particular cases, the stratum may display great variations of type. If a priestly stratum is decisive, it will aim at making the disciple a scribe, or at least an intellectual, likewise of greatly varying character. In reality, none of these types ever occurs in pure form. The numerous combinations and intermediary links cannot be discussed in this context. What is important here is to define the position of Chinese education in terms of these forms.

The holdovers of the primeval charismatic training for regeneration, the milk name, the previously discussed initiation rites of youth, the bridegroom's change of name, and so on, have for a long time in China been a formula (in the manner of the Protestant confirmation) standing beside the testing of educational qualifications. Such tests have been monopolized by the political authorities. The educational qualification, however, in view of the educational means employed, has been a 'cultural' qualification, in the sense of a general education. It was of a similar, yet of a more specific nature than, for instance, the *humanist* educational qualification of the Occident.

In Germany, such an education, until recently and almost exclusively, was a prerequisite for the official career leading to positions of command in civil and military administration. At the same time this *humanist* education has stamped the pupils who were to be prepared for such careers as belonging socially to the *cultured* status group. In Germany, however – and this is a very important difference between China and the Occident – rational and specialized *expert* training has been added to, and in part has displaced, this educational status qualification.

The Chinese examinations did not test any special skills, as do our modern rational and bureaucratic examination regulations for jurists, medical doctors or technicians. Nor did the Chinese examinations test the possession of charisma, as do the typical 'trials' of magicians and bachelor leagues. To be sure, we shall presently see the qualifications which this statement requires. Yet it holds at least for the technique of the examinations.

The examinations of China tested whether or not the candidate's mind was thoroughly steeped in literature and whether or not he possessed the *ways of thought* suitable to a cultured man and resulting from cultivation in literature. These qualifications held far more specifically with China than with the German humanist gymnasium. Today one is used to justifying the gymnasium by pointing to the practical value of formal education through the study of antiquity. As far as one may judge from the assignments[6] given to the pupils of the lower grades in China, they were rather similar to the essay topics assigned to the top grades of a German gymnasium, or perhaps better still, to the select class of a German girls' college. All the grades were intended as tests in penmanship, style, mastery of classic writings,[7] and finally – similar to our lessons in religion, history and German – in conformity with the prescribed mental outlook.[8] In our context it is decisive that this education was on the one hand purely secular in nature, but, on the other, was bound to the fixed norm of the orthodox interpretation of the classic authors. It was a highly exclusive and bookish literary education.

The literary character of education in India, Judaism, Christianity and Islam resulted from the fact that it was completely in the hands of Brahmans and Rabbis trained in literature, or of clerics and monks of book religions who were professionally trained in literature. As long as education was Hellenic and not 'Hellenist', the Hellenic man of culture was and remained primarily ephebe and hoplite. The effect of this was nowhere thrown into relief more clearly than in the conversation of the Symposium, where it is said of Plato's Socrates that he had never 'flinched' in the field, to use a student term. For Plato to state this is obviously at least of equal importance with everything else he makes Alcibiades say.

During the Middle Ages, the military education of the knight, and later the genteel education of the Renaissance salon, provided a corresponding though socially different supplement to the education transmitted by books, priests, and monks. In Judaism and in China, such a counterbalance was, in part altogether, and in part as good as altogether, absent. In India, as in China, the literary means of education consisted substantially of hymns, epic tales and casuistry in ritual and ceremony. In India, however, this was underpinned by cosmogonic as well as religious and philosophical speculations. Such speculations were not entirely absent from the classics and from the transmitted commentaries in China, but obviously they have

6. Themes for them are given by Williams. See also Zi (1896).

7. This held especially for the examinations for the master's degree, where the theme of the dissertation often called for an erudite, philological, literary, and historical analysis of the respective classical text. See the example given by Zi (1896, p. 144).

8. This held especially for the highest degree ('doctorate') for which the emperor, often in person, gave the themes and for which he classified the graduates. Questions of administrative expediency, preferably connected with one of the 'six questions' of Emperor Tang, were customary topics (see Biot, 1847, p. 209, note 1, and Zi, 1896, p. 209, note 1).

always played only a very minor role there. The Chinese authors developed rational systems of social ethics. The educated stratum of China simply has never been an autonomous status group of scholars, as were the Brahmans, but rather a stratum of officials and aspirants to office.

Higher education in China has not always had the character it has today. The public educational institutions (*Pan kung*) of the feudal princes taught the arts of the dance and of arms in addition to the knowledge of rites and literature. Only the pacification of the empire into a patrimonial and unified state, and finally, the pure system of examinations for office, transformed this older education, which was far closer to early Hellenic education, into what has existed into the twentieth century. Medieval education, as represented in the authoritative and orthodox *Siao-Hio*, that is 'schoolbook', still placed considerable weight upon dance and music. To be sure, the old war dance seems to have existed only in rudimentary form, but for the rest, the children, according to age groups, learned certain dances. The purpose of this was stated to be the taming of evil passions. If a child did not do well during his instruction, one should let him dance and sing. Music improves man, and rites and music form the basis of self-control.[9] The magical significance of music was a primary aspect of all this. 'Correct music' – that is, music used according to the old rules and strictly following the old measures – 'keeps the spirits in their fetters.'[10] As late as the Middle Ages, archery and charioteering were still considered general educational subjects for genteel children.[11] But this was essentially mere theory. Going through the schoolbook one finds that from the seventh year of life, domestic education was strictly separated according to sex; it consisted essentially of instilling a ceremonial, which went far beyond all Occidental ideas, a ceremonial especially of piety and awe towards parents and all superiors and older persons in general. For the rest, the schoolbook consisted almost exclusively of rules for self-control.

This domestic education was supplemented by school instruction. There was supposed to be a grade school in every *Hsien*. Higher education presupposed the passing of the first entrance examination. Thus two things were peculiar to Chinese higher education. First, it was entirely non-military and purely literary, as all education established by priesthoods has been. Second, its literary character, that is, its *written* character, was pushed to extremes. In part, this appears to have been a result of the peculiarity of the Chinese script and of the literary art which grew out of it.[12]

9. See Chu Hsi (1889),V, III, I. Cf. the quotation from Chu Hsi, p. 46. Concerning the question of generations, cf, 1, 13.

10. Chu Hsi (1889), 1, 25, also 2. Introduction no. 5f.

11. There were literary prescriptions also for this.

12. It need hardly be mentioned that what is here said about language and script

As the script retained its pictorial character and was not rationalized into an alphabetical form, such as the trading peoples of the Mediterranean created, the literary product was addressed at once to both the eyes and the ears, and essentially more to the former. Any 'reading aloud' of the classic books was in itself a translation from the pictorial script into the (unwritten) word. The visual character, especially of the old script, was by its very nature remote from the spoken word. The monosyllabic language requires sound perception as well as the perception of pitched tone. With its sober brevity and its compulsion of syntactical logic, it stands in extreme contrast to the purely visual character of script. But in spite of this, or rather – as Grube has shown in an ingenious way – in part because of the very rational qualities of its structure, the Chinese tongue has been unable to offer its services to poetry or to systematic thinking. Nor could it serve the development of the oratorical arts as have the structures of the Hellenic, Latin, French, German and Russian languages, each in its own way. The stock of written symbols remained far richer than the stock of monosyllabic words, which was inevitably quite delimited. Hence, all phantasy and ardour fled from the poor and formalistic intellectualism of the spoken word and into the quiet beauty of the written symbols. The usual poetic speech was held fundamentally subordinate to the script. Not speaking but writing and reading were valued artistically and considered as worthy of a gentleman, for they were receptive of the artful products of script. Speech remained truly an affair of the plebs. This contrasts sharply with Hellenism, to which conversation meant everything and a translation into the style of the dialogue was the adequate form of all experience and contemplation. In China the very finest blossoms of literary culture lingered, so to speak, deaf and mute in their silken splendour. They were valued far higher than was the art of drama, which, characteristically, flowered during the period of the Mongols.

Among the renowned social philosophers, Meng Tse (Mencius) made systematic use of the dialogue form. That is precisely why he readily appears to us as the one representative of Confucianism who matured to full 'lucidity'. The very strong impact upon us of the 'Confucian Analects' (as Legge called them) also rests upon the fact that in China (as occasionally elsewhere) the doctrine is clothed in the form of (in part, probably authentic) sententious responses of the master to questions from the disciples. Hence, to us, it is transposed into the form of speech. For the rest, the epic literature contains the addresses of the early warrior kings to the army; in their lapidary forcefulness, they are highly impressive. Part of the didactic *Analects* consists of speeches, the character of which rather corresponds to pontifical 'allocutions'. Otherwise speech plays no part in the official literature. Its

reproduces *exclusively* what such eminent sinologists, as especially the late W. Grube, teach the layman. It does *not* result from the author's own studies.

lack of development, as we shall see presently, has been determined by both social and political reasons.

In spite of the logical qualities of the language, Chinese thought has remained rather stuck in the pictorial and the descriptive. The power of *logos*, of defining and reasoning, has not been accessible to the Chinese. Yet, on the other hand, this purely scriptural education detached thought from gesture and expressive movement still more than is usual with the literary nature of any education. For two years before he was introduced to their meaning, the pupil learned merely to paint about two thousand characters. Furthermore, the examiners focused attention upon style, the art of versification, a firm grounding in the classics, and finally, upon the expressed mentality of the candidate.

The lack of all training in calculation, even in grade schools, is a very striking feature of Chinese education. The *idea* of positional numbers, however, was developed (Edkins, n.d.)[13] during the sixth century before Christ, that is, during the period of warring states. A calculative attitude in commercial intercourse had permeated all strata of the population, and the final calculations of the administrative offices were as detailed as they were difficult to survey, for reasons mentioned above. The medieval schoolbook (Chu Hsi, 1889) enumerates calculation among the six 'arts'. And at the time of the warring states, there existed a mathematics which allegedly included trigonometrics as well as the rule of three and commercial calculation. Presumably this literature, apart from fragments, was lost during Shi-Hwang-Ti's burning of the books (Chu Hsi, 1889, p. 42, note 3). In any case, calculation is not even mentioned in later pedagogy. And in the course of history, calculation receded more and more into the background of the education of the genteel mandarins, finally to disappear altogether. The educated merchants learned calculation in their business offices. Since the empire had been unified and the tendency toward a rational administration of the state had weakened, the mandarin became a genteel literary man, who was not one to occupy himself with the '$\sigma\chi o\lambda\acute{\eta}$' of calculation.

The mundane character of this education contrasts with other educational systems, which are nevertheless related to it by their literary stamp. The literary examinations in China were purely political affairs. Instruction was given partly by individual and private tutors and partly by the teaching staffs of college foundations. But no priest took part in them.

The Christian universities of the Middle Ages originated from the practical and ideal need for a rational, mundane and ecclesiastic legal doctrine and a rational (dialectical) theology. The universities of Islam, following the model of the late Roman law schools and of Christian theology,

13. The Chinese abacus used the (decimal) positional value. The older positional system which has fallen into oblivion seems to be of Babylonian origin.

practised sacred case law and the doctrine of faith; the Rabbis practised interpretation of the law; the philosophers' schools of the Brahmans engaged in speculative philosophy, in ritual, as well as in sacred law. Always ecclesiastic dignitaries or theologians have formed either the sole teaching staff or at least its basic corps. To this corps were attached mundane teachers, in whose hands the other branches of study rested. In Christianity, Islam and Hinduism, prebends were the goals, and for the sake of them educational certificates were striven after. In addition, of course, the aspirant wished to qualify for ritual activity and the curing of souls. With the ancient Jewish teachers (precursors of the Rabbis), who worked 'gratis', the goal was solely to qualify for instructing the laymen in the law, for this instruction was religiously indispensable. But in all this, education was always bound by sacred or cultic scriptures. Only the Hellenic philosophers' schools engaged in an education solely of laymen and freed from all ties to scriptures, freed from all direct interests in prebends, and solely devoted to the education of Hellenic 'gentlemen' (*Caloicagathoi*).

Chinese education served the interest in prebends and was tied to a script, but at the same time it was purely lay education, partly of a ritualist and ceremonial character and partly of a traditionalist and ethical character. The schools were concerned with neither mathematics nor natural sciences, with neither geography nor grammar. Chinese philosophy itself did not have a speculative, systematic character, as Hellenic philosophy had and as, in part and in a different sense, Indian and Occidental theological schooling had. Chinese philosophy did not have a rational-formalist character, as Occidental jurisprudence has. And it was not of an empirical casuist character, as Rabbinic, Islamite and, partly, Indian philosophy. Chinese philosophy did not give birth to scholasticism because it was not professionally engaged in logic, as were the philosophies of the Occident and the Middle East, both of them being based on Hellenist thought. The very concept of logic remained absolutely alien to Chinese philosophy, which was bound to script, was not dialectical, and remained oriented to purely practical problems as well as to the status interests of the patrimonial bureaucracy.

This means that the problems that have been basic to all Occidental philosophy have remained unknown to Chinese philosophy, a fact which comes to the fore in the Chinese philosophers' manner of categorical thought and above all in Confucius. With the greatest practical matter-of-factness, the intellectual tools remained in the form of parables, reminding us of the means of expression of Indian chieftains rather than of rational argumentation. This holds precisely for some of the truly ingenious statements ascribed to Confucius. The absence of speech is palpable, that is, speech as a rational means for attaining political and forensic effects, speech as it was first cultivated in the Hellenic *polis*. Such speech could not be developed in a bureaucratic patrimonial state which had no formalized justice. Chinese justice remained, in part, a summary Star Chamber procedure (of the high officials), and, in part, it relied solely on documents. No oral pleading of cases existed, only the written petitions and oral hearings of the parties concerned. The Chinese bureaucracy was interested in conventional propriety, and these bonds prevailed and worked in the same direction of obstructing forensic speech. The bureaucracy rejected the argument of 'ultimate' speculative problems as practically sterile. The bureaucracy considered such arguments improper and rejected them as too delicate for one's own position because of the danger of innovations.

If the technique and the substance of the examinations were purely mundane in nature and represented a sort of 'cultural examination for the literati', the popular view of them was very different: it gave them a magical-charismatic meaning. In the eyes of the Chinese masses, a successfully examined candidate and official was by no means a mere applicant for office qualified by knowledge. He was a proved holder of magical qualities, which, as we shall see, were attached to the certified mandarin just as much as to an examined and ordained priest of an ecclesiastic institution of grace, or to a magician tried and proved by his guild.[14]

The position of the successfully examined candidate and official corresponded in important points, for example, to that of a Catholic chaplain. For the pupil to complete his period of instruction and his examinations did not mean the end of his immaturity. Having passed the 'baccalaureate', the candidate came under the discipline of the school director and the examiners. In the case of bad conduct his name was dropped from the lists. Under certain conditions his hands were caned. In the localities' secluded cells for examinations, candidates not infrequently fell seriously ill and suicides occurred. According to the charismatic interpretation of the examination as a magical 'trial', such happenings were considered proof of the wicked conduct of the person in question. After the applicant for office had luckily passed the examinations for the higher degrees with their strict seclusion, and after, at long last, he had moved into an office corresponding to the number and rank of examinations passed and depending on his patronage, he still remained throughout his life under the control of the school. And in addition to being under the authority of his superiors, he was under the constant surveillance and criticism of the censors. Their criticism extended even to the ritualist correctness of the very Son of Heaven. The impeachment of the officials[15] was prescribed from olden times and was valued as meri-

14. Also, Timkovski (1820–21) emphasizes this.

15. For such a self-impeachment of a frontier officer who had been inattentive, see no. 567 of Aurel Stein's documents, edited by de Chavannes (1913). It dates from the Han period, hence long before the introduction of examinations.

torious in the way of the Catholic confession of sins. Periodically, as a rule every three years, his record of conduct, that is, a list of his merits and faults as determined by official investigations of the censors and his superiors, was to be published in the *Imperial Gazette*.[16] According to his published grades, he was allowed to retain his post, was promoted, or was demoted.[17] As a rule, not only objective factors determined the outcome of these records of conduct. What mattered was the 'spirit', and this spirit was that of a life-long penalism by office authority.

16. The beginnings of the present *Peking Gazette* go back to the time of the second ruler of the Tang dynasty (618–907).

17. Actually one finds in the *Peking Gazette*, with reference to the reports partly of censors, partly of superiors, laudations and promotions (or the promise of such) for deserving officials, demotions of insufficiently qualified officials for other offices ('that he may gather experiences', 31 December 1897 and many other issues), suspension from office with half pay, expulsion of totally unqualified officials, or the statement that the good services of an official are balanced by faults which he would have to remedy before further promotion. Almost always detailed reasons are given. Such announcements were especially frequent at the end of the year but there was also a great volume at other times. There are also to be found posthumous sentences to be whipped for (obviously) posthumously demoted officials (*Peking Gazette*, 26 May 1895).

References

BIOT, E. C. (1847), *Essai sur l'histoire de l'instruction publique en Chine et de la corporation des lettres depuis les anciens temps jusqu'à nos jours*, Paris.

CHU HSI (1889), *Le Siao Hio, ou Morale de la Jeunesse*, trans. C. de Harlez, Annals du Musée Guimet, vol. 15.

DE CHAVANNES, E. (1913), *Les documents Chinois découverts par Aurel Stein dans les sables du Turkestan oriental*, Oxford University Press.

EDKINS, J. (n.d.), 'Local values in Chinese arithmetical notation', *J. Peking Oriental Soc.*, vol. 1, no. 4, p. 161.

TIMKOVSKI, E. F. (1820–21), *Reise Durch Chine*, Leipzig.

ZI, E. (1896), 'Pratique des examens militaires en Chine', *Variétés Sinologiques*, no. 9.

14 L. Althusser

Ideology and Ideological State Apparatuses
'Notes towards an investigation'

Excerpt from L. Althusser, *Lenin and Philosophy and Other Essays*, New Left Books, 1971, pp. 123–73.

On the reproduction of the conditions of production[1]

I must now expose more fully something which was briefly glimpsed in my analysis when I spoke of the necessity to renew the means of production if production is to be possible. That was a passing hint. Now I shall consider it for itself.

As Marx said, every child knows that a social formation which did not reproduce the conditions of production at the same time as it produced would not last a year (Marx to Kugelmann, 11 July 1868; Marx, 1955, p. 209). The ultimate condition of production is therefore the reproduction of the conditions of production. This may be 'simple' (reproducing exactly the previous conditions of production) or on 'an extended scale' (expanding them). Let us ignore this last distinction for the moment.

What, then, is *the reproduction of the conditions of production*?

Here we are entering a domain which is both very familiar (since *Capital* Volume Two) and uniquely ignored. The tenacious obviousnesses (ideological obviousnesses of an empiricist type) of the point of view of production alone, or even of that of mere productive practice (itself abstract in relation to the process of production) are so integrated into our everyday 'consciousness' that it is extremely hard, not to say almost impossible, to raise oneself to the *point of view of reproduction*. Nevertheless, everything outside this point of view remains abstract (worse than one-sided: distorted) – even at the level of production, and, *a fortiori*, at that of mere practice.

Let us try and examine the matter methodically.

To simplify my exposition, and assuming that every social formation arises from a dominant mode of production, I can say that the process of production sets to work the existing productive forces in and under definite relations of production.

It follows that, in order to exist, every social formation must reproduce

1. This text is made up of two extracts from an ongoing study. The sub-title 'Notes towards an investigation' is the author's own. The ideas expounded should not be regarded as more than the introduction to a discussion.

the conditions of its production at the same time as it produces, and in order to be able to produce. It must therefore reproduce:

1. The productive forces.
2. The existing relations of production.

Reproduction of the means of production

Everyone (including the bourgeois economists whose work is national accounting, or the modern 'macroeconomic' 'theoreticians') now recognizes, because Marx compellingly proved it in *Capital* Volume Two, that no production is possible which does not allow for the reproduction of the material conditions of production: the reproduction of the means of production.

The average economist, who is no different in this than the average capitalist, knows that each year it is essential to foresee what is needed to replace what has been used up or worn out in production: raw material, fixed installations (buildings), instruments of production (machines), etc. I say the average economist = the average capitalist, for they both express the point of view of the firm, regarding it as sufficient simply to give a commentary on the terms of the firm's financial accounting practice.

But thanks to the genius of Quesnay who first posed this 'glaring' problem, and to the genius of Marx who resolved it, we know that the reproduction of the material conditions of production cannot be thought at the level of the firm, because it does not exist at that level in its real conditions. What happens at the level of the firm is an effect, which only gives an idea of the necessity of reproduction, but absolutely fails to allow its conditions and mechanisms to be thought.

A moment's reflection is enough to be convinced of this: Mr X, a capitalist who produces woollen yarn in his spinning-mill, has to 'reproduce' his raw material, his machines, etc. But *he* does not produce them for his own production – other capitalists do: an Australian sheep-farmer, Mr Y, a heavy engineer producing machine-tools, Mr Z, etc., etc. And Mr Y and Mr Z, in order to produce those products which are the condition of the reproduction of Mr X's conditions of production, also have to reproduce the conditions of their own production, and so on to infinity – the whole in proportions such that, on the national and even the world market, the demand for means of production (for reproduction) can be satisfied by the supply.

In order to think this mechanism, which leads to a kind of 'endless chain', it is necessary to follow Marx's 'global' procedure, and to study in particular the relations of the circulation of capital between Department I (production of means of production) and Department II (production of means of consumption), and the realization of surplus-value, in *Capital*, Volumes Two and Three.

We shall not go into the analysis of this question. It is enough to have mentioned the existence of the necessity of the reproduction of the material conditions of production.

Reproduction of labour power

However, the reader will not have failed to note one thing. We have discussed the reproduction of the means of production – but not the reproduction of the productive forces. We have therefore ignored the reproduction of what distinguishes the productive forces from the means of production, i.e. the reproduction of labour power.

From the observation of what takes place in the firm, in particular from the examination of the financial accounting practice which predicts amortization and investment, we have been able to obtain an approximate idea of the existence of the material process of reproduction, but we are now entering a domain in which the observation of what happens in the firm is, if not totally blind, at least almost entirely so, and for good reason: the reproduction of labour power takes place essentially outside the firm.

How is the reproduction of labour power ensured?

It is ensured by giving labour power the material means with which to reproduce itself: by wages. Wages feature in the accounting of each enterprise, but as 'wage capital',[2] not at all as a condition of the material reproduction of labour power.

However, that is in fact how it 'works', since wages represents only that part of the value produced by the expenditure of labour power which is indispensable for its reproduction: sc. indispensable to the reconstitution of the labour power of the wage-earner (the wherewithal to pay for housing, food and clothing, in short to enable the wage-earner to present himself again at the factory gate the next day – and every further day God grants him); and we should add: indispensable for raising and educating the children in whom the proletarian reproduces himself (in n models where $n = 0, 1, 2,$ etc. . . .) as labour power.

Remember that this quantity of value (wages) necessary for the reproduction of labour power is determined not by the needs of a 'biological' Guaranteed Minimum Wage (*Salaire Minimum Interprofessionnel Garanti*) alone, but by the needs of a historical minimum (Marx noted that English workers need beer while French proletarians need wine) – i.e. a historically variable minimum.

I should also like to point out that this minimum is doubly historical in that it is not defined by the historical needs of the working class 'recognized'

2. Marx gave it its scientific concept: *variable capital*.

by the capitalist class, but by the historical needs imposed by the proletarian class struggle (a double class struggle: against the lengthening of the working day and against the reduction of wages).

However, it is not enough to ensure for labour power the material conditions of its reproduction if it is to be reproduced as labour power. I have said that the available labour power must be 'competent', i.e. suitable to be set to work in the complex system of the process of production. The development of the productive forces and the type of unity historically constitutive of the productive forces at a given moment produce the result that the labour power has to be (diversely) skilled and therefore reproduced as such. Diversely: according to the requirements of the socio-technical division of labour, its different 'jobs' and 'posts'.

How is this reproduction of the (diversified) skills of labour power provided for in a capitalist regime? Here, unlike social formations characterized by slavery or serfdom, this reproduction of the skills of labour power tends (this is a tendential law) decreasingly to be provided for 'on the spot' (apprenticeship within production itself), but is achieved more and more outside production: by the capitalist education system, and by other instances and institutions.

What do children learn at school? They go varying distances in their studies, but at any rate they learn to read, to write and to add – i.e. a number of techniques, and a number of other things as well, including elements (which may be rudimentary or on the contrary thoroughgoing) of 'scientific' or 'literary culture', which are directly useful in the different jobs in production (one instruction for manual workers, another for technicians, a third for engineers, a final one for higher management, etc.). Thus they learn 'know-how'.

But besides these techniques and knowledges, and in learning them, children at school also learn the 'rules' of good behaviour, i.e. the attitude that should be observed by every agent in the division of labour, according to the job he is 'destined' for: rules of morality, civic and professional conscience, which actually means rules of respect for the socio-technical division of labour and ultimately the rules of the order established by class domination. They also learn to 'speak proper French', to 'handle' the workers correctly, i.e. actually (for the future capitalists and their servants) to 'order them about' properly, i.e. (ideally) to 'speak to them' in the right way, etc.

To put this more scientifically, I shall say that the reproduction of labour power requires not only a reproduction of its skills, but also, at the same time a reproduction of its submission to the rules of the established order, i.e. a reproduction of submission to the ruling ideology for the workers, and a reproduction of the ability to manipulate the ruling ideology correctly for the agents of exploitation and repression, so that they, too, will provide for the domination of the ruling class 'in words'.

In other words, the school (but also other state institutions like the church, or other apparatuses like the army) teaches 'know-how', but in forms which ensure *subjection to the ruling ideology* or the mastery of its 'practice'. All the agents of production, exploitation and repression, not to speak of the 'professionals of ideology' (Marx), must in one way or another be 'steeped' in this ideology in order to perform their tasks 'conscientiously' – the tasks of the exploited (the proletarians), of the exploiters (the capitalists), of the exploiters' auxiliaries (the managers), or of the high priests of the ruling ideology (its 'functionaries'), etc.

The reproduction of labour power thus reveals as its *sine qua non* not only the reproduction of its 'skills' but also the reproduction of its subjection to the ruling ideology or of the 'practice' of that ideology, with the proviso that it is not enough to say 'not only but also', for it is clear that *it is in the forms and under the forms of ideological subjection that provision is made for the reproduction of the skills of labour power*.

But this is to recognize the effective presence of a new reality: *ideology*.

Here I shall make two comments.

The first is to round off my analysis of reproduction.

I have just given a rapid survey of the forms of the reproduction of the productive forces, i.e. of the means of production on the one hand, and of labour power on the other.

But I have not yet approached the question of the *reproduction of the relations of production*. This is a *crucial question* for the Marxist theory of the mode of production. To let it pass would be a theoretical omission – worse, a serious political error.

I shall therefore discuss it. But in order to obtain the means to discuss it, I shall have to make another long detour.

The second comment is that in order to make this detour, I am obliged to re-raise my old question: what is a society?

Infrastructure and superstructure

On a number of occasions (1969, 1970) I have insisted on the revolutionary character of the Marxist conception of the 'social whole' in so far as it is distinct from the Hegelian 'totality'. I said (and this thesis only repeats famous propositions of historical materialism) that Marx conceived the structure of every society as constituted by 'levels' or 'instances' articulated by a specific determination: the *infrastructure*, or economic base (the 'unity' of the productive forces and the relations of production) and the *superstructure*, which itself contains two 'levels' or 'instances': the politico-legal (law and the state) and ideology (the different ideologies, religious, ethical, legal, political, etc.).

Besides its theoretico-didactic interest (it reveals the difference between Marx and Hegel), this representation has the following crucial theoretical advantage: it makes it possible to inscribe in the theoretical apparatus of its essential concepts what I have called their *respective indices of effectivity*. What does this mean?

It is easy to see that this representation of the structure of every society as an edifice containing a base (infrastructure) on which are erected the two 'floors' of the superstructure, is a metaphor, to be quite precise, a spatial metaphor: the metaphor of a topography (*topique*).[3] Like every metaphor, this metaphor suggests something, makes something visible. What? Precisely this: that the upper floors could not 'stay up' (in the air) alone, if they did not rest precisely on their base.

Thus the object of the metaphor of the edifice is to represent above all the 'determination in the last instance' by the economic base. The effect of this spatial metaphor is to endow the base with an index of effectivity known by the famous terms: the determination in the last instance of what happens in the upper 'floors' (of the superstructure) by what happens in the economic base.

Given this index of effectivity 'in the last instance', the 'floors' of the superstructure are clearly endowed with different indices of effectivity. What kind of indices?

It is possible to say that the floors of the superstructure are not determinant in the last instance, but that they are determined by the effectivity of the base; that if they are determinant in their own (as yet undefined) ways, this is true only in so far as they are determined by the base.

Their index of effectivity (or determination), as determined by the determination in the last instance of the base, is thought by the Marxist tradition in two ways: (1) there is a 'relative autonomy' of the superstructure with respect to the base; (2) there is a 'reciprocal action' of the superstructure on the base.

We can therefore say that the great theoretical advantage of the Marxist topography, i.e. of the spatial metaphor of the edifice (base and super-structure) is simultaneously that it reveals that questions of determination (or of index of effectivity) are crucial; that it reveals that it is the base which in the last instance determines the whole edifice; and that, as a consequence, it obliges us to pose the theoretical problem of the types of 'derivatory'

3. *Topography* from the Greek *topos*: place. A topography represents in a definite space the respective *sites* occupied by several realities; thus the economic is *at the bottom* (the base), the superstructure *above it*.

effectivity peculiar to the superstructure, i.e. it obliges us to think what the Marxist tradition calls conjointly the relative autonomy of the super-structure and the reciprocal action of the superstructure on the base.

The greatest disadvantage of this representation of the structure of every society by the spatial metaphor of an edifice, is obviously the fact that it is metaphorical: i.e. it remains *descriptive*.

It now seems to me that it is possible and desirable to represent things differently. NB, I do not mean by this that I want to reject the classical metaphor, for that metaphor itself requires that we go beyond it. And I am not going beyond it in order to reject it as outworn. I simply want to attempt to think what it gives us in the form of a description.

I believe that it is possible and necessary to think what characterizes the essential of the existence and nature of the superstructure *on the basis of reproduction*. Once one takes the point of view of reproduction, many of the questions whose existence was indicated by the spatial metaphor of the edifice, but to which it could not give a conceptual answer, are immediately illuminated.

My basic thesis is that it is not possible to pose these questions (and therefore to answer them) *except from the point of view of reproduction*.

I shall give a short analysis of law, the state and ideology *from this point of view*. And I shall reveal what happens both from the point of view of practice and production on the one hand, and from that of reproduction on the other.

The state

The Marxist tradition is strict, here: in the *Communist Manifesto* and the *Eighteenth Brumaire* (and in all the later classical texts, above all in Marx's writings on the Paris Commune and Lenin's on *State and Revolution*), the State is explicitly conceived as a repressive apparatus. The State is a 'machine' of repression, which enables the ruling classes (in the nineteenth century the bourgeois class the 'class' of big landowners) to ensure their domination over the working class, thus enabling the former to subject the latter to the process of surplus-value extortion (i.e. to capitalist exploitation).

The State is thus first of all what the Marxist classics have called *the State apparatus*. This term means: not only the specialized apparatus (in the narrow sense) whose existence and necessity I have recognized in relation to the requirements of legal practice, i.e. the police, the courts, the prisons; but also the army, which (the proletariat has paid for this experience with its blood) intervenes directly as a supplementary repressive force in the last instance, when the police and its specialized auxiliary corps are 'outrun by events'; and above this ensemble, the head of State, the government and the administration.

Presented in this form, the Marxist–Leninist 'theory' of the State has its finger on the essential point, and not for one moment can there be any question of rejecting the fact that this really is the essential point. The State apparatus, which defines the State as a force of repressive execution and intervention 'in the interests of the ruling classes' in the class struggle conducted by the bourgeoisie and its allies against the proletariat, is quite certainly the State, and quite certainly defines its basic 'function'.

From descriptive theory to theory as such

Nevertheless, here too, as I pointed out with respect to the metaphor of the edifice (infrastructure and superstructure), this presentation of the nature of the State is still partly descriptive.

As I shall often have occasion to use this adjective (descriptive), a word of explanation is necessary in order to remove any ambiguity.

Whenever, in speaking of the metaphor of the edifice or of the Marxist 'theory' of the State, I have said that these are descriptive conceptions or representations of their objects, I had no ulterior critical motives. On the contrary, I have every grounds to think that great scientific discoveries cannot help but pass through the phase of what I shall call *descriptive 'theory'*. This is the first phase of every theory, at least in the domain which concerns us (that of the science of social formations). As such, one might – and in my opinion one must – envisage this phase as a transitional one, necessary to the development of the theory. That it is transitional is inscribed in my expression: 'descriptive theory', which reveals in its conjunction of terms the equivalent of a kind of 'contradiction'. In fact, the term theory 'clashes' to some extent with the adjective 'descriptive' which I have attached to it. This means quite precisely:

1. that the 'descriptive theory' really is, without a shadow of a doubt, the irreversible beginning of the theory; but

2. that the 'descriptive' form in which the theory is presented requires, precisely as an effect of this 'contradiction', a development of the theory which goes beyond the form of 'description'.

Let me make this idea clearer by returning to our present object: the State.

When I say that the Marxist 'theory' of the State available to us is still partly 'descriptive', that means first and foremost that this descriptive 'theory' is without the shadow of a doubt precisely the beginning of the Marxist theory of the State, and that this beginning gives us the essential point, i.e. the decisive principle of every later development of the theory.

Indeed, I shall call the descriptive theory of the State correct, since it is perfectly possible to make the vast majority of the facts in the domain with which it is concerned correspond to the definition it gives of its object. Thus, the definition of the State as a class State, existing in the repressive State apparatus, casts a brilliant light on all the facts observable in the various orders of repression whatever their domains: from the massacres of June 1848 and of the Paris Commune, of Bloody Sunday, May 1905 in Petrograd, of the Resistance, of Charonne, etc., to the mere (and relatively anodyne) interventions of a 'censorship' which has banned Diderot's *La Réligieuse* or a play by Gatti on Franco; it casts light on all the direct or indirect forms of exploitation and extermination of the masses of the people (imperialist wars); it casts light on that subtle everyday domination beneath which can be glimpsed, in the forms of political democracy, for example, what Lenin, following Marx, called the dictatorship of the bourgeoisie.

And yet the descriptive theory of the State represents a phase in the constitution of the theory which itself demands the 'supersession' of this phase. For it is clear that if the definition in question really does give us the means to identify and recognize the facts of oppression by relating them to the State, conceived as the repressive State apparatus, this 'interrelationship' gives rise to a very special kind of obviousness, about which I shall have something to say in a moment: 'Yes, that's how it is, that's really true!'[4] And the accumulation of facts within the definition of the State may multiply examples, but it does not really advance the definition of the State, i.e. the scientific theory of the State. Every descriptive theory thus runs the risk of 'blocking' the development of the theory, and yet that development is essential.

That is why I think that, in order to develop this descriptive theory into theory as such, i.e. in order to understand further the mechanisms of the State in its functioning, it is indispensable to *add* something to the classical definition of the State as a State apparatus.

The essentials of the Marxist theory of the State

Let me first clarify one important point: the State (and its existence in its apparatus) has no meaning except as a function of *State power*. The whole of the political class struggle revolves around the State. By which I mean around the possession, i.e. the seizure and conservation of State power by a certain class or by an alliance between classes or class fractions. This first clarification obliges me to distinguish between State power (conservation of State power or seizure of State power), the objective of the political class struggle on the one hand, and the State apparatus on the other.

We know that the State apparatus may survive, as is proved by bourgeois 'revolutions' in nineteenth-century France (1830, 1848), by *coups d'état* (2 December, May 1958), by collapses of the State (the fall of the Empire in 1870, of the Third Republic in 1940), or by the political rise of the petty bourgeoisie (1890–95 in France), etc., without the State apparatus being

4. See p. 264, *On Ideology*.

affected or modified: it may survive political events which affect the possession of State power.

Even after a social revolution like that of 1917, a large part of the State apparatus survived after the seizure of State power by the alliance of the proletariat and the small peasantry: Lenin repeated the fact again and again.

It is possible to describe the distinction between State power and State apparatus as part of the 'Marxist theory' of the State, explicitly present since Marx's *Eighteenth Brumaire* and *Class Struggles in France*.

To summarize the 'Marxist theory of the State' on this point, it can be said that the Marxist classics have always claimed that (1) the State is the repressive State apparatus, (2) State power and State apparatus must be distinguished, (3) the objective of the class struggle concerns State power, and in consequence the use of the State apparatus by the classes (or alliance of classes or of fractions of classes) holding State power as a function of their class objectives, and (4) the proletariat must seize State power in order to destroy the existing bourgeois State apparatus and, in a first phase, replace it with a quite different, proletarian, State apparatus, then in later phases set in motion a radical process, that of the destruction of the State (the end of State power, the end of every State apparatus).

In this perspective, therefore, what I would propose to add to the 'Marxist theory' of the State is already there in so many words. But it seems to me that even with this supplement, this theory is still in part descriptive, although it does now contain complex and differential elements whose functioning and action cannot be understood without recourse to further supplementary theoretical development.

The State ideological apparatuses

Thus, what has to be added to the 'Marxist theory' of the State is something else.

Here we must advance cautiously in a terrain which, in fact, the Marxist classics entered long before us, but without having systematized in theoretical form the decisive advances implied by their experiences and procedures. Their experiences and procedures were indeed restricted in the main to the terrain of political practice.

In fact, i.e. in their political practice, the Marxist classics treated the State as a more complex reality than the definition of it given in the 'Marxist theory of the State', even when it has been supplemented as I have just suggested. They recognized this complexity in their practice, but they did not express it in a corresponding theory.[5]

5. To my knowledge, Gramsci is the only one who went any distance in the road I am taking. He had the 'remarkable' idea that the State could not be reduced to the (Repressive) State Apparatus, but included, as he put it, a certain number of in-

I should like to attempt a very schematic outline of this corresponding theory. To that end, I propose the following thesis.

In order to advance the theory of the State it is indispensable to take into account not only the distinction between *State power* and *State apparatus*, but also another reality which is clearly on the side of the (repressive) State apparatus, but must not be confused with it. I shall call this reality by its concept: *the ideological State apparatuses.*

What are the ideological State apparatuses (ISAs)?

They must not be confused with the (repressive) State apparatus. Remember that in Marxist theory, the State Apparatus (SA) contains: the Government, the Administration, the Army, the Police, the Courts, the Prisons, etc., which constitute what I shall in future call the Repressive State Apparatus. Repressive suggests that the State Apparatus in question 'functions by violence' – at least ultimately (since repression, e.g. administrative repression, may take non-physical forms).

I shall call Ideological State Apparatuses a certain number of realities which present themselves to the immediate observer in the form of distinct and specialized institutions. I propose an empirical list of these which will obviously have to be examined in detail, tested, corrected and reorganized. With all the reservations implied by this requirement, we can for the moment regard the following institutions as Ideological State Apparatuses (the order in which I have listed them has no particular significance):

The religious ISA (the system of the different Churches).
The educational ISA (the system of the different public and private 'Schools').
The family ISA.[6]
The legal ISA.[7]
The political ISA (the political system, including the different Parties).
The trade-union ISA.
The communications ISA (press, radio and television, etc.).
The cultural ISA (Literature, the Arts, sports, etc.).

---

stitutions from '*civil society*': the Church, the Schools, the trade unions, etc. Unfortunately, Gramsci did not systematize his institutions, which remained in the state of acute but fragmentary notes (see Gramsci, 1971, pp. 12, 259, 260–63; see also the letter to Tatiana Schucht, 7 September 1931, in Gramsci, 1968, p. 479. English translation in preparation).

6. The family obviously has other 'functions' than that of an ISA. It intervenes in the reproduction of labour power. In different modes of production it is the unit of production and/or the unit of consumption.

7. The 'Law' belongs both to the (Repressive) State Apparatus and to the system of the ISAs.

I have said that the ISAs must not be confused with the (Repressive) State Apparatus. What constitutes the difference?

As a first moment, it is clear that while there is *one* (Repressive) State Apparatus, there is a *plurality* of Ideological State Apparatuses. Even presupposing that it exists, the unity that constitutes this plurality of ISAs as a body is not immediately visible.

As a second moment, it is clear that whereas the – unified – (Repressive) State Apparatus belongs entirely to the *public* domain, much the larger part of the Ideological State Apparatuses (in their apparent dispersion) are part, on the contrary, of the *private* domain. Churches, parties, trade unions, families, some schools, most newspapers, cultural ventures, etc., etc., are private.

We can ignore the first observation for the moment. But someone is bound to question the second, asking me by what right I regard as Ideological *State* Apparatuses, institutions which for the most part do not possess public status, but are quite simply *private* institutions. As a conscious Marxist, Gramsci already forestalled this objection in one sentence. The distinction between the public and the private is a distinction internal to bourgeois law, and valid in the (subordinate) domains in which bourgeois law exercises its 'authority'. The domain of the State escapes it because the latter is 'above the law': the State, which is the State *of* the ruling class, is neither public nor private; on the contrary, it is the precondition for any distinction between public and private. The same thing can be said from the starting-point of our State Ideological Apparatuses. It is unimportant whether the institutions in which they are realized are 'public' or 'private'. What matters is how they function. Private institutions can perfectly well 'function' as Ideological State Apparatuses. A reasonably thorough analysis of any one of the ISAs proves it.

But now for what is essential. What distinguishes the ISAs from the (Repressive) State Apparatus is the following basic difference: the Repressive State Apparatus functions 'by violence', whereas the Ideological State Apparatuses *function 'by ideology'*.

I can clarify matters by correcting this distinction. I shall say rather that every State Apparatus, whether Repressive or Ideological, 'functions' both by violence and by ideology, but with one very important distinction which makes it imperative not to confuse the Ideological State Apparatuses with the (Repressive) State Apparatus.

This is the fact that the (Repressive) State Apparatus functions massively and predominantly *by repression* (including physical repression), while functioning secondarily by ideology. (There is no such thing as a purely repressive apparatus.) For example, the army and the police also function by ideology both to ensure their own cohesion and reproduction, and in the 'values' they propound externally.

In the same way, but inversely, it is essential to say that for their part the Ideological State Apparatuses function massively and predominantly *by ideology*, but they also function secondarily by repression, even if ultimately, but only ultimately, this is very attentuated and concealed, even symbolic. (There is no such thing as a purely ideological apparatus.) Thus schools and churches use suitable methods of punishment, expulsion, selection, etc., to 'discipline' not only their shepherds, but also their flocks. The same is true of the family. . . . The same is true of the cultural IS Apparatus (censorship, among other things), etc.

Is it necessary to add that this determination of the double 'functioning' (predominantly, secondarily) by repression and by ideology, according to whether it is a matter of the (Repressive) State Apparatus or the Ideological State Apparatuses, makes it clear that very subtle explicit or tacit combinations may be woven from the interplay of the (Repressive) State Apparatus and the Ideological State Apparatuses? Everyday life provides us with innumerable examples of this, but they must be studied in detail if we are to go further than this mere observation.

Nevertheless, this remark leads us towards an understanding of what constitutes the unity of the apparently disparate body of the ISAs. If the ISAs 'function' massively and predominantly by ideology, what unifies their diversity is precisely this functioning, in so far as the ideology by which they function is always in fact unified, despite its diversity and its contradictions, *beneath the ruling ideology*, which is the ideology of 'the ruling class'. Given the fact that the 'ruling class' in principle holds State power (openly or more often by means of alliances between classes or class fractions), and therefore has at its disposal the (Repressive) State Apparatus, we can accept the fact that this same ruling class is active in the Ideological State Apparatuses in so far as it is ultimately the ruling ideology which is realized in the Ideological State Apparatuses, precisely in its contradictions. Of course, it is a quite different thing to act by laws and decrees in the (Repressive) State Apparatus and to 'act' through the intermediary of the ruling ideology in the Ideological State Apparatuses. We must go into the details of this difference – but it cannot mask the reality of a profound identity. To my knowledge, *no class can hold State power over a long period without at the same time exercising its hegemony over and in the State Ideological Apparatuses*. I only need one example and proof of this: Lenin's anguished concern to revolutionize the educational Ideological State Apparatus (among others), simply to make it possible for the Soviet proletariat, who had seized State power, to secure the future of the dictatorship of the proletariat and the transition to socialism.[8]

8. In a pathetic text written in 1937, Krupskaya relates the history of Lenin's desperate efforts and what she regards as his failure.

This last comment puts us in a position to understand that the Ideological State Apparatuses may be not only the *stake*, but also the *site* of class struggle, and often of bitter forms of class struggle. The class (or class alliance) in power cannot lay down the law in the ISAs as easily as it can in the (repressive) State Apparatus, not only because the former ruling classes are able to retain strong positions there for a long time, but also because the resistance of the exploited classes is able to find means and occasions to express itself there, either by the utilization of their contradictions, or by conquering combat positions in them in struggle.[9]

Let me run through my comments.

If the thesis I have proposed is well-founded, it leads me back to the classical Marxist theory of the State, while making it more precise in one point. I argue that it is necessary to distinguish between State power (and its possession by . . .) on the one hand, and the State Apparatus on the other. But I add that the State Apparatus contains two bodies: the body of institutions which represent the Repressive State Apparatus on the one hand, and the body of institutions which represent the body of Ideological State Apparatuses on the other.

But if this is the case, the following question is bound to be asked, even in the very summary state of my suggestions: what exactly is the extent of the role of the Ideological State Apparatuses? What is their importance based on? In other words: to what does the 'function' of these Ideological State Apparatuses, which do not function by repression but by ideology, correspond?

On the reproduction of the relations of production

I can now answer the central question which I have left in suspense for many long pages: *how is the reproduction of the relations of production secured?*

9. What I have said in these few brief words about the class struggle in the ISAs is obviously far from exhausting the question of the class struggle.

To approach this question, two principles must be borne in mind:

The first principle was formulated by Marx in the Preface to *A Contribution to the Critique of Political Economy*: 'In considering such transformations [a social revolution] a distinction should always be made between the material transformation of the economic conditions of production, which can be determined with the precision of natural science, and the legal, political, religious, aesthetic or philosophic – in short, ideological forms in which men become conscious of this conflict and fight it out.' The class struggle is thus expressed and exercised in ideological forms, thus also in the ideological forms of the ISAs. But the class struggle *extends far beyond* these forms, and it is because it extends beyond them that the struggle of the exploited classes may also be exercised in the forms of the ISAs, and thus turn the weapon of ideology against the classes in power.

This by virtue of the *second principle*: the class struggle extends beyond the ISAs because it is rooted elsewhere than in ideology, in the Infrastructure, in the relations of production, which are relations of exploitation and constitute the base for class relations.

In the topographical language (infrastructure, superstructure), I can say: for the most part,[10] it is secured by the legal-political and ideological superstructure.

But as I have argued that it is essential to go beyond this still descriptive language, I shall say: for the most part,[10] it is secured by the exercise of State power in the State Apparatuses, on the one hand the (Repressive) State Apparatus, on the other the Ideological State Apparatuses.

What I have just said must also be taken into account, and it can be assembled in the form of the following three features:

1. All the State Apparatuses function both by repression and by ideology, with the difference that the (Repressive) State Apparatus functions massively and predominantly by repression, whereas the Ideological State Apparatuses function massively and predominantly by ideology.

2. Whereas the (Repressive) State Apparatus constitutes an organized whole whose different parts are centralized beneath a commanding unity, that of the politics of class struggle applied by the political representatives of the ruling classes in possession of State power, the Ideological State Apparatuses are multiple, distinct, 'relatively autonomous' and capable of providing an objective field to contradictions which express in forms which may be limited or extreme, the effects of the clashes between the capitalist class struggle and the proletarian class struggle, as well as their subordinate forms.

3. Whereas the unity of the (Repressive) State Apparatus is secured by its unified and centralized organization under the leadership of the representatives of the classes in power executing the politics of the class struggle of the classes in power, the unity of the different Ideological State Apparatuses is secured, usually in contradictory forms, by the ruling ideology, the ideology of the ruling class.

Taking these features into account, it is possible to represent the reproduction of the relations of production[11] in the following way, according to a kind of 'division of labour'.

The role of the repressive State apparatus, in so far as it is a repressive apparatus, consists essentially in securing by force (physical or otherwise) the political conditions of the reproduction of relations of production which are in the last resort *relations of exploitation*. Not only does the State apparatus contribute generously to its own reproduction (the capitalist

10. For the most part. For the relations of production are first reproduced by the materiality of the processes of production and circulation. But it should not be forgotten that ideological relations are immediately present in these same processes.

11. *For that part* of reproduction to which the Repressive State Apparatus and the Ideological State Apparatus *contribute*.

State contains political dynasties, military dynasties, etc.), but also and above all, the State apparatus secures by repression (from the most brutal physical force, via mere administrative commands and interdictions, to open and tacit censorship) the political conditions for the action of the Ideological State Apparatuses.

In fact, it is the latter which largely secure the reproduction specifically of the relations of production, behind a 'shield' provided by the repressive State apparatus. It is here that the role of the ruling ideology is heavily concentrated, the ideology of the ruling class, which holds State power. It is the intermediation of the ruling ideology that ensures a (sometimes teeth-gritting) 'harmony' between the repressive State apparatus and the Ideological State Apparatuses, and between the different State Ideological Apparatuses.

We are thus led to envisage the following hypothesis, as a function precisely of the diversity of Ideological State Apparatuses in their single, because shared, role of the reproduction of the relations of production.

Indeed we have listed a relatively large number of ideological State apparatuses in contemporary capitalist social formations: the educational apparatus, the religious apparatus, the family apparatus, the political apparatus, the trade-union apparatus, the communications apparatus, the 'cultural' apparatus, etc.

But in the social formations of that mode of production characterized by 'serfdom' (usually called the feudal mode of production), we observe that although there is a single repressive State apparatus which, since the earliest known ancient states, let alone the absolute monarchies, has been formally very similar to the one we know today, the number of Ideological State Apparatuses is smaller and their individual types are different. For example, we observe that during the Middle Ages, the Church (the religious ideological State apparatus) accumulated a number of functions which have today devolved on to several distinct ideological State apparatuses, new ones in relation to the past I am invoking, in particular educational and cultural functions. Alongside the Church there was the family Ideological State Apparatus, which played a considerable part, incommensurable with its role in capitalist social formations. Despite appearances, the Church and the family were not the only Ideological State Apparatuses. There was also a political Ideological State Apparatus (the Estates General, the *Parlement*, the different political factions and Leagues, the ancestors of the modern political parties, and the whole political system of the free Communes and then of the *Villes*). There was also a powerful 'proto-trade-union' Ideological State Apparatus, if I may venture such an anachronistic term (the powerful merchants' and bankers' guilds and the journeymen's associations, etc.). Publishing and communications, even, saw an indisputable development, as did the theatre; initially both were integral parts of the Church, then they became more and more independent of it.

In the pre-capitalist historical period which I have examined extremely broadly, it is absolutely clear that *there was one dominant Ideological State Apparatus, the Church*, which concentrated within it not only religious functions, but also educational ones, and a large proportion of the functions of communications and 'culture'. It is no accident that all ideological struggle, from the sixteenth to the eighteenth century, starting with the first shocks of the Reformation, was *concentrated* in an anti-clerical and anti-religious struggle; rather this is a function precisely of the dominant position of the religious ideological State apparatus.

The foremost objective and achievement of the French Revolution was not just to transfer State power from the feudal aristocracy to the merchant-capitalist bourgeoisie, to break part of the former repressive State apparatus and replace it with a new one (e.g. the national popular Army) – but also to attack the number-one Ideological State Apparatus; the Church. Hence the civil constitution of the clergy, the confiscation of ecclesiastical wealth, and the creation of new ideological State apparatuses to replace the religious ideological State apparatus in its dominant role.

Naturally, these things did not happen automatically: witness the Concordat, the Restoration and the long class struggle between the landed aristocracy and the industrial bourgeoisie throughout the nineteenth century for the establishment of bourgeois hegemony over the functions formerly fulfilled by the Church: above all by the schools. It can be said that the bourgeoisie relied on the new political, parliamentary-democratic, ideological State apparatus, installed in the earliest years of the Revolution, then restored after long and violent struggles, for a few months in 1848 and for decades after the fall of the Second Empire, in order to conduct its struggle against the Church and wrest its ideological functions away from it, in other words, to ensure not only its own political hegemony, but also the ideological hegemony indispensable to the reproduction of capitalist relations of production.

That is why I believe that I am justified in advancing the following thesis, however precarious it is. I believe that the ideological State apparatus which has been installed in the *dominant* position in mature capitalist social formations as a result of a violent political and ideological class struggle against the old dominant ideological State apparatus, is the *educational ideological apparatus*.

This thesis may seem paradoxical, given that for everyone, i.e. in the ideological representation that the bourgeoisie has tried to give itself and the classes it exploits, it really seems that the dominant ideological State apparatus in capitalist social formations is not the Schools, but the political ideological State apparatus, i.e. the regime of parliamentary democracy combining universal suffrage and party struggle.

However, history, even recent history, shows that the bourgeoisie has been and still is able to accommodate itself to political ideological State apparatuses other than parliamentary democracy: the First and Second Empires, Constitutional Monarchy (Louis XVIII and Charles X), Parliamentary Monarchy (Louis-Philippe), Presidential Democracy (de Gaulle), to mention only France. In England this is even clearer. The Revolution was particularly 'successful' there from the bourgeois point of view, since unlike France, where the bourgeoisie, partly because of the stupidity of the petty aristocracy, had to agree to being carried to power by peasant and plebian '*journées révolutionnaires*', something for which it had to pay a high price, the English bourgeoisie was able to 'compromise' with the aristocracy and 'share' State power and the use of the State apparatus with it for a long time (peace among all men of good will in the ruling classes!). In Germany it is even more striking, since it was behind a political ideological State apparatus in which the imperial Junkers (epitomized by Bismarck), their army and their police provided it with a shield and leading personnel, that the imperialist bourgeoisie made its shattering entry into history, before 'traversing' the Weimar Republic and entrusting itself to Nazism.

Hence I believe I have good reasons for thinking that behind the scenes of its political Ideological State Apparatus, which occupies the front of the stage, what the bourgeoisie has installed as its number-one, i.e. as its dominant ideological State apparatus, is the educational apparatus, which has in fact replaced in its functions the previously dominant ideological State apparatus, the Church. One might even add: the school–family couple has replaced the Church–family couple.

Why is the educational apparatus in fact the dominant ideological State apparatus in capitalist social formations, and how does it function?

For the moment it must suffice to say:

1. All ideological State apparatuses, whatever they are, contribute to the same result: the reproduction of the relations of production, i.e. of capitalist relations of exploitation.

2. Each of them contributes towards this single result in the way proper to it. The political apparatus by subjecting individuals to the political State ideology, the 'indirect' (parliamentary) or 'direct' (plebiscitary or fascist) 'democratic' ideology. The communications apparatus by cramming every 'citizen' with daily doses of nationalism, chauvinism, liberalism, moralism, etc., by means of the press, the radio and television. The same goes for the cultural apparatus (the role of sport in chauvinism is of the first importance), etc. The religious apparatus by recalling in sermons and the other great

ceremonies of birth, marriage and death, that man is only ashes, unless he loves his neighbour to the extent of turning the other cheek to whoever strikes first. The family apparatus . . . but there is no need to go on.

3. This concert is dominated by a single score, occasionally disturbed by contradictions (those of the remnants of former ruling classes, those of the proletarians and their organizations): the score of the Ideology of the current ruling class which integrates into its music the great themes of the humanism of the great forefathers, who produced the Greek miracle even before Christianity, and afterwards the glory of Rome, the Eternal City, and the themes of interest, particular and general, etc. nationalism, moralism and economism.

4. Nevertheless, in this concert, one ideological State apparatus certainly has the dominant role, although hardly anyone lends an ear to its music: it is so silent! This is the school.

It takes children from every class at infant-school age, and then for years, the years in which the child is most 'vulnerable', squeezed between the family State apparatus and the educational State apparatus, it drums into them, whether it uses new or old methods, a certain amount of 'know-how' wrapped in the ruling ideology (French, arithmetic, natural history, the sciences, literature) or simply the ruling ideology in its pure state (ethics, civic instruction, philosophy). Somewhere around the age of sixteen, a huge mass of children are ejected 'into production': these are the workers or small peasants. Another portion of scholastically adapted youth carries on: and, for better or worse, it goes somewhat further, until it falls by the wayside and fills the posts of small and middle technicians, white-collar workers, small and middle executives, petty bourgeois of all kinds. A last portion reaches the summit, either to fall into intellectual semi-employment, or to provide, as well as the 'intellectuals of the collective labourer', the agents of exploitation (capitalists, managers), the agents of repression (soldiers, policemen, politicians, administrators, etc.) and the professional ideologists (priests of all sorts, most of whom are convinced 'laymen').

Each mass ejected *en route* is practically provided with the ideology which suits the role it has to fulfil in class society: the role of the exploited (with a 'highly-developed' 'professional', 'ethical', 'civic', 'national' and a-political consciousness); the role of the agent of exploitation (ability to give the workers orders and speak to them: 'human relations'), of the agent of repression (ability to give orders and enforce obedience 'without discussion', or ability to manipulate the demagogy of a political leader's rhetoric), or of the professional ideologist (ability to treat consciousnesses with the respect, i.e. with the contempt, blackmail and demagogy, they deserve, adapted to the accents of morality, of virtue, of 'transcendence', of the nation, of France's world role, etc.).

Of course, many of these contrasting virtues (modesty, resignation, submissiveness on the one hand, cynicism, contempt, arrogance, confidence, self-importance, even smooth talk and cunning on the other) are also taught in the family, in the church, in the army, in good books, in films and even in the football stadium. But no other ideological State apparatus has the obligatory (and not least, free) audience of the totality of the children in the capitalist social formation, eight hours a day for five or six days out of seven.

But it is by an apprenticeship in a variety of know-how wrapped up in the massive inculcation of the ideology of the ruling class that the *relations of production* in a capitalist social formation, i.e. the relations of exploited to exploiters and exploiters to exploited, are largely reproduced. The mechanisms which produce this vital result for the capitalist regime are naturally covered up and concealed by a universally reigning ideology of the school, universally reigning because it is one of the essential forms of the ruling bourgeois ideology: an ideology which represents the school as a neutral environment purged of ideology (because it is ... lay), where teachers respectful of the 'conscience' and 'freedom' of the children who are entrusted to them (in complete confidence) by their 'parents' (who are free, too, i.e. the owners of their children) open up for them the path to the freedom, morality and responsibility of adults by their own example, by knowledge, literature and their 'liberating' virtues.

I ask the pardon of those teachers who, in dreadful conditions, attempt to turn the few weapons they can find in the history and learning they 'teach' against the ideology, the system and the practices in which they are trapped. They are a kind of hero. But they are rare and how many (the majority) do not even begin to suspect the 'work' the system (which is bigger than they are and crushes them) forces them to do, or worse, put all their heart and ingenuity into performing it with the most advanced awareness (the famous new methods!). So little do they suspect it that their own devotion contributes to the maintenance and nourishment of this ideological representation of the school, which makes the school today as 'natural', indispensable-useful and even beneficial for our contemporaries as the Church was 'natural', indispensable and generous for our ancestors a few centuries ago.

In fact, the Church has been replaced today *in its role as the dominant Ideological State Apparatus* by the school. It is coupled with the family just as the Church was once coupled with the family. We can now claim that the unprecedentedly deep crisis which is now shaking the education system of so many States across the globe, often in conjunction with a crisis (already proclaimed in the *Communist Manifesto*) shaking the family system, takes on a political meaning, given that the School (and the school–family couple) constitutes the dominant Ideological State Apparatus, the Apparatus playing a determinant part in the reproduction of the relations of production of a mode of production threatened in its existence by the world class struggle.

On ideology

When I put forward the concept of an Ideological State Apparatus, when I said that the ISAs 'function by ideology', I invoked a reality which needs a little discussion: ideology.

It is well known that the expression 'ideology' was invented by Cabanis, Destutt de Tracy and their friends, who assigned to it as an object the (genetic) theory of ideas. When Marx took up the term fifty years later, he gave it a quite different meaning, even in his Early Works. Here, ideology is the system of the ideas and representations which dominate the mind of a man or a social group. The ideologico-political struggle conducted by Marx as early as his articles in the *Rheinische Zeitung* inevitably and quickly brought him face to face with this reality and forced him to take his earliest intuitions further.

However, here we come upon a rather astonishing paradox. Everything seems to lead Marx to formulate a theory of ideology. In fact, *The German Ideology* does offer us, after the *1844 Manuscripts*, an explicit theory of ideology, but . . . it is not Marxist (we shall see why in a moment). As for *Capital*, although it does contain many hints towards a theory of ideologies (most visibly, the ideology of the vulgar economists), it does not contain that theory itself, which depends for the most part on a theory of ideology in general.

I should like to venture a first and very schematic outline of such a theory. The theses I am about to put forward are certainly not off the cuff, but they cannot be sustained and tested, i.e. confirmed or rejected, except by much thorough study and analysis.

Ideology has no history

One word first of all to expound the reason in principle which seems to me to found, or at least to justify, the project of a theory of ideology *in general*, and not a theory of particular ideolog*ies*, which, whatever their form (religious, ethical, legal, political), always express *class positions*.

It is quite obvious that it is necessary to proceed towards a theory of ideolog*ies* in the two respects I have just suggested. It will then be clear that a theory of ideolog*ies* depends in the last resort on the history of social formations, and thus of the modes of production combined in social formations and of the class struggles which develop in them. In this sense it is clear that there can be no question of a theory of ideolog*ies in general*, since ideolog*ies* (defined in the double respect suggested above: regional and class) have a history, whose determination in the last instance is clearly situated outside ideologies alone, although it involves them.

On the contrary, if I am able to put forward the project of a theory of ideology *in general*, and if this theory really is one of the elements on which theories of ideolog*ies* depend, that entails an apparently paradoxical proposition which I shall express in the following terms: *ideology has no history*.

As we know, this formulation appears in so many words in a passage from *The German Ideology*. Marx utters it with respect to metaphysics, which, he says, has no more history than ethics (meaning also the other forms of ideology).

In *The German Ideology*, this formulation appears in a plainly positivist context. Ideology is conceived as a pure illusion, a pure dream, i.e. as nothingness. All its reality is external to it. Ideology is thus thought as an imaginary construction whose status is exactly like the theoretical status of the dream among writers before Freud. For these writers, the dream was the purely imaginary, i.e. null, result of 'day's residues', presented in an arbitrary arrangement and order, sometimes even 'inverted', in other words, in 'disorder'. For them, the dream was the imaginary, it was empty, null and arbitrarily 'stuck together' (*bricolé*), once the eyes had closed, from the residues of the only full and positive reality, the reality of the day. This is exactly the status of philosophy and ideology (since in this book philosophy is ideology *par excellence*) in *The German Ideology*.

Ideology, then, is for Marx an imaginary assemblage (*bricolage*), a pure dream, empty and vain, constituted by the 'day's residues' from the only full and positive reality, that of the concrete history of concrete material individuals materially producing their existence. It is on this basis that ideology has no history in *The German Ideology*, since its history is outside it, where the only existing history is, the history of concrete individuals, etc. In *The German Ideology*, the thesis that ideology has no history is therefore a purely negative thesis, since it means both:

1. Ideology is nothing in so far as it is a pure dream (manufactured by who knows what power: if not by the alienation of the division of labour, but that, too, is a *negative* determination).

2. Ideology has no history, which emphatically does not mean that there is no history in it (on the contrary, for it is merely the pale, empty and inverted reflection of real history) but that it has no history *of its own*.

Now, while the thesis I wish to defend formally speaking adopts the terms of *The German Ideology* ('ideology has no history'), it is radically different from the positivist and historicist thesis of *The German Ideology*.

For on the one hand, I think it is possible to hold that ideolog*ies have a history of their own* (although it is determined in the last instance by the class struggle); and on the other, I think it is possible to hold that ideology *in general has no history*, not in a negative sense (its history is external to it), but in an absolutely positive sense.

This sense is a positive one if it is true that the peculiarity of ideology is that it is endowed with a structure and a functioning such as to make it a non-historical reality, i.e. an *omni-historical* reality, in the sense in which that structure and functioning are immutable, present in the same form through-out what we can call history, in the sense in which the *Communist Manifesto* defines history as the history of class struggles, i.e. the history of class societies.

To give a theoretical reference-point here, I might say that, to return to our example of the dream, in its Freudian conception this time, our proposition: ideology has no history, can and must (and in a way which has absolutely nothing arbitrary about it, but, quite the reverse, is theoretically necessary, for there is an organic link between the two propositions) be related directly to Freud's proposition that the *unconscious is eternal*, i.e. that it has no history.

If eternal means, not transcendent to all (temporal) history, but omni-present, trans-historical and therefore immutable in form throughout the extent of history, I shall adopt Freud's expression word for word, and write *ideology is eternal*, exactly like the unconscious. And I add that I find this comparison theoretically justified by the fact that the eternity of the un-conscious is not unrelated to the eternity of ideology in general.

That is why I believe I am justified, hypothetically at least, in proposing a theory of ideology *in general*, in the sense that Freud presented a theory of the unconscious *in general*.

To simplify the phrase, it is convenient, taking into account what has been said about ideologies, to use the plain term ideology to designate ideology in general, which I have just said has no history, or, what comes to the same thing, is eternal, i.e. omnipresent in its immutable form throughout history (= the history of social formations containing social classes). For the moment I shall restrict myself to 'class societies' and their history.

Ideology is a 'representation' of the imaginary relationship
of individuals to their real conditions of existence

In order to approach my central thesis on the structure and functioning of ideology, I shall first present two theses, one negative, the other positive. The first concerns the object which is 'represented' in the imaginary form of ideology, the second concerns the materiality of ideology.

Thesis 1. Ideology represents the imaginary relationship of individuals to their real conditions of existence.

We commonly call religious ideology, ethical ideology, legal ideology, political ideology, etc., so many 'world outlooks'. Of course, assuming that we do not live one of these ideologies as the truth (e.g. 'believe' in God, duty, justice, etc. . . .), we admit that the ideology we are discussing from a critical point of view, examining it as the ethnologist examines the myths of a 'primitive society', that these 'world outlooks' are largely imaginary, i.e. do not 'correspond to reality'.

However, while admitting that they do not correspond to reality, i.e. that they constitute an illusion, we admit that they do make allusion to reality, and that they need only be 'interpreted' to discover the reality of the world behind their imaginary representation of that world (ideology = *illusion/allusion*).

There are different types of interpretation, the most famous of which are the *mechanistic* type, current in the eighteenth century (God is the imaginary representation of the real king), and the *'hermeneutic'* interpretation, inaugurated by the earliest Church fathers, and revived by Feuerbach and the theologico-philosophical school which descends from him, e.g. the theologian Barth (to Feuerbach, for example, God is the essence of real man). The essential point is that on condition that we interpret the imaginary transposition (and inversion) of ideology we arrive at the conclusion that in ideology 'men represent their real conditions of existence to themselves in an imaginary form'.

Unfortunately, this interpretation leaves one small problem unsettled: why do men 'need' this imaginary transposition of their real conditions of existence in order to 'represent to themselves' their real conditions of existence?

The first answer (that of the eighteenth century) proposes a simple solution: priests or despots are responsible. They 'forged' the beautiful lies so that, in the belief that they were obeying God, men would in fact obey the priests and despots, who are usually in alliance in their imposture, the priests acting in the interests of the despots or *vice versa*, according to the political positions of the 'theoreticians' concerned. There is therefore a cause for the imaginary transposition of the real conditions of existence: that cause is the existence of a small number of cynical men who base their domination and exploitation of the 'people' on a falsified representation of the world which they have imagined in order to enslave other minds by dominating their imaginations.

The second answer (that of Feuerbach, taken over word for word by Marx in his Early Works) is more 'profound', i.e. just as false. It, too, seeks and finds a cause for the imaginary transposition and distortion of men's real conditions of existence, in short, for the alienation in the imaginary of the representation of men's conditions of existence. This cause is no longer Priests or Despots, nor their active imagination and the passive imagination of their victims. This cause is the material alienation which reigns in the conditions of existence of men themselves. This is how, in *The Jewish Question* and elsewhere, Marx defends the Feuerbachian idea that men make themselves an alienated (= imaginary) representation of their conditions of existence because these conditions of existence are themselves alienating (in the *1844 Manuscripts*: because these conditions are dominated by the essence of alienated society – '*alienated labour*').

All these interpretations thus take literally the thesis which they presuppose, and on which they depend, i.e. that what is reflected in the imaginary representation of the world found in an ideology is the conditions of existence of men, i.e. their real world.

Now I can return to a thesis which I have already advanced: it is not their real conditions of existence, their real world, that 'men represent to themselves' in ideology, but above all it is their relation to those conditions of existence which is represented to them there. It is this relation which is at the centre of every ideological, i.e. imaginary, representation of the real world. It is this relation that contains the 'cause' which has to explain the imaginary distortion of the ideological representation of the real world. Or rather, to leave aside the language of causality it is necessary to advance the thesis that it is the *imaginary nature of this relation* which underlies all the imaginary distortion that we can observe (if we do not live in its truth) in all ideology.

To speak in a Marxist language, if it is true that the representation of the real conditions of existence of the individuals occupying the posts of agents of production, exploitation, repression, ideologization and scientific practice, does in the last analysis arise from the relations of production, and from relations deriving from the relations of production, we can say the following: all ideology represents in its necessarily imaginary distortion not the existing relations of production (and the other relations that derive from them), but above all the (imaginary) relationship of individuals to the relations of production and the relations that derive from them. What is represented in ideology is therefore not the system of the real relations which govern the existence of individuals, but the imaginary relation of those individuals to the real relations in which they live.

If this is the case, the question of the 'cause' of the imaginary distortion of the real relations in ideology disappears and must be replaced by a different question: why is the representation given to individuals of their (individual) relation to the social relations which govern their conditions of existence and their collective and individual life necessarily an imaginary

apparatus, be it only a small part of that apparatus: a small mass in a small church, a funeral, a minor match at a sports' club, a school day, a political party meeting, etc.

Besides, we are indebted to Pascal's defensive 'dialectic' for the wonderful formula which will enable us to invert the order of the notional schema of ideology. Pascal says more or less: 'Kneel down, move your lips in prayer, and you will believe.' He thus scandalously inverts the order of things, bringing, like Christ, not peace but strife, and in addition something hardly Christian (for woe to him who brings scandal into the world!) – scandal itself. A fortunate scandal which makes him stick with Jansenist defiance to a language that directly names the reality.

I will be allowed to leave Pascal to the arguments of his ideological struggle with the religious ideological State apparatus of his day. And I shall be expected to use a more directly Marxist vocabulary, if that is possible, for we are advancing in still poorly explored domains.

I shall therefore say that, where only a single subject (such and such an individual) is concerned, the existence of the ideas of his belief is material in that *his ideas are his material actions inserted into material practices governed by material rituals which are themselves defined by the material ideological apparatus from which derive the ideas of that subject*. Naturally, the four inscriptions of the adjective 'material' in my proposition must be affected by different modalities: the materialities of a displacement for going to mass, of kneeling down, of the gesture of the sign of the cross, or of the *mea culpa*, of a sentence, of a prayer, of an act of contrition, of a penitence, of a gaze, of a hand-shake, of an external verbal discourse or an 'internal' verbal discourse (consciousness), are not one and the same materiality. I shall leave on one side the problem of a theory of the differences between the modalities of materiality.

It remains that in this inverted presentation of things, we are not dealing with an 'inversion' at all, since it is clear that certain notions have purely and simply disappeared from our presentation, whereas others on the contrary survive, and new terms appear.

Disappeared: the term *ideas*.

Survive: the terms *subject, consciousness, belief, actions*.

Appear: the terms *practices, rituals, ideological apparatus*.

It is therefore not an inversion or overturning (except in the sense in which one might say a government or a glass is overturned), but a reshuffle (of a non-ministerial type), a rather strange reshuffle, since we obtain the following result.

Ideas have disappeared as such (in so far as they are endowed with an ideal or spiritual existence), to the precise extent that it has emerged that their existence is inscribed in the actions of practices governed by rituals defined in the last instance by an ideological apparatus. It therefore appears that the subject acts in so far as he is acted by the following system (set out in the order of its real determination): ideology existing in a material ideological apparatus, prescribing material practices governed by a material ritual, which practices exist in the material actions of a subject acting in all consciousness according to his belief.

But this very presentation reveals that we have retained the following notions: subject, consciousness, belief, actions. From this series I shall immediately extract the decisive central term on which everything else depends: the notion of the *subject*.

And I shall immediately set down two conjoint theses:

1. There is no practice except by and in an ideology.
2. There is no ideology except by the subject and for subjects.

I can now come to my central thesis.

Ideology interpellates individuals as subjects

This thesis is simply a matter of making my last proposition explicit: there is no ideology except by the subject and for subjects. Meaning, there is no ideology except for concrete subjects, and this destination for ideology is only made possible by the subject: meaning, *by the category of the subject* and its functioning.

By this I mean that, even if it only appears under this name (the subject) with the rise of bourgeois ideology, above all with the rise of legal ideology,[13] the category of the subject (which may function under other names: e.g. as the soul in Plato, as God, etc.) is the constitutive category of all ideology, whatever its determination (regional or class) and whatever its historical date – since ideology has no history.

I say: the category of the subject is constitutive of all ideology, but at the same time and immediately I add that *the category of the subject is only constitutive of all ideology in so far as all ideology has the function (which defines it) of 'constituting' concrete individuals as subjects*. In the interaction of this double constitution exists the functioning of all ideology, ideology being nothing but its functioning in the material forms of existence of that functioning.

In order to grasp what follows, it is essential to realize that both he who is writing these lines and the reader who reads them are themselves subjects, and therefore ideological subjects (a tautological proposition), i.e. that the author and the reader of these lines both live 'spontaneously' or 'naturally' in ideology in the sense in which I have said that 'man is an ideological animal by nature'.

13. Which borrowed the legal category of 'subject in law' to make an ideological notion: man is by nature a subject.

That the author, in so far as he writes the lines of a discourse which claims to be scientific, is completely absent as a 'subject' from 'his' scientific discourse (for all scientific discourse is by definition a subject-less discourse, there is no 'subject of science' except in an ideology of science) is a different question which I shall leave on one side for the moment.

As St Paul admirably put it, it is in the 'Logos', meaning in ideology, that we 'live, move and have our being'. It follows that, for you and for me, the category of the subject is a primary 'obviousness' (obviousnesses are always primary): it is clear that you and I are subjects (free, ethical, etc. . . .). Like all obviousnesses, including those that make a word 'name a thing' or 'have a meaning' (therefore including the obviousness of the 'transparency' of language), the 'obviousness' that you and I are subjects – and that that does not cause any problems – is an ideological effect, the elementary ideological effect.[14] It is indeed a peculiarity of ideology that it imposes (without appearing to do so, since these are 'obviousnesses') obviousnesses as obviousnesses which we cannot *fail to recognize* and before which we have the inevitable and natural reaction of crying out (aloud or in the 'still, small voice of conscience'): 'That's obvious! That's right! That's true!'

At work in this reaction is the ideological *recognition* function which is one of the two functions of ideology as such (its inverse being the function of *misrecognition – méconnaissance*).

To take a highly 'concrete' example, we all have friends who, when they knock on our door and we ask, through the door, the question 'Who's there?', answer (since 'it's obvious') 'It's me'. And we recognize that 'it is him', or 'her'. We open the door, and 'it's true, it really was she who was there'. To take another example, when we recognize somebody of our (previous) acquaintance ((*re-*)*connaissance*) in the street, we show him that we have recognized him (and have recognized that he has recognized us) by saying to him 'Hello, my friend', and shaking his hand (a material ritual practice of ideological recognition in everyday life – in France, at least; elsewhere, there are other rituals).

In this preliminary remark and these concrete illustrations, I only wish to point out that you and I are *always already* subjects, and as such constantly practice the rituals of ideological recognition, which guarantee for us that we are indeed concrete, individual, distinguishable and (naturally) irreplaceable subjects. The writing I am currently executing and the reading you are currently[15] performing are also in this respect rituals of ideological

14. Linguists and those who appeal to linguistics for various purposes often run up against difficulties which arise because they ignore the action of the ideological effects in all discourses – including even scientific discourses.

15. NB: this double 'currently' is one more proof of the fact that ideology is 'eternal', since these two 'currentlys' are separated by an indefinite interval; I am writing these lines on 6 April 1969, you may read them at any subsequent time.

recognition, including the 'obviousness' with which the 'truth' or 'error' of my reflections may impose itself on you.

But to recognize that we are subjects and that we function in the practical rituals of the most elementary everyday life (the hand-shake, the fact of calling you by your name, the fact of knowing, even if I do not know what it is, that you 'have' a name of your own, which means that you are recognized as a unique subject, etc.) – this recognition only gives us the 'consciousness' of our incessant (eternal) practice of ideological recognition – its consciousness, i.e. its *recognition* – but in no sense does it give us the (scientific) *knowledge* of the mechanism of this recognition. Now it is this knowledge that we have to reach, if you will, while speaking in ideology, and from within ideology we have to outline a discourse which tries to break with ideology, in order to dare to be the beginning of a scientific (i.e. subjectless) discourse on ideology.

Thus in order to represent why the category of the 'subject' is constitutive of ideology, which only exists by constituting concrete subjects as subjects, I shall employ a special mode of exposition: 'concrete' enough to be recognized, but abstract enough to be thinkable and thought, giving rise to a knowledge.

As a first formulation I shall say: *all ideology hails or interpellates concrete individuals as concrete subjects*, by the functioning of the category of the subject.

This is a proposition which entails that we distinguish for the moment between concrete individuals on the one hand and concrete subjects on the other, although at this level concrete subjects only exist in so far as they are supported by a concrete individual.

I shall then suggest that ideology 'acts' or 'functions' in such a way that it 'recruits' subjects among the individuals (it recruits them all), or 'transforms' the individuals into subjects (it transforms them all) by that very precise operation which I have called *interpellation* or hailing, and which can be imagined along the lines of the most commonplace everyday police (or other) hailing: 'Hey, you there!'[16]

Assuming that the theoretical scene I have imagined takes place in the street, the hailed individual will turn round. By this mere one-hundred-and-eighty-degree physical conversion, he becomes a *subject*. Why? Because he has recognized that the hail was 'really' addressed to him, and that 'it was *really him* who was hailed' (and not someone else). Experience shows that the practical telecommunication of hailings is such that they hardly ever miss their man: verbal call or whistle, the one hailed always recognizes that it is really him who is being hailed. And yet it is a strange phenomenon, and

16. Hailing as an everyday practice subject to a precise ritual takes a quite 'special' form in the policeman's practice of 'hailing' which concerns the hailing of 'suspects'.

one which cannot be explained solely by 'guilt feelings', despite the large numbers who 'have something on their consciences'.

Naturally for the convenience and clarity of my little theoretical theatre I have had to present things in the form of a sequence, with a before and an after, and thus in the form of a temporal succession. There are individuals walking along. Somewhere (usually behind them) the hail rings out: 'Hey, you there!' One individual (nine times out of ten it is the right one) turns round, believing/suspecting/knowing that it is for him, i.e. recognizing that 'it really is he' who is meant by the hailing. But in reality these things happen without any succession. The existence of ideology and the hailing or interpellation of individuals as subjects are one and the same thing.

I might add: what thus seems to take place outside ideology (to be precise, in the street), in reality takes place in ideology. What really takes place in ideology seems therefore to take place outside it. That is why those who are in ideology believe themselves by definition outside ideology: one of the effects of ideology is the practical *denegation* of the ideological character of ideology by ideology: ideology never says, 'I am ideological'. It is necessary to be outside ideology, i.e. in scientific knowledge, to be able to say: I am in ideology (a quite exceptional case) or (the general case): I was in ideology. As is well known, the accusation of being in ideology only applies to others, never to oneself (unless one is really a Spinozist or a Marxist, which, in this matter, is to be exactly the same thing). Which amounts to saying that ideology *has no outside* (for itself), but at the same time *that it is nothing but outside* (for science and reality).

Spinoza explained this completely two centuries before Marx, who practised it but without explaining it in detail. But let us leave this point, although it is heavy with consequences, consequences which are not just theoretical, but also directly political, since, for example, the whole theory of criticism and self-criticism, the golden rule of the Marxist–Leninist practice of the class struggle, depends on it.

Thus ideology hails or interpellates individuals as subjects. As ideology is eternal, I must now suppress the temporal form in which I have presented the functioning of ideology, and say: ideology has always-already interpellated individuals as subjects, which amounts to making it clear that individuals are always-already interpellated by ideology as subjects, which necessarily leads us to one last proposition: *individuals are always-already subjects*. Hence individuals are 'abstract' with respect to the subjects which they always-already are. This proposition might seem paradoxical.

That an individual is always-already a subject, even before he is born, is nevertheless the plain reality, accessible to everyone and not a paradox at all. Freud shows that individuals are always 'abstract' with respect to the subjects they always-already are, simply by noting the ideological ritual that surrounds the expectation of a 'birth', that 'happy event'. Everyone knows how much and in what way an unborn child is expected. Which amounts to saying, very prosaically, if we agree to drop the 'sentiments', i.e. the forms of family ideology (paternal/maternal/conjugal/fraternal) in which the unborn child is expected: it is certain in advance that it will bear its Father's Name, and will therefore have an identity and be irreplaceable. Before its birth, the child is therefore always-already a subject, appointed as a subject in and by the specific familial ideological configuration in which it is 'expected' once it has been conceived. I hardly need add that this familial ideological configuration is, in its uniqueness, highly structured, and that it is in this implacable and more or less 'pathological' (presupposing that any meaning can be assigned to that term) structure that the former subject-to-be will have to 'find' 'its' place, i.e. 'become' the sexual subject (boy or girl) which it already is in advance. It is clear that this ideological constraint and pre-appointment, and all the rituals of rearing and then education in the family, have some relationship with what Freud studied in the forms of the pre-genital and genital 'stages' of sexuality, i.e. in the 'grip' of what Freud registered by its effects as being the unconscious. But let us leave this point, too, on one side.

Let me go one step further. What I shall now turn my attention to is the way the 'actors' in this *mise en scène* of interpellation, and their respective roles, are reflected in the very structure of all ideology.

An example: the Christian religious ideology

As the formal structure of all ideology is always the same, I shall restrict my analysis to a single example, one accessible to everyone, that of religious ideology, with the proviso that the same demonstration can be produced for ethical, legal, political, aesthetic ideology, etc.

Let us therefore consider the Christian religious ideology. I shall use a rhetorical figure and 'make it speak', i.e. collect into a fictional discourse what it 'says' not only in its two Testaments, its Theologians, Sermons, but also in its practices, its rituals, its ceremonies and its sacraments. The Christian religious ideology says something like this:

It says: I address myself to you, a human individual called Peter (every individual is called by his name, in the passive sense, it is never he who provides his own name), in order to tell you that God exists and that you are answerable to Him. It adds: God addresses himself to you through my voice (Scripture having collected the Word of God, Tradition having transmitted it, Papal Infallibility fixing it for ever on 'nice' points). It says: this is who you are: you are Peter! This is your origin, you were created by God for all eternity, although you were born in the 1920th year of Our Lord! This is your place in the world! This is what you must do! By these means, if you observe the 'law of love' you will be saved, you, Peter, and will become part of the Glorious Body of Christ! etc. . . . .

Now this is quite a familiar and banal discourse, but at the same time quite a surprising one.

Surprising because if we consider that religious ideology is indeed addressed to individuals,[17] in order to 'transform them into subjects', by interpellating the individual, Peter, in order to make him a subject, free to obey or disobey the appeal, i.e. God's commandments; if it calls these individuals by their names, thus recognizing that they are always-already interpellated as subjects with a personal identity (to the extent that Pascal's Christ says: 'It is for you that I have shed this drop of my blood!'); if it interpellates them in such a way that the subject responds: '*Yes, it really is me!*'; if it obtains from them the *recognition* that they really do occupy the place it designates for them as theirs in the world, a fixed residence: 'It really is me, I am here, a worker, a boss or a soldier!' in this vale of tears; if it obtains from them the recognition of a destination (eternal life or damnation) according to the respect or contempt they show to 'God's Commandments', Law become Love; – if everything does happen in this way (in the practices of the well-known rituals of baptism, confirmation, communion, confession and extreme unction, etc. . . .), we should note that all this 'procedure' to set up Christian religious subjects is dominated by a strange phenomenon: the fact that there can only be such a multitude of possible religious subjects on the absolute condition that there is a Unique, Absolute, *Other Subject*, i.e. God.

It is convenient to designate this new and remarkable Subject by writing Subject with a capital S to distinguish it from ordinary subjects, with a small s.

It then emerges that the interpellation of individuals as subjects presupposes the 'existence' of a Unique and central Other Subject, in whose Name the religious ideology interpellates all individuals as subjects. All this is clearly[18] written in what is rightly called the Scriptures. 'And it came to pass at that time that God the Lord (Yahweh) spoke to Moses in the cloud. And the Lord cried to Moses, "Moses!" And Moses replied, "It is (really) I! I am Moses thy servant, speak and I shall listen!" And the Lord spoke to Moses and said to him, "*I am that I am*"'.

God thus defines himself as the Subject *par excellence*, he who is through himself and for himself ('I am that I am'), and he who interpellates his subject, the individual subjected to him by his very interpellation, i.e. the

17. Although we know that the individual is always already a subject, we go on using this term, convenient because of the contrasting effect it produces.
18. I am quoting in a combined way, not to the letter but 'in spirit and truth'.

individual named Moses. And Moses, interpellated-called by his Name, having recognized that it 'really' was he who was called by God, recognizes that he is a subject, a subject *of* God, a subject subjected to God, *a subject through the Subject and subjected to the Subject*. The proof: he obeys him, and makes his people obey God's Commandments.

God is thus the Subject, and Moses and the innumerable subjects of God's people, the Subject's interlocutors-interpellates: his *mirrors*, his *reflections*. Were not men made *in the image* of God? As all theological reflection proves, whereas He 'could' perfectly well have done without men, God needs them, the Subject needs the subjects, just as men need God, the subjects need the Subject. Better: God needs men, the great Subject needs subjects, even in the terrible inversion of his image in them (when the subjects wallow in debauchery, i.e. sin).

Better: God duplicates himself and sends his Son to the Earth, as a mere subject 'forsaken' by him (the long complaint of the Garden of Olives which ends in the Crucifixion), subject but Subject, man but God, to do what prepares the way for the final Redemption, the Resurrection of Christ. God thus needs to 'make himself' a man, the Subject needs to become a subject, as if to show empirically, visibly to the eye, tangibly to the hands (see St Thomas) of the subjects, that, if they are subjects, subjected to the Subject, that is solely in order that finally, on Judgement Day, they will re-enter the Lord's Bosom, like Christ, i.e. re-enter the Subject.[19]

Let us decipher into theoretical language this wonderful necessity for the duplication of *the Subject into subjects* and of *the Subject itself into a subject-Subject*.

We observe that the structure of all ideology, interpellating individuals as subjects in the name of a Unique and Absolute Subject is *speculary*, i.e. a mirror-structure, and *doubly* speculary: this mirror duplication is constitutive of ideology and ensures its functioning. Which means that all ideology is *centred*, that the Absolute Subject occupies the unique place of the Centre, and interpellates around it the infinity of individuals into subjects in a double mirror-connexion such that it *subjects* the subjects to the Subject, while giving them in the Subject in which each subject can contemplate its own image (present and future) the *guarantee* that this really concerns them and Him, and that since everything takes place in the Family (the Holy Family: the Family is in essence Holy), 'God will *recognize* his own in it', i.e. those who have recognized God, and have recognized themselves in Him, will be saved.

Let me summarize what we have discovered about ideology in general.

19. The dogma of the Trinity is precisely the theory of the duplication of the Subject (the Father) into a subject (the Son) and their mirror-connection (the Holy Spirit).

The duplicate mirror-structure of ideology ensures simultaneously:

1. The interpellation of 'individuals' as subjects.

2. Their subjection to the Subject.

3. The mutual recognition of subjects and Subject, the subjects' recognition of each other, and finally the subject's recognition of himself.[20]

4. The absolute guarantee that everything really is so, and that on condition that the subjects recognize what they are and behave accordingly, everything will be all right: Amen – 'So be it'.

Result: caught in this quadruple system of interpellation as subjects, of subjection to the Subject, of universal recognition and of absolute guarantee, the subjects 'work', they 'work by themselves' in the vast majority of cases, with the exception of the 'bad subjects' who on occasion provoke the intervention of one of the detachments of the (repressive) State apparatus. But the vast majority of (good) subjects work all right 'all by themselves', i.e. by ideology (whose concrete forms are realized in the Ideological State Apparatuses). They are inserted into practices governed by the rituals of the I S As. They 'recognize' the existing state of affairs (*das Bestehende*), that 'it really is true that it is so and not otherwise', and that they must be obedient to God, to their conscience, to the priest, to de Gaulle, to the boss, to the engineer, that thou shalt 'love thy neighbour as thyself', etc. Their concrete, material behaviour is simply the inscription in life of the admirable words of the prayer: '*Amen – So be it*'.

Yes, the subjects 'work by themselves'. The whole mystery of this effect lies in the first two moments of the quadruple system I have just discussed, or, if you prefer, in the ambiguity of the term *subject*. In the ordinary use of the term, subject in fact means: (1) a free subjectivity, a centre of initiatives, author of and responsible for its actions; (2) a subjected being, who submits to a higher authority, and is therefore stripped of all freedom except that of freely accepting his submission. This last note gives us the meaning of this ambiguity, which is merely a reflection of the effect which produces it: the individual *is interpellated as a (free) subject in order that he shall submit freely to the commandments of the Subject, i.e. in order that he shall (freely) accept his subjection*, i.e. in order that he shall make the gestures and actions of his subjection 'all by himself'. *There are no subjects except by and for their subjection.* That is why they 'work all by themselves'.

'*So be it! . . .*' This phrase which registers the effect to be obtained proves

20. Hegel is (unknowingly) an admirable 'theoretician' of ideology in so far as he is a 'theoretician' of Universal Recognition who unfortunately ends up in the ideology of Absolute Knowledge. Feuerbach is an astonishing 'theoretician' of the mirror connection, who unfortunately ends up in the ideology of the Human Essence. To find the material with which to construct a theory of the guarantee, we must turn to Spinoza.

that it is not 'naturally' so ('naturally': outside the prayer, i.e. outside the ideological intervention). This phrase proves that it *has* to be so if things are to be what they must be, and let us let the words slip: if the reproduction of the relations of production is to be assured, even in the processes of production and circulation, every day, in the 'consciousness', i.e. in the attitudes of the individual-subjects occupying the posts which the socio-technical division of labour assigns to them in production, exploitation, repression, ideologization, scientific practice, etc. Indeed, what is really in question in this mechanism of the mirror recognition of the Subject and of the individuals interpellated as subjects, and of the guarantee given by the Subject to the subjects if they freely accept their subjection to the Subject's 'commandments'? The reality in question in this mechanism, the reality which is necessarily *ignored* (*méconnue*) in the very forms of recognition (ideology = misrecognition/ignorance) is indeed, in the last resort, the reproduction of the relations of production and of the relations deriving from them.

January–April 1969

P.S. If these few schematic theses allow me to illuminate certain aspects of the functioning of the superstructure and its mode of intervention in the infrastructure, they are obviously *abstract* and necessarily leave several important problems unanswered, which should be mentioned:

1. The problem of the *total process* of the realization of the reproduction of the relations of production.

As an element of this process, the ISAs *contribute* to this reproduction. But the point of view of their contribution alone is still an abstract one.

It is only within the processes of production and circulation that this reproduction is *realized*. It is realized by the mechanisms of those processes, in which the training of the workers is 'completed', their posts assigned them, etc. It is in the internal mechanisms of these processes that the effect of the different ideologies is felt (above all the effect of legal-ethical ideology).

But this point of view is still an abstract one. For in a class society the relations of production are relations of exploitation, and therefore relations between antagonistic classes. The reproduction of the relations of production, the ultimate aim of the ruling class, cannot therefore be a merely technical operation training and distributing individuals for the different posts in the 'technical division' of labour. In fact there is no 'technical division' of labour except in the ideology of the ruling class: every 'technical' division, every 'technical' organization of labour is the form and mask of a *social* (= class) division and organization of labour. The reproduction of the relations of production can therefore only be a class undertaking. It is realized through a class struggle which counterposes the ruling class and the exploited class.

The *total process* of the realization of the reproduction of the relations of production is therefore still abstract, in so far as it has not adopted the point of view of this class struggle. To adopt the point of view of reproduction is therefore, in the last instance, to adopt the point of view of the class struggle.

2. The problem of the class nature of the ideolog*ies* existing in a social formation.

The 'mechanism' of ideology *in general* is one thing. We have seen that it can be reduced to a few principles expressed in a few words (as 'poor' as those which, according to Marx, define production *in general*, or in Freud, define *the* unconscious *in general*). If there is any truth in it, this mechanism must be *abstract* with respect to every real ideological formation.

I have suggested that the ideologies were *realized* in institutions, in their rituals and their practices, in the ISAs. We have seen that on this basis they contribute to that form of class struggle, vital for the ruling class, the reproduction of the relations of production. But the point of view itself, however real, is still an abstract one.

In fact, the State and its Apparatuses only have meaning from the point of view of the class struggle, as an apparatus of class struggle ensuring class oppression and guaranteeing the conditions of exploitation and its reproduction. But there is no class struggle without antagonistic classes. Whoever says class struggle of the ruling class says resistance, revolt and class struggle of the ruled class.

That is why the ISAs are not the realization of ideology *in general*, nor even the conflict-free realization of the ideology of the ruling class. The ideology of the ruling class does not become the ruling ideology by the grace of God, nor even by virtue of the seizure of State power alone. It is by the installation of the ISAs in which this ideology is realized and realizes itself that it becomes the ruling ideology. But this installation is not achieved all by itself; on the contrary, it is the stake in a very bitter and continuous class struggle: first against the former ruling classes and their positions in the old and new ISAs, then against the exploited class.

But this point of view of the class struggle in the ISAs is still an abstract one. In fact, the class struggle in the ISAs is indeed an aspect of the class struggle, sometimes an important and symptomatic one: e.g. the anti-religious struggle in the eighteenth century, or the 'crisis' of the educational ISA in every capitalist country today. But the class struggles in the ISAs is only one aspect of a class struggle which goes beyond the ISAs. The ideology that a class in power makes the ruling ideology in its ISAs is indeed 'realized' in those ISAs, but it goes beyond them, for it comes from elsewhere. Similarly, the ideology that a ruled class manages to defend in and against such ISAs goes beyond them, for it comes from elsewhere.

It is only from the point of view of the classes, i.e. of the class struggle, that it is possible to explain the ideolog*ies* existing in a social formation. Not only is it from this starting-point that it is possible to explain the realization of the ruling ideology in the I S As and of the forms of class struggle for which the I S As are the seat and the stake. But it is also and above all from this starting-point that it is possible to understand the provenance of the ideologies which are realized in the I S As and confront one another there. For if it is true that the I S As represent the *form* in which the ideology of the ruling class must *necessarily* be realized, and the form in which the ideology of the ruled class must *necessarily* be measured and confronted, ideologies are not 'born' in the I S As but from the social classes at grips in the class struggle: from their conditions of existence, their practices, their experience of the struggle, etc.

April 1970

References

ALTHUSSER, L. (1969), *For Marx*, Allen Lane the Penguin Press.
ALTHUSSER, L. (1970), *Reading Capital*, New Left Books.
GRAMSCI, A. (1968), *Lettere del Carcere*, Einaudi.
GRAMSCI, A. (1971), *Selections from the Prison Notebooks*, Lawrence and Wishart.
MARX, K. (1955), *Selected Correspondence*, Foreign Languages Publishing House, Moscow.

15 N. Morris

State Paternalism and *laissez-faire* in the 1860s

Excerpt from *Studies in the Government and Control of Education since 1860*,
History of Education Society, Methuen, 1970, pp. 13–25.

Teachers of history tend, of necessity, to make certain assumptions and to attach certain labels or descriptions to people and events. What I want to do here is to consider two generalizations that are frequently made about the history of education in the nineteenth century.

In the first place, we agree that the nineteenth century saw successive acts of governmental intervention which culminated in state assumption of collective responsibility for education. This represented a move from individualism to collectivism. But we also believe that the ethos of the nineteenth century was predominantly individualistic and anti-collectivist. Since there is a contradiction here we go on to conclude that acts of state intervention in education must have been made reluctantly, by people who were gradually pushed along that road against their better judgement.

The second generalization is a related one. Since the nineteenth century saw the emergence of conscious, and even aggressive, *laissez-faire* theory in the economic sphere, it is assumed that this theory must be woven into our interpretation of educational development. Thus, Robert Lowe was a free-trader; therefore, payment by results, the product of a free-trade mind, must reflect a free-trade philosophy.

From these generalizations there derives the following interpretation: mid-nineteenth-century politicians were predominantly *laissez-faire* in outlook but were forced by circumstances, and probably against their will, into acceptance of collective action in the educational field.

Sketching this approach in another way, we often say that eighteenth-century paternalism, which survived into the early nineteenth century, gave way to *laissez-faire* in the expansionist mid-century period; and *laissez-faire* was itself superseded by collectivism towards the end of the century. It might be a mistake, however, to suppose that this progression – even if it took place – happened evenly over all aspects of life. What I want to suggest is that to read educational history against a picture of a generalized progression of this sort may obscure more than it explains.

If any government was ever influenced by free-trade principles, and likely to carry them over into the field of education, it was indeed the government in which Robert Lowe was Minister of Education. It was under Lowe's ministry that the Kay-Shuttleworth system was abandoned and payment by results initiated. This, it is said, inaugurated the sad years during which the state attempted to obtain efficiency in education by purchase. Lowe was a celebrated free-trader and therefore his system represented the triumph of a *laissez-faire* attitude towards state intervention in education.

Now I find this line of thought difficult to follow. It overlooks the fact that the prime object of the Kay-Shuttleworth system itself had been to buy efficiency, by offering money to managers to stimulate school building, by using the purse to nudge managers into buying materials and equipment, by paying teachers to become better qualified, and so on. The whole purpose of making grants-in-aid which foster development is to promote efficiency by the use of money. The argument in 1861 was not whether public money should be used for the first time to promote efficiency, but what was the most effective and least objectionable way in which to continue conducting the purchase of efficiency.

The Kay-Shuttleworth system paid out money for specified purposes but its weakness had been that it lacked sanction. Conditions of grant had no statutory basis and were only enforceable under normal civil contract law. Even this would probably not be used against a defaulter since managers were voluntary workers and, if proceeded against, had only to walk out in order to defeat the whole grant-aid exercise. The grant was simply a carrot for willing horses; in effect, the state offered to double whatever was put in locally, but if the managers defaulted the money was, for practical purposes, irrecoverable. Inspectors were sent round to see if schools were complying with conditions of grant but they were not enforcement officers since there was no law to enforce: all they could do was suggest and report. Now it is not necessary to be a free marketeer, or a butcher of educational expenditure, to find this sort of situation unsatisfactory.

Historians of education have slipped too easily into identifying a system which tried to reward efficiency with a free-market system. It is true that under payment by results the efficiency of teachers was tested by outsiders and the amount of profit earned was geared to the verdict of the testers. But this is far removed from a free-market system. Payment was made from public money, under conditions closely defined by the state. The fact that the state was cost-conscious does not alter the fact that this was still a publicly provided and publicly controlled service. Economic deployment of resources, and the desire to get value for money expended, are not the hall-marks of free-traders. These things are important to anyone – a communist government or a private venture businessman – who is spending money.

There is also a tendency to describe the Lowe system as *competitive*. This too can be misleading. The Revised Code re-introduced free bargaining between employer and employed; there may, therefore, have been an element of competition between employers to purchase the services of the best teachers, or between teachers to obtain posts by under-selling their services, and there may have been competition between teachers to achieve results which would enhance their own market value. But the payments themselves were not earned competitively. The state did not establish a fixed fund and set the schools to compete against one another, to see which could get most out of it. Payment on results was a productivity award.

To call the system competitive is to tar it with the *laissez-faire*, market economy brush. Call it a system of organized productivity awards and it becomes respectable, even to collectivists and socialists. In fact, the government in 1862 deliberately rejected any suggestion of state withdrawal from education and any reversion to a free market in schools. It was firmly opposed to relaxation of state-imposed standards and the reasons for this attitude were firmly embedded in the context of the times.

If nineteenth-century society was to avoid breakdown under the strains of developing urbanization, it was urgent to evolve new techniques for enforcing civil discipline. Organized education was part of the answer to this problem. Society was construed as a comity of social ranks, each of which had its place in the whole, and the preservation of society was equated with preservation of those ranks. It was not a question of the state reluctantly intervening in education, whether for the working class or middle class. Maintaining the structure of society meant control and regulation of the ranks of society and this was freely regarded as an essential part of the state's duties, concomitant with civil law and order. As an important agent of control, the educational system was therefore a legitimate state interest. To leave the supply of schools to the market, according to demand, could leave a particular social class with a deficiency of normative facilities; without a system of controls and checks, such schools as were created might also fall short of the standard of social conditioning which they were expected to purvey.

The instructions to Her Majesty's Inspectors issued on 4 July 1840, under the name of the Lord President of Council (Lord Lansdowne), are significant: 'No plan of education ought to be encouraged in which intellectual instruction is not subordinate to the *regulation of the thoughts and habits of the children* by the doctrines and precepts of revealed religion' (Minutes of the Committee of Council on Education, 1840–41). 'Regulation of the thoughts and habits of the children' – nothing could have less to do with *laissez-faire*, or be more paternalistic (if not autocratic) than this. Here was the main object of the state in elementary education – to control the thoughts and habits of the labouring poor. The obvious instruments to this end were the churches, but it was the state's responsibility to ensure that the job was properly done.

Lowe is frequently blamed for basing part of his new grant system on examination results and, at the same time, ignoring altogether the Newcastle proposal to increase the number of elementary schools by use of a county rate. Here, it is said, Lowe revealed himself in his true colours as a cheese-paring anti-collectivist, to whom education of the poor meant nothing more than minimal proficiency in reading, writing and arithmetic in a limited number of schools. This must be one of history's most ironic verdicts. The object of the Newcastle Commission's county rate proposal was to make public money available to those church and private schools which were unable to conform to the conditions under which state aid was awarded and so failed to qualify for government grant. The state's conditions, on the other hand, were designed as a guarantee that public money should be funnelled only to responsible bodies who could be trusted not only to discharge the academic requirements of education but also to form the 'thoughts and habits' of the children according to acceptable principles. For this purpose, it was a condition of grant that schools had to be in connection with a religious denomination or provide for the daily reading of the scriptures and also had to be in the charge of a state-certified teacher. The Newcastle Commission would have abandoned those safeguards. Whilst agreeing that existing grant conditions were wise and should continue to apply to exchequer aid, the commissioners proposed that locally levied money should be paid over on the results of examination in the Three Rs to any school which conformed to some very rudimentary building standards, with scarcely any reference to the school's moral atmosphere, to the influence of the schoolmaster or to the general arrangements and course of instruction. Rate assistance was to be prize money for secular achievement and could be won by private as well as church schools. Historians seem to have forgotten that it was the Newcastle Commission, not Robert Lowe, which said:

assistance given by the state to education should assume the form of a bounty paid upon the production of certain results by any person whatever. We consider it unfair to exclude the teachers of private schools from a share in this bounty, if they can prove that they have produced the result (Report of the Commissioners appointed to inquire into the State of Popular Education in England, vol. 1, p. 96, B.P.P., 1861, XXI).

It was Lowe who refused to hand public money to 'any person whatever'. To have done so would, indeed, have established a kind of free trade in education, but in this instance it was Lowe who insisted on a measure of protection. The Newcastle proposal would have abrogated the main object for which parliament voted grants – namely, to ensure that children were not merely intellectually instructed but were subject to a total atmosphere conducive to right moral and social discipline. The government for which Lowe spoke had no doubt that to offer rewards for intellectual success without safeguarding moral tone would lead to a general decline in character-training. It refused to be moved from its policy of supporting and working through agencies – and only those agencies – which had an objectively assessed capacity to carry through the state's 'civilizing' mission. When it became clear that the will and the resources of the sects were inadequate to perform this role to the degree that was needed, the state created additional trustworthy and publicly-controlled agencies – the school boards – to fill the gaps.

Lowe, then, continued a paternalistic policy; but was he not, nevertheless, an economist and the author of a system designed to reduce educational expenditure? As most textbooks point out (following, I suspect, Bartley's analysis, 1871), the amount of parliamentary grant declined in the years following the introduction of the Revised Code and this fact has become the basis of the belief that in 1862 the state tried to contract out of its financial commitment to education, using payment on results as the means by which to effect its escape. Lowe and his colleagues could, of course, have been both paternalistic in attitude and parsimonious in practice, but the effect of the former would be nullified by the latter; such schizophrenia is so remarkable as to require closer examination.

First of all, what effect was the payment-on-results system likely to have on the exchequer grant? It can be said at once that the government made no change in one of the main principles on which it had paid grant since 1833 – that the annual disbursement should not be a sum fixed beforehand by policy decision, but should be geared to local demand. Textbooks point out (and students tirelessly reiterate in almost every essay on this period) that the first government allocation of £20,000 to education in 1833 was only one-tenth of the sum voted in the same year for repairing the royal stables. But this was not necessarily evidence of educational miserliness in high places. The education grant was to be 50 per cent of the cost of new schools built by the denominations; the total charge falling on the government depended, therefore, on the number and value of projects initiated by the denominations. In order to meet its part of the offer, the Treasury had to make provision for it in its estimates. In arriving at the figure of £20,000 it had regard both to the volume of school building which the National and British Societies had undertaken in recent years, and also to an estimation of what they were likely to build in the coming year. As the amount of building subsequently expanded, so the annual exchequer subsidy increased. Grants for other educational purposes, in 1846 and later, were based on the same principle: the exchequer simply met an agreed proportion of costs incurred not by itself, but by the schools. The Revised Code contained the same feature. It committed the government to payments based on whatever average attendance and whatever number of examination passes could be achieved by those schools which were on its approved list. The charge which fell on central funds as a result of this system could not be foreseen; the only way in which the exchequer could have affected the total call made upon it was by manipulating the unit amounts offered in the grant formula and the conditions under which those amounts were payable. Fiscally, payment by results was itself nothing more than a variation of previous grant conditions, without alteration of the principle of open-ended payment, which persisted (through a variety of further changes in grant conditions) until 1958. That best-known quotation in all educational history – 'If the system is expensive it will at least be efficient; if it is not efficient it will at least be cheap' – expresses not so much a cynical desire to reduce educational costs as a feeling of exasperation at a system which placed the exchequer at the mercy of an outside spender; it was akin to Winston Churchill's complaint in 1926 that the exchequer's only function in local government expenditure was to calculate the price of the tune called by the local authorities.

The global demand made upon government resources was, therefore, just as unpredictable under the new system as it had been before. Did the new grant formula, however, contain some built-in factor which would automatically reduce the amount which schools received? Under the Revised Code each child could, theoretically, earn up to 12s. annually for his school; was this figure realistic and how had it been arrived at?

The Newcastle Commission, which preceded the introduction of the Revised Code, had given considerable thought to the question of unit payment. The latest figures available to it indicated that the specific grants which it was proposed to consolidate into a new block grant (and this is what the Revised Code later effected), were running at approximately 10s. per pupil in average attendance. The Commission accepted this as reasonable and suggested that in order to maintain an average 10s., the earnable maximum per child should be fixed at 15s. This was, of course, just a guess.

It is true that in the financial year ending 31 December 1861, the average grant earned per pupil jumped by 15 per cent over the previous year's figure. But even if this had been fully realized by the government in the early months of 1862, when a figure for the new formula was under consideration, the 1861 result was so far out of line with previous experience, and presented a sudden increase of such magnitude, that no government could have accepted it unquestioningly as the basis for future payment. As it was, the government adopted the Newcastle Commission's recommended 10s. average, but took the gamble that this would be achieved by fixing the earnable maximum at 12s., instead of the 15s. suggested by the Commission. In the outcome, neither was precisely right; it would have been surprising if they had been. The 15s. of the Newcastle Commission would have produced an average well above 10s. Lowe's figure produced an average of only 9s., but after five years' experience the earnable maximum was adjusted to 13s. 4d., with additional specific payments for pupil teachers. In other words, there is no reason to suppose that either Lowe or his governmental colleagues had had any intention of reducing the education grant in 1862; on the contrary, the evidence is that they took great care to maintain the level at which the grant had been running in recent years, whilst simplifying (and, they believed, improving) its administration.

To sum up, the Revised Code reduced the volume of centralized activity in Whitehall. The number of schools dealt with individually by the central office had trebled in the ten years preceding 1861. In the circumstances, the Kay-Shuttleworth method of making a variety of ad hoc grants to each school separately had become unmanageable and further extension under that system was impossible; the Revised Code, which offered each school a block grant calculated on a common formula, was designed to cope with expansion. It also ended the system under which money could be pumped into schools with no viable means of securing that it was spent efficiently or for the purpose for which it was given; money had now to be earned before it was received. At the same time the principle of open-ended subsidy was maintained: the more schools that qualified for grant-aided status the greater the call on the exchequer; the greater the proficiency of the scholars and the better their attendance the more the Treasury would pay. But Treasury support was still reserved for those schools (and only those schools) which provided a satisfactory moral, as well as intellectual, environment. In all this, it is difficult to discern any new *laissez-faire* intention; on the contrary, Lowe's system exuded paternalism.

It is, of course, understandable that the establishment classes should want to control the lower orders, and even that they should use education as an instrument of regulation. When we come to the area of upper- and middle-class schools, however, state intervention is less obviously explicable. Here, it might be thought, was a field where private enterprise and market economy would be self-sufficient; and, of course, there were many – then, as now – who thought they should be.

Let me quote a letter written in 1867 by a senior clerk in the Colonial Office, replying to a proposal to apply public funds to a middle-class school in Trinidad:

I have always thought it questionable whether the taxpayer at large should be made to pay for the education of the rich. It is no doubt of great importance for the poor that the rich should be educated, and if rich colonists would not have their children educated without a school supported from public funds, it might be right that a school for the rich should be so supplied. But it is a remark as old as Adam Smith that this sort of support is the anodyne of educational institutions and that they are only kept aware and alert when their support depends upon their exertions and their customers whom their reputation attracts (quoted in Furlonge, 1968, p. 110).

In other words, subsidies are the opium of private enterprise; here is the very essence of *laissez-faire* philosophy.

It is clear, however, that by 1870 the state had already relegated Adam Smith and adopted the alternative put forward – if not supported – in the first part of the Colonial Office reply. Since it was of paramount importance to the equilibrium and advancement of society that the rich – the natural leaders and providers in all walks of life – should be educated as befitted their station, and since they were failing to supply their own schools, it followed that the state must step in. The Taunton Commission had already taken it for granted that secondary education, for girls as well as boys, was, in its own words, a matter of 'public concern', and had made a series of recommendations for state regulation of upper- and middle-class schools. By 1869, the government had introduced legislation in line with those recommendations.

It is a matter for debate whether historians have given proper emphasis to the real significance of the Taunton Report and the 1869 Bill. Almost all who have written on the work of the Taunton Commission, for example, contrive to give the impression, perhaps unwittingly, that the concept of three classes of school to match three upper and middle social classes was the Commission's own brain-child and that, although the idea was sufficiently interesting to merit the passing attention of scholars, it really had little effect on the main-stream of educational development. I think that this popular view requires more examination than it has hitherto received.

In the absence of public intervention, all schools above the elementary were subject to market pressures. These forces applied not only to private and proprietary schools dependent on the price which their customers were willing to pay, but almost equally, as the Taunton Commission itself demonstrated, to schools endowed with an independent income. Inevitably, the supply of schools and the type of work conducted in them followed demand. The Taunton Report did not invent schools for the classes; they existed long before the Commission was appointed. Nor was it novel to believe that the preservation of social ranks above the labouring poor depended on the existence of a satisfactory stock of efficient schools geared to the education and training of the various middle- and upper-class groups. What was new in the 1860s was not the concept, but the state's willingness to devise and create the machinery necessary to convert the idea into reality. This is what the Taunton Commission and 1869 Bill were about.

The question of what institutions should best be established for the regulation of middle-class schools was one to which much thought had already been given. It seems to have been assumed that apparatus would take the familiar paternalistic form of a government department working through agencies. This was the pattern already set in the field of elementary education and, indeed, the Newcastle Commission had suggested, in 1861, that the Privy Council, responsible for elementary schools, should simply extend its activities to other schools. It would, of course, be necessary for grant conditions to be modified to suit the circumstances of the endowed school, and it was also thought that a special method would have to be devised for certificating endowed school teachers; but the general machinery operating in the elementary field could, it was suggested, be employed.

Instead of accepting this proposal (which was, in any case, outside the Newcastle Commission's brief) the government passed the whole issue to a new body, the Taunton Commission. The object of this was twofold: to create a climate of opinion favourable to state intervention above the elementary level and to produce a viable scheme which the state could operate.

In 1869 – that is to say, in little more than a year after receiving the Taunton Report – the government tabled a major education bill designed to ensure a sufficient supply of schools catering for the needs of each middle- and upper-class group in all parts of the country and proposing an elaborate complex of statutory institutions (based on the Taunton recommendations) for providing and supervising them. The fact that this bill preceded legislation for elementary education is in itself indicative of the priority which the government gave to state action in schools beyond those for the poor. The full Taunton proposals would have created a new structure in four tiers, each with its own particular responsibilities. Starting at the bottom, the school head was to be charged with maintenance of discipline, with appointment and dismissal of assistant staff, and supervision of teaching methods. Above the head, the governing body would be responsible for financial management, appointment and dismissal of the head, and determination of the curriculum. Next, the country was to be divided into eleven provinces, each with a provincial authority whose function would be to designate the class or grade to which each school was to be assigned, to ensure that the province had a sufficiency of each grade and to decide whether a school should be a boarding or a day school. Fourthly, a Central Council would be responsible to Parliament for coordinating the work of the provincial authorities, inspecting schools, examining pupils, examining and certificating teachers, keeping a register of teachers and presenting an annual report. The 1869 Bill dropped the Provincial Councils and added another body, the Endowed Schools Commissioners, for the purpose of carrying out an initial rationalization of endowments. It was envisaged that this work could be completed in some three years, after which the task of keeping the revised pattern of endowments under review would pass to the Central Council. In the event, the 1869 Act set up only the temporary body of Endowed Schools Commissioners, but in withdrawing the other proposals from his bill, Forster made it clear that he was postponing rather than abandoning them; legislation to deal with them would be re-introduced in about three years' time when the Endowed Schools Commissioners had reconstituted the finances of the schools and provided the provincial and central councils with a base from which they could operate effectively.

It is not my purpose to write the history of this period but only to suggest that there is little evidence here of government aversion to intervention. The meticulous systematization of middle-class schools, envisaged by the Taunton Commissioners and embodied in the 1869 Education Bill, parallels the detail in the 1862 Revised Code for elementary education. We have come, during the twentieth century, to regard education as a social dynamic and to equate increased state activity in it as progress; but the activists of the 1860s were not necessarily looking beyond the society they knew; much of the call for greater state participation in education arose, indeed, from a simple desire to preserve and bring out the best in each social rank by soaking it in its appropriate ethos. For this purpose, different types of school were needed. Society had its greatest success with the upper classes and the public schools. It was fairly successful in the elementary field. That the state failed to move quickly enough to foster sufficient satisfactory schools for the middle classes before the pattern of society itself broke up was due, very largely, to the context in which it had chosen to work. State paternalism, operating deviously through agents, is not the most direct way of achieving an objective; the father-role has its own trials and difficulties. The churches in both elementary and secondary education, and the universities, governing bodies and headmasters in middle-class education, were not the easiest of partners. The state advised, exhorted and offered assistance, but left initiative in private hands. The chosen agents quarrelled amongst themselves, and the state had to be extremely careful how it apportioned its favours. Even more seriously, they frequently reacted against state intervention with all the self-righteousness of adolescents in rebellion against a parent. But, of course, they were not adolescents; they formed some of the most powerful pressure groups in the country, and politicians, coming from the same social class, were rarely ready to apply a heavy hand. This was a situation which was not peculiar to education. Much of our history, in all fields, turns on the ambivalence of sectional interests which need the protection and support of organized society, and even accept its money, but which, at the same time, for reasons of profit or privilege, cling avidly to private power and resent the interference which they themselves invoke; they take what society offers but carry on a love–hate dialogue with the community; they want to remain petty baronies within the state and regard conditions on which they accept public aid as infringements of their own liberty. We are familiar with the forty years' delay in achieving a national system of elementary education, brought about by the unwillingness of the sects to surrender their freedom to the state, whilst carrying on their own internecine war. There has been less study of the forty years' delay in establishing a system of secondary schools, but it is likely that there is a strong parallel between the two stories; the sectional interests which the state hoped to prod into providing an efficient system of middle-class schools wanted the order which could only come from public regulation, but refused to sacrifice their private rights. And the state, for its part, was reluctant to coerce them because it is rarely advisable to bludgeon powerful interests, particularly if they belong to your own class. This, after all, is the secret of the stability of British government.

Professor S. H. Beer, of Harvard, sees the Education Act of 1870, at the end of the decade, as a leading instance of what he calls the 'drift from *laissez-faire*', associated with increasing 'radical' influence on policy. 'Radical' policy, he suggests, involved specific, exceptional acts of state intervention in order to provide a service or to correct particular undesirable consequences of the free economy. Unlike later 'collectivist' policy, it was not an effort to reshape the economic system or to alter its foundations (Beer, 1965). This, I think, is fair comment – with the rider that the state had rarely been *laissez-faire* in education. I know that there is a familiar textbook bromide to the effect that the nineteenth century abhorred government. But the belief that the less government the better was never intended to be applied to the field of civil discipline. This is why I find little difference in spirit between the Education Act of 1870 and events which took place over the preceding years. State intervention was indeed radical and not collectivist; but throughout the 1860s its motivation was anxiety to control, to regulate and to promote. In dealing with the social order the paternal syndrome was stronger than economic principle.

What I am trying to say is probably just this: directly or indirectly, the state has normally been interventionist in education because it is one of the prime objects of government to prevent the breakdown of society, and one of the main instruments for accomplishing this objective is education. The common interpretation of nineteenth-century educational history, which sees a reluctant state dragged into participation by events and pressures, should, perhaps, be turned the other way round: the state was willing enough; it was the difficulty of harnessing churchmen and academics to the task which caused delay.

References

BARTLEY, G. C. T. (1871), *The Schools for the People*.
BEER, S. H. (1965), *Modern British Politics*, Knopf.
FURLONGE, E. A. (1968), 'Secondary education in Trinidad and Tobago', unpublished Ph.D. thesis, University of Sheffield.

Acknowledgements

Permission to reproduce the following readings in the volume is acknowledged to the following sources:

1 Professor William G. Bowen
2 American Sociological Association
3 Cambridge University Press
4 The Brookings Institution
5 Doubleday & Co. Inc.
6 Doubleday & Co. Inc.
7 St Martin's Press Inc.
8 Routledge & Kegan Paul Ltd
9 Andre Deutsch and Houghton Mifflin Co.
10 George Allen & Unwin Ltd
11 American Sociological Association
12 The Free Press
13 Oxford University Press Inc.
14 Editions Sociales, Paris
15 Methuen & Co. Ltd.

Author Index

Subject Index

Ivy League, 190, 191
  as status symbol, 194, 226
  in US, 193–4
  see also Professions
College graduates, 26, 31, 56
  and job selection, 189
  non-monetary attractions of jobs, 27, 52
  unemployment of, 89–92, 94
  see also Professions: overcrowding and unemployment
Colleges of Advanced Technology, 114
Committee of Council on Education 1840–41, 283
Committee on Scientific Education, 1868, 77
Communication, 126
Communist Manifesto, 248, 261, 264
Competition
  in educational system, 282–3
  industrial, 110, 112–13, 131, 169–70
Comprehensive institutions, 101, 104
Conant, Dr James B., 105
Conflict theory, 173, 175, 178, 185, 193, 195
Confucius, 230, 231, 237, 239
Contribution to the Critique of Political Economy, A, 255
Controls
  normative, 189–90, 192, 193
  performance, 182–3, 184, 196
  remunerative, 190
Cost–benefit analysis, 64, 65, 66, 67
Council of Economic Advisers, 87–8, 93
Cousin, Victor, 73
Couzens, James, 136
Critique of the Gotha Programme, 13

Darwin, Charles, 126, 130, 151
Democracy and bureaucracy, 225, 227
Department of Science and Art, 110, 117
Descriptive theory, 249–50
De Staël, Germaine, 73
Devonshire Commission, 111

Discrimination, 56, 183
Dodge Brothers, 135, 136
Drake, Sir Francis, 138

Earning power, 11, 23, 25–6
Earnings, foregone, 52, 58, 78
École Polytechnique, 115, 192
Economic analysis and education, 40–41
Economic contribution of education, 46, 50
  assessment of, 15–41
    inter-country comparisons, 16–17
    inter-temporal correlations, 17–18
    residual approach, 20–22, 179
    returns-to-education approach *see* Rate-of-return techniques
Economic development and educational activity, 16, 179–81
Economic growth, 11, 35, 49–50
  and education, 59, 94
  in US, 21, 102
Economic output *see* Residual input
Economic power, 211–12
Economics of Education, The, 43
Economic system of nineteenth century, 131
Edinburgh University, 112
Education
  as consumer good, 17, 19
  cultural contributions of, 31–3, 37
  demand for, 17
  economic contribution of *see* main entry
  and G N P, 16–18, 29, 37
  indirect benefits of, 29–30
  investment orientation to *see* Investment
  and lifetime earnings, 23, 25, 33, 56
  as means of cultural selection, 189, 195, 225
  non-monetary contributions of, 26–9, 37, 46
  public, 171
  and social conflict, 148–9
  state intervention *see* State paternalism

material existence of, 267–70
recognition function, 271–2, 275, 278
ruling, 245–6, 254, 256–7, 260, 261, 278–80
theory of, 262–4
see also State: ideological apparatuses
Imperial College of Science and Technology, 114
Imperial Gazette, 241
Income and educational attainments, 36, 55–6, 59, 65, 80
in US and Europe, 82, 84
Income-elasticity, 17
Income streams, 46, 52–3, 58
Industrial Revolution, 71, 97, 108, 121, 131, 151–4
Industrial system *see* Labour force; Technology; Unemployment
Industry
and commerce, 121–2
and machinery *see* Machines; Automation
mechanical requirements, 124
research and development, 18
and science *see* Science
and society, 160, 165–9
Industry and education, 18–20, 167
profitability criterion, 18–19, 35
in UK and Germany, 71–9
International Exhibition Paris 1867, 112
International Labor Office, 61
Investment in education, 44–67, 94
aggregate input–output analysis, 48–51
governmental, 33–4, 57, 95–6
individual, 34, 51–2, 53, 95
and individual satisfactions, 57
microdecision theory, 51, 56–7
and migration, 56–7, 149
rate of return *see* Rate-of-return techniques
see also Educational planning; Manpower planning; On-the-job training
Iron and steel, 124–5, 126–7, 132, 135, 160

Jewish Question, The, 266
Job categories
changes in requirements, 194, 195–6
educational and skill requirements, 178–9, 181, 182, 190
Job placement, 105
Junior colleges, 56, 65

Kay–Shuttleworth system, 282, 287
Kennedy, President John, 95
'Know-how', 112, 114, 245–6, 260, 261

Labour
and automation *see* Automation
and capitalism, 163–5, 166, 167–9
child, 168–70, 172
division of, 134, 155–8, 162–3, 165–7, 278
inputs, 20–21
price of, 216
'Labour efficiency units', 65–6
Labour force, 140–41
average years of schooling, 84–6, 89, 145
blue collar, 143, 144, 189–90, 192
demand for, 36, 59–60, 88–94, 101, 105, 141
educational requirements, 176, 177, 182
educational training, 19, 45, 95, 136, 141, 143–4
improved quality through education, 80–84, 148–9, 179
participation rates, 82, 90–92, 94
reproduction of, 244
reproduction of skills, 245–6
white collar, 143, 144, 189–90, 192
see also Manpower planning; Manpower projections; Unemployment
Labour-market imbalance, 88–90
Labour power *see* Labour force
Labour theory of value, 48
Laissez-faire, 120, 131, 281–2, 283, 287–8, 291
Lenin, Vladimir I., 248, 250, 251, 254
Lernfreiheit, 115

Unemployment, 96, 99, 102, 140
  due to shortage of demand, 147–8
  structural, 87–8, 141, 146–8
  tax reduction as remedy to, 87, 93, 147
  of youth, 105, 145
Unemployment rates, 85-91, 92-4, 96, 145
UNESCO, 59
University College, London, 112
University education *see* College education
University Extension Movement, 116
University Grants Committee, 117
Universities
  in France, 115
  in Germany, 114, 115
  medieval, 238–9
  in UK, 111–14, 115, 116

Vocational education, 61, 64, 66, 179, 180–81, 193

major issues, 101–3
new program, 104
in UK, 75, 77
in US, 99–100

Wage capital, 244
Wage structures, 26
WASP, 186–7, 188–9, 190–91
Watt, James, 127, 129, 154–5, 158, 167
Wealth of Nations, 45
Whitney, Eli, 128
Wilson, George, 112
Work
  education for, 103–4
  technological change of, 97–8
Wyalt, John, 151

Zuckerman Committee, 38